Global University for Sustainability Book Series

Series Editors
Lau Kin Chi, Department of Cultural Studies, Lingnan
University, Hong Kong, China
Sit Tsui, Institute of Rural Reconstruction of China,
Southwest University, Chongqing, China

D0743509

The book series aims to publish books and monographs drawing on the expertise of the Global U Founding Members by offering a succinct analysis of global crises affecting the ecological, social, political, and economic aspects, as well as to explore transformative visions and praxis for sustainability. Some books may be translated from their original language into English.

More information about this series at
http://www.palgrave.com/gp/series/16706

Wen Tiejun

Ten Crises

The Political Economy of China's Development (1949–2020)

Wen Tiejun
Beijing, China

With Contrib. by
Lau Kin Chi
Hong Kong, China

Sit Tsui
Chongqing, China

Global University for Sustainability Book Series
ISBN 978-981-16-0457-7   ISBN 978-981-16-0455-3   (eBook)
https://doi.org/10.1007/978-981-16-0455-3

Cover credit: Alex Linch shutterstock.com

This Palgrave Macmillan imprint is published by the registered company Springer Nature Singapore Pte Ltd.
The registered company address is: 152 Beach Road, #21-01/04 Gateway East, Singapore 189721, Singapore

Foreword

This book is the first one of the Global University for Sustainability Book Series published with Palgrave Macmillan.

Global University for Sustainability (Global U) is an international network of around 200 renowned scholars/activists, with a substantial number from Asia, Africa, and Latin America, apart from those from Europe and North America. They are academic scholars, peace activists, community workers, food producers, and rural reconstruction promoters, among others (please see https://our-global-u.org/oguorg/en/founding-members/). The book series aims to publish books and monographs drawing on the expertise of Global U Founding Members by offering a succinct analysis of global crises affecting the ecological, social, political, and economic aspects, as well as to explore transformative visions and praxis for sustainability.

The three main categories falling under this series are:

- General analysis (e.g., history of political economy of a country; issue of sustainability; issue of nuclear disasters); with a focus on China but not only on China.

- Biographies or autobiographies of eminent thinkers from around the world, especially from Asia, Africa and Latin America, connecting their personal trajectory to their thought and the larger context.
- Analysis and interpretation of on-the-ground experiences highlighting how local communities negotiate with economic and other forces impacting on them and organize in alternative ways.

Professor Wen Tiejun, the author of this book, has a wide readership across official institutions, academics, mass media, and grassroots communities. Apart from being a well-known expert of agrarian issues and policy advisor, he is a scholar/activist who has initiated the rural reconstruction movement in contemporary China (2000—the present), particularly promoting agro-ecology, sustainability, and rural regeneration. He is deeply involved in defending the livelihoods of small peasantry in his whole life. In 1968, when he was 17 years old, he was sent to mountain areas in Shanxi Province to work as a peasant. Then he worked as a truck driver for 2 years and later as service worker for 4 years. He entered university when he turned 28 years old. His world vision has been shaped by 11 years of working with and learning from peasants and workers. These grassroots experiences have great influence on his rural sustainability experiments and policy research. He is named by the media as an expert of *sannong* issues (three agrarian issues: peasant, village, and agriculture), who is "doing studies by foot". He has delivered lectures and provided training programs to tens of thousands of students, peasants, peasant workers, and government officers. He has also delivered dozens of lectures and interviews overseas. Recently, Professor Wen won the award of FAO-China food hero (one of five winners) through online popular voting. One live-streamed lecture he delivered in August 2020 attracted 550,000 online watchers. Global U is organizing the English translation project of his biography: *A Life with No Regrets: Life and Thought of Wen Tiejun*, translated by Alice Chan.

The book, *Ten Crises: The Political Economy of China's Development (1949–2020)*, that presents itself to the readers here is a collective endeavour, the culmination of over 12 years of research, discussion, translation, and writing. Soon after the 2008 global financial crisis, the project team headed by Professor Wen Tiejun and Professor Lau Kin Chi began a comparative study of the impact of the financial crisis on developing countries, which included empirical trips to a dozen countries in Asia, Africa and Latin America, apart from Europe and North America, as well as many academic conferences and forums to discuss and debate the theme. In February 2011, a project on comparing Seven Emerging Countries, namely China, India, Indonesia, Brazil, Venezuela, South Africa and Turkey, was launched, which had the support of UNDP-China, Renmin University of China, Lingnan University, along with a couple of institutions. In December of the same year, the first South South Forum on Sustainability was organized, inviting most of the 100 participants from over 40 countries to one of the four 10-day field trips to different regions of China before or after the Forum which was held in Lingnan University in Hong Kong. (see https://our-global-u.org/ogu org/en/the-first-south-south-forum-on-sustainability/) The South South Forum on Sustainability has become an annual activity since 2016, and the Seventh Forum was convened in July 2020. The Global U, fermenting since 2008 and officially launched in 2015, has been the key institution coordinating these forums and research projects. Through the Global U network, Professor Wen and his team have continuously presented new insights and new findings on China's development.

In the comparative study of Seven Emerging Countries, we had a country research team for each country. For China, the core research team members were Professor Wen Tiejun, Professor Dong Xiaodan, Professor Lau Kin Chi, Professor Sit Tsui, and Dr. Erebus Wong. A basic framework and ample materials were taken from a project that Professor Wen Tiejun began in 1998–2000. At that time, he returned to research work in the Ministry of Agriculture after being transferred from his on-the-ground work to promote institutional changes in rural areas in China, and after the completion of his Ph.D. on "A Research on the Basic Economic System of Rural China". He received a grant from the deputy director of a Chinese state-owned financial corporation to take up research and writing of the part on Economic History of a four-part "History of 20th Century China" project. After three years of research, the outline of the research report that he presented was considered inappropriate for continuation and publication due to it being too frank and blunt as regards the presentation of this history. The entire project was shelved. A short paper on the findings of this project was published in the Chinese journal *Dushu*, no. 3, 2001, titled "China's Century-Long Quest for Industrialization: Four Bends in a River".

Thus, when the country report on China was initiated for the Seven Emerging Countries project, the research team based itself on these materials, conducted further research, and produced the Chinese book *Eight Crises: The Real Experience of China's Economic History 1949–2009*. Published in January 2013, this became a bestseller, rather rare for an academic book, and had 25 prints as of June 2020.

English translation of the book *Eight Crises* began in 2013, and was planned to be completed by 2016. However, on further discussion among the research team, it was felt that presentation of the crisis 1949–1950 would be necessary for it gives an analysis on how new China responded to the economic problems inherited from the Nationalist Party regime. The first crisis written in Chinese, a lengthy book version, was published in 2019 entitled *Delinking: The True Experiences of How China Resolved the First Economic Crisis 1949–1952*. With the first crisis being added to the original eight crises, and the global and domestic conditions taking a new turn towards crisis, it was then decided that the post-2013 period should be added as the tenth crisis. To support the team's research and articulation, Professor Wen Tiejun came to Hong Kong in 2017 to video record, initially in English, and subsequently in Chinese (in 2017–2019), ten lectures of the ten crises, plus an overall introduction. (see https://our-global-u.org/oguorg/en/series-no-5-chi nas-real-experiences-professor-wen-tiejun-on-ten-cyclical-economic-cri ses-in-china-1949-2016/) The English subtitled edition of the lecture series will accompany the publication of this book.

The book sets to debunk a highly simplistic but prevalent method-ological or ideological perspective of reading China's development, which generally divides the nation's economic development by 1978 or the so-called Reform and Opening Up. By this view, before the Reform, China was caught up with the idea of socialism and was underdeveloped. After the Reform, economic vitality was unleashed by the force of market and hence the legacy of its dazzling development. Contradicting this view, this book contextualizes China's 70 years of contemporary history against one coherent backdrop: a late developing country endeavouring at all costs to industrialize, be it named socialism or capitalism. China's de facto ideology is indeed developmentalism. We can see a red thread running through China's torrential path of development: a series of crises arising out of its developmentalist effort. This path is complicated by China getting caught in the geo-political confrontation of two superpowers in the twentieth century: The Soviet Union and the USA. It illuminates how China has dealt with the crises by resolving them or deferring to the next ones. Unlike developed countries which transferred their costs of development to others in less favourable status, China, the book argues, could only cope with these costs by internalizing them. As Professor Wen has been one of the leading researchers of the agrarian problem in China, he emphasizes the role of the rural sector being a source of surplus extraction for industrialization and receptor of cost of development being transferred by the urban sector.

Ten Crises: A Summary

Some mainstream grand narrative would divide China's development into two periods marked by the year 1978. According to this narrative, the Chinese economy before 1978 had been strangled by institutional constraints; afterwards, China took off because of the Reform and Open Up as its developmental momentum was released. This book does not take this mainstream narrative, but instead looks into China's development as a process with various disruptions. As a late developing country with below average per capita resources, China has taken the path of introvert accumulation whereas the western model of expansionary and predatory development could not be followed. Under a condition of capital scarcity, China has relied on foreign investment in different periods with varied manners and therefore had to bear the cost, both financial and institutional, including foreign debts and institutional contradictions (urban-rural dual structure, conflicts of interests between central and local governments, institutional adaption and transition in order to accommodate foreign investment, be it sovietisation in the 1950s or Americanization since the 1980s). These costs and contradictions were expressed as social, economic and social tensions, as well as cyclic fiscal and financial crises at particular moments. The major events since the 1950s in China have to be contextualized in the economic and geopolitical global background.

The book comprises of five chapters:

Chapter 1: *The First Crisis 1949–1950: This chapter describes how China in 1949–1950 dealt with the decade-long hyperinflation crisis that had crumbled the old regime. The crux was how to keep the speculative economy at bay by consolidating a real economy.*

The first crisis confronting China's new regime was in essence a continuation of the monetary crisis plaguing the republic for nearly two decades. The silver crisis triggered by the great depression in the 1930s had compelled the *Kuomintang* (The Nationalist Party) government to push through currency modernization with the silver standard withering and fiat paper currency as replacement. However, war and other socio-economic factors had steered the reform toward hyperinflation and monetary breakdown. According to the doctrine of New Democracy as advocated by the ruling party in the early days of the people's republic, private capital was given a role to play in national industrialization. Nevertheless, the innate profit-seeking of private capital was prone to speculative behaviour along with the economic cycle. The new regime that barely held a footing made use of its nation-wide logistic capacity built during the revolution to curb the crisis with the assistance of strong-handed administration.

The experience of stable supplies-based currency in circulation in liberated zones during the revolution was heeded by the central government. The stability and creditability of the newly installed RMB was consolidated by having its value anchored to essential supplies. The land reform had also stabilized the rural sector and expanded the monetary demand by the peasants, which laid the ground for expansionary monetary measure by the government to solve the fiscal problem.

Chapter 2: *The Second to Fourth Crises 1958–1976: This chapter describes how China got an opportunity to receive technological aid from the Soviet Union and therefore achieved rapid development in industry. After breaking up with the Soviet Union, China sank into persistent economic crises, which induced its tragic decade of political turmoil. However, China also took the occasion to become a sovereign country even though it got caught in animosity by both superpowers.*

China's involvement in the Korean War consolidated its alliance with the USSR. With the Soviet aid, China rapidly laid the groundwork of heavy and military industry. However, the aid also strengthened the model of state capitalism. The tension between state monopoly capital and private capital became aggravated during war-time economy, hence the political campaigns to counter corruption in the early years of the people's republic. Private capital eventually was banned in 1956 when state capital controlled three essential factors: land, labor and capital, which was known as the socialist transition. What emerged was the government corporatism with Chinese characteristics, in which capital became embedded into the state.

Moreover, in order to accommodate the Soviet aid, China had to promote institutional transition according to the soviet model in government, army and higher education, which was later known and criticized as "total sovietization". The short-lived alliance with the USSR soon turned sour as China insisted on intact sovereignty. As a punishment, the USSR withdrew all financial and technological aid. The Chinese economy, already dependent on the soviet mode, dived into recession. The aid turned into foreign debt and became a source of fiscal deficits.

In order to relieve the fiscal pressure in the urban sector, the Going to Mountain and Villages campaign was mobilized in the name of socialist cause through the charisma of revolutionary legend as a way to transfer the unemployed population to villages, which was in essence a transfer of cost (expressed as crisis) to the rural sector.

After delinking from the USSR, China made large-scale use of labor force as a substitute to capital in scarcity through a centralized system. This historical experience of nation-wide, large-scale mobilization through a centralized system proved to be an effective institutional advantage in response to the crisis for China.

The soviet system without a corresponding USSR aid became alienated from the economic base. Many subsequent political events had to be contextualized in this institutional contradiction for a more objective understanding and evaluation.

Similarly, the Third Frontier Construction which was much criticized for its economic inefficiency had to be contextualized in the harsh geopolitical condition China faced in that period for a better evaluation.

Chapter 3: *The Fifth to Seventh Crises 1978–1996: This chapter describes how China once again got a chance to acquire technology from advanced countries through rapprochement with the West. However, over-investment also led to fiscal deficits and foreign debts. Radical reforms were taken to deal with the crises incurred.*

Since the early 1970s, China resumed the introduction of foreign investment by turning to the West and Japan. Like the case of Soviet investment, it instantly led to mounting foreign debt and therefore increasing fiscal deficit. The crisis of 1979–1981 was overcome by the resuscitation of *sannong* (Three Agrarian Sectors) by rural industrialization with township enterprises as the major agents.

A series of institutional costs due to fiscal reform (which in fact was the shrugging off of the government's responsibilities) and over investment by local governments resulted in the 1988–1990 crisis. After the political and social unrest, China plunged into recession in 1990.

During 1992–1993, the central government accelerated monetarization and liberated the capital market in order to come out of the depression. Before long, serious deficits in three major sectors (fiscal, financial, and balance of payment) were recorded at the same time in 1993–1994. To deal with the crisis, China pushed through radical reforms such as taxation reform, privatization of state-owned enterprises, banking commercialization, and commodification of housing, education as well as medical care, etc. The Chinese economy became increasingly export-oriented. Structural imbalance also emerged in three major realms, namely rural-urban disparity, regional disparity, and widening social income gap.

As rural industrialization was suppressed in favour of export and the shrinking local budget, the *sannong* problem deteriorated and so did rural governance.

Chapter 4: *The Eighth and Ninth Crises 1997 and 2008: After increasing integration into globalization, China's economy shifted from scarcity to overcapacity. Previous crises were mostly endogenous despite the external factors.*

However, the eighth and ninth crises were mostly exogenous. China also faced the challenge of inherent and global financialization.

The 1997 Asia Financial Crisis and the 2008 Global Financial Crisis were wake-up calls to the Chinese leadership. As China's domestic economy was highly dependent on export, growth and employment were instantly affected when international demand declined.

Unlike the contractionary measures responding to endogenous crises in previous occasions, the Chinese government now took expansionary fiscal measures to deal with crises, increasing investment, pulling domestic demand and keeping the growth.

Since 2003, the central government continuously increased its pro-*sannong* financial investment, succeeding in not only bringing capital and labor back to rural areas and thus partly restoring the regulative capacity of rural labor pool but also in constructing the second capital pool in the county level economy.

These experiences of responding to crisis show that the government's proactive intervention through counter-cycle macro regulation has been effective in alleviating the impact of crisis.

However, China, deeply embedded into the globalization dominated by the USA, had over capacity in labor force, industrial capacity and finance. The economic troika of investment, consumption and export became increasingly imbalanced.

The corporatist local governments heavily relied on land revenues in their fiscal budget. The formula "high investment + high indebtedness = high growth rate" led to a series of structural problems plaguing China till this day.

Chapter 5: *The Tenth Crisis, 2013-the present. This chapter gives a brief evaluation of the unfolding situation since 2013. It presents the idea of ecological civilization which may serve as an alternative to the developmentalism that has captivated China for more than 150 years.*

The tenth crisis was in fact a continuation of the last crisis. After the 2008 crisis, the US Fed launched three rounds of Quantitative Easing, flooding the global financial market with hot money. China had also launched a 4 trillion yuan stimulation package. We saw a market boom during 2009–2012 in emerging economies around the world because of the liquidity. As the third QE ended in 2013, many emerging countries dived into recession.

The USA elites have long identified China as the USA's rival in the future. However, after the fall of the USSR, a series of events had taken China temporarily off the priority target in the USA's geopolitical agenda. It was not until the Asia-Pacific Rebalance and TPP in the Obama administration that the USA obviously targeted China. The Trump administration took a further step to make China its major strategic rival. Since 2018, the USA has launched the trade war, technology sanction and a series of geopolitical manoeuvres putting pressure on China. After several relatively peaceful decades, China is once again confronted with a hostile geopolitical situation.

Whether it was facing the two superpowers in the old cold war and the unipolar power in the post cold war, China had played the role of secondary contradiction (opponent). Now suddenly cast as the major rival, would an inexperienced China be equipped to face the challenge?

On the domestic side, China has been troubled by an array of structural problems: over financialization crowding out industry (de-industrialization), asset bubbles, speculative financial capital's rent seeking impulse, technological dependence due to insufficient R&D investment and underdevelopment in core technologies, the Americanized knowledge production blinding intellectuals from the reality, widening social wealth gap, long term local governments' budget deficits (over reliance on land revenues), the economy being increasingly indebted, a non-labor-friendly taxation encouraging assets hoarding, regional disparity widening again, aging population structure....

Facing a series of challenges, the Chinese leadership proposed the idea of Double Circulation in 2020. The success of this new strategy would depend on two conditions. Firstly, the vitality of domestic circulation would depend on how weak domestic consumption can be improved. It depends on improving the wealth disparity and the imbalanced asset allocation with a too heavy portion on real estates. Secondly, the viability of international circulation would rely on a successful industrial upgrade and building a de-dollarized regional trading system.

In summary, the concern is how to terminate the rough and extensive development model relying on rent-seeking and externality-transferring, and steer toward a pro-people, creative ecological civilization with a balanced and organic rural-urban co-habitation.

This book is authored by Professor Wen Tiejun. While the first nine crises were mostly written in Chinese and then rendered into English by Dr. Erebus Wong and Ms. Alice Chan, the tenth crisis was drafted in English by Dr. Erebus Wong based on multiple sessions of discussions of the team. As a collective endeavour, it has contribution from members of the Global U research team, including the following: Professor Lau Kin Chi, Professor Sit Tsui, Dr. Kho Tungyi, Ms. Jin Peiyun, Dr. Yan Xiaohui, Mr. He Zhixiong, Mr. Lau Kin Ching, Ms. Auyeung Lai Seung, Mr. Lee Kiu Chi, Mr. Kelven Cheung, and Ms. Pan Tingting.

The following research team members had contributed to the publication of the first nine crises in Chinese: Professor Dong Xiaodan, Dr. Liu Haiying, Ms. Gu Xin, Professor Chen Chuanbo, Professor Yang Shuai, Dr. Shi Yan, Dr. Cheng Cunwang, Dr. Li Chenjie, Dr Wang Ping, Dr. Qiu Jiansheng, Dr. Lan Yonghai, Ms. Zeng Tianyun, Ms. Zhang Qin, Mr. Wu Guanghan, Ms. Xu Mengqiu, Dr. Zhang Yiying, Mr. Zhou Huadong, among others.

Lau Kin Chi
Hong Kong, China

Sit Tsui
Chongqing, China

Professor Lau Kin Chi teaches cultural studies in Lingnan University, Hong Kong, China. She is currently coordinator of the Programme on Cultures of Sustainability, Centre for Cultural Research and Development, Lingnan University, Hong Kong. She is a founding member of the Global University for Sustainability, and heads the Global U executive team. She has been involved in the rural reconstruction movement in China for almost three decades, and is board member of PeaceWomen across the Globe, and Asian Regional Exchange for New Alternatives.

Professor Sit Tsui is associate professor at the Institute of Rural Reconstruction of China, Southwest University, Chongqing, China. She is board member of Asian Regional Exchanges for New Alternatives. She is also one of the founding members of Global University for Sustainability. She has been actively involved in the rural reconstruction movement in China since 2000.

Preface

Rural Reconstruction (or revitalization) is an effort to promote non-elitist popular democracy. It is also a theoretical reflection on radical modernization in modern Chinese history. In nearly two decades, we may summarize our theoretical intervention in five major aspects:

1. Theory of Civilization Diversity

    Climate cycle with subsequent change in natural environment is decisive in shaping civilization diversity. At least before the global expansion of western colonization, the processes of civilizations in different parts of the continents did not necessarily follow the escalating modes of production theory suggested by western thinkers. This perspective is instructive for us to present an alternative ecological view of history.
2. Derived Institution and Path-dependency Theory

    Under different geographical conditions and resources profiles, civilizations were endogenous and diversified before modern globalization, hence having taken different paths of primitive accumulation for modernization in history. As a result, different institutional arrangements emerged respectively, along with the path dependency in later institutional change. It is an important perspective for comparative studies in countries and regions.

3. Theory of Successive Cost Transfer

In modern world system, core nations and dominant social groups have made gains by constantly transferring institutional cost outwards, through which advanced nations completed primitive capital accumulation, accomplished industrial capital expansion, then elevated itself to financial capitalism. However, many developing countries and lower class have been caught in "underdevelopment trap" after incessantly having to bear the transfer of cost. Contemporary globalization is in essence a system dominated by parasitic financial capital successively transferring its cost outwards to make gains. In this system, different interest blocs compete fiercely in profit-making. Before the incontinent greed of human beings, the eco-systems which are absent in negotiation become the ultimate bearers of the costs, hence the imminent danger of unsustainability of human societies.

4. Theory of Sovereignty Externality in Developing Countries

After the Second World War, most of the developing countries gained sovereignty through negotiation with former suzerains, which may be regarded as a sort of "transaction". Like any transaction, it usually implies risk of information asymmetry. The party which monopolizes information takes the benefits and at the same time transfers costs to the other party. Sovereignty gained through negotiation often entails negative externality. Therefore, developing countries find it hard to totally unshackle themselves from dependency.

5. Theory of Externality Internalization in Rural Society

China has completed industrialization as a developing country with a population of over a billion. It is a rare achievement. We believe it may be attributed to the traditional social foundation of "internalizing externality within rural community". Rural community rationality and government rationality, in contrast to individual rationality as championed by economic theories, may be regarded as China's comparative institutional advantage. However, the government is at the same time an alienation of human creation, which in turn rules human beings at high costs. Negative externalities in economy, society, culture, resources and environment have been the aftermaths of radical modernization pushed forward by the alliance of capital and government. These undesirable negative externalities stand as towering obstacles in China's path to achieve sustainability. Rural reconstruction is therefore a movement to involve people to revitalize the *sannong* (三农：农业、农民、农村, literally, three agrarian sectors: the agriculture, the villages, the peasants) to continue to function as the carrier of "soft-landing" of crisis in China.

With the above in mind, we engage in researches in five major fields, locally and internationally:

1. How to Face the Challenge of Globalization

    During the three stages of capitalism—primitive accumulation, industrial expansion and financial capitalism, core nations (advanced countries) constantly transfer the cost of capitalist development outwards through new ways. This remains to be the biggest challenge confronting developing countries and ecological sustainability.

2. Comparative Studies of Developing Countries

    We have cooperated with the United Nations Development Programme to take part in the Global South Knowledge Sharing Network. One of our researches in this aspect is Seven Emerging Countries Comparative Studies which compares the experiences and paths of China, Brazil, India, Indonesia, Turkey, South Africa and Venezuela.

3. Regional Studies within China

    China is a continental country. The geographical and human conditions of different regions are extremely diversified. Apart from the historical studies of China as a whole (represented by this book), we also engage in studying the development experiences of different regions in China. So far we have completed researches on South Suzhou, South China, Chongqing, Hangzhou and Suzhou Industrial Zone, etc. These works lay the foundation to construct a holistic picture of China's experiences.

4. China's National Security

Globalization poses great challenge to national security of developing countries. This book explores how China's new socialist regime established itself through land revolution and took the advantage of *sannong*'s internationalization mechanism to deal with economic crises. On its path of modernization (industrialization + urbanization), China has undergone ten major economic crises (with one unfolding). Based on historical comparison, we find that whenever the government succeeded in mobilizing peasants to bear the cost of crisis, it would achieve "soft-landing". Otherwise the crisis might take hard-landing in urban sector. The consequences were social and political unrest, along with subsequent radical institutional transformation. Therefore, how to promote and improve rural governance is pivotal to national security as a whole.

5. *Sannong* and Three Governances

After the central government accepted our ideas of *sannong* problem, we have spent more than a decade to research the problem of governance on three levels (county, township and village). After the disintegration of rural organizations during the 1980s, the *sannong* as economic base became increasingly debilitated. However, on the contrary, the cost of "three governances" as super-structure became increasingly unbearable. This disparity resulted in social conflicts and problems in ecology, food safety and culture, which were detrimental to national security as a whole. How could we break through this "prisoner's dilemma"?

Rural reconstruction is a quixotic attempt to mobilize people to search for a way. It might end in failure. However these social experiments in themselves are worthy of historical record and studies. The movement stands as one of the alternative social histories people are taking part to create.

The slogan of the World Social Forum is "Another World is Possible." Here in China, we hesitate to raise one more slogan. Maybe a better way is to show people by our unyielding praxis: another world is here.

Wen Tiejun
Beijing, China

Contents

List of Figures

Chapter 4

Chapter 5

Chapter 6

List of Tables

1

Introduction

China's experience defies logical self-consistency if deciphered through the discourse forged by advanced countries in the stage of financial capitalism. This book endeavors to contextualize China's 'particular' historical experience in the general process of capitalist development. China's progress in the past 60 years is thus depicted as a completion of primitive capital accumulation and then procession into industrial expansion and adjustment.

In its pursuit of industrialization, China has endured cyclical macroeconomic fluctuation, which is unexceptional to most of the industrialized countries. China has experienced ten such crises since the founding of the New Republic. With the exception of the first crisis in 1949–1950 at the beginning of national founding, which was a continuation of the monetary crisis of the former Republic of China since 1935, the other nine cyclical alternations between economic peaks and troughs since 1958 have occurred during New China's late industrialization. Over the past 60 years, these have occurred in a context where China has been subject to untenable foreign debt pressure on four occasions. It was under a relatively

© The Author(s) 2021
Wen Tiejun, *Ten Crises*, Global University for Sustainability Book Series,
https://doi.org/10.1007/978-981-16-0455-3_1

passive circumstance of debt and deficit crisis that China embraced an "open policy."

1   Key Concepts

Capital and Government

In the historical stage of capitalism characterized by the western civilization, human beings have created two "alienating products": capital and government, the former on the side of the economic base, the latter, on that of the superstructure. They are highly costly and in turn put human beings under their yoke. Governments in various forms (including representative democracy or many socialist regimes) serve as the hand-maiden of capital, which expresses the general rule of the superstructure being derived from and submitted to the economic base. In relation to this generality, there is a specific form of capital directly controlled or monopolized by governments, which is known as state capital. It is intrinsically integrated into the government, leading to "government corporatization," or the capitalization of power.

It should be commonsense. However the elites seem to be puzzled by it. The problem is less about their recognition of this regularity than how the elite bloc takes measures to constrain itself in accord with the regularity.

Urbanization and Cycle of Crises

The development of capitalism and urbanization concur. As capital concentrates in cities, the expansion of capital synchronizes with urbanization. The overspill of capital has a bearing on the evolving urban culture. As governments are stationed in cities, they accelerate the institutional changes brought about by urbanization. Associated with the capitalization of cities, urban culture becomes politicized and developmentalism becomes the politically correct mainstream tenet.

Nevertheless, the accumulation and concentration of capital entails a commensurate level of risk. In its pursuit of the institutional gains by urban capital, the government pushes for urbanization and inevitably increases the risk inherent in the concentration of capital. Periodic crises break out as a consequence. Hence, the acceleration of the deepening of capital in cities and the increasing inherent risk, as well as the outbursts of crises, has forged an alliance of economic, political and cultural powers. As a power-bloc "for itself," it exerts a universal bearing on other social groups "in itself".

Elite blocs and other social groups obsessed with developmentalism never get tired of this path even after numerous blows of crisis.

Political Modernization and Debt Crisis

The global crisis caused by the credit crunch on Wall Street, the core zone of financial capital, is the result of an overexpansion of credit, or too large externalities. This expansion of credit is based on currency power, which is a direct combination of capital and government, the two alienated products of human beings in the stage of financial capitalism. On the one hand, it is the aftermath of a rapacious "financialized bubble economy" catalyzed by the virtualization of the economic base. On the other hand, it is also the repercussion of the "debt mechanism" implied in western political system of high cost and therefore high debt. Any developing country that follows the Eurocentric and ideologized model of globalization and blindly duplicates the western political system would face a similar or worse situation.

As early as in 1996, the author pointed out that the over expansion of derivatives by international financial capital was bound to lead to a financial crisis. It is an inevitable law. At that time, China was not ready for this critical point of view. It was only after 1997 when East Asia was hit hard by financial crisis that people learnt the lesson and accepted this regularity.

The third regular pattern revealed here has more or less been recognized by the intellectuals responsible for knowledge production at the critical moment during the 2007–2011 crisis. However, the interest-distribution mechanism underpinning the discursive system has prevented the discourses from renovating themselves.

The scale of the impact of the 2008 crisis was greater than any previous financial crisis. Financial capital ignited the global crisis by transferring its cost to the real economy. It was an all-round crisis of western capitalist modernization. Once again its cost was being transferred to developing countries.

Theory of Cost Transfer

Capitalism characterized by the West has created crises throughout its different stages. The costs have been transferred to its colonies or developing countries, which is the main cause of the latter's poverty. The theory of cost transfer refers to this general contradiction between the western powers and developing countries. After WWII and the subsequent tide of decolonization, over 100 new nations were born. They generally took the model of capitalism as characterized by the West and pursued a developmentalist industrialization. However, unlike their western predecessors, they could not transfer the corresponding costs to other nations, and therefore most of them got ensnarled in the "development trap". Those countries which succeeded in getting out of the trap usually had the social conditions to transfer the costs internally. Before the Reform, most of the crises in urban China were resolved by transferring the cost to the collectivized rural communities. The crises could therefore take a "soft-landing" in the cities. Afterward, when a crisis took a "hard-landing," the so called "reform" emerged as a response.

Learning from the history of capitalism in which the West transfers the costs of its capitalist crises to the rest of the world, we have come up with a theory of cost transfer, a basic theory that explains the widening wealth gap in the world economy at different stages of capitalism (Wen 2012).

This theory of cost transfer is the conceptual tool we use to analyze the ten crises that broke out during the four rounds of foreign capital inflow for China's industrialization. We have come up with two viewpoints. First, if less developed countries take the advanced countries as their target of catching up and emulation, then they must consider if it is possible to duplicate the latter's development path under the same conditions. If it is impossible, then the development experience of advanced countries is not of universal significance. Second, core nations will remain on the institutional path of transferring the cost of global crisis to other countries, which is the cause of less developed countries falling into the development trap. China, as a nation with an aboriginal population of more than a billion making it through the age of classical colonialism, is the only industrialized country which has accomplished primitive accumulation without pursuing the course of external colonial expansion like the West. We are afraid that it is impossible to explain it through western theoretical/ideological frameworks and concepts, which leaves much room for theoretical innovation.

Crisis Soft-Landing and Empowering the Three Agrarian Sectors

China was a "less-developed" country with extreme scarcity of capital. In order to push for national industrialization in the cities, it took various forms of "pro-capital" measures at different stages, first in the primitive accumulation of capital, and then in the expansion of industrial capital. At a particular stage where there was no capital investment, China applied the strategy of "replacing capital with intensive and concentrated labor investment". In 2005, the "Building New Socialist Countryside" was adopted as a national strategy. After then, a few thousand billion RMB was invested into the rural areas. Tens of millions of peasants have been absorbed into the "non-agricultural" sector for employment. This is the reason why China could make it through the crisis in 2009. It is an important first instance of "win-win" soft-landing in both the rural and urban sectors.

The fifth key concept revealed in this book is still an inference from empirical regularities. It is not a well articulated theory. In challenging the ideological discourse system, the authors have come up with several new innovations. However, we do not believe that analysis based on economic rules alone can formulate a logically consistent explanation of contemporary Chinese history.

2   Development Trap and China's Experience

In the tide of decolonization during and after the Second World War, many developing countries attempted to push for industrialization by duplicating the model of their former "suzerains" ("developed countries"). However, among them, only a handful of nations succeeded in realizing the goal, thanks to the reconfiguration of geopolitics dominated by two superpowers. Most of the others, following their former suzerains in the path of industrialization, found themselves ensnarled in a "development trap" in different ways.

If we are willing to free ourselves from the "ideologized" interpretation of developmentalism after WWII and look into objective experiences, we may find that: amongst countries with an aboriginal population of over 100 million,[1] China is the only developing nation which has accomplished primitive capital accumulation and proceeded into industrial expansion and adjustment. It can be said that China has moved into the later stage of industrialization and in recent years, propelled by industrial capital excess, been leaping towards the stage of financial capitalism.

Before its integration into global competition, China's general industrialization can be divided into three stages according to the general development pattern of industrial capital: primitive accumulation, industrial expansion and structural adjustment. This development is indicated by its 8% average annual growth rate that has been sustained for over 70 years since 1949.

In a global politico-economic setting dominated by advanced countries, New China depended on foreign capital from the USSR for primitive accumulation at the initial stage of industrialization. However,

---

[1] Here "aboriginal" is in contrast to the "colonized". Accordingly, there are five developing countries with over a hundred million aboriginal population, all Asian nations: China, India, Indonesia, Pakistan and Bengal.

this process was soon interrupted. It became extremely difficult to go on without external capital investment. On the one hand, it had to face serious resource constraints and population pressure; on the other, it had to break through the blockade in the cold war seeking the opportunities pertaining to capital, technology and the market.

We must emphasize this point: China pushed for industrialization during a time when its internal and external circumstances were extremely unfavorable.

Apart from resource limits, China was confronted by two harsh institutional constraints.

First, the peasants were geographically highly dispersed. After three agrarian revolutions in the early twentieth century, China finally succeeded in setting up the foundation of nation-building. However, in 1950, it was a country with peasants making up 80% of its population, 500 million strong. The main economy revolved around traditional agriculture, a mode of production that ran against the logic of industrialization. 100 million rural households were involved in small-scale farming and animal husbandry. As the state pushed for industrialization, it had to rely heavily on extracting a considerable surplus from the rural sector. With the peasants so dispersed spatially, the transactions cost was extremely high.

Second, capital was absolutely scarce in China. In such a condition, China had to open itself up to attract foreign capital in order to pursue its industrialization. To attract foreign capital, it had to construct its superstructure and ideology to build an institution adaptable to the operation of foreign capital. For a nation that had bathed in blood for nearly a century to restore its full sovereignty, the institutional cost of such measures to attract foreign capital was enormous.

Compared with those advanced countries that accomplished primitive accumulation through colonization, China had to face the above two constraints. In the course of its industrialization, crises broke out frequently as a feature of the interaction of economy and politics.

After a century of invasion and internal turmoil, the Chinese believed that they had to follow the path of industrialization of western powers in order to maintain its sovereignty. However, they were well aware that China lacked the proper conditions for industrialization. For this reason, the leaders of the Communist Party of China proposed the tenet of New Democracy in 1947 and the *Common Program* in 1951 which was equivalent to a constitution. The basic policies were to advance gradual industrialization under national capitalism. The idea was to promote private industry and commerce in cities, develop middle-class peasants and preserve the well-to-do rural households in rural areas, so as to form a commodity circulation between light textile industry in cities and the rural sector. The industrial base would be expanded gradually to facilitate primitive accumulation for large industry. At that time, Mao Zedong emphasized that he opposed populism or "peasant socialism" and stressed that only after the completion of industrialization and socialized production would the Communist Party push for socialism with the consensus of the people.

These thoughts, which were in line with the economic pattern of developmentalism in less advanced countries as well as the guidelines of national capitalism in developing privatization and market, are still praised today. So the younger generations would believe that the CPC later gave up this reasonable development strategy of New Democracy simply because of the faults of leftist heeling. And this book will argue that it is not that simple.

After an analysis of historical materials and statistics, we find that there have been ten rounds of major economic crises in China since 1949. The book is entitled as *Ten Crises* because of the following considerations.

Firstly, the first crisis of hyper inflation during 1949–1950 was a continuation of the inflation the Republic of China faced after the 1929–1933 crisis in the West. In 1935, the Chinese government had to adopt a paper currency reform due to a lack of precious metals after the 1929 crisis. The consequence was long-term serious inflation. Therefore this crisis was not directly related with the other nine crises (six endogenous periodic crises before and three exogenous crises after China integrated into the global system) associated with China's industrialization in contemporary history.

Secondly, the nine crises of alternating peaks and ebbs after 1958 were attributed to the fact that Chinese leaders in different periods introduced foreign capital which resulted as foreign debts. The playing out of the economic cycle was common in many less developed countries in the process of industrialization. The interpretation of contemporary Chinese history as a series of periodic economic crises is not a totally new innovation. It is the conclusion of two decades of research after the author proposed the "theory of crisis" in 1988, which had drawn controversies and criticism.

In fact, continuous and steady long-term economic growth during industrialization is impossible for any country. Periodic economic fluctuation is a normal pattern, even for those advanced countries which had succeeded by exploiting colonies.

What this book attempts to do is to reveal the ideological discourses for what they are and to proceed in step-by-step fashion to come up with a theoretical innovation: the generality of the "theory of cost transfer," *i.e.,* the costs of crises in urban industrialization are transferred to the rural sector, which is a condition for the "soft-landing" of the crisis in cities.

It is a theoretical innovation in the studies of critical policy. Although based on Immanuel Wallerstein's world system theory and Samir Amin's dependence theory, we do not confine ourselves to one school. We take political economy as our analytical framework and the transaction cost theory of new institutional economics as an auxiliary tool. We endeavor to make the theory of cost transfer a theoretical tool to de-construct the economic histories of contemporary China and world capitalism.

The analytical object of Immanuel Wallerstein's world system theory is the modern capitalist world system rising from Europe in the sixteenth century. Its contents include capitalist world economy, inter-states system and geo-culture. He believes that since human history moves into the stage of capitalist civilization as stated by Marx, all nations and people in the world are being incorporated into a world economic system by the core nations, forming a "core—semi-periphery—periphery" structure. Through unequal exchange, the surpluses from the semi-periphery and periphery are being channeled into core regions. In this process, the dominance of the core nations is fortified while the periphery is debilitated (Wallerstein 2004).

World system theory is not based on China's experience. However, the persisting non-equilibrium structure of "core—semi-periphery—periphery" has deteriorated into a "lose-lose" game if China's situation is taken into further consideration. Peripheral or semi-peripheral countries like China (also known as "emerging" or "developing" countries) are feeding core nations through two channels. One the one hand, China delivers physical products to the West. The trade surplus in turn increases its money supply. China, on the other hand, can only use its accumulated foreign exchange reserve to purchase the bonds of western governments. In this way its trade surplus is channeled into western capital markets to create a bigger financial bubble.

Accordingly, the global economic crisis incurred by the credit crunch in the capitalist core zone in 2008 tallies with the general historical pattern of capitalism marching into the stage of financial capitalism.

The integration of China into the world system should be reflected by questioning: what is the status of China (or less developed regions) that is being incorporated into the world economic system? By whom is the system being dominated? The Anglo-American financial empire taking London-New York as its axis may come straight to the point: since the 1990s, they have succeeded in integrating the dismantled Soviet Union, Eastern Europe and the developing China into a western currency system. Any physical economy being incorporated will bring new blood into this failing system.

The concept of "delinking" in this book is taken from Samir Amin's dependence theory. In the 1960s China succeeded in pushing for indus-trialization on its own after the disruption of foreign investment and support. Amin sings high praise for China's experience. However, what he refers to is the stage of autarkic industrialization. If we take the late 1990s into consideration, that becomes a different story. The increas-ingly excessive industrial capacity is the sword of Damocles hanging over the capitalist world. Driven by capacity excess, China joins globaliza-tion. No matter how it is dressed ideologically, this integration is in essence a "re-linking" and afterwards an output of surplus through new dependence.

After China's integration into the world economy system, any researcher who investigates the situation from the perspective of devel-oping countries will find that the "core-periphery" relationship in the capitalist world system was of a "dominance-dependence" structure. Peripheral countries function as suppliers of raw materials and primary products. Their domestic industries heavily rely on advanced (mainly western) industrialized nations. Those countries that adopted a strategy of import substitution would find the strategy ineffective when on the one hand confronting the tariff barriers of advanced countries and on the other hand challenged by domestic conservative interest blocs, thereby finding themselves under the thumb of others.

After completing the primitive accumulation for industrialization and undertaking industrial capital expansion, China made an effort to partake of what in recent times has been popularly known as 'globalization'. A painful process for China as it is, it is not peculiar. When most of the politicians in the world yield to the vulgar political pressure of justifying their political legitimacy by economic growth, we must understand level-headedly that the past 70 years of China's historical trajectory has been a choice without alternatives.

3   China's Economic Crises and the Conditions of "Soft-Landing"

Industrialization is less about an economic process of yielding industrial products through input of factors such as capital, labor and technology, as propounded by economic theories, than a political goal of post-colonial nation-states striving for sovereignty. Most of the developing countries have constantly faced extreme capital scarcity. By the criteria of economic efficiency under the premise of general market equilibrium, it is difficult to comprehend why these countries have implemented 'pro-capital' policies and provided institutional arrangements to the extent they have in order to accomplish primitive capital accumulation for industrialization at all costs, let alone to be judged by the ideological discourse in service of global financial capital expansion dominated by developed countries.

China's industrialization involved internally extracting surplus from the agricultural sector to support industrial accumulation. Nevertheless, the dominant dynamics in China's industrialization have been subject to the shifting parameters of the global geo-political and economic landscape. It is because of these geopolitical shifts that China has been afforded the opportunities to break with the usual development obstacles. Indeed, although access to foreign capital accrued debt, it also provided much needed capital and technology for industrialization. Still, the accrual of debt meant that China has continually had to confront the danger of being caught in a "development trap".[2]

New China's two waves of industrialization can both be attributed to catching up with the unprecedented historical opportunities of industry transfer from developed to developing countries after WWII. The first occasion was the Korean War in the 1950s. On the condition of getting itself involved in the war, China was in return offered aid in the form of a transplant of military-heavy industry from the Soviet Union. The second wave of industrialization took place after the 1970s when China undertook a rapprochement with the West and Japan. To a certain extent China had taken advantage of its rising geopolitical importance in the Asia–Pacific when the USA and the Soviet Union struggled for supremacy in the region. China could therefore complete its structural adjustment from an economic structure too weighted to military-heavy industry before the Reform to the production of consumer goods.

The particularity of China's industrialization and the later Open-up lies in the following facts. At the end of 1950s the Soviet Union withdrew investment from China. During the subsequent crisis, which lasted from the late 50s to the early 60s, China eventually achieved 'delinking,' unlike many developing countries under similar circumstances where industrialization was directed under the aegis of foreign power and when the process was forced to intermit; on some occasions this might lead to social disasters. The delinking allowed China's primitive accumulation for industrialization while paying back foreign debts to the Soviet Union,

---

[2]After WWII, developing countries were under a submissive geo-political position. Their developments were often determined by the shifting of international geo-political strategies dominated by their economic "suzerains." Developing countries in pursuit of industrialization generally had to depend on foreign investment due to lack of domestic capital and technology. The sovereignty debts in the South were mainly results of pursuing industrialization by foreign debts from developed countries.

For most developing countries, that might be the beginning of disaster. Unlike most developed countries they could not externalize the institutional cost of primitive accumulation. More dangerously, whenever international geo-politics changed, foreign investment and aids might break off abruptly. That might lead to economic crisis, political and social turmoil, and even human disaster. It could be regarded as a development trap.

thus breaking its economic and political dependency. Such a dependency on the "suzerain" or foreign investor was a common fate among many Third World nations.

Hence, the study of China's development experience brings forth a question which is worthy of reflection. In as much as China had suffered from various serious economic crises, how could it manage to avoid a chain reaction of political and social turmoil, even total breakdown, and therefore escape the 'development trap'?

The analysis of world-system theory, which divides up the world in terms of "core—semi-periphery—periphery," according to their respective positions in sharing the benefits from global production, basically coheres with Mao Zedong's conclusion about the "Three Worlds." Both elaborate the underlying mechanism by which the costs and benefits of the global economic system are distributed: the institutional costs of economic growth and social development in developed countries are typically transferred to developing countries by way of dominant institutional arrangements overseen by the core countries.

As for the question of how China has managed to avoid the "development trap" faced by many developing countries, generations of politicians in the East have scribed the answer in their praxis. Yet most of the theories that have emerged from the west seem to have neglected what is essential and as such, misinterpreted China's experience.

In principle, the different subjects of urban and rural sectors should have their own representatives in the government to represent their interests. However, any late industrializer facing extreme capital scarcity has had to embrace pro-capital policies. Those who represent the interests of the urban sector where industrial capitals concentrate have long exerted considerably more influence on governmental policy-making than their rural counterparts. Even though the central government sometimes embraces positively pro-rural policies, their implementation has often been difficult under constraints of institutional transition, which represents the interests of industrial capital.

Nevertheless, traditional rural China has been prone to stability in contrast to the situation with modern Chinese cities. Since the early twentieth century in China, economic crises endogenous to industrial civilization have tended to break out in the cities. The impact of the crises of capitalism on the urban sector have depended on the extent to which their costs could be transferred to the rural sector and to peasants, since unlike the USA, China could not transfer the institutional costs of the crisis abroad.

During the breakout of economic crises, based on the basic institutional contradiction of a dual structure (urban and rural), China can thus diversify its various economic and social costs. Although enormous costs have been borne, an uninterrupted industrialization has been essentially maintained.

It has been observed throughout China's 70-year history of industrialization that as a rule whenever the cost of crisis could be transferred to the rural sector, the capital-intensive urban industry sector could achieve a "soft-landing" and the existing institution could be maintained. When the cost of the crisis was not transferable to the rural sector, it manifested as a "hard-landing" in the urban sector, giving rise to major reforms in the economic system.

China's economic reform therefore originated from policy adjustments in response to economic crises. Nevertheless, because of the obfuscations caused by ideology, people have failed to see the problem from this perspective.

In terms of social stabilization, Rural China (comprising three irreducible dimensions: the peasants, the rural areas and the agriculture, known as the "*sannong*", the three agrarian sectors) has played an important role as a shock absorber to the cyclical economic crises (approximately one in every ten years) caused by urban industrial capital in the last 70 years. This has been the case especially in the last 40 years of reform, which has seen China turning crises into opportunities. This is the crux of this book, which elaborates on China's 70 years of industrialization during which there were four occasions of serious indebtedness, ten crises and their subsequent soft-landings and hard-landings.

At the initial stage of industrialization, China's understanding of the regularity of crises was simplistic while its reaction to them was passive. In the crisis of 2008–2009 we saw the **Chinese government proactively implementing a pro-peasant policy with an increased infusion of fiscal fund. The three agrarian sectors again appears to be forged as a vehicle of soft-landing in the event of crisis.**

2

1949–1952: 'Land Reform Dividend'—Old Crisis Plus New Crisis

How the rural sector under the new communist regime contributed to resolve the crisis lasting from the old republic; the transition of the New Democracy (national capitalism) to socialism; geopolitical environment and the rapid industralization of China.

1 Overview

The economic fluctuation in the early years (1949–1952) of the People's Republic of China was the culmination of new problems breaking out on top of old ones. On the one hand, China had had to deal with persistent hyperinflation since the old republic; on the other hand, a new crisis had to be tackled, namely, the contradiction innate to primitive capital accumulation for the development of 'national capitalism'.

The enormous institutional cost of modernization and its derivative, the urban crisis unfolding as hyperinflation in the age of the Republic of China, could not be resolved by adopting the same old economic means by the new regime whose success of revolution was marked by the occupation of cities.

© The Author(s) 2021
Wen Tiejun, *Ten Crises*, Global University for Sustainability Book Series,
https://doi.org/10.1007/978-981-16-0455-3_2

The new republic resolved this chronic crisis (as a result of a half-a-century pursuit of modernization since the late Qing dynasty) by fully restoring the traditional peasant economy through agrarian reform, thus gaining the 'land reform dividend'.[1] Colloquially, this was expressed as, 'Nine peasants are capable of supporting one urban citizen.'[2]

Agrarian reform is not only about relieving the crisis of modernization through the restoration of a traditional institution. It also involved the extension of revolution experience (the military strategy of encircling cities from villages) to economic realm in peaceful times. Moreover, it lays the foundation of the *sannong* (三农)[3] as a means to resolve the urban industrial capital crisis under a persistent dual urban–rural structure.

The substance of the land revolution in China is 'even distribution of land and tax exemption', which was the goal of all peasants supporting the founding emperors during dynasty change. History shows that as long as rulers maintained the basic economic institution of land to the tillers, Chinese rural society, characterized as a 'sponge society', could

---

[1]The policy of redistributing agrarian land to rural households has long been an effective measure to resolve urban crises. It worked not only in 1950 in Mao Zedong's age, but also 30 years later in Deng Xiaoping's time. Furthermore, most of the countries and regions in East Asia that have been influenced by Confucian culture have adopted this measure and thereby maintained long-term stability, including China, Japan, South and North Koreas, and Taiwan. Clearly, it is of universal importance to those Asian countries that have the dual rural–urban structure as the basic institution. Moreover, in China's history, those dynasties that had implemented a policy of land distribution and tax exemption generally sustained long-term stability. Only radical reformers in mainland China attempted to fundamentally change this institution.

[2]This expression is inspired by the late Du Runsheng (杜润生). As a leader of agrarian policy (being deputy director of the National Agriculture Committee) in the early 1980s, he had not only interpreted the distribution of land to households practised by the rural grassroots as 'Household Joint Production Contract Responsibility System' but also as a realization of the rural collective economy characterized by a double layer management and a combination of unity and division. In persuading the central leadership, he expressed it in a way that those leaders who were under a serious deficit crisis could understand: 'Eight peasants are capable of supporting two urban citizens.'

[3] *Sanrong* (the three agrarian sectors, namely, peasants, villages and agriculture) is a non-mainstream perspective that the author has insisted on for years, which had also been marginalized for a long time until it was adopted by the ruling leadership after a presentation on 25 December 2001. In 2002 it was confirmed to be of utmost importance in the national strategy. See Wen Tiejun (2009).

secure about 200 years of stability in the dynastic cycle.[4] Apparently, this has been the historical experience of Asian agrarian societies with populations that are mostly aboriginal (unlike for example Latin America where most of the aboriginal population were exterminated and replaced by European immigrants). In this regard, we borrow from Marx's Asiatic Mode of Production hypothesis to propose the concept of East Asian Stable Society. We submit that China, Japan, North and South Koreas, as well as Vietnam all belong to the East Asian Confucian Cultural Sphere. No matter the political and ideological system they claim to adopt, they all strive to build a sponge society through the even distribution of agrarian land among peasants. They are therefore more stable than the developing societies of Latin America and Africa, for example.

This historical experience was once again demonstrable in mainland China in the twentieth century. The land revolution, which had been disrupted by the Second World War and then resumed during 1946–1949, can therefore be called the Third Land Revolutionary War.[5] Since China regained its sovereignty through this war after having been partitioned by imperialist powers, it is also known as the independence war that granted it political autonomy from its semi-colonial status.

The new government that emerged from the revolutionary war implemented agrarian reform in the entire country, achieving an even distribution of land for nearly 90% of the population. Nevertheless, in order to extract agricultural surplus to support industrialization, the central government deliberately procrastinated on tax exemption, which most new dynasties would immediately implement along with land distribution.

---

[4] 'Sponge society' refers to rural society's capacity to absorb enormous negative externality like a sponge. Rural economy is composed of millions of peasant households having diverse livelihoods that combine agriculture, husbandry, handicraft, labour, etc. This concept is inspired by 'sponge city' in contemporary sustainable development studies. A sponge city can absorb water during rain. It holds and purifies water through filtration and then releases it for use. Collection, filtration and purification are three functions of a sponge city.

[5] On 4 May 1946, the Chinese Communist Party issued a document known as *The May Fourth Instruction*, which proposed to change the policy of tax and interest alleviation to land to the tillers. Later, *Outlines of Land Law* was formulated. Land Reform Task Forces consisting of tens of thousands of cadres were sent to rural regions to mobilize peasants to struggle against landlords.

As a consequence, this fundamental institutional transition in property relationship by means of revolutionary war achieved three results. First, a vast and diversified physical economy was created by letting about a 100 million rural households return to their traditional mode of production and to delink from the process of modernization so that the subsistence of urban residents (about 10% of the total population) could be secured. The hyperinflation in cities since the last years of the old republic was then greatly ameliorated. Second, as long as peasants could be mobilized by the ideology of land reform, sufficient amount of material products could be collected and transported to the cities. This represented the first triumph of state capital over private capital through revolutionary mobilization. Third, the state established its fiscal and financial system, which was necessary for economic regulation of the real economy. The experiences gained from the process became the foundation on which the state constructed its basic economic institutions.

Achieving these three results by means of a single policy involved a transplantation of the military strategy learnt during the revolution (encircling cities from villages) into the realm of economy. The institutional heritage of so-called rural socialism with Chinese characteristics therefore took shape long before the final victory and involved the development of the real economy by self-reliance in the 'liberated' regions. We will return to discuss this further.

After the regime change, China faced a new economic crisis. The old crisis of developing national capitalism as led by the Nationalist Party (*Kuomintang*, KMT) was yet to be overcome when the new government led by the Communist Party faced a new crisis in its effort to develop its own version of national capitalism. It was a case of old wine in new bottles, leading to the same problems.

The constant threat of imperialist invasion would have prompted any modern Chinese government to pursue modernization regardless of the ideology it officially identified with. Nevertheless, as long as the institutional cost of primitive capital accumulation necessary for industrialization could not be transferred outwards, internal crisis would break out.

The political-economic structure of New Democracy (新民主主义), as promulgated by the new regime, was represented by the national flag of the People's Republic of China. The large star represented the leadership of the Communist Party (including the state capital controlled by the party). The other four stars represented the working class (less than 5% of the population), the peasant class (petit landowners or rural petit property owners, 88%), urban petit bourgeois and national capitalists. State capital, private capital and petit property owners constituted the major political sectors of the country. Workers and the urban proletariat, which according to classical Marxism should have the consciousness of a class revolution, represented less than 7% of the total population.

In short, China had long been an agricultural country composed mainly of geographically scattered peasants. What took place in 1949 then was a pre-capitalist peasant revolution, asserted both by the Communist International headed by the Soviet Union and the Chinese Communist Party. Both agreed that China should develop national capitalism (which means capitalism of and for the nation as opposed to domination by foreign capital). Only after establishing mass industrial production could China be transformed into a socialist country.

Accordingly, the new government, which was midwifed by a violent revolution to overthrow the oppressive old system in 1949, not only openly advocated market capitalism (as Mao said, 'New Democracy is national capitalism under the leadership of the Communist Party') but also took for granted the swift accomplishment of industrialization (pursuing modernization had become the preference since the late Qing dynasty). As a consequence, China inevitably had to face the internal contradiction of a peasant country striving for primitive capital accumulation despite its scarcity of resources. This was the reality no matter how the national predicament resulting from this was presented ideologically.

As a matter of fact, the new republic managed to resolve the crisis through three institutional arrangements, along with the interaction of three sectors: politics, economy and society. First, the overall land reform allowed peasants (88% of the population) to delink themselves from the urban crisis of modernization and return to the traditional peasant economy. An extensive and vastly diversified physical economy took shape in rural regions. In the process, China managed to resolve the hyperinflation crisis. From then on, rural sector served as a vehicle for the 'soft-landing' of urban sector in case of crisis. Second, a national fiscal-financial system was built upon the rural economy, which was centred on real physical goods/production. This system was connected directly with the policy of physical goods and supplies distribution, enabling the government to perform counter-cycle economic regulation.[6] Third, the government used military means, with the aid of a political campaign, to forcibly put down the speculative behaviour of urban private capital at the lowest cost. It successfully put out the economic crisis instigated by private enterprises, which would have followed the trend of economic cycle out of individualistic economic rationality.

To summarize, right after the success of the revolution (which was marked by the occupation of cities), China faced severe crises in cities where capital was concentrated. It was a great challenge to the new regime whose political subjects comprised peasantry moving into cities. At the same time, the government had political problems like bureaucratization and cadre corruption, which could be viewed as the internal crisis of peasantry politics. That's why we define the economic fluctuations during the early years of the new republic as the first crisis.

The subsequent political campaigns were derived from this. The hyperinflation (as a result of budget deficits and monetary oversupply) was quickly suppressed, partly due to the fact that about one-third of the oversupplied money was absorbed by the peasant household economy like a sponge. However, as a result, the rural economy was monetized and polarized, which led to problems within the cooperative movement.

Considering that many developing countries might be confronted with crises right after becoming independent, sovereign states, the experience of China's first crisis may be of universal significance (Image 1).

---

[6]Capitalists, following their impulse of profit-making, will dive into a booming market, therefore adding oil to an overheated economy. On the contrary, during economic downturn, they will jump ship by cutting production or selling their depreciating assets, thus aggravating the trend. This individual economic rationality many often leads to irrational economic trend at macro level. A government, free of the compulsion to seek profit, may regulate the economy by doing the opposite, for example promoting production during economic downturn. This is what the US government was doing during the New Deal the Quantitative Easing and the Chinese government likewise during many occasions of crisis. We call it counter-cycle economic regulation.

Image 1 The land reform staff publicizing the Land Reform Law to peasants in 1950

2   An Interpretation of the Crisis in the Three Years of National Economic Restoration

According to the official narrative, the three years (1949–1952) before the first Five-Year Plan were never described as undergoing cyclic economic crisis. Instead, they were known as the Three Years of National Economic Restoration (Gu 1992: 151). Researchers of historical studies would usually compare the statistical data of these three years with the initial days (1949) of the republic, and the best days of the previous republic (around 1936).

We must agree with this comparison when we interpret these three years as being in crisis. This is because the Chinese leadership at that time openly admitted that in this period China followed the strategy of developing national capitalism known as New Democracy (Ren 2011: 104–106). This means that at the beginning of the new republic, the economy operated mainly according to the laws of market capitalism as dominated by capital expressed both in their state and private forms.

The function of the government was to perform counter-cycle regulation during economic recession. Therefore, the nature of its economic base was comparable with the old republic.

It's well known that the development of capitalism in its initial phase entails the enormous cost of the primitive accumulation of capital. This general law was also embodied in 1949–1952. The author has suggested that the traditional peasant economy resolved the crisis of modernization, which we believe is once again proven by the 1949–1952 crisis.

It should be understood that the definition of New Democracy, with private capital as main catalyst, is not contradictory to the ideological discourse of national economic restoration. However, we wish to highlight two important questions that seem to have been neglected. First, how did the new republic get out of the chronic hyperinflation crisis that had been persisting since 1937? Resolving hyperinflation allowed the new republic to avoid the development trap and to proceed towards the establishment of national capitalism. Second, if the new regime had really committed itself to developing national capitalism, why did it later launch highly charged political campaigns that have generally been generally regarded as targeting private capital?

We believe that clarifying these two questions are of significance to China and other developing countries in the new millennium.

First, let's address the question of how China got out of hyperinflation. What concerns us is that hyperinflation is a common phenomenon in developing countries, no matter which ideology they officially declare adherence to. China has to a certain extent succeeded in resolving the crisis of urban inflation by transferring the costs of development to rural society. However, many developing countries without a land revolution still appear caught in the development trap.[7]

Once a country gains political independence after de-colonization, it often finds itself in an economic predicament. One of the key factors is that when a developing country achieves independence through

---

[7]Development economics finds that many countries (or regions) may face the development trap (interruption of development in various forms) during its progress from a low-income level towards middle- and high-income levels. Even if a country reaches a high-income level, the development trap might still be inevitable. Economic development and national welfare improvement are processes of breaking through development traps one after the other.

non-violent or non-revolutionary de-colonization, it generally has to reach a deal with its former colonial master or the hegemonic power through negotiations that involve conceding a part of its economic right (sovereignty). Usually, what transpires alongside the declaration of independence is the signing of an economic agreement or treatise with its former colonial master. Although a developing country aspires to achieve modernization as quickly as possible, the continuation of a colonial mono-economic structure often makes it impossible to de-colonize the economy.

We may call this the colonial 'original sin' of developing countries. No matter what kind of ideology their political leaders subscribe to, they have to face the problem of what we call the negative externality of sovereignty.

Through comparative studies, we come to the theory that any developing nation gaining sovereignty through non-violent negotiations has to go through a transaction process (in terms of institutional economics) with its former master state. Sovereignty gained by this kind of transaction would lead to a structural imbalance of interests due to informational and power asymmetries between the two parties. Accordingly, most developing nations with political sovereignty gained through negotiations have to face the problem of negative externality of sovereignty. After independence, the nation must concede to its former suzerain (or transnational corporations) a part of its right to gains in economic resources and/or fiscal-financial aspects. As a result, it must continue to depend on its former master state economically or politically. Such is the 'original sin' causing the developing countries falling into the development trap.

We find that the fundamental difference between the general state of developing country dependence (according to Samir Amin's Dependence Theory) and China's success in delinking resides in whether a country manages to resolve the general negative externality of sovereignty independence negotiations usually result at. People are familiar with the wisdom that we must clean our house before inviting guests. The problem is whether it is possible to have a non-violent revolution that sees the guests off if they occupy the house by their comparative advantage due to colonization and outward-bound cost transfer.

Hence, research into how China cleaned the hyperinflation in its house of semi-colonization may contribute to development economics. It can also serve as an instructive experience of the practice of delinking to many developing countries.

The second problem is about the nature of the first political campaign in the new republic: *San Fan Wu Fan* (三反五反, literally struggle against three harms [corruption, wastefulness and bureaucratization] and five venoms [bribery, theft of state property, tax evasion, shoddiness and economic spying]).

While the economic achievement of 1949–1952 is generally praised, the initiation of socialist transformation in 1953 remains contentious. It was a widely-held belief that as long as the Chinese kept to the path of New Democracy in the initial years, economic fluctuation and hence political turmoil would then be avoidable. Yet one must remember that this belief is sustained by historical de-contextualization and selective memory. While the development of national capitalism in these three years was admirable, the political campaign that was going on simultaneously was widely considered reprimandable. Moreover, the counter-cycle economic regulation effort by the government had almost completely sunk into oblivion. In the general criticism, these three issues (economic development, political campaign and economic regulation) seem to have taken place in different times and spaces as if they were totally unrelated.

Therefore, an attempt to explore the nature of *San Fan Wu Fan* must take three factors into consideration. First, the consistency of background with the first question (how China resolved the crisis of hyperinflation?). According to the chronology of the mainstream narrative, 1956 was the end of New Democracy after the completion of the socialist reform of private capital. However, according to our analysis, the market economy with private capital as major economic agent lasted for less than three years. During these years, under the strategy of New Democracy, China had cautiously gone through the minefield of inflation, economic imposture (especially in supplies to government) and recession.

The correlation between these three problems could be summarized as follows: all Chinese governments since the late Qing dynasty have promoted the concentration of capital in cities, which proportionately also incurs the concentration of risk. As a consequence, cities become the place where institutional cost accumulates.[8] Furthermore, under the pressure of high inflation, the real economy becomes less profitable. Private capital, driven by economic rationality, tends to turn away from the physical economy and towards speculation. Therefore, the phrase following inflation is always recession. The narrow escape out of hyperinflation with a resulting deflation is necessarily followed by the misfortune of industrial and commercial recession.[9] Without governmental intervention or a strong counter-cycle regulation, this pro-cyclical economic roller coaster in an unstable economy would lead to a drastic collapse. For this reason, the new regime implemented the first counter-cycle regulation by tackling the economic anarchism of private capital, which is regarded as the first industrial and commercial regulation.

Second, the essences of the first and second questions are in common. We must accept the fact that aiming at modernization through industrialization requires primitive capital accumulation for the formation, expansion and constant upgrading of industries, no matter the ideology adhered to, or political system in place. The negative externality generated by capital pursuing profits is inevitable. National capitalism composed of Chinese private enterprises is not an exception. The downstream consumption end of the real economy must endure indirect exploitation by accepting overpriced, low-quality products as a way to contribute surplus value to primitive capital accumulation as much and as fast as possible.[10] Hence, the key question becomes: who is going to play the role of the consumption end in order to bear the institutional cost of primitive capital accumulation?

---

[8]By institutional cost, we mean the cost generated by various state institutional arrangements for industrialization. Apart from the direct cost of capital accumulation, it also includes related indirect cost of all kinds.

[9]Besides, after land reform, villages returning to the traditional peasant economy became relatively independent from the cities of the modern market economy. On the one hand, villages provided firm support to the government's effort to manage urban inflation. On the other hand, the household subsistence economy could not serve as a source of surplus value for primitive capital accumulation for industrialization, which aggravated the predicament of the urban industrial sector.

[10]The American development economist Ragnar Nurkse was among the earliest to propose the theory of domestic need. See Ragnar Nurkse, *Problems of Capital Formation in Underdeveloped Countries*. Oxford University Press, 1953.

A well-known viewpoint is that China could push forward industrialization only by extracting surplus from the rural sector. However
after land reforms, the peasant economy became 'unembedded' from the
urban economy.[11] Capital therefore could not accomplish its "precipitous
leap" to complete its movement. Since the rural sector could not play this
role spontaneously, the government had to take it up. The government
applied a loose fiscal and monetary policy in 1950, performing a counter-
cyclical regulation by placing orders and purchasing, and so on. Nevertheless, it implied that the government directly absorbed the institutional
cost of primitive capital accumulation without changing the innate characteristics of private capital. Attempts to accelerate capital accumulation
through collusion with government officers, counterfeiting, poor quality,
and tax evasion prevailed, which not only exacerbated fiscal difficulty but
also harmed the new regime's political credibility.

Hence, whereas the new government aiming to develop national capitalist industry and commerce had to concede to private capital under
conditions of capital scarcity, its tolerance for the institutional cost of
accumulation and expansion of private capital had to be limited because
of fiscal constraints and the consideration of its own legitimacy. Besides,
there was no room for poor quality and counterfeit products in the
provision of supplies to the Korean War which China got involved in
beginning in June 1950.

For a regime born out of revolution, still self-conscious and self-
disciplined, *San Fan Wu Fan* was a self-cleansing political movement.
It was an effort to solve economic problems by political means after
the land reform and an attempt to block the path of institutional cost
transfer by capital in urban and government sectors.

Therefore, this political movement was quite significant in suppressing
the over-concentration of capital risk in cities.

---

[11] 'Unembeddedness' is a term from Karl Polanyi's *The Great Transformation*. He believes that
after land, money and labour—the three fictitious commodities—become tradeable commodities
in the market, the economy becomes unembedded from society, as contrast with its previous
embeddedness into the latter. When industry and commerce developed rapidly in the Republic
of China, peasant household production and livelihood became more and more commercialized
and monetized. The peasant economy became interwoven with capital movement into villages.
After land reform, and before the establishment of a new commodity economic relationship,
villages became unembedded from the urban-centric modern market economy.

The collusion between officers and merchants during the government's effort to save the economy could be viewed as the impact of the economic base mainly comprised of private capital upon the new superstructure constructed out of a violent revolution. In this sense, *San Fan Wu Fan* was the active reaction of the superstructure to the economic base, representing a dialectical movement driven by the contradiction between them. This political movement was an effort to lessen the accumulated institutional cost of primitive accumulation of capital. However, as it did not touch upon the fundamental contradiction of how capital accomplished primitive accumulation in urban sector, a recession took place after *San Fan Wu Fan* in cities where capital was concentrated.

As a response, the central government made the second effort to resuscitate industry and commerce by policy adjustment (Zhu 1999: 104–107).

During 1949–1952, the government acted as a purchaser to relieve recession. At the same time, it played the role of a commercial negotiator to regulate and limit the profits of manufacturing while acting as a political agent to crush misbehaviours and collusion. If we take the previous efforts to suppress hyperinflation and accommodate old civil servants into consideration, the policy of the New Democracy during 1949–1952 could be viewed as a consistent combination of reservation, constraint and suppression.

In view of this complicated history, we endeavour to generalize two concepts.

The first of these is 'land reform dividend'. In a traditionally agricultural country with a large population, land is the most important property for peasants. The even distribution of land—or the principle of land to the tillers—is of vital political and economic significance for national mobilization. The internal mobilization thus achieved becomes an important tool for developing countries to delink from dependency and realize absolute sovereignty among the nations of the world. In circumstances of negative externalities of (or incomplete) sovereignty, the ability to internalize cost based on common landownership offers an institutional advantage.

The second concept is of 'government rationality'. An economic agent who is seeking profit guided by individualistic economic rationality usually has a shorter investment time-frame. He or she will go along with the economic cycle. When the economy is booming investors will jump into the market, adding oil to a maybe already over-heated carnival. While the market is turning down, they may turn to short-selling. However, a government which is non profit-seeking should not be bound by this narrow rationality. On the contrary, a government should take counter-cycle measures for the greater benefit of the society as a whole. We call it "government rationality," an expanded form of rationality with much longer time-frame and larger inclusive concern of interests.

As long as a nation pursues developmentalism, it incurs various kinds of negative externalities, no matter its political system.[12] The government can act as an economic agent, directly taking counter-cyclical policies in the market to mitigate the cost of such externalities. Moreover, the experience of this period can supplement the deficiency in the theory of the separation of government and enterprises, which has been emphasized as an orthodoxy by economics and political science since the late 1990s. These experiences of government rationality learnt during the economic development of China provide rich content to be explored for the general theory of government behaviour (He 2014). Thirty years later in the age of Reform, local governments actively took part into economic activities and competed with each other, a condition known as local government corporatism.[13] The rendering of political momentum into

---

[12]We define developmentalism as an idea and mentality by which people pursue economic growth in spite of problems in social ethics, environment and ecology. As Hui (1999) puts it, 'developmentalism is a belief that economic growth is the pre-condition of social progress.' It is also approximate to the old developmentalism in Ye (2012).

[13]The author has conducted research on the development model of the Jiangsu regions. We find that the value of development in these regions lies on the combination of local government rationality and rural community rationality, due to which social stability could be maintained despite intensive extraction of surplus value during primitive capital accumulation in the industrialization of rural areas of the regions. The accumulation has been completed in a short period of time. The subsequent reform of village and township enterprises, which marks the end of the Sunan model, was a result of the local government transferring the cost to rural society under pressure of an economic crisis (Wen 2011). A follow-up study further investigates the experiences of local governments in the regions, including counter-cycle economic regulation through state credit replacement and enterprise-public services, as well as increasing total land rent in the regions and innovations in 'total rent' (Dong 2015). Furthermore, Huang (2011) proposes the concept of the 'third hand' in the pursuit of equitable development in his studies on the local government in Chongqing. The third hand is different from Adam Smith's 'first hand', which is an imaginary hand of self-regulation and optimization of the market economy by rational

economic advantage by the government's involvement in the economy has been constantly replicated and reinvented.

3   Resolving the Modern Financial Crisis of the Old Republic

Analysing the crisis of stagflation confronting the new republic in 1949 is a challenging task. Stagflation involved the simultaneous occurrence of inflation and rising unemployment, which is an inversion of conventional economic wisdom. It was a situation China was forced to bear as a semi-colony, the result of the negative externality of sovereignty. To fully understand it, we must put aside the cold war ideology which still informs value judgement in social sciences. We must trace its origin to the general crisis of overproduction during 1929–1933 in the West, which was followed by the Second World War. Only by doing so can we hope to understand how China managed to resolve this exogenous crisis by a land revolution, which brought to fruition the millennium-long appeal of land to the tillers by the traditional peasant economy. Therefore, we must start with the monetary reform of establishing a modern financial system in the old Republic of China.

From Silver Crisis to Paper Currency Crisis

In the initial period, the Republic of China did have a golden decade. During 1920–1930, China recorded high economic growth under the capitalist economy (Faribank 1992). However, it ended due to internal conflict and exogenous crisis.

---

homo economicus pursuing individual self-interest. It is also distinct from the intervening 'second hand' of government regulation in order to perfect the market economy. The economic agent of the third hand is state-owned enterprise instead of private enterprise. However, it is different from previous state-owned enterprise because its aim is not profit but rather social equity and public goods.

The republic experienced a silver crisis in 1935 and chronic inflation after 1937. We believe that it was an after-effect of the West transferring cost outwards in order to get out of the crisis of 1929–1933. It was another lesson the Chinese had to learn while aspiring to modernize in the footsteps of the West since the late Qing dynasty.

First, let us look into the Silver Purchase Act of 1934 as a response to the Great Depression in the USA and its consequent influence on China.

President Franklin D. Roosevelt put forth the Silver Purchase Act of 1934 due to the lobbying and pressure of seven silver-producing states and related interest blocs. Accordingly, the treasury purchased silver till the end of 1961. The act was eventually abolished in 1963. During 1934–1949, the US government had spent US$ 1.5 billion to purchase silver, more than the New Deal's subsidy to agriculture (see Box 1).[14]

Box 1: United State's Silver Purchase Act of 1934

The United States of America is traditionally a major silver producing country. In the 1930s, US capital controlled 66% of silver production and 77% of silver smelting of the world. Yet the silver industry did not have an important position in the US economy. According to 1934 data, the total value of silver production was only US$ 32 million, lower than that of peanuts and potatoes, and much lower than that of wheat and cotton. Nevertheless, for the seven western states where silver production was concentrated (Utah, Idaho, Arizona, Montana, Nevada, Colorado and New Mexico) it was highly important, and the senators from these seven silver-producing states had control of one-seventh of the votes in the Senate. These senators, the Democrat senators in particular, along with the producers of copper, lead and zinc that had silver as a by-product, formed the so-called silver bloc. The US government and politicians found that only by pleasing the silver bloc could they smoothly implement their policies or pass legislations.

The Great Depression in 1929 brought serious setbacks to the silver producers. The price of silver dropped drastically, from US$ 0.58 per ounce in 1928 to US$ 0.38 in 1930. By the second half of 1932 it

---

[14]https://weibo.com/1197745300/Ddd8NleKO?from=singleweibo&mod=recommand_weibo&sudaref=www.baidu.com&type=comment#_rnd1454125302430.

had dropped even more to US$ 0.25 per ounce. In that situation, the silver bloc immediately launched lobbying activities to prop up the price of silver, such as convening international conferences, requesting the government to purchase and reserve silver at higher than market price, to mint and issue silver coinage, and so on. However, these lobbying actions did not have much effect during the administration of President Hoover. In November 1932, not only was Roosevelt, a Democrat, elected president of the United States, but the Democrats also won a major victory in the Congress. At the same time close allies of the silver bloc—Democrat senators from agricultural states—also saw their force strengthened. As a result, the space for and the impact of lobbying actions by the silver bloc rose to an unprecedented height. President Roosevelt needed the support of the silver bloc in order to pass a series of legislations related to the New Deal, and thus had to indulge the silver bloc's activities. The famous silver senator Pittman, chairman of the Senate's Foreign Relations Committee, had said that if President Roosevelt did not raise the subsidy on silver production, he would request the Senate not to put the Neutrality Act to vote. The Silver Purchase Act that was passed in June 1934 signified the apex of the silver bloc's lobbying activities.

The main content of the Silver Purchase Act was to authorize the Department of Treasury to purchase silver in the overseas market until the silver price reached US$ 1.29 per ounce or until the value of silver in the US Treasury reserve reached one-third of the value of the gold reserve. During the process of purchasing, the Department of Treasury had widespread discretionary power.

Key measures included:

- The Department of Treasury decided the timing and terms for purchasing silver in the overseas market based on whether or not it would be beneficial to US public interest.
- When silver price reached US$ 1.29 per ounce or when the value of silver in the currency reserve reached one-third of the value of gold in the currency reserve, silver purchase should stop.
- On 1 May 1934, the domestic silver price in the US should not be lower than US$ 0.50 per ounce.
- When the value of silver in the currency reserve exceeded one-third of the gold in the reserve, the treasury should sell silver.

- The face value of the silver certificate should not be lower than the cost of the silver content.
- The Department of Treasury was authorized to control import and export, as well as other trading activities in relation to silver.
- The president announced the nationalization of silver.
- Profit tax of 50% would be imposed on trading gains relating to the purchase and sale of silver.

Source: Liu Yunzhong 'Impact and Implications to the Chinese Economy Of the U.S. "Silver Purchase Act" in 1934', State Council Development Research Center, *Research Report*, 28 November, 2005, Issue 200.

At the beginning of the Great Depression, for about two to three years, most of the nations trading with China adopted the gold standard. The demand for gold was higher than silver. The general commodity prices in these countries, including silver, were falling after 1929, though the silver price fell by a greater extent than the general price. Based on the value of gold, the value of silver fell by 40% in the international market during 1929–1931, while the US wholesale price index declined by 26%. Therefore, the high economic growth during 1920–1930 in China was at the mercy of the West before the wave of financial globalization. China avoided the immediate impact of the crisis in the West due to its adoption of a different currency system. Thanks to the silver standard, China enjoyed a golden decade. Pegged to silver, the Chinese currency devalued in the world market, which greatly mitigated the conductive effect of the international economic crisis.

Even though China also recorded a decline in export, it was relatively less serious compared to the fall in import and compared to global export. In 1930–1931, when the crisis in the West was at its peak, China recorded a trade surplus. In 1931, China imported 45.45 million taels of silver. While other nations were hit hard by deflation, China on the contrary recorded mild inflation.

However, in 1931, the UK, Japan and India abandoned the gold standard in succession. Still on the silver standard, China's currency appreciated against other major currencies and it faced an international payment deficit. In 1932, the net export of silver was 7.35 million taels due to the trade deficit. The domestic price index started to decline. When the US abandoned the gold standard in 1933, the Chinese currency started to appreciate against the dollar, from US$ 0.19 in 1932 to US$ 0.33. The export in 1932 was merely 58% of 1930. The trade deficit had to be balanced by exporting precious metals such as gold and silver.

Now when the world economy and trade began to recover, China stumbled into recession.

Generally, a colonized or semi-colonized country in dependency would pursue modernization according to the model of its master state, unaware of the fact that modernization was achieved in the latter by external colonization. Similarly, when China suffered from the exogenous crisis that originated in the master state, its modern economy was hit hard in the 1930s.

The most serious impact on China was the Silver Purchase Act. From its implementation in June 1934 to 30 June 1935, the US government purchased 294 million ounces of silver. The silver price was rocketing to US$ 0.81 by April 1935. The rise in the international silver price was higher than the domestic price in China. By mid-October 1934, the difference between international and domestic prices was greater than 25%. By the spring of 1935, it became greater than 50%. A profit of US$ 300–400 could be made by exporting US$ 1,000 worth of silver. Tax on silver export failed to curb the draining of silver (Liu 2005). From April 1934 to November 1935, the silver reserve in China dropped from 6.02 to 2.88 trillion yuan[15] (part of which was exported to Japan and then smuggled aboard) (Xu 2010: 73).

The consequence of silver draining was an exogenous deflation. A chain reaction led to a vicious circle, which can be represented with the following flow Chart 1.

When silver started to drain out of China in 1932, the physical economy rapidly went into recession, while private capital in the urban sector flowed from industry towards speculation. In this way, statistics

---

[15]元: unit of Chinese currency.

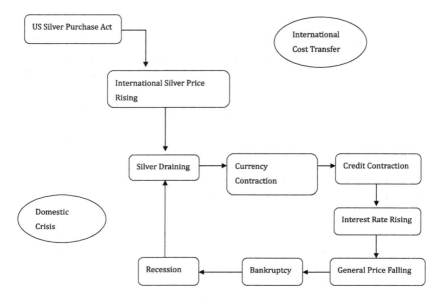

Chart 1 The economic crisis in China caused by the Silver Purchase Act

still showed the national economy as booming.[16] Therefore, the period 1927–1937 is generally known as the Golden Decade of the Republic of China.

Rural regions suffered most from the impact of deflation and asset depreciation. Agricultural product price dropped by 6.9% in 1934 and 3.7% in 1935. As price dropped and demand for agricultural products declined, together with the impact of drought, agricultural production amounted to merely 13.1 billion yuan, a drop of 46% compared with 1931. A member of the Nationalist Party (KMT) Li Tianni conducted a survey in Shandong in 1934 and reported:

> Shandong East is traditionally a rich region. However, land price which used to be a hundred yuan per *mu* is now worth only about 40–50

---

[16]After 80 years, China in 2015 faces a similar situation. After the end of Quantitative Easing in the USA, rise in interest rate has driven foreign exchange reserve out of China. Chasing speculation, private capital has left the physical economy and is rushing towards real estate and the stock market. The GDP is represented as recording high growth rate.

yuan. In the western and southern poorer regions, land price that used to be 50 yuan is now as low as 20 or even 10 yuan per *mu*, yet nobody wants to purchase land. Peasant bankruptcy is prevailing. The agony is unprecedented. (Li 1934)[17]

At the same time, the interest rate was rocketing. In July 1934, the market rate was 5%. In September it became 12%. Many enterprises closed down. In 1935 alone, 1,065 enterprises went bankrupt in Shanghai, and 20 banks closed down or halted business in the whole country. The production of yarn, the largest industry of China was cut by 60%. (The whole situation is similar to the impact of the policy of US Federal Reserve since 2008, which cut then raised the interest rate.)[18]

Under such severe economic pressure, the government had to abandon the silver standard and establish the modern paper currency system. The financial reform of shifting towards a modern fiat currency is somehow similar to contemporary 'deep reform' as strongly advocated by liberal and neo-liberal economists, both as a response to an exogenous crisis.

In fact, China had long been perplexed by the fluctuation of the international silver supply since it took the silver standard in the mid-sixteenth century (Han 2009). The fiat currency reform not only ended the silver currency system that was in function since the Ming dynasty but also skipped the gold standard prevalent in the West after the silver standard. China moved directly into paper currency. Many view this as the beginning of modernization of China's currency system. (The mentality of advocating swift and radical modernization is similar to those who nowadays advocate radical financial reform.) Yet, the effect

---

[17] *Mu* 畝, unit of area (1 *mu* = 0.0667 hectares).

[18] Someone reviewed this history on the internet. It is worth quoting here: "The Silver Purchase Act was actually similar to the making of Petrodollar later. The timing is 1934 when the USA needed to get out of the Great Depression. Purchasing silver with dollar pushed up the international price of silver. So doing would control the economy of silver standard nations like China and Mexico. Franklin D. Roosevelt made this decision after pondering on his difference in advantage against the Führer [Adolf Hitler]. Mexico and the southwest seven states were the major places producing silver in the world. The Americans could control silver flow easily. The change of currency credit from silver to the dollar made China dependent on importing American goods. The resuscitation of American industry was thus secured. Before 1934 the Führer knocked open Chinese market through barter trading. Afterward Germany was squeezed out by the United States.".

of this reform was underestimated and China soon ran into a free fall of hyperinflation. The crisis as a result of the malicious cost of modernization continued till 1950 after a new regime was established (Liu 2005).

China at that time had a fiat currency system that was based on foreign exchange reserve (the US dollar). It was not a sovereign currency system based on the credit of the state's political power, as China had a semicolonial relationship with major Western powers. Any currency system based on foreign reserve implies a high level of dependency, which may erode a nation's currency sovereignty.

The lesson should be learnt nowadays. If exports do not weigh much in a nation's economy, when the ratio of foreign exchange reserves and domestic currency value corresponding with the circulation of goods and services is lower than a certain level, the monetary policy may fail when foreign reserves are inadequate to regulate domestic money supply. In another case, when exports constitute a large part of a nation's economy, the hard earned wealth is given to the master nation of foreign reserve as a form of seigniorage. Furthermore, the domestic economy may be constrained by external factors like external demand and foreign exchange rate. Before 1949, China was in the former situation whereas today it is in the latter. Worse still, military expenditure due to chronic wars (invasion and civil war) put great pressure on the fiscal balance. Arms purchase led to a drop in foreign reserve. The KMT government was powerless in monetary regulation. As a consequence, a booming speculative economy and hyperinflation went into a vicious circle.

The reason China managed to maintain a relatively good economy during the 1929–1933 crisis in the West is because it did not adopt the gold standard. And because the silver standard had become obsolete in the West, it helped China to avoid currency competition with the rest of the world (Li 2005). The Chinese took this precious chance to develop heavy and chemical industries, which lay the foundation of resistance against the Japanese invasion. State capital was formed in the process and continued to become a dominant force in China's economic construction after 1949.

But for all that, the financial reform in 1936 ushered China into the international paper currency club and at the same time the international parade of economic crisis.

Currency War and Hyperinflation in the Republic of China

Prior to military defeat, the failure of modern financial reform became the major factor in the KMT regime's downfall. In 1935, the KMT government, confronted with the problems of silver draining and deflation, put forth an important reform in the financial system. The traditional silver standard was replaced by the modern paper currency system. On the one hand, it was an important step in the modernization of the economy. On the other, it began the collapse of the modern financial system because of consequent hyperinflation and other complications.

When a developing country pushes forth paper currency reform without cutting its connection with foreign finance (which was impossible for China at that time), it has to rely on foreign support in terms of capital and policy. Otherwise, it cannot establish the credit foundation of its currency. At that time, the USA, UK and Japan all wanted China to peg its fiat currency with theirs since doing so would put China into their sphere of influence. Eventually, the KMT government opted for the US dollar (Chen 2015). It became one of the factors triggered Japan to accelerate its invasion of China. Japan, which aspired to monopolize interests in China, invaded North China in 1935 when the KMT government put forth the fiat currency reform. In 1937, the invasion began in earnest. Military expenditure put great pressure on the KMT government's fiscal budget as overseas arms purchase cut into its foreign reserve and it became difficult to sustain a stable exchange rate. The war was also conducted in the field of currency. Japan issued a huge amount of counterfeit currency in the occupied regions in order to transfer the cost of its domestic fiscal deficit (see Box 2).

The KMT failed to resolve its internal contradictions even after the victory in 1945. Monetary regulation and anti-regulation became means of struggle by different partisan sects. The fiscal budget was further burdened by civil war. Hyperinflation, born together with the fiat currency, became uncontrollable after 1945, till the beginning of the new republic.

Box 2: Legal Currency, Resistance Currency and Puppet-Regime Currency in Shandong Liberated Regions During the Sino-Japanese War

In addition to military battles during the years of the Sino-Japanese War, there were also battles between the legal currency (issued by the KMT government), the resistance currency (issued by the anti-Japanese democratic government) and the puppet-regime currency (issued by the puppet regime, set up and controlled by the Japanese imperialists).

The currency battles among the antagonists during the war could generally be divided into two phases:

Before the eruption of the Pacific War in 1941, legal currency was freely circulated both in the liberated and occupied regions, and had a preferred status in the latter. At that time, with support from countries like the USA and the UK, its value had not declined significantly. Japan then issued a large amount of currency under the puppet regime in the occupied areas in exchange for legal currency. The collected legal money was then taken to American and British banks in places such as Shanghai to exchange for foreign currencies (US dollar and British pound) to purchase various needed materials from the international market. Because of that, they still allowed free circulation of legal currency and did not wish to see it depreciating rapidly.

During the Pacific War, Japan plundered billions of legal currency from areas like Shanghai and took over foreign banks in these regions. The channel to convert legal currency into dollars and pounds was therefore disrupted. Following that, Japan changed its strategy. In deciding to eliminate the KMT legal currency, it sent billions of it to KMT's regions for the acquisition of large quantities of supplies. At the same time, Japan also issued large amounts of currency under the puppet regime to replace the legal currency in order to cover fiscal deficits. As a result, legal currency rapidly depreciated in value. Yet, since the KMT government had the support of the USA, UK and others, the value of legal currency could still be stabilized from time to time. Besides, given that the Japanese invaders had issued the puppet currency recklessly, the latter's value started to decline sharply from 1944, even more seriously than the legal currency.

Source: Xue (2006).

The first complete fiscal year after the fiat currency reform was 1936. The fiscal deficit in that year was 33%, which was serious enough by today's standard. (During 1987–1989, China's overall fiscal deficit reached 25%; in 1988 the inflation rate was 18.5%.) However, in 1940, fiscal deficit reached 87%. In 1945, the year of victory, it was 81%. That was only one year during 1940–1945 that recorded a figure lower than 70%. In the following two years during the civil war, the deficit stayed above 60%.[19]

During the Sino-Japanese War, fiscal budget was out at the elbows. The discount rate of the national bond was up to 45–50%. Increasing the money supply became the only source of revenue (Coble 1987: 43). Consequently, the value of paper currency in circulation expanded from 1.3 billion yuan in January 1937 to 556.9 billion in August 1945, just before Japan surrendered. At the end of 1948, it rocketed to 24,558,999 billion yuan. The subsequent inflation rate became one of the highest recorded in history. Take the general price in 1936–1937 as the base of 1. In June 1945, it became 2,133. In August 1948, before the currency reform (yuan being backed by US dollar reserve the government held at hand), it became 7.25 million. Before liberation, it was 316.67 million. While the purchasing power of 100 yuan in 1937 was two cows, in 1941 it was a pig, in 1943 a chicken, in 1945 a fish, in 1946 an egg, and in May 1949 0.00245 grain of rice.[20] The period 1937–1945 was of relatively mild inflation. During 1945–1948, prices increased by 30% every month. After 1948, money supply and inflation went out of control.

---

[19]Gilbert Rozman, *The Modernization of China* (Chinese translation). Shanghai People's Press, 1989, pp. 372–373, 432. Quoted in Cheng (1998: 41).

[20]Renmin University Agricultural Economics Department, 中国近代农业经济史 (*Modern Agricultural Economic History of China*). Beijing: Renmin University Press, 1980, p. 203. Quoted in Cheng (1998: 41).

From August 1948 to April 1949, the money supply expanded 4,524 times, which was twice the increment that took place during the eight years of the resistance war. The price index in Shanghai at that time was 13,574,200% (Xu 2008: 515). Such was the historical background when East China was liberated and the renminbi entered into Shanghai in 1949.

The Birth of Renminbi: The Continuation or End of the Crisis?

Since its foundation, the Communist Party of China (CPC) was identified as a 'peasant party' by the Soviet Communist Party. The former accepted the theory proposed by the latter that China had to develop national capitalism first. In the 1940s, national capitalism was formulated as the strategy of New Democracy. However, after the new regime occupied the cities, it immediately found itself in a predicament. It was almost impossible to achieve industrialization on a shabby economic foundation by private capital under conditions of hyperinflation. The peasant economy accounted for the major part of the Chinese economy at the time, which consisted of geographically scattered peasants with little surplus to offer. To push forth industrialization under this condition, the state had to face the problem of an excessively high transaction cost between urban capital and rural peasants. It was a fundamental contradiction regardless of how this new regime, which was born out of a peasant revolution, defined itself.

The condition of the new republic was like that of many poor developing countries nowadays. In 1949, the total industrial and agricultural production in China was 45.6 billion yuan, 84.18 yuan per capita; the total social production was worth 54.8 billion yuan, 101.17 yuan per capita; and the gross national income was 35.8 billion yuan, 66 yuan per capita.[21] The industrial foundation was weak, and agriculture constituted the predominant mode of production of the national economy. However, most of the agricultural production was conducted by traditional means.

---

[21] *China Statistics Yearbook 1984*, pp. 23–25. Quoted in Wu and Dong (2001: 942–945).

In the same year, the average production of staple grain in China was 142 catties per *mu*, while the world's average was 154 (Zhang 1997: 35–37). Total foodstuffs production was 225 billion catties. A historical comparison shows that industrial production had been cut by half, heavy industry by 70% and light industry by 30%. National per capita income was merely US$ 27, about two-thirds of the average of Asian countries (Zhou 2005). Total unemployment, including workers and intellectuals, amounted to about 1.5 million, besides which there was also a huge semi-employed population (Zhen 2001).

In short, even if the new government had decided to stay on the path of national capitalism that the old regime failed to make a success of, it would not have had the required economic foundation to get out of the lasting hyperinflation.

While the civil war was still raging on, the new regime found itself caught in the same dilemma as its predecessor: serious fiscal deficit required an expanding money supply, which in turn increased the pressure of currency devaluation. According to Chen Yun (陈云), then deputy premier and director of the Financial and Economic Committee, the fiscal revenue in 1949 was equivalent to 30.3 billion catties of foodstuffs, whereas the fiscal expenditure was 56.7, with a deficit of 26.4 catty or 46.56%. Excluding Northeast China, which was the major grain-producing region, the fiscal deficit would have gone up to 65.97%. In other words, beyond the Northeast, only one-third of the expenditure was covered by revenues. The other two-thirds had to rely on money issuance. Since its circulation from December 1948 onwards, the supply of RMB increased by 160 times in a year and 270 times by February 1950 (He 2008) (see Box 3).

Box 3: The Pressure of Fiscal Deficits During the Early Establishment of New China

When the civil war was still raging in October 1949, direct military expenses alone had taken over 60% of the total fiscal expenditure of the new government. Moreover, the new government had adopted the policy of retaining the former regime's military and government personnel who were willing to submit to the new government. In addition, the number of military, government and administrative personnel in the liberation areas had also increased from 6 million in August to 7 million in November. Such an enormous expenditure had mainly been sustained by the issuance of paper currency.

Chen Yun, in his speech on 8 August 1949 to the Shanghai Financial and Economics Conference, mentioned that:

> The total amount of paper money issued up to the end of July 1949 was 280 billion yuan, which constituted the monetary base. To ensure disbursements for military battles, subsidies on grain and food in new liberated regions, repairs of the railroad, as well as funds for investment in shipping and transportation, in postal & telecommunication, and mining, for operation of state-owned enterprises, purchase of cotton yarn and so on, it would be necessary to issue 163.3 billion yuan every month between August to October. That is before taking into account industrial investment and the purchase of agricultural produce. In November and December, there would be the need to purchase cotton and other material supplies on top of military expense. Taking all into account, the monthly issuance necessary would be 169.2 billion yuan.

In fact, the actual amount far exceeded the plan. On 13 November, in the draft report on inflation to be presented to the State Council Fiscal and Economics Committee, Chen Yun had mentioned that the total amount of currency issued at the end of September and October was 810 billion and 1.1 trillion yuan respectively, and that on 13 November it had reached 1.6 trillion yuan.

The new money supply was mainly to make up for the fiscal deficit. According to Chen Yun's estimate, from August to November fiscal expenditure had reached 5.43 trillion yuan while fiscal revenue was only 1.88 trillion yuan, with a deficit of 3.55 trillion yuan.* Total revenue could only cover 34.6% of the total expenditure. For every 3 yuan of expenditure, revenue accrued was 1 yuan, leading to a 2 yuan deficit. The total expenditure for three months, December 1949 to February 1950, was over 3.14 trillion yuan, while revenue was estimated to be 0.64 trillion yuan, with a deficit of 2.5 trillion yuan.

Sources: Jin and Chen (2005: 642–656) and Chen (1995a: 1–8).
Note: *In the original article, these figures were 543 million, 188 million and 355 million yuan respectively, and have been converted

> into trillion taking into consideration other materials and the need to keep data logical.

Furthermore, the economy had to be rebuilt from scratch. The money issued by the new government corresponded even less to real economic wealth than under the previous regime.

Due to years of wars and natural disasters, the number of livestock was reduced by one-third and major farming tools were reduced by 30%. Rural labour decreased remarkably too; in north China alone, it was cut by one-third. The amount of land affected by disasters was 12.795 million *mu*, which constituted about 8.71% of the total arable land. Total foodstuff production decreased from the pre-war historical height of 150 million tonnes to 112.18 tonnes in 1949. Cotton production dropped from 849,000 tonnes in 1936 to 444,000 in 1949. Edible oil production dropped from 5,078,000 tonnes in 1933 and 1,934,000 to 2,564,000 in 1949. The number of large livestock decreased from 71.57 million in 1935 to 60.02 million in 1949.[22] There were 40 million people affected by natural disaster and 7 million by famine. In the flood and drought-stricken East and North China, according to conservative estimates, there were less than 2,900 million catties of grain (Jin and Chen 2005: 669).

By 1949, enormous amount of materials for industrial production had been destroyed in war. Post-war industrial capacity was remarkably low. The general price difference between industrial and agricultural products expanded by 45.3%. Total industrial production value, especially of heavy industry, decreased by half compared with 1936; steel production dropped by 90% compared with 1943; and coal production decreased by 50% compared with 1942. At the birth of the new republic, the whole steel industry in China was equipped with only 7 open hearth furnaces and 22 small electric furnaces. Total electricity capacity was merely about

---

[22] *China Rural Statistics Yearbook 1989*. Beijing: China Statistics Press, 1989; *Thirty Years of National Agricultural Statistics (1949–1979)*. National Bureau of Statistics, 1980.

1,146,000 kilowatt. Total industrial fixed assets of the nation were worth only 12.4 billion yuan.[23]

Moreover, the KMT government had transferred a substantial part of its faculties and materials to Hong Kong, of which there were 29 state-owned monopoly enterprises, including China Airlines and Central Airlines; China Merchants Steam Navigation Company (Hong Kong); the largest ocean shipping companies in old China; the bodies of minerals export; and nine banks and offices in its financial system. The total assets amounted to 243 million Hong Kong dollars.[24]

Moreover, a great part of the infrastructure was destroyed by the war. Transportation became difficult, which aggravated regional scarcity. In 1949, railways in China covered merely 26,878 km, including 913.7 km in Taiwan (Wu and Dong 2001: 442). Motorways were in a poor condition and total mileage was short. According to statistics, total motorways were 149,000 km, of which 86,000 km were accessible.[25] On average, there were only 1.6 kms of motorway in every 100 square kilometre stretch. Only 30% of motorways were paved, mostly with low quality gravel or cobbles. Over 60% was unpaved road (ibid: 454). As for shipping, in the liberated regions (not including Southwest and South China), there were 2,357 vessels of 38,100 total tonnage, whereas in Hong Kong, Taiwan and overseas there were 448 vessels of 78,200 tonnes. Aviation was at its initial stage. Therefore, the total traffic mileage of modern goods transportation was 229.6 tonne-km, merely 52.7% of 1936 (Li and Zou 1993: 215) (Table 1).

---

[23]Ceng Peiyan (ed.) 中国投资建设五十年 (*Fifty Years of Investment and Construction in China*). Beijing: China Planning Press, 1999, p. 1. Quoted in Wu and Dong (2001: 69).

[24]After much negotiation, the new regime managed to take back aeroplanes, machineries, means of transportation, bank deposits, minerals and cotton amounting to a total of 200 million Hong Kong dollars in value. Part of the assets of the two airlines confiscated by Hong Kong became a suspense issue in Sino-British diplomacy. After long-term negotiations from July 1952 to October 1985, the two governments signed an agreement on 5 June 1987. The British government paid China 3.8 million US dollars as part of the compensation. See Liu Jingfang, '建国初期发生在香港的一场特殊运动' (*A Special Movement in Hong Kong at the Birth of the Nation*), in 百年潮 (*A Century of Tide*), 1997(3). Quoted in Wu and Dong (2001: 71).

[25]As shown in Table 1, this figure was given as 80,700 km. Inconsistency in data was found in Wu and Dong (2001).

Table 1 Transportation route length of China in 1949 (unit: 10,000 km)

	Railway	Motorway	Canal	Aviation (1950)	Post Road
Accessible mileages in 1949	2.2	8.07	7.36	1.14	93[*]
Historical high	2.68	14.9			

Note: [*]Includes 250,000 km of rural post road in North China
Source: China Economic Yearbook 1981, 1949–52 中华人民共和国经济档案选编·交通通讯卷 (Selection from People's Republic of China Economic Archives 1949–1952: Transportation). Beijing: China Supplies Press (1996: 7, 487, 957). Quoted in Wu and Dong (2001: 70)

Additionally, the KMT government transferred all of the country's gold reserves when retreating to Taiwan. There were no hard currency reserves in the Central Bank. The new regime had no means to withdraw currency from circulation. According to a report by *Renmin Daily*, KMT took 2.775 million taels of gold and 15.2 million silver yuan to Taiwan.[26] At the end of 1948, Chiang Kai-shek ordered all the gold, silver yuan and foreign reserves of about 500 million US dollars transferred to Taiwan.[27] After liberation, the Central Bank was taken over. There remained 6,180 taels of gold, 1,546,643 silver coins and a little foreign exchange reserve (Li 1993: 7; Shanghai CPC History Research Office 1993: 1086).

The consequence of issuing a large amount of paper money due to the deficiency of materials and hard currency was severe. General prices marked by RMB rocketed from the very beginning. From April 1949 to February 1950, four rounds of substantial price fluctuations were recorded (see Box 4). From December 1948 to December 1949, the wholesale price index in 13 cities including Beijing was up to 7,384%. On every occasion, the price spike started in the cities, and then spread to the whole nation. Two essential consumer goods, staple food and

---

[26] *Renmin Daily*, 8 January 1990. The values from different sources vary. This is the most quoted source.
[27] 李宗仁回忆录 (*Memoirs of Li Zongren*). Nanning: Guangxi People's Press, 1980, p. 948. Quoted in Wu and Dong (2001: 70).

cotton gauze, were always leading the rise (He 2008). As money supply accumulated, the inflation rate accelerated.

Box 4: The Four Instances of Renminbi Devaluation During the Early Years of the PRC[#]

1. The first instance of devaluation

In 1949 there was a severe spring drought in North China and the harvest fell short. A wave of price fluctuations occurred in April in North and Northwest China, impacting Shandong, north Suzhou, Beijing, Tianjin and so on. In April and May, the areas mentioned above recorded a general price hike of around 50%. Using the wholesale price index (WPI) in 13 major cities in the country, including Beijing and Shanghai as example, and with December 1948 as the base index of 100, in March 1949, WPI had inflated to 234.3, in April 287.0, and to 494.8 in May. For month-over-month comparison, April was 122.5 and May had risen to 172.4.[*]

2. The second instance of devaluation

This time, the wave of price fluctuations occurred in Shanghai soon after liberation. It started with silver coin speculation, and then led to attacks on other major commodities such as grain and cotton yarn, causing price levels in Shanghai to spike. During the 13 days between 17 May 1949 and 9 June 1949, the general price index rose by more than 2.7 times. The gold price rose by 2.11 times, silver by 1.98 times, rice 2.24 times and yarn 1.49 times. The status of paper currency was almost completely supplanted by gold and silver coins. From 23 June to 21 July, within the course of a month, the price of yarn rose from 325,000 to 615,000, increased by 89%.[##] The hike was even worse for grain. From 23 June to 16 July, the price of rice rose from 11,700 per Chinese stone [1 Chinese stone = 100 catties] to 59,000, an increase of 404%. The extent of price inflation was high overall. The price index in July was 204.6, higher than June by 104.6. All major commodities had a price increase of 50–200% in July as compared to June. Price levels in Beijing and Tianjin also spiked. The wave of inflation spread precipitously like wildfire across the country.

3. The third instance of devaluation

This was the most severe and most widespread price inflation after the establishment of New China. It also lasted the longest. On 1 October 1949, the People's Republic of China was established. From 15 October, with Shanghai and Tianjin in the lead, followed by Central and Northwest China, the price of imported industrial material such as metal and chemicals steadily rose. After that the price of yarn and grain jumped, leading to a rapid increase in the overall prices. The daily increase was between 10 and 30%. The renminbi declined in value drastically. The wholesale price index, which was 100 in June 1949, rose to 302.5 by October, 720.9 in November and 998.3 by December. The 13 major cities including Beijing and Tianjin had the wholesale price index going up from 1,667.5 in September to 2,179.4 in October, then to an unprecedented 5,376.6 in November, rising further to 7,484.2 in December.** With the July price level as base, in the four cities of Shanghai, Tianjin, Hankou and Xian, the price level on 10 December rose by an average of more than 3.2 times. The peak of the price fluctuation was seen on 24 November, when it was 3.7 times more than it was at the end of July.

4. The fourth instance of devaluation

Around the Chinese New Year in early 1950, speculators in Shanghai got the chance to exploit the old pattern of favourable market openings as well as opportunities in consumer commodity due to a shortage in supplies to meet increased demand. This shortage was caused by the disruption in operations of factories and electric plants that had suffered serious damage during the air bombing of Shanghai by the KMT, prompting another assault on the prices of grain and yarn. This had once again led to countrywide inflation. The wholesale price index of 25 commodities in 15 large- and medium-sized cities, with December 1949 as a base, had risen to 126.6 in January 1950, 203.3 in February and 226.3 in March. On a regional basis, Chongqing had an increase of 186%, Xian 132%, Guangzhou 73%, Tianjin 83%, Wuhan 68% and Shenyang 57%. At the later stage, the rate of increase of the price level had far exceeded the increase in the money supply.

Notes:
#Apart from specified quotes, other data is taken from He (2008).

> ##The unit of weight for yarn has not been specified in the original article.
> Sources:
> *1949–1952 中华人民共和国经济档案资料选编·综合卷 (Selection from People's Republic of China Economic Archives 1949–1952: General). Beijing: China Urban Economy & Society Press, 1990, p. 111.
> **Ibid.

In summary, the newborn RMB was the sovereign currency of the People's Republic of China. In order to consolidate its credit foundation as a sovereign currency, the government had to increase its credibility by solving fundamental economic difficulties. If the national currency could not establish its credibility, then the political power of the state would be seriously diminished and incomplete.[28]

How could an economic foundation for political sovereignty be built upon a wasteland of recession and speculation? This problem remained unsolved for the KMT government, because of which they lost the battle. How could the new government manage to achieve this goal? We will attempt to offer an explanation below. The mechanisms at work could then help shed light on the ever-changing difficulties people face nowadays.

Here, we emphasize two theses. First, inflation always takes place in cities where capital is concentrated. Second, in situations of crises, private capital always veers away from the physical economy towards speculation according to its economic rationality. These were apparent at the very beginning of the new republic.

---

[28]We call it 'governance deficiency' in another research.

Stabilizing the RMB: 'Material Supplies Standard' Resolved the Crisis of Paper Currency

It is well known that the communist regime in China completely eradicated the decade-long problem of hyperinflation in one year, to the surprise of many.

The new republic was in a state of destitution. It was a yet-to-be-unified nation embroiled in the Korean War, on top of being confronted by armies from 16 countries and completely blockaded by the West. Troubled by domestic problems and external aggression, how did it achieve the political and economic goal of an independent nation with its sovereignty intact?

The actions of going to war while trying to maintain people's livelihoods are somewhat contradictory. Securing supplies for war required the expansion of the money supply, which naturally led to inflation. Under these conditions, the economy could not function well.

Accordingly, citing inflation as a reason, Dong Biwu (董必武) and Bo Yibo (薄一波) suggested in April 1949 that the new government should not expand the money supply. In other words, they suggested going along with the cycle by 'selling short' when the market was heading downward. However, the CPC leaders finally adopted Chen Yun's point of view, which involved the counter-cycle measure of 'going long'. He thought that in the long term, as the regime consolidated its footing in the whole country and resumed production, the government could act proactively in the economy. Then the expansion in the money supply would not run out of control. Besides, the government's purchase of supplies did require expanding the money supply.

In other words, an economic agent who is seeking profit in the market and guided by economic rationality with a shorter time-frame will go along with the cycle by selling while the market is turning down. However, a government which is non profit-seeking and guided by "government rationality" with much longer time-frame and larger inclusive concern of interests should take counter-cycle measures.

What followed has proven that the government's move to carry out counter-cycle regulation by directly 'going long' is a practical way to resolve an economic crisis.

However, counter-regulation based on government rationality requires certain rather specific conditions, otherwise different results could ensue. After many experiences of crises, and especially after the 2008 credit crunch when the US, Japan and China one after the other successively adopted a quantitative easing policy, people started to understand that Chen Yun's proposal was actually an expression of government rationality in the face of crisis. It is only on the condition that a government directly confers credit upon paper money (fiat currency) using its political power that it can perform counter-cycle regulation.

In comparison, the KMT had failed in counter-cycle regulation through the enormous expansion of the money supply. We propose this is because full and intact national sovereignty is a necessary and sufficient condition for effective counter-cyclical regulation. The new government succeeded because it viewed itself as a people's government, having its footing in national mobilization through revolution and taking unlimited responsibility for the welfare of the people. It is owing to such background political factors that it could achieve such an effective and desirable result.

The major mechanisms of the RMB currency battle at the birth of the new republic included, in the short term, a dependence on military-political authority. The state took military control over cities where capital was concentrated, appropriating all state capital and transnational capital. A state-owned system based on capital was therefore developed at the least cost and enabled it to concentrate its power. Second, the government directly organized large-scale material supplies throughout the entire nation. It was a direct battle against the hard currency control of speculators, enabling the government to modify the foundation of the value of material supplies controlled by speculative capital. Besides, the long-term problem of regional compartmentalization by local powers and vested interests was also an issue. Almost all the big cities occupied by different field armies suffered from hyperinflation and speculation. Were it not for this condition, the central government could not have successfully adopted a counter-cyclical regulation policy when the country was permeated by a byzantine network of complicated local and partisan interests.

In the mid-term, the key was the economic regulative tools established by the central government. The government anchored the value with physical commodities essential to daily life in three domains: public bonds, savings and salaries (see below). The RMB was then linked with material supplies in the urban distribution of goods as well as with fiscal and financial systems. Its credit foundation to function as a currency was thereby consolidated.

Furthermore, there were two essential factors. First was the expansion of production. The new government emphasized agricultural production. People were mobilized to build large-scale agricultural infrastructure. Water conservation and irrigation facilities were constructed on rivers that used to be plagued by floods. This made thousands of acres of fields stable for producing crops. During 1949–1952, total arable land area increased by 10.25% and grain production increased by 46.1%.[29] It is noteworthy that in many cases funds for irrigation facilities were delivered as loans. Without the extensive mobilization of peasants, local governments would generally have found it difficult to overcome the high transaction cost of dealing with peasants individually and had to take up all the cost of irrigation. That would have eventually been rendered a fiscal burden to the national budget.

The second factor was frugality. Production expansion went hand in hand with frugality. Together with the *San Fan Wu Fan* movement, the efficiency of the fiscal fund was remarkably improved. Despite the continuation of the war, China had recorded a fiscal budget surplus consecutively in 1951 and 1952.

Because value was anchored, the floating interest rate was expected to stabilize. The RMB therefore became accepted by the people and became a source of savings in the People's Bank of China. Increasing social savings bestowed on the new banking sector the capability of credit creation for investment. It was an institutional innovation of material supplies-based currency (see following introduction),[30] different from

---

[29]1949–1952 中华人民共和国经济档案资料选编·商业卷 (Selection from *PRC Economic Archives 1949–1952: Commerce*). Beijing: China Supplies Press, 1995, pp. 365, 338. Quoted in Wu and Dong (2001: 656).

[30]This generalization was first given by Xue Muqiao (薛暮桥) in an interview with the foreign media in the liberated zone of Shandong. See the discussion below.

precious metal standard or foreign exchange-based currency. According to this experience, we may propose a hypothesis on the correlation between the value discount of material supplies and currency credibility:

The core concept of the economics of development, namely Saving = Investment[31] could only be validated under the condition of 3P + 3S.[32]

In 1953, China started to launch large-scale industrialization projects with the aid of the Soviet Union. The state accordingly began to implement the united purchasing and selling system. The RMB, which had just begun circulating smoothly, lost the status of an independently functioning currency. Otherwise, the supplies-based currency would become an important experience of constructing currency sovereignty, the core of economic sovereignty, for developing countries hoping to get out of a financial crisis.

In summary, we elaborate on two concepts put forward so far, namely, the revolution dividend and government rationality. Land revolution has paid the institutional cost of total mobilization, which can be regarded as a bonus of revolution. The government, guided by the interests of sustaining its institutional gain, instead of profit-seeking economic rationality, forms a 'comprehensive rationality' in which different aspects such as politics and economy, the physical economy and finance, short-term and long-term profits coordinate and balance themselves.

We start with the stabilization of the financial order in a short period.

---

[31]The lesson of most of the developing countries is proving the invalidity of S = I under post-colonial conditions. Developing countries are generally forced to maintain a colonized mono-economic structure, relying on resources export. High value-added fields such as logistics and financing are controlled by transnational corporations. As a result, it is difficult to increase social saving. The banking sector therefore is short of a funding source for credit creation. Similarly, the savings of developing countries become a major contributor to investment in developed countries, whereas these investments are to a great extent stimulated by war. See Dong et al. (2011).

[32]3P includes people's livelihood, people's solidarity and people's cultural diversity. 3S includes resource sovereignty, social solidarity and sustainable security. These are general principles we formulated in our exploration into the Trap of the South during the First South–South Forum on Sustainability at Lingnan University, Hong Kong in 2011.

The Great Currency Defence Battle

Confronted with the four instances of 'short selling' against the RMB at the beginning of the republic, as mentioned in Box 4, the new government started to fight the currency defence battle in the second instance and was successful in the third. The two battles took place in Shanghai, where speculative capital was concentrated.

In the Silver Yuan Battle during the second instance, the major means used by the new regime was a combination of military and political power. The Communist Party deployed military force to close down the silver coins market, politically declaring trading in silver coins as illegal. The RMB became the only legal currency. However, this did not fundamentally repress inflation. Then the government realized that the chief enemy of the RMB was no longer KMT's Jinyuanjuan[33] (bank note based on US dollar reserve), which had lost their credit base as the old regime collapsed, but the silver coins, which had a long history of

---

[33]After learning this lesson, various regions had adopted the approach of freezing the conversion price of silver and gold at a low level. 'At the same time of banning the trading of silver dollar and prohibiting the use of silver and gold in pricing, the people's government in various regions had also adopted the measure of having the People's Bank of China (PBOC) set conversion rates for silver and gold. Given that the quantity of silver and gold was relatively abundant in the society, in order to avoid having to issue large quantity of RMB pursuant to the conversion which could in turn worsen inflation, the people's government had implemented the policy of freezing at a low price (in south-western regions, since the quantity of silver was relatively abundant while the goods controlled by the government was insufficient, to avoid impacting the market the approach was simply to suspend conversion of silver and gold on a temporary basis). That meant the conversion rate set by PBOC would be lower than that in the black market by a rather wide margin, thus making it unattractive for wealthy people to convert their gold and silver into RMB. Nevertheless, that price was not unreasonably low. It would also give consideration to the interest of the converters. In line with the rise in price levels, the government had also adjusted the conversion rates upward several times. By the end of 1949, Shanghai had collected more than 1.08 million pieces of silver yuan and Beijing more than 220,000. In March 1950, after the stabilization of price levels, the state also adjusted upward the conversion rates of gold and silver. Given that the value of RMB had been stable, the amount of gold and silver collected by the state increased substantially. As an example, in 1950 Guangdong had converted and collected 7.455 million teals [1 teal = 37.5 gm] of gold (with 71.1% in the second half of the year), 1.012 million pieces of silver yuan (with 73.7% in second half of the year) and 53.236 million teals of pure silver (with 98.2% in second half of the year)' (Wu 1995).

circulation and potential of appreciation under inflation.[34] The credit
foundation of silver coins remained robust (see Box 5).

Box 5: The Shanghai Silver Yuan Battle

Shanghai was liberated on 27 May 1949. On the following day, the
Shanghai Military Control Commission announced the regulations for
using renminbi and the abolition of Jinyuanjuan, the old republic
currency. One RMB (old) was equivalent to 10,000 Jinyuanjuan. After
5 June, the latter was strictly prohibited from being circulated in the
market. Given that the latter's credibility was already close to zero,
the conversion was conducted very smoothly. In seven days a total of
35.9 trillion Jinyuanjuan was collected, approximately 53% of the total
amount issued by the KMT government.

Yet, the newly issued 200 million RMB existed only superficially in
the market and did not enter into actual circulation—in reality, without
equivalent commodities the conversion of the currency had simply
amounted to taking over the depreciation pressure of the Jinyuanjuan.

Given that silver still functioned as currency, while the RMB could
only have a supplementary role in low-value transactions, silver became
the target of speculation. To start with, one silver yuan was equivalent to 100 RMB. By 3 June it had appreciated to 720 RMB. On 4
June, it suddenly spiked to 1,100 RMB and the trend went on. On 5
June, the Eastern China Financial Commission and Shanghai Municipal
Committee released 100,000 silver yuan in an attempt to suppress speculation on silver coins, but it was like a drop in the ocean. On 7 June,
the value of a silver coin had even gone up to 1,800 RMB.

The failure of market-based measures was too much and it was a big
lesson for the new government. It was not until 10 June, when the
Shanghai Military Control Committee sent troops to close down the
securities exchange building and arrested a number of speculators, that
a heavy blow was dealt to speculation. At the same time, the government announced 'Measures for Management of Gold, Silver and Foreign
Currency in Eastern China', prohibiting the free circulation and private

---

[34]The KMT government's legal paper money after the currency reform, the value of which
was supported by the government's US dollar reserve, hence the name Jinyuanjuan (金圆券),
literally 'Dollar Bank Notes'.

trading of gold, silver and foreign currencies. Then, starting 14 June, the banks launched value-anchored deposits. Using these kinds of low-cost, direct intervention measures, the government was able to mitigate price inflation for the time being.

Source: Jin and Chen (2005: 569).

After the failure of silver coins speculation, private capital turned to speculation on staple grain and cotton. Through hoarding and market manipulation, speculators aspired to make windfall profits. It turned out to be the 'Battle of Rice and Cotton' (see Box 6).

The victory in the battle during the third instance of speculation was decisive in consolidating the status of the RMB. The key was not to rely on the communist government having more hard currency, the silver yuan or foreign reserve, but rather more hard commodities, the essential supplies of livelihood. As Chen Yun put it, 'people's confidence relies on staple grain in cities, on cotton gauzes in rural regions…. how much we were able to get hold of determined our capacity to regulate market' (Chen 1995a: 118–120).

This battle against the selling short of the RMB can be presented as the best manoeuvre of government rationality combining political power and economic operation. It was the first muscle-flexing of the Communist Party of China in the economy. Henceforth, people understood that what stood behind the RMB was more than the state's political power, but also an enormous reserve of material supplies stocked by the mobilization of the whole nation in the land revolution.

Therefore, the success of this battle not only established the RMB's status in the currency system but also facilitated the policy of anchoring value to essential commodities for consolidating the RMB's credibility in the middle term. When the credibility of the RMB was still weak, people would accept it only when its credit was backed up by essential supplies. And the success of this policy was guaranteed by the CPC's power to secure material supplies through popular mobilization across the whole nation. Therefore, Mao Zedong praised it highly, comparing it with one of CPC's most decisive military victories, the Huaihai Campaign.

Box 6: The Battle of Rice and Cotton: Dealing with the Third Wave of RMB Devaluation

From mid-June to late July 1949, in Shanghai, where there was the highest concentration of Chinese private sector capital, a wave of speculative activity took place targeting essential commodities. They took advantage of the KMT's military blockade against the CPC government and the disorders caused by the agents of the former, as well as natural disasters like flooding and storms in certain areas to trigger speculation on grain, cottons and so on, deploying enormous sums of money. Led by the price of rice, followed by the price of yarn, an across-the-board inflation emerged. The price of rice in Shanghai increased drastically by four times, while that of yarn doubled. At the same time, it also affected the entire Eastern and Northern China, as well as regions in Central and South China. The average price level in July rose by 1.8 times as compared to June.

Faced with the onslaught of the third wave of inflation, the person in charge of the fiscal faculty of the central government, Chen Yun, noticed that speculators in Shanghai were hoarding mainly yarn, while in Northern China speculators focused on grain. To avoid being attacked simultaneously on two fronts, he first turned his attention to the north. Starting from 15 November, a daily shipment of 10 million catties [1 catty = 600 gm] of grain was sent from the northeast to supply the Beijing and Tianjin regions. At the same time, 16 traders speculating on grain were arrested and punished. These measures overwhelmed the speculators and pacified the people. After sorting this problem, Chen Yun focused all his efforts towards suppressing the inflation trend in Shanghai.

To deal with this issue, he convened a financial conference from 27 July to 15 August concerning the five major regions—Eastern China, Northern China, Central, Northeast and Northwest—to discuss solutions for the severe economic situation facing Shanghai and the entire country. Chen Yun suggested that the key to solving the problem in Shanghai and stabilizing the price level nationwide was to take control of the 'two white, one black' (i.e., rice, yarn and coal). And within the 'two white, one black', the crucial ones were rice and cotton gauze. 'The extent of control we had on these would determine the control over the market.... The key to maintaining calmness in cities is staple grain and in rural regions it is cotton yarn.'

After analysing the sources of supplies and the conditions for transportation, Chen Yun believed it was completely possible to deploy supplies to Shanghai to ensure price stability there. The population in Shanghai at the end of 1948 was 5.05 million, and by May 1949 it had reached 5.5 million. Of this, urban population was 4.4 million. There were around 400,000 people who were staying there temporarily after liberation, which meant that the permanent urban population was 4 million. Based on a monthly supply of around 11 kg per person, the daily need in Shanghai would be around 1.5 million catties, which could be deployed from the old liberated regions (Xu and Li 2003: 9–11).

Therefore, even though Chen Yun accepted that the increased money supply by the CPC was the main reason for the inflation, he believed that through deployment of goods (from the old CPC bases to big cities) the inflation would be controllable.

Before November, the CPC fully exerted its well-organized system to raise material supplies from around the country. With grain, for example, the plan was to deploy 400 million catties from Sichuan and 10 million catties from Northeast China to Shanghai on a daily basis (for a duration of half a month). Furthermore, liberated areas in Northern and Central China, in Shandong, and so on also supplied grain to various big cities on an ongoing basis. The scale of this deployment, in terms of vastness and quantity, far exceeded that of the Huaihai Campaign. By the end of November, the quantity of grain mobilized by the CPC was no less than 5 billion catties, while the Huaihai Campaign had mobilized only 1 billion catties. The quantity of cotton yarn and cotton cloth controlled by the state-owned China Textile Company reached half of the total nationwide production.

Through a series of successive small price level increases to attract investors to purchase the commodities, the People's Bank of China had absorbed 800 billion liquid funds in the society.

On 24 November, the general price level was 2.2 times compared to that at the end of July. At this level, the quantity of goods under the central government's control was equivalent to the amount of monetary circulation in the market.

On 25 November, the central government directed a unified action in big cities across the nation to sell commodities. In addition to large-scale selling off, other coordinating measures in terms of taxation, credit and so on put tremendous pressure on speculative capital. The Central Committee of Finance and Economy stipulated that funds of all state-owned enterprises must be deposited in state-owned banks, and must not be loaned to private banks or private enterprises; private-owned factories were not permitted to close down operations and had to pay normal wages to workers; tax collection was intensified and no delays were permitted; at the same time, underground banks were banned to block sources of funds to speculators.

The speculators had acquired commodities in large quantities, even borrowing to do so. Yet from that day on, price levels did not increase further; rather they declined, to the shock of speculators. After 10 days of continuous selling off by the government, the speculators could no longer hold their positions and had to sell at a low price. Because of this, price levels dropped by 30–40%. By then, the inflation storm that had lasted for 50 days finally came to an end under the CPC's command and coordinated actions. That was known as the "Battle of Rice and Cotton".

Sources: Bo Yibo (1991), Jin and Chen (2005: 642–645), and "中共当年金融战之霸气" ('The CPC's Domineering Financial War in Years Back') https://www.360doc.com/content/16/0302/12/194 1668_538784910.shtml.

In adhering to individual economic rationality under a market economy, private capital tends to withdraw from the physical economy and turn towards speculation under pressure of long-term inflation. The economic failure of China before 1949 was due to the fact that the KMT government, having limited stock of foreign exchange, precious metals and staple grain and cotton, had been incapable of carrying out counter-cyclical regulation against speculation. The government selling to suppress price rises had amounted to subsidizing speculative merchants. Capital related with the government had also sneaked into speculation through different means, leading to corruption. Eventually, the official credit system had collapsed.

We can see the difference between the two governments in dealing with crisis.

Notably, in the two instances of inflation, the opponent of the RMB was no longer the old fiat money which had lost its credibility, but rather silver yuan which was hard currency generally welcomed by the people. That meant the new paper money (the credit of which was conferred by the state) had to compete with the credibility of silver coins. Under that condition, the credit of the RMB could only be backed by material supplies. In order to win this defence battle in one effective strike, the government had to concentrate staples and cotton in overwhelming quantity in a short period of time. It was impossible to suppress speculation by selling a limited amount of supplies in the market.

For example, on 5 June, the government sold 100,000 silver yuan to the market to suppress silver coin speculation. However it was to no avail. On the contrary, the price of silver yuan rose from 100 RMB (before short-selling up to 1,100 RMB) to 1,800 RMB on 7 June. On 10 October, the government started a new round selling off staples and cotton. In one month, 30 billion yuan of currency were withdrawn from circulation by selling cotton gauzes, staple grain, sugar, etc. However, these supplies were hoarded by speculative merchants in different cities. Material supplies failed to reach consumers. Speculators even made profits by purchasing supplies in a city and then hoarding them in another.

Against such circumstances of market failure, the CPC was forced to change its strategy. It moved from counter-market regulation to temporarily and strategically going along with the trend. Market prices were gradually pushed up, attracting speculators towards buying material supplies. Then at the end of November, the state started to sell supplies in major cities at the same time. Compared with the currency that was in circulation, the value of supplies held by the CPC had exceeded the total value of capital in society. State-owned facilities stocked more than half of the nation's total production of cotton gauze. Therefore, the government could give a decisive blow to speculation in a short period.

After the victory, the stock of staple grain and cotton in Shanghai far exceeded demand for more than half a year, which served as a precaution against speculation making a comeback. As Chen Yun stated, these supplies were not necessary to be put on the market; however, they had to be ready. Furthermore, in Beijing and Tianjin regions, a large amount of backup reserve was prepared. Chen said, 'We must be determined to stock up about 400 million catties of rice in Shanghai around Chinese New Year. '400 million catties of reserve should be maintained' until autumn harvest (Jin and Chen 2005: 671).

It was not until the beginning of 1950 when the CPC suppressed the fourth inflation by an unbeatable amount of material supplies that the RMB began to earn its credibility and the people started accepting the RMB as a saving currency. Before this, a vital policy involved anchoring the value of savings to essential supplies.

The State-Conferred Credibility on RMB by Supplies-Based Value System in Three Domains

The Silver Yuan Battle and the Battle of Rice and Cotton were both strategic responses to speculation and they were executed by a state under the military's control. Anchored value in three domains was to secure the value of surplus money held in common people's hands: (i) salaries of civil servants; (ii) savings in banks; and (iii) public bonds. The credit base of national financial capital was thereby consolidated.[35]

It is unimaginable today that in 1949 the accounting unit of the national fiscal budget was millets instead of the RMB. But this was in fact a long tradition in the liberated regions before 1949. Xue Muqiao, later director of the National Bureau of Statistics, recalled that despite diversity in species and supply volume, the total quantity of money in liberated regions was generally maintained around the average of 30 catty of millet per capita. Money would devalue if supply exceeded this amount; otherwise, money supply would be insufficient and peasants would be harmed by deflation.

As the CPC entered the cities, the value of the RMB was still unstable. Therefore, millet remained to serve as the accounting unit in the whole state system. For example, during the age of Soviet Aid, the annual salary

---

[35]A comparable case of commodity-goods serving as money is offered by the example of opium, which served as the medium of exchange in the later years of the Qing dynasty and the early years of the Republic of China. After the eradication of opium, rice and cloth, essential supplies for people's livelihood, were used instead.

of an expert from the Soviet Union working in China was 18,000–20,000 catty of millet, whereas the chairman and vice chairman were paid 3,400 catty, a minister 2,400 catty and a bureau director 1,800 catty of millet.

Taking millet instead of money as a unit of pricing was actually a way of anchoring value. The new regime anchored the value of money to essential supplies in three domains. The market was stabilized in this way to facilitate withdrawing newly issued money from circulation.

Despite differences in the domains, the strategy was basically anchoring value to material supplies. The RMB served not only as a medium of exchange but also as a unit of account and a store of value, which are the classical functions of money. What secured its value were in fact essential supplies, including staple grain, cotton and coal.

The following is an introduction to the practices in the three domains.

1. Public Bonds. Public bonds were sold at a price based on a basket of essential supplies (like rice, millet and flour), then redeemed at the current price of the same amount of supplies according to different maturities. The purchasing power of the money invested was thus guaranteed. Here, public bonds as a means of saving were similar to its equivalent products in other countries. What was really creative was the credibility of bonds secured by essential supplies (Jin and Chen 2005: 652). See Box 7 for the process of public bonds offering.

Box 7: China's First Public Bonds Offering

The offering of public bonds had been under consideration well before the establishment of the state. Yet, within a short span of five months, between initial planning to final implementation, the scale of the public bonds offering had increased by five times.

1. Proposed plan on public bonds offering of RMB 240 billion yuan

   To stabilize finance and price, and to resolve fiscal difficulty, the plan for the first public bonds offering was drawn up under the direction of Chen Yun in July–August 1949.

   Based on Chen Yun's report in the planning meeting as well as subsequent supplementary explanations, the scale of this offering was to be 240 billion yuan, about a quarter of the fiscal deficit of the time.

The rationale put forward by Chen Yun was that the liberated zone had been expanding continuously and the liberated population increasing steadily. In addition, with railroad repairs, battles and so on, fiscal disbursements had consistently grown, while revenue could not go up in that short span. Between August and December, the nationwide fiscal deficit was estimated to be at 580 billion yuan. Moreover, to ensure ongoing production of textile and agricultural produce, funds for acquiring materials could not be spared. After autumn, the purchase of cotton wool and other materials would require 350 billion yuan worth of cash. The two items totalled 930 billion yuan.

If all of these disbursements were to be resolved by issuing currency, it would be difficult to sustain a stable price level. In Southern China and small towns, the use of rice for exchange of goods had already led to an abnormal price level for rice. The plan was to issue public debt of 240 billion yuan. Although it was only a quarter of the issued currency, it could still exert a major impact on finance. Besides making up the deficit and reducing price fluctuations, it could also facilitate the purchase of local produce and currency circulation in rural regions.

The value of public bonds would be anchored to essential commodities. The amounts to be issued would be 120 billion yuan in Eastern China, 70 billion in Central China and 40 billion in Northern China. The targets would mainly be urban industrial and commercial entrepreneurs, as well as landowners in new regions that had not yet experienced land reform. The regulations for the debt would have to be worked on urgently and announced as early as possible in August. The offer period would end in October, with September as the focal point for collecting funds. The terms were to repay the debt by a third every year and to fully repay it in three years. Interest and principal repayments would start in the following year (1950) in November, and the annual interest rate would be fixed at 4% (equivalent to the half-year fixed interest rate for anchored value savings deposit) (Chi 2003).

However, due to disagreements with the national capitalist class, the central government decided to delay the issuance (Bo 1991: 76).

2. Issuance of the People's Victory Bond

The first public debt plan had not been implemented due to opposition from national capitalists. Yet it was at the initiation of national capitalists that public debt offering was put on the agenda for a second time.

To date the reason for this given in various literatures was that price-level inflation had had a major impact on industry and commerce, hence the request for public debt from all sides. Yet, based on the historical background, one could see that inflation had already continued for 13 years since 1937. Further, at the discussions that took place only three to four months ago on public debt offering to alleviate price fluctuation, the national capitalists had been against the proposition. Why would they turn around just after three or four months?

The view in this book is that, in late November, the CPC was able to succeed in combating the violent onslaught of price inflation, relying on nationwide mobilization to deploy physical goods and material (see the Battle of Rice and Cotton described earlier), hence taking away the abnormal speculative profit margins by private capital. That had been a significant turn in China's modern history of paper money. Therefore, the agents of capital turned around and requested the government to use public debt to compensate for the deficit, 'to maintain a stable currency environment'.

To put it precisely, between September and November, the CPC purchased and transported grain as well as other goods around the country. On 25 November, these were put up for unified sale in various big cities, and the price level began to decline from that day on. Three days later, the CPC began to discuss issuance of public debt pursuant to requests from all sides. It was presided over by the top leaders of the country: on 28 November 1949, Mao Zedong chaired the Chinese Central Politburo meeting to work on the estimates for the 1950 revenue and expenditure, as well as the issuance of the People's Victory Bond. On 2 December, Mao Zedong convened the fourth meeting of the Central People's Government Committee, passed the 'Draft Report on 1950 National Fiscal Budget Estimation' as well as the plan to issue public debt.

Based on Bo Yibo's explanation of the 'Draft Report on 1950 National Fiscal Budget Estimation' as well as the report by Chen Yun and Bo Yibo to the CPC Central, 'The Plan for Issuing Bank Notes and Bonds', the 1950 budget deficit was estimated to be 7 billion catty of millet, accounting for 18.7% of the total disbursement. The two ways to resolve the deficit were: first to issue bonds to cover 38.4% of the deficit; and second to expand money supply to cover the remaining 61.6%.

The public offering of People's Victory Bond was planned to be 200 million shares, to be phased in during 1950. The first offering would be between January and March. The collection of funds and repayments of principal and interests would be computed based on the prices of a basket of physical goods. The unit was 'share'. The price of each share would be computed based on the average total wholesale price of 6 catty of rice, 1.5 catty of flour, 4 Chinese feet (=1.33 m) of white fine cloth and 16 catty of coal in six big cities (Shanghai, Tianjin, Hankou, Xian, Guangzhou and Chongqing). This average market price would be announced by the People's Bank of China once every 10 days. The debt would be repaid in 5 years, 10% in the first year then increased by 5% every successive year.[#] On every annual maturity, the principal would be repaid once by drawing lots. The annual interest rate would be 5%, also to be computed based on a basket of physical goods, payable once a year after completion of one full year counting from the cut-off date. Upon issuance of the debt, there would be appropriate expansion of the money supply so that liquidity would not become too tight. That would facilitate the sale of debts and the withdrawal of currency, as well as avert a price-level decline that would depress industry and commerce.

On 16 December, the state council passed the regulations for the first phase of issuing 100 million shares, to be launched on 5 January.

Based on the price level at the time, every share of debt was equivalent to approximately RMB 12,000 yuan. With the first phase of 100 million shares, the public debt plan had amounted to 1.2 trillion yuan.

The completion of the first phase of debt issuance was better than expected. As for the second phase, given that the national fiscal economic situation had already improved it was no longer issued (Jin and Chen 2005: 654–655).

Note:
[#]This meant that the repayment from year 1 to year 5 would be 10, 15, 20, 25 and 30%, respectively).

As mentioned in Box 7, the value-anchored bond was put on the agenda when the CPC was dealing with the silver yuan impact in Shanghai during July–August 1949. However, after consulting economists, Mao thought that the timing was not right for issuing public bonds as New China was yet to be born. It was only after the victory of the Battle of Rice and Cotton, by which time the new government had succeeded in defending the RMB by state capital three times, that value-anchored bonds were ready.

On 4 December 1949, the *Renmin Daily* announced the decision of offering value-anchored bonds. The unit of value-anchored bonds was based on the values of a basket of essential supplies. It included the sum of average retail prices of 6 catty of rice (millet in Tianjin), 1.5 catty of flour, 4 feet of white fine cloth and 16 catty of coal in six major cities: Shanghai, Tianjin, Hankou, Xian, Guangzhou and Chongqing. The prices were announced by the People's Bank every 10 days. The annual interest rate was 5%, which was also marked at the values of the above supplies (Jin and Chen 2005: 654–655). Since the issuance of the bonds on 5 January 1950, the total sale amount was 9.15 million units, 91.6% of the target. The budget deficit was thereby reduced by 40% (Wu and Dong 2001: 345).[36]

2. Salary. After liberation, the value of the RMB was very unstable. Public and private enterprises generally applied the method of supplies-based value. There were many ways of determining supplies-based value. Units of salary were different even in the same city. The new government employed a large number of employees and workers in the public sector (see Box 8). In order to secure their basic livelihood, the Department of Labour and the Central Committee of Finance and Economy successively proposed solutions and suggestions for salary reform. After 1952, salary reform was implemented in major regions in North China, East China, South Central China, Southwest China and Northwest China. Taking 'salary point' as the unit of salary was the main content of the reform.

---

[36]According to Jin and Chen (2005: 655), the sale exceeded the quota of the first issuance, reaching 70.4% of the target of two issuances. However, as the fiscal budget balance improved the second issuance was not offered.

The salary point was set by five major supplies essential to livelihood: staple grain, edible oil, cloth, salt and coal. Every salary point included 0.8 catty of staple food, 0.2 feet of white cloth, 0.05 catty of edible oil, 0.02 catty of salt and 2 catties of coal. The amount was constant in the whole country. However, content could vary in different places. For example, in the south of the Yangtze River, rice was the staple, while in North China the staple was composed of 40% white flour and 60% coarse grain. In Northeast China it was 20 and 80%, respectively. The types and brands of cloth, oil, salt and coal varied from place to place. Workers at the same skill level were paid at the same salary point; however, the equivalent amount of RMB in cash could be different.

Box 8: Background of the 'Taking On' Policy

In comparison with many policy adjustments executed since the 1980s of contracting out that were in essence the shrugging off of fiscal burdens, the new government that took over in 1949 had adopted a 'taking on' policy towards former public service personnel and bureaucratic capital enterprise personnel

On the eve of the establishment of the state, following successive liberations of large and medium cities, the question of how to handle former public service personnel in the KMT government as well as personnel in bureaucratic capital enterprises that had been taken over became a tricky problem that the CPC faced. A comprehensive acceptance would most certainly lead to a heavy burden on the new government, while unrestricted dismissals would increase unemployment and social instability. Based on the experience of taking over cities in the north-eastern region during early liberation, the conclusion was to take them on as is in order to facilitate the establishment of new governance as quickly as possible. After the liberation of Beijing and the Tianjin region, the CPC Central accepted this policy after weighing the pros and cons. As such, the Party and the People's government kept 6 million people employed

On 24 September 1949, the CPC Central issued guidelines on handling former personnel, putting forward that:

(i) Except for a small number of war criminals, spies and malicious persons among former personnel, most of the others have generally pinned their hopes on us. Their basic requirement was simply to be fed. After the liberation of Nanjing, Shanghai and Hangzhou, the dismissal of over 27,000 former personnel had led to high instability. With the peaceful liberation of Beijing, the 17,000 former military personnel being laid off had mostly fled to Suiyuan, full of bitterness and grievances, and now we still have the responsibility of resolving it. All such experiences indicate that former personnel should not be handled by means of dismissals and lay-offs. They must be given a way out in terms of work and livelihood.

(ii) The Party and the People's government have the responsibility to reform and feed these people through providing work. We are prepared, within a specific period after nationwide liberation, to retain 9 to 10 million people, including new and former military and administrative personnel. It most certainly would be difficult for the fiscal budget, but it is solvable, and politically it is essential

Source: Wu and Dong (2001: 314).

A third of the supplies-based salary corresponded to the levy of public staples in real grain. This levy and payment in material supplies without the medium of money helped to greatly suppress the room for speculation in essential supplies. Therefore, salary point as an accounting unit was an important and effective measure in stabilizing employees' livelihood (Wu and Dong 2001: 906).

3. Savings. Value-anchored savings catered to people's preference for material supplies over money. This way of saving had been first tried by Huabei Bank in North China. The RMB was rendered into a unit of essential supplies and the value of the savings was secured by the amount of this unit. When money was deposited into a bank account, the value was rendered into certain units of essential supplies. In case the unit price rose, the difference in the value of money would be subsidized by the bank (the state) (see Box 9).

Box 9: The Implementation of Value-Anchored Savings[*]

In order to implement the value-anchored business, the People's Bank of China (PBC) announced temporary rules on fixed-term savings deposits on 20 April 1949. This was done to regulate the four types of value-anchored savings—lump sum deposit and withdrawal, deposit by instalment and lump sum withdrawal, lump sum deposit and withdrawal by instalment, as well as principal deposit with interest payments. Each equivalent unit of essential goods would be the total price of one catty of flour, one catty of maize or millet noodle and one Chinese foot (= 0.33 m) of cloth. The price would be based on price levels published in local newspaper, calculated as the average price over the previous five days before the deposit or withdrawal.[**]

Since there would be a big differential in the unit price between deposits and withdrawals during the inflation period, current and term deposits less than one month would only be offered to workers, teachers and so on during its early implementation to prevent speculation by businessmen. Deposits for more than 3 months would be offered to all.

On 18 March 1950, the PBC established unified terms for value-anchored deposits, stipulating that the equivalent unit would be constituted based on appropriate goods to be selected by the local PBC in each region. In addition to the four types of common value-anchored deposits, there were also fixed term deposits and special deposits for organizations, joint enterprises and cooperatives. Compared to 1949, there was no longer a limit on target depositors based on the duration of the deposit. In rural regions, single item deposit was implemented. This type of deposit was based on one single item, using the retail price announced by the local trading organization as the standard for computing the equivalent unit. Upon maturity, withdrawals would reflect the rise but not the fall in price. There were three types of deposits for rural regions: (i) Production and Livelihood: deposit by instalment and withdrawal in lump sum; (ii) Patriotic Savings: deposit with reward; and (iii) Rural Fixed Sum Savings.

Sources:

[*]Wu and Dong (2001: 779–780).

[**]*Selection from People's Republic of China Economic Archives 1949–1952: Finance* (1996: 286–287).

Apart from value-anchored savings, there were also loans denominated in real supplies, or loan and repayment denominated by real supplies. This was as a way to stabilize prices. These supplies included staple grain, cotton, cotton cloth and oil. This type of loan was more prevalent in the liberated regions in North China. Usually the loan was specific to agricultural investment. For example, in the northern liberated regions, the monthly interest for a general agricultural loan in cash was 10–100%, 50–100% for industry and 70–100% for commerce. On the other hand, the monthly interest rate for real supplies savings was much lower at 5–10%.[37]

As inflation subsided and savings in cash increased, value-anchored savings were eventually cancelled at the end of 1950. All in all, anchoring value to essential supplies in finance, banking and salary afforded the state a standard method of fighting inflation by firmly standing on the heavily agriculturally-based physical economy.

Agricultural tax in the form of grain levies corresponded with the payment of civil servants' salaries by rationing supplies. Under a tight fiscal budget, the pressure of inflation due to expanding demand in the cities was relieved. Thanks to value-anchored savings, the wealth effect of holding money became positive again for the first time after a long period. The price of a commodity is determined by the volume of money in circulation and the amount of that commodity in the market. The more supplies the government held in stock, the easier it was to withdraw money from circulation. Similarly, supplies-based bonds also played an important role in relieving the fiscal budget tension, withdrawing money and suppressing inflation.

Supplies-based value system was applied with modification in three domains. It was practical and easy to operate. The new government applied it to effectively regulate economy.

In 1952, the general prices of essential and industrial materials became stable and gradually declined. That meant China succeeded in eradicating inflation due to speculation by private capital. General prices in

37华北解放区财政经济史资料选编 (*Selected Materials of Fiscal and Economic History in North China Liberated Regions vol. 2*). Beijing: China Fiscal and Economic Press, 1996, p. 264.

important resource commodities such as food, fuels and industrial materials recorded deflation in December 1952, an unprecedented situation since the Sino-Japanese War, which marked the decisive victory of the People's Republic of China over inflation.[38] The CPC already had a strong footing in the cities where capital interest blocs colluded to seek speculative profits. From now on, it could focus on solving the problem of depression in the real economy.

'Supplies Standard' Currency System in Practice in Liberated Regions

The concept of taking essential supplies as the credit base of currency was not invented in 1949 when the new regime was born. It had been successfully put into practice in the liberated regions during the Sino-Japanese War. An analysis of these practices should be included in the experience of the strategy of 'encircling cities from villages' in the Chinese revolution.

In the liberated regions of Shandong, Xue Muqiao had suggested the idea of a supplies standard and confidently believed in the efficacy of using essential supplies of livelihood as the basis of monetary issuance. Xue argues that it is much better than silver and gold which you cannot not eat or wear for warmth: "People in our base areas welcome this currency system. They don't need gold, much less dollars or pounds." (Xue 1992: 153) (see Box 10).

Box 10: 'Supplies Standard' Currency in Shandong Liberated Regions

During the Sino-Japanese War the Shandong base region adopted measures of lowering rent and tax, which resulted in a significant increase in peasants' productivity. Agricultural production led to good harvests year after year. Food grain, cotton and oil were in abundance, and in

---

[38] 上海解放前后物价资料汇编 (1921–1957 年) (*Collected Data on Prices in Shanghai Before and After the Liberation, 1921–1957*). Shanghai: People Publishing House, 1958, p. 390.

some regions there were even surpluses that could be exported. The coastline of Shandong was long and thus rich in salt production. On both sides of the Jin-Pu Railway and Jiao-Ji Railway, there were more than 10 million Japanese soldiers and people in the occupied zones who needed salt. The resistance government implemented a monopoly on salt, making use of salt export to earn large amounts of legal currency and puppet-regime currency, then exchange them for all kinds of supplies and materials from the occupied zones, to suppress the relative value of both these currencies. Daily necessities like food grain and cotton yarn that were controlled by the resistance government were the most reliable for the resistance government's currency. There was no need for gold backing. The people who held the resistance government's currency were not concerned with how much gold or silver—and even less how many US dollars or British pounds—they could exchange the money for. Rather they were more focused on what quantity of daily necessities they could get from the money.

During the Liberation War, a US journalist who came to the Shandong liberated regions noted that the resistance currency had neither legal gold content, nor gold or silver reserves, nor the backing of the US dollar and British pound. Yet it was able to maintain its value as well as price stability. He thought it was an enigmatic miracle. He asked Xue Muqiao who was in charge of monetary policy in Shandong what the standard was for the resistance currency. The latter told him that it was the material supplies standard. He said:

> The resistance government regulates the amount of money supply so it does not exceed the amount needed for market circulation. Out of every 10,000 yuan of currency, at least 5,000 is used to purchase essential goods such as grain, cotton wool, cotton cloth, peanuts, etc. If prices go up, we sell these goods to withdraw money and depress the price level. On the other hand if prices decline, we issue more currency to buy the goods. We use daily necessities as reserves for currency issuance, and it is much better than using gold or silver which cannot be eaten as food when hungry or worn as clothes for warmth. The people in the base regions welcome our currency system. They do not want gold, and even less US dollars or British pounds.

Practice had shown that although Shandong did not have gold or foreign exchange reserves to back the money supply, yet their currency value as well as general prices in the market were very stable. This was because the industrial and commercial bureaus in the base region held enormous quantities of material supplies. If general prices were found to rise, it indicated that the quantity of goods in circulation was lower while of the circulating currency was higher, and there was a danger of inflation. The bureau then sold off large quantities of the supplies at hand, like rice, cotton wool, cotton cloth, salt, peanut and peanut oil, to withdraw the currency. And if the price level declined, it indicated that there were more goods in the market when money in circulation decreased. This carried the risk of depressing the price of produce and hurting the peasants. The government then increased monetary supply and printed more money to buy up goods and supplies, filling up the stockpile. With the innovative monetary policy that relied on large quantities of material goods reserve and control over currency circulation, the currency of the government in the Shandong base had achieved the same level of stability as the US dollar backed by gold.

As a result, Shandong money started to circulate in the occupied areas surrounding the Shandong liberation base. From businessmen to common folk, everyone in the occupied areas wanted to sell their goods to the Shandong base in exchange for Shandong money which they would then save up to buy salt, peanut oil and so on from Shandong. Even those people who did not need to buy salt and peanut right away wanted to convert large amounts of Shandong money and save it for the preservation of its value. In this way, the predecessor of the renminbi—shandongbi—became the reserve currency of the surrounding regions, and because of that, even though shandongbi did not have any gold or foreign currency reserves, it was able to achieve relative stability in value.

Sources: Xue (2006: 166–172; 1992: 151–159).

In the border regions of Shaanxi, Ganxu and Ningxia, Zhu Lizhi (朱理治) and Chen Yun had made remarkable achievement in restoring and developing the economy and consolidating currency credit, while avoiding a repeat of the bankruptcy of the Chinese Soviet government in Jinggangshan in the early 1930s.[39]

---

[39]In 1940, Mao Zedong, in a letter to Peng Dehuai (彭德怀), mentioned: 'The worst part of the tasks in our base areas is the problem of finance and economy. In many other aspects

The establishment of a new currency system in the aforementioned base areas was achieved under extremely difficult fiscal circumstances condition. The fiscal background was similar to the whole of China in 1949 (see Box 11).

Box 11: Fiscal Difficulties in the Border Regions of Shaanxi, Gansu and Ningxia After 1940

Shaanxi, Gansu and Ningxia in the loess plateau of the north-western border regions were rich in natural resources like salt, coal, oil, ores, forests, medicinal plants, etc. and also suitable for agriculture and husbandry. Yet the population there was low and habitation was scattered. The economy and technology were also backward. If the economy could not be developed, the CPC could not gain a footing there and turn the regions into the rear headquarters for resisting the Japanese.

In the first few years of the resistance war, the main fiscal sources for the border regions had been part of the funds given to the Eighth Route Army by the KMT government, as well as monetary and material subsidies from progressive people both overseas and domestic. In 1937 and 1938, the only levies had been of 10,000 Chinese stones (1 stone = 100 catties) of grain each year. Taxation was also low. In 1940, the KMT government stopped military funding to the Eighth Route Army and blocked all donations (domestic and overseas) to the border regions. In 1941, after the Wannan Incident (the attack on the New Fourth Army by the KMT army in southern Anhui) channels of external assistance to the border regions were completely cut off. The economic and fiscal situation fell into severe difficulty. Mao Zedong said, 'The biggest hardship had been in 1940 and 1941—both incidents of KMT's anti-Communist campaign had occurred in this period. Our situation had become so bad that there were almost no clothing, no edible oil, no paper and no vegetables. Soldiers had no boots and socks. Staff had no quilts for winter.'

Under these circumstances the border government started production for subsistence, tightened expenses and increased taxation. The grain

---

we have learnt the lesson of failures in the Soviet period. However, only in the domain of finance we have yet to learn any lesson. If we fail to pay attention, we would be doomed to bankruptcy' (Geng and Zhu 2015).

levy in 1940 was 90,000 Chinese stones and, in 1941, it increased to 200,000. This was too burdensome for the people and some of them were upset. In that year, when a county mayor died after he was struck by lightning, the common folk said, 'Why didn't it strike Mao Zedong?'

After several years of all-out production efforts, the scarcity of food grain was resolved, which led to better self-sufficiency. However, the fiscal situation was becoming increasingly problematic for various reasons. The trade deficit with other regions, investment of large amounts of funds in production, and increase in military spending for the deployment of the army, all added to the problem.

In May 1940, Cao Juru, the president of the Bank of Border Regions pointed out, 'We should have a self-sufficient fiscal budget but we still have deficits. We need 170,000 yuan every month. The shortfall is over 40,000 yuan.' The fiscal situation was difficult. Bank loans became an important way for the government to cover the deficit in public finance. In 1940, loans to support fiscal budget accounted for 69.2% of the total loans taken by the bank (in 1938 and 1939 it was 21.6 and 18% respectively). Out of that, the loan to directly support public finance was as high as 93.1%. In November 1940, the central authority of the border region requested the bank to increase money issuance by 4 million yuan to subsidize the Office of Finance's production fund and operating costs.

In the first half of 1941, due to the demands of fiscal expenditure and investments in government-operated production, the bank expanded the money supply. As recorded in 陕甘宁边区社会经济史 (*Social Economic History of Shaanxi, Gansu and Ningxia Border Regions*) by Wang Zhenglin, from March to June 1941, the border currency issued each month was 3,095,410 yuan, 2,760,500 yuan, 2,780,000 yuan and 2,373,600 yuan respectively; the average monthly increase rate was 31.9%. From July to December, the issuance each month was 1,076,625 yuan, 1,413,900 yuan, 2,438,600 yuan, 2,688,015 yuan, 1,051,725 yuan and 3,344,975 yuan; the average monthly increase rate was below 10%. At the same time, the price equivalence between the price of commodities and the border currency also went up. For example, in Yan'an the rate of increase in the price level went from 12.9% in March to 26.7% in June, while the price equivalence went up from 6.6 to 14.6%. In this regard, the bank adopted a tightening policy in July and August. The rate was 7% in July and 8.5% in August. In September and October, due to investment in salt production, the money supply again went up, with the rate of increase at 16.9 and 13.2% respectively. In December, because of the need to compete for the purchase of goods, launch agricultural loans and for fiscal turnover, the rate of increase in money supply again went up sharply from 4.5% in November to 13.9% in December.

Sources: Jin and Chen (2005: 351–401), Geng (2015: 6).

Under the new leadership of Zhu Lizhi, the Bank of Border Regions emphasized the real productivity of loans, and increased their disbursal for agricultural production and trading. Loans adopted a variety of forms to anchor value to essential supplies. In 1942, the bank decided to conduct lending through real supplies. Industrial lending was done through purchasing orders and payments were made in goods. Commercial lending, except relief aid loan, also took the form of goods purchasing order. Take agricultural loan as an example. A peasant wanted a loan from the bank to buy farm cattle and tools. The loan was valued at the market price of material supplies (such as staples or cotton). After the harvest, the peasant repaid the loan in the form of real goods of equivalent value. Different regions adopted variations to this template of loan finance. Some banks lent physical farming tools and then received repayment in the form of agricultural products. Some allowed borrowing and repayment both in terms of millet. This form of lending 'solved the difficulty of peasants and promoted production. The value of the loan was secured. The turnover of the agricultural loan was maintained in this way. The policy was reasonable both for the government and peasants' (Geng 2015).

In 1943, the issuance of currency and trading again fell into difficulty. The problems of trade, finance and the fiscal budget became increasingly serious (Jin and Chen 2005: 351–401).

In order to tackle the fiscal difficulty in these border regions, Chen Yun implemented a series of measures in 1944, including trade management, import substitution and issuing the 'salt note' (formally known as the Commercial Circulation Note). All of these became important experiences in inflation management later through circulating supplies and increasing production (see Box 12).

Box 12: How the Border Regions of Shaanxi, Gansu and Ningxia Stabilized the Currency in 1944–1945

External trade surplus was the main channel for building up the reserve for the border bank's currency. In regional trade at the time, the largest export was salt, accounting for two-thirds of the total export of the border regions. Cotton and cloth were the largest import commodities, taking care of 65% of the total import into the border regions. Therefore, salt, cotton and cloth played a key role in balancing imports and exports, as well as in stabilizing price levels. In 1944, the border region won a glorious salt hoarding battle. On 18 April, the battle of Henan, Hunan and Guangxi erupted as the Japanese army attacked Henan. This led to the disruption of the channel for salt distribution by the border region. Yet, the Northwest Financial Office decided to stock additional quantities of salt. Along with the initial loan of 300 million yuan to the Salt Sales and Transportation Cooperative, a further 300 million was allotted to launch the salt hoarding battle, which led to more than 10 million catties of salt being stocked up. In the beginning, traders from the KMT territories did not come to the border regions to buy salt. But the territories in Shaanxi could only hold on for about two weeks and other north-western regions for two months before they had to come to the border regions for salt. The price of salt went from the loss-making 12,000 yuan (legal currency) per 100 catties to the break-even price of 13,000 yuan, travelling further up to the profitable 16,000 yuan. Afterwards, because of changes in the war situation, the source of sea salt to the KMT territories was completely cut off. The border salt price rose further. Salt from Xihuachi rose to 18,000–19,000 yuan per 100 catties, while in Liulin it went up to 36,000–37,000 yuan. When it came to the import of cotton wool and cloth, on the one hand, the border regions during harvest time offered a price 1.5 times higher than the KMT authority to buy cotton wool before the latter did. On the other hand, they actively developed production, planting cotton and weaving cloth during idle time in winter. In September and October, when new cotton wool from the Guanzhong Plain went on the market, the price of cotton wool in the KMT territories was 11,000 yuan per 100 catties, while the purchase price offered by the border regions was 28,000 yuan per 100 catties, higher than the former by 17,000 yuan. As a result, not only were merchants selling cotton to the borders, even the Kuomintang army blockading the border regions sold cotton wool to seek profit. KMT platoon commanders would bring their entire platoons to carry cotton wool over. Some would make even more than three trips in one night. The border regions achieved an import of over a million catty of high-quality new cotton wool within two months, collecting sufficient raw material in preparation for developing the textile industry to produce clothes and linen. The border regions further produced 3 million catty of cotton wool: common folk weaved gauze during winter so that the need to buy from outside was reduced. 'Without planting cotton wool and having to buy cloth completely from outside, there would be a need to spend 225 million yuan (border currency), amounting to 26–27 million yuan in legal currency.'

Given that the price ratio was well controlled for import and export of cotton and salt, in 1944, the border regions were able to realize a trade surplus of 1.9 billion in terms of border currency. In 1945, they continued to have surplus, turning around the disadvantaged trade deficit situation. They then formed the basis for stabilizing the border currency.

To stabilize the border currency, Chen Yun, after much consideration, came up with the solution of the 'salt coupon':

> In order to bring the exchange rate of the border currency at par with the legal currency without disrupting financial transactions in the market, there has to be a 'replacement' method. Is it possible to have the salt company issue a kind of circulation coupon, with a price at par with the legal currency and at a fixed rate of exchange of 1:9 with the border currency? Then it can be circulated in the border regions while gradually withdrawing the border currency. When it reaches the intended level the border currency can be raised to be at par with the legal currency in one go, and then the issuance of salt coupons can be stopped by using the border currency to replace and withdraw the salt coupons. In this way, the goal of raising the border currency to be at par with the legal currency can be reached and financial activity in the market would not be affected. Moreover it would expel the legal currency so that the border regions are not disadvantaged.

Based on this line of thinking, on 23 May 1944, the Northwest Financial Office met and decided to issue the Border Trading Company

Commercial Circulation Coupon, pointing out that although it had been nominally issued by the trading company, in reality it had been issued by the border bank. Every circulation coupon converted to 20 yuan in border currency; the latter was to be withdrawn gradually. In future, all business trading and debt clearance in the border regions were to be conducted based on the circulation coupon. The face value of the commercial circulation coupon was 50 yuan, which could be exchanged with the border currency (Jin and Chen 2005: 369).

Pursuant to the effect of the various aspects described earlier, the exchange rate between the border currency and the legal currency declined from the initial 12:1 and 10:1 down to 8.5:1 after June 1944, at which level it basically stabilized. After December, the circulation coupon as the chief medium for specialized loans and trade investments to purchase salt and local produce effectively supported external trade. Moreover, it supported the liquidity of funds in banks, maintaining outflows and inflows in an orderly manner. By being used to exchange old border currency notes of smaller value, the coupon also improved convenience for people in their daily life.

In 1961, this was Zhou Enlai's assessment of the border region's achievement:

> The peak period of production engagement in the Shaanxi, Gansu and Ningxia border regions had only lasted three years from 1943 to 1945. At the time we put forward the goal of saving up one year's crop out of three years' yield... that goal was indeed achieved. In March 1947 when Hu Zongnan attacked Yan'an, we retreated from Yan'an to fight guerrilla battles in north Shaanxi. Wherever we went, even in the mountain region of Hengshan where conditions were the hardest, grain reserves in peasants' homes were full. That was the support based upon which we were able to fight the 3 years' liberation war. The troops of Hu Zongnan could not do anything about it.

Source: Jin and Chen (2005: 351–401).

RMB Put on a Firm Footing by the Organization of Rural Regions After Land Reform

This book analyses the experience of the new regime's resolution of crisis through the revolution dividend. To take it a step further, we must emphasize that as a newly independent nation, the earlier discussed measures could not be implemented in isolation, despite the curbing of hyperinflation in a short time period or the setting up of the fiscal and financial system by value-anchoring. In fact, the strategy was an extension of Mao's revolutionary strategy of encircling cities from villages being implemented in the economy during peaceful times.

First, peasants who had land distributed to them returned to work in the traditional self-sufficient economy. That meant that 88% of the population was immune to modern economic crises in cities and that the government could focus their attention only on the cities to deal with them. The case of the previous republic was different. The major agents of industrial capital were absentee landlords controlling commerce and industry. They had a high demand for agricultural raw materials. Cash cropping therefore became a big part of peasant production. The result was greater commercialization of peasant livelihoods and mone-tization of peasant incomes. Peasant livelihoods were in turn hit hard by the devaluation of the legal tender (Wen and Feng 1999). Second, due to the accomplishment of the land revolution, the state succeeded in politically mobilizing almost all peasants, which supported the policy of supply-based value-anchoring of the fiscal and financial system. That is to say, a historically unprecedented yet rigorous rural organizational system comprising 88% of the total population became the means by which inflation in cities was stabilized.

During 1949–1950, the government focused on dealing with hyper-inflation. Even though the state had yet to announce the land reform law, the reform had been implemented in the liberated regions of North-east and North China since 1947. The combination of land reform and peasant mobilization was a basic principle formulated by the CPC during revolutionary struggle. Total mobilization of the population enabled middle-class and poor peasants, which comprised a majority of the peasant population, to sunder their dependence on the landlord class. For the first time in history, peasants gained the consciousness of polit-ical subjects playing an active part in the nation's polity and new forms of rural political practice began to take shape.

But how was the political subjectivity of peasants being expressed? This was determined by whether it was necessary to mobilize peasants in the state's strategies and, accordingly, which group of peasants (rich, middle-income, poor or tenant) needed to be mobilized. Through selective mobilization, the new regime extended state power into natural villages for the first time in Chinese history (Wen 1993; Wang 2015).[40] Properties inside villages, such as land, houses and livestock, were redistributed by way of revolutionary politics. A form of incomplete property rights compared to individualized private property rights took shape. Thereby, the state later found an institutional breach to intervene to reshape property relationship.

Afterwards, the state faced little resistance from local interest blocs in implementing its will in villages, for example when establishing a state-monopolized purchasing and selling system in the name of state-owned unit or cooperatives, as well as the cooperative movement in the 1950s. It was a sort of revolution dividend. The state's supreme political power was based on its right to regulate the collective interests of all social groups.

The most important function of land reform lay in the reduction of transaction costs when collecting surplus staple grain from self-sufficient and geographically scattered peasants. In the name of revolution, it became relatively easy for the state in taxing and purchasing supplies from villages.

Whether the state managed to collect enough staple grain and supplies was vital to its success in curbing speculation and hyperinflation. After speculation and hyperinflation were stamped out, the staples and supplies stocked by the state were redistributed to peasants through wage payment as a form of aid and investment into irrigation infrastructure, etc. On the one hand, agricultural production could be greatly improved and, on the other, surplus workforce could be prevented from flowing out of the villages during famines. In this way, a crisis could be quickly resolved before it resulted in social turmoil.

So, can the countryside continue to bear the costs of urban crises? It depends on whether the property relationship in villages is equitable and to what extent the peasants can organize themselves. With these

---

[40]In Chinese history, state power rarely went down to the village level. Villages usually maintained a sort of autonomy regulated by local gentry.

two factors realised, the vast rural areas can insulate against the crisis of inflation by providing basic supplies to cities.

Redistribution of Property Relationship and Organization of Peasants Reduced the Cost of Levying Staple Grain

After land reform, poor peasants (52.2% of the total population) owned 47.1% of arable land, 2.93 *mu* per capita on average; middle-income peasants (39.9%) owned 44.3%, 3.67 *mu* per capita; rich peasants (5.3%) owned 6.4%, 3.8 *mu* per capita; and landlords (2.6%) owned 2.2%, 2.52 *mu* per capita (Xu 2007: 10). According to some studies, the level of unevenness was not as serious as expected (Wen and Feng 1998).[41] Nevertheless, after land reform, the fairness of landownership had indeed improved. The institutional cost of land reform was a certain loss in terms of the economy of scale. The institutional benefit was the state's capacity for political mobilization of over half of the rural population.

Regarding support by rural areas, after land reform, peasants in the liberated regions still had a relatively heavy tax and levy burden of about 20%. During the Sino-Japanese War, the average grain levy per capita was about 32 catty of rice. In some areas it was as low as 18–19 catty per capita. In 1948, the average grain levy was 40 catty per capita. In 1949, it became 56 catty, about 18.2% of the total agricultural production. During the Sino-Japanese War, besides grain levy, peasants had to pay some money without other additional charges. In 1949, the burden on the peasants increased. In some provinces, it was 5–15% more. Then the average total tax per capita was 58–64 catty of fine grains, about 20.6–22.7% of the total agricultural production in that year. Additionally, peasants had to bear a salt tax, a custom tax, civilian war service and the invisible loss of currency depreciation.

---

[41]In a letter to Mao Zedong, Dong Shijin (董时进) mentioned that according to a survey by the Land Committee of the ROC on 1.75 million peasant households in 163 counties of 16 provinces, 35.6% of peasant households owned arable land under 5 *mu*, 24% 5–10 *mu*, 13% 10–15 *mu*. Big landlords owning land over 1,000 *mu* accounted for only 0.02% of the rural population. *Source*: Dong Shijin, 论共产党的土地改革 (On CPC's Land Reform). Hong Kong: Freedom Press, 1951, pp. 111–113. Quoted in Xiong (2010).

Table 2 1950–1952 Agricultural Taxes and Other Levies (RMB 10,000)

	#	Agricultural taxes	Other levies	Sub-total	* (%)	※ (%)
1950	2,431,212	229,277	56,093	285,370	9.43	11.74
1951	2,660,171	307,312	95,728	403,040	11.55	15.15
1952	3,227,600	329,853	47,819	377,672	10.22	11.70
Total	8,318,983	866,442	199,640	1,066,082	10.42	12.82

Notes:
#Net value of agricultural and sideline production
*Agricultural taxes as percentage of total net value of agricultural and sideline production
※Agricultural taxes and other levies as percentage of total net value
Source: Li (1962: 153)
Table 2 Illustration:
1. Net value of agricultural and sideline production was calculated according to the net value given by the National Bureau of Statistics minus the value of preliminary processing and handicraft for self-subsistence. The reduction of material consumption was 21.32%
2. Other agricultural taxes included: animal husbandry tax, rural industry and commerce tax, land certificate fee and various other levies. The last item might not be precise

The burden imposed on peasants after liberation was due to the pressure of the fiscal budget. In November 1949, non-productive personnel paid by fiscal revenues numbered more than nine million. As the war raged on, fiscal expenditure increased.[42] China's participation in the Korean War in October 1950 only made the economic situation more difficult.

As industry and commerce were just recovering from war, revenues from these sectors were not substantial. In consideration of the nation as a whole, the new government had to continue burdening peasants (Tables 2 and 3).

Although the CPC decided to reduce the tax burden on peasants in 1950, the policy was not implemented because of the Korean War. In general, due to the need for fiscal revenues, the tax burden on peasants became relatively heavy in the liberated regions till the restoration of the national economy.

---

[42] 1949–1952 中华人民共和国经挤档案资料选编·财政卷 (Selection from PRC Economic Archives: Fiscal). Beijing: Economic Management Press (经济管理出版社), 1995, p. 186. Quoted in Wu and Dong (2001: 327).

Table 3   1949–1952 Agricultural taxes

	1949	1950	1951	1952
Agricultural population (10,000)	44,726	46,059	47,626	49,191
Farm land area (10,000 *mu*)	146,822	150,534	155,507	161,878
Real agricultural production (fine grains 100 million catty)	1,847.1	2,195.4	2,493.2	2,924.2
Taxable production (fine grains 100 million catty)	1,809.6	1,860.0	2,090.4	2,374.2
Per cent of production	97.97	84.72	83.84	81.19
Real levy (fine grains 10,000 catty)	248.8	269.7	361.5	357.8
Per cent of taxable production	13.8	14.5	17.3	15.1
Per cent of agricultural production	13.5	12.3	14.5	12.2
Average per capita (catty)	56	59	76	73
Average per *mu* (catty)	17	18	23	22

Source: Ministry of Finance of the People's Republic of China (1994: 119)

Historically, tax below tithe was bearable for peasants, and an incidence of 20% tax would definitely have amounted to an imposition. Were it not for peasant mobilization and the successful deployment of appropriate ideology associated with the land revolution, it seems unlikely that they would have acquiesced to such a tax burden so readily and peacefully.

We could examine this situation with some cases in Southwest China, which was liberated relatively late. Although the total amount of grain levy was not particularly large, the levy did increase. By that time land reform was yet to be implemented and local grassroots organization was absent. As a result, a large number of hungry peasants became bandits or violently resisted the grain levy. Banditry was quite rampant after liberation in the southwest (Box 13).

Box 13: Banditry and Grain Levy in the South-Western Region in the Early Years of the PRC

Since the liberation war progressed rapidly, when the troops entered the newly liberated regions the democratic government was not in place or perhaps had just been put in place. As a result the conditions were poor for implementing certain necessary policies. Rural land reform could not be done in time, hence the agricultural taxation system could not be put in place temporarily. To ensure grain supply to the troops, in addition to seizing it from the reserves of the local KMT government in battles, the CPC adopted the approach of levying on-site, and announced 'Regulations Regarding the Collection of Grain' on 21 March 1949. The main targets to levy and borrow from were first landlords and wealthy peasants, and then middle-class peasants. The levying and borrowing was based on the total grain harvest: landlord 40–50 per cent, wealthy peasants 25–35 per cent, wealthy tenant peasants 20 per cent, and middle-class peasants 10–15 per cent. Poor peasants had to lend very little or not at all. Hay for horses was requested in proportion to the grain levy. Former Bao Jia Head [the team head of the local rural administration and security system] monitored and executed the implementing of the policy. For regions that were liberated a little earlier, even though they had already started the agricultural taxation system, yet many places had still not been able to set up a formal system nor announced comprehensive regulations in that regard. Without a set of comprehensive rules, different places had different approaches (totally over 30). Certain places had situations in which the burden was placed on limited portion of people or the marginal levying rate too high or too much to the extremes at both ends.[*]

From 17 November 1949 to 25 March 1950 there were 29 incidents of grain robbing in the mid-southern regions. Also in the southwestern regions, due to 'bandits in Sichuan disturbing and blockading the region, the scope of grain levying was not wide', and all the major cities had insufficient food grain.[**] According to statistics, in 1950 there was a loss of agricultural tax of 1.46 billion catty, of which over 65 million catty was grabbed or burnt by bandits. Moreover, in the process of levying over 3,000 cadres had sacrificed their lives.[***]

Sources:
[*]Wu and Dong (2001: 327–328).
[**]1949–1952 中华人民共和国经济档案资料选编·综合卷 (Selection from People's Republic of China Economic Archives 1949–1952: General). Beijing: China Supplies Publishing House, (1996: 340); quoted from Wu and Dong (2001: 308).
[***]1949–1952 中华人民共和国经济档案资料选编·商业卷 (Selection from People's Republic of China Economic Archives 1949–1952: Commerce). Beijing: China Supplies Publishing House, 1996, 18; quoted from: Wu and Dong (2001: 308).

Judged on the basis of numbers alone, the cost of transferring staple grain from Yunnan to other regions was much lower than the cost of transporting them from Central and Northeast China, even if the cost of transportation was double that of production. However, as the Northeast was liberated earlier and land reform completed, publicly-run commerce and cooperatives developed rapidly. Therefore, in the region the capacity to sell commodities and transportation became strong, which substantially contributed towards stabilizing supply–demand and price in the market (see Box 14). For example, in early 1950 the Central Committee of Finance and Economy planned to transfer two billion catty of staple grain from Central and Northeast China to famine-stricken regions, much higher than the 400 million catty from the Southwest.

Box 14: Development of Government-Operated Commerce in the North-Eastern Regions

Before 1947, in the north-eastern liberated regions only the bases in Northern Manchuria and Western Manchuria (now Heilongjiang) had a relatively large government-operated business. In late April 1946, the city of Harbin started to conduct government-operated business centring on the purchase of grain and sale of cloth and salt. In the same year, Harbin established the Northern Manchuria Trading Company and Dongxin Company. Trading companies were also established by various provinces (back then the north-eastern base was divided into five provinces, Songjiang, Heilongjiang, Nenjiang, Kejiang and Mudanjiang, and the special municipality of Harbin). In August 1947, the Northeast Trading Management Bureau was set up to coordinate the operation. Harbin Department Store, set up in August 1948, was the first large-scale shop during the history of the base region. By 1948, the north-eastern liberated region government had government-operated shops set up in over 80% of cities and towns.

Source: Wu and Dong (2001: 100).

A major function of the rural cooperative at the beginning of the PRC was to purchase supplies for the state. It showed that a cooperative could cut transaction costs of collecting supplies from peasants (see Table 4). It is clear that in regions that were liberated earlier and where land reform was implemented, cooperatives developed better, which may be regarded as an institutional benefit.

In summary, the central government collected staple grain from the whole nation in order to suppress inflation in cities. The state regime that was based in cities therefore enjoyed the institutional benefit of social stability. However, in rural areas which were yet to be organized, the institutional cost in terms of social instability increased. The above analysis demonstrates that fair distribution of properties and grassroots organizing were pivotal to the villages' capacity to bear institutional costs.

Table 4 Rural cooperatives purchase products for the state as ratio of total state purchasing

Year	Purchasing	Staple food	Ginned cotton	Linen for gunny bag	Tobacco	Tea
1951	Purchase for the state (10,000 catty)	559,854	70,292	13,695	6,918	1,176
	As per cent of total cooperative purchasing	71.7	84.8	65.2	79.6	71.5
	As per cent of state purchasing	31.0	45.8	43.7	52.9	14.5
1952	Purchase for the state (10,000 catty)	1,502,100	158,982	32,075	18,408	6,168
	As per cent of total cooperative Purchasing	82.0	95.0	80.8	88.9	85.4
	As per cent of state Purchasing	49.7	79.9	72.6	51.8	56.1

Source: *1949–1952* 中华人民共和国经济档案资料选编·工商体制卷 (Selection from People's Republic of China Economic Archives 1949–1952: Industrial and Commercial Institutions). Beijing: China Social Sciences Press, 1993: 422. Quoted in Wu and Dong (2010: 189)

Irrigation Infrastructure Construction Through State-Mobilized Labour to Secure Food Production

The building of irrigation infrastructure proved remarkably effective in increasing food production. This was closely related to the organization and mobilization of peasants during land reform.

In the early years of the republic, under conditions of material scarcity, the most effective way to increase food production in a short period of time was through mobilization of the workforce, which was a way to earn labour rent at a relatively low cost. During the restoration of the national economy, irrigation was a crucial component of infrastructural investment, second only to transportation and communication (Table 5).

During 1949–1952, the total investment in agriculture, forestry and irrigation was 1.03 billion RMB, 13.14% of the total infrastructure investment, most of which was used in irrigation construction.

In 1950, the value of loans for irrigation investment was equivalent to 500 million catty of rice, which was allocated to 21 million *mu* of arable land; and 320,000 soldiers were organized by the state to participate in irrigation construction (see Box 15).

Box 15: Mobilization of Labour to Construct Irrigation Infrastructure in New China (Examples of Several Large-Scale Irrigation Projects)
In dealing with the problem of flooding of River Huai, the state mobilized 220,000 workers to build dams. It was a large-scale irrigation

---

Table 5 Irrigation infrastructure in China 1949–1952

	Unit	1950	1951	1952
Infrastructure investment	10,000 RMB	9,206	19,508	32,799
Large lock gates built	Number	–	–	3
Enlarged irrigated areas	10,000 *Mu*	1,204	2,796	4,017
Irrigation canals over 10,000 *Mu*	Place	1,254	1,279	1,346

Source: *1949–1952*   中华人民共和国经济档案资料选编·基本建设投资与建筑业卷 (Selection from People's Republic of China Economic Archives 1949–1952: Infrastructure & Construction) (1989: 942)

construction rarely seen in the history of China. In 1951, before the expected start of flooding season, a preliminary regulation of River Huai was achieved. Except for certain parts that faced mountain torrents or waterlogging, most rivers in the region went through the flooding season safely. The result was an unprecedentedly rich harvest in the River Huai basin. Compared with 1950, flooded area was reduced by 65%, while irrigated area increased by 21%.

In October 1951, construction work started on the Guanting Reservoir located in upper Yongding River. More than 40,000 workers and peasants participated in the construction of the project. It was essentially completed before floods came in 1953. No sooner was the main dam completed than it blocked a particularly bad flood, the second largest on record.

As for the pre-1952 project to channel the flood water of the Jingjiang, on the one hand, it strengthened the Jiangjiang dam that was 114 km from the left shore of the Changjiang (Yangtze River), and on the other hand, it secured the flood channelling region, that is, the low-lying areas to the right shore of the Changjiang, east of Hudu River, west of the dam on the right shore of the Jingjiang, and north of Anxiang River, a total area of 921 sq. km. A water entrance gate that was 1,054.3 m long as well as a 336.6 m control gate were built to control and manage the water flow. In the two-and-a-half-month period from 5 April to 20 June 1952, the project had mobilized 300,000 labourers, including troops, workers and engineers, supplied on a timely basis close to 1 million tonnes of engines, equipment and material, and invested 5 million on the construction project as well as 10.5 million on relocation. The water entrance gate with 54 holes and water control gate with 32 holes were built in accordance with the plan. At the same time, the project of constructing a dam for the flood channelling area to take in up to 5–6 billion m^3 of water, as well as the project on strengthening the 133 km dam along the Jingjiang were also completed. These had the effect of safeguarding the lives and properties of eight million people on either sides of the Jingjiang, ensuring rich harvests in that vast region, and facilitating transportation for the country along the Changjiang. Given that such an enormous project was completed within such a short duration, it was referred to by some international friends as a 'world wonder' of the time.

Source: Wu and Dong (2001: 479–483).

During 1950–1952, 420,000 km of embankments along rivers across China were repaired and reinforced. In the three years, 20 million people directly took part in irrigation infrastructural construction. The earthwork was estimated to be over 1.7 billion cu. m, equivalent to the construction of 10 Panama Canals or 23 Suez Canals. Up to 107 projects involved land over 10,000 *mu*. Collective construction work was being undertaken in 2.08 million places. Irrigation areas were extended by 32.4 million *mu*, 24 million of which reaped the benefits in the same year.

Flood-stricken areas rapidly decreased in the country. In 1949, there were over 100 million *mu* of them, about 60 million in 1950, 21 in 1952, and down to 16 in 1952. Meanwhile, extended irrigated areas were 49.5 million *mu*. A rough estimate had it that food production increased by a few million tonnes due to flood prevention and increased irrigation facilities (Wu and Dong 2001: 479–483).

Irrigation infrastructural construction became another tool for extensive mobilization in rural regions after land reform.

The experience of the low-cost mobilization of labour force was formed in having soldiers build the railway, which was Sun Yat-sen's idea that was not realized during his time. At the eve of the new republic, the task of railway restoration was heavy. Peng Dehuai (彭德怀) suggested having sappers to do earthwork and cave digging to build the Tianshui–Lanzhou railway line. The Central Committee of Finance and Economy also suggested using surplus troops for roadbed work and cave digging. Earlier, the CPC had mobilized people in the liberated regions to build railway lines. Before leaving for Moscow in December 1949, Mao Zedong called Chen Yun and Bo Yibo to say: 'It is imperative to deploy troops to build Tianshui–Lanzhou, Tianshui–Chengdu, Chengdu–Chongqing, Yibin–Kunming, Yunnan–Guizhou, Guizhou–Guangxi, Hunan–Guangxi railway connections. Please work on it immediately.' Consequently, despite a very tight fiscal budget, the state invested as much as possible in building railway lines in the early years of new China. With limited funds and heavy tasks, sappers were irreplaceable in this undertaking. In 1950, 286,546 people were mobilized for the construction of Baoji–Tianshui, Tianshui–Lanzhou, Tianshui–Chengdu, Chengdu–Chongqing lines. The fund was equivalent to 997,475,095 catty of millet. The cost of dynamite was equivalent to 27,725,000 catties of millet, most of which was taken from captured ammunition. The salary budget was originally 379,147,426 catties of millet. It was later cut substantially. The total cost was reduced almost by half because of the participation of sappers.[43]

Labour force mobilization was also applied in other domains, for example, 'disaster relief through work', which helped to achieve part of the government's relief task and also prevented famine-stricken people from flocking towards cities. In 1950, 1,532 million catties of staple grain were used for refugee relief. Out of this, 545.64 million catties was relief in the form of remuneration to pay the peasants working in irrigation construction and other projects, 37% of total aid (Jin and Chen 2005: 672). According to incomplete statistics, 123,854 people worked for relief allowance in 1950, 59,639 in 1951 and 85,128 in September 1952 (Wu and Dong 2001: 873).

The rural economy in China has always been diversified. The peasant household economy has long been comprised of different businesses besides farming. After land reform, sideline production in the rural sector developed, which became an effective way to absorb surplus labour force in disaster-stricken times. This has been a feature of the village as a 'sponge society' capable of resolving disasters and crises.

In order to relieve the impact of extensive natural disasters, the government implemented a series of supportive policies and measures to revitalize and develop sideline production and the handicrafts industry in rural regions. In the winter of 1949 and spring of 1950, a great part of the 766 million catties of relief grain were used to support peasants in developing sideline production and the handicrafts industry. Rural sideline production increased from 1.16 billion RMB in 1949 to 1.83 RMB in 1952, an increment of 57.8%, annual growth of 16.4% on average, which was a little higher than the average growth of gross agricultural production (see Box 16).[44]

---

[43]1949–1952 中华人民共和国经济档案资料选编·交通通讯卷 (Selection from People's Republic of China Economic Archives 1949–1952: Transportation and Communication) Beijing: China Supplies Publishing House, 1996, pp. 169–170. Quoted in Wu and Dong (2001: 450–451).

[44]1949–1952 中华人民共和国经济档案资料选编·农业卷 (Selection from People's Republic of China Economic Archives 1949–1952: Agriculture). Beijing: Social Sciences Literature Press, 1991, p. 982. Quoted in Wu and Dong (2001: 531).

Box 16: The Implementation of Relief Through Work in Various Regions, 1949–1952[*]

To resolve the difficulty of transporting food grain from producing regions to stations, piers and transportation lines, people were actively mobilized. This approach of providing relief through work allowed peasants to earn a certain portion of their subsistence by delivering grain.

For example, in the Changde region of Hunan, where flooding was severe, the organization of peasants to deliver food grain enabled over 880,000 of them to receive income through labour, thereby securing their livelihood.[**]

In the process of organizing grain transportation in the central and southern regions, the fiscal disbursement on shipping charge was equivalent to around 250 million catties of grain, and the amount paid out by the Bureau of Trade was equivalent to around 200 million catties. These transportation charges could provide for one month's consumption for 10 million people.

The supplementary production arising from disaster aids achieved notable results everywhere. For example, in Wen'an and Wuqing counties in Hebei, 90,000 peasants were mobilized into fishing and mattress weaving, with a monthly income of 600,000 catties of millet. In addition, over 60,000 people were organized to weave willow baskets, knit sacks, operate mills and so on, with income sufficient to sustain the livelihood for 200,000. In the Anqing region of Anhui, 100,000 victims were organized to self-help, engaging in such activities as gathering wood, fishing and delivering goods. The basic livelihood for 500,000 people was thus secured.[***] Victims numbering 300,000 in the coastal regions of Shandong and 450,000 in Hauiyin region of northern Suzhou relied on supplementary production to live through the spring famine.[****] The Duyang Lake area in the mid-southern region had actively organized peasants to engage in supplementary production and transportation activities, and 500,000 people were able to earn their living.[*****] Such practices have shown that wherever there was effective organization, the results of self-help among victims were good.

Notes:

[*]*1949–1952* 中华人民共和国经济档案资料选编·商业卷 (Selection of People's Republic of China Economic Archives 1949–1952:

Commerce). Beijing: China Supplies Publishing House, 1995, 126–127; quoted in Wu and Dong (2001: 310).

**Xinhua News Agency, '全国调粮任务接近全部完成' (Country-wide Mission on Deployment of Food grain Close to Full Completion); 1942–1952 中华人民共和国经济档案资料选编·商业卷 (Selection of People's Republic of China Economic Archives 1942–1952: Commerce). Beijing: China Supplies Publishing House, 1995, p. 126; quoted in Wu and Dong (2001: 319).

***1949–1952 中华人民共和国经济档案资料选编·农业卷 (Selection of People's Republic of China Economic Archive 1949–1952: Agriculture). Beijing: Social Sciences Literature Press, 1991, p. 54; quoted in Wu and Dong (2001: 54).

****Sun Encheng, 与空前严重的灾荒奋斗中的华东人民 (People of Eastern China Struggling with Unprecedentedly Severe Famine); 1949–1952 中华人民共和国经济档案资料选编·农业卷 (Selection of People's Republic of China Economic Archives 1949–1952: Agriculture). Beijing: Social Sciences Literature Press, 1991, p. 77; quoted in Wu and Dong (2001: 319).

*****1949–1952   中华人民共和国经济档案资料选编·农业卷 (Selection of People's Republic of China Economic Archive 1949–1952: Agriculture). Beijing: Social Sciences Literature Press, 1991, p. 54; quoted in Wu and Dong (2001: 54).

Preliminary Completion of State Regime Building

The central government's strong capacity for supplies allocation, on the one hand, profited from its experience mobilizing people in the base areas. Grassroots organizations that came into existence during land reform became the pillar of mobilization. On the other hand, it was the consequence of a highly centralized system, which was built by the CPC during the war for military command and unified local construction of the base areas (see Box 17). Confronting the pervasive challenge of inflation, the Central Committee of Finance and Economy was sanctioned by the top military authority to work across regions and departments. It was therefore capable of collecting incredible amounts of supplies from different parts of the country.

The political and economic authority of the central government was rebuilt in a short time, which was an anomaly in the history of the centre–local relationship, particularly, the lack of control of the central government over local regions since the late Qing dynasty.

Box 17: Focusing Power on Large-Scale Tasks—The Formation of a Unified System of Nationwide Financial-Economic Work

During the war, various liberated areas had been situated in isolation from one another, each taking care of their respective fiscal and economic works, and issuing their respective currencies. After Mao Zedong, Zhou Enlai and Ren Bizhi came to Xibaipo. Zhou Enlai suggested that finance and economy in the liberated areas should no longer work on the basis of 'united' governments, but a 'unified' government. He wanted to eliminate agency offices, establish Central Ministry of Finance and Economics, and set up People's Bank of China to issue currency on a unified basis (Jin and Chen 2005: 595–596).

Yet the financial and economic tasks in the various liberated areas were far from coordinated. For example, in October, after Jinan was liberated, the northern and eastern liberated areas united. Given that price levels in the two regions differed quite substantially, in the town of Linqing (located on the border of the two liberated areas, it was a major trading post before the liberation of Jinan) there emerged a major bidding battle for cotton material between the trading units of Northern China and Eastern China. More than 20 government-owned shops took part in the bidding for over 1.5 million catty of cotton material, with the result that the price level surged abruptly and private businessmen were able to make use of the opportunity and profit through dishonest practices. It was estimated that the cotton material purchased by government-owned businesses was on average 10% soaked, causing serious losses to the government (Wu and Dong 2001: 102).

On 4 June 1949, in the inauguration ceremony of the Central Committee of Finance and Economy, Liu Shaoqi clearly indicated that a highly centralized management on finance and economy was needed. Chen Yun also pointed out that with the liberation battle continuously gaining ground, the problems of finance and economy had increased. Moreover the problems were often nationwide, thereby requiring one organization to handle these problems (Jin and Chen 2005: 609–611).

The Central Committee of Finance and Economy had been set up just before the establishment of the PRC, led by the Central Military Committee. Under this committee, in each local region, a Committee of Finance was set up. In this way, the institutional structure of focusing power on large-scale tasks was formed.

This institutional advantage of centralization with Chinese characteristics facilitated the enormous supplies allocation and mobilization in the whole nation. In a work meeting in Shanghai, Chen Yun emphasized the coordination within and among regions:

On the matter of finance and economy, local governments would have their own agendas. However, if each local government has its own plan, our force will be too diffused to deal with the present situation. It is now impossible to concentrate all the reserve power. However, major reserve power must be used in a unified and systematic way. (Jin and Chen 2005: 624)

In the meeting, a decision was made to form unified enterprises for purchasing. The allocation of supplies in different regions, which used to be under the command of the field army, was now centralized. Large amounts of supplies allocation were to be made through the Central Committee of Finance and Economy (ibid.: 625–626).

In order to make up for a shortage of 2.9 billion catties of staple grain due to a natural disaster at the end of 1949, the Central Committee of Finance and Economy decided to allocate grain from Central, Northeast and Southwest China to East and North China. Out of this, 1.5 billion catties was from Northeast China and 1.1 billion catties from Central China. To secure the supply of food and cotton in major cities, grain were transferred from Sichuan regardless of cost. At that time, the grain reserve in Shanghai was less than 100 million catties. In order to prevent speculative merchants from making trouble, a stock of 400 million catties was needed. Grain were transported to Shanghai from different regions. Furthermore, 600–800 million catties of reserve was ready between Suzhou and Nanjing. After liberation, Shanghai had merely 20 million catties of staple grain. In the first half of 1950, the state managed to mobilize 1.7 billion catties of grain, enough for one-and-a-half years (Jin and Chen 2005: 669–673). The scale of supplies allocation for this purpose was enormous. Till the end of July 1950, 6 billion catties of staple grain were allocated in the whole nation.[45]

Furthermore, through land reform with extensive rural grassroots mobilization, the CPC managed a feat unparalleled in Chinese history: a complete arable land survey.

Land was the foundation of tax for every dynasty throughout China's history. However, the total area of arable land was unknown to the rulers. Measurement of land was always a difficult task for politicians and reformers who hoped to suppress ownership concentration by landlords and land appropriation by powerful families. In history only the founding emperor could have successfully implemented even distribution of land and tax exemption based on relatively transparent information. In comparison, poll tax was much easier to operate. For example, Zhang Juzheng (张居正), the chancellor of the Ming Emperor Wanli,[46] took on the task of putting the tax problem in order. In 1580, measurement of land in the whole country was promulgated in the name of the emperor. The goal was to survey the total amount of farmland. However, the task had not even started when Zhang passed away in 1582. In some counties and districts, no land survey had ever been done for centuries (Huang 1997: 33).

---

[45] 1949–1952 中华人民共和国经济档案资料选编·商业卷 (*Selection of People's Republic of China Economic Archives 1949–1952: Commerce*). Beijing: China Supplies Publishing House, 1995: 24.

[46] Zhang's post was the emperor's secretary or chief assistant (首辅), but at that time his duty was that of a chancellor.

In the new republic, land reform through total mobilization achieved an outcome that exceeded expectations. From statistics, the ratio of agricultural tax on real production decreased in 1950, then rose up in 1951 and declined substantially in 1952. In 1951, the real agricultural tax (including formal tax and additions by local governments) was more than 36 billion catties, an increase of 34% compared to 1950. Besides the additional tax prepared for the Korean War, one of the reasons was an addition of 60 million *mu* of 'invisible' farmland found in the survey. The taxable production was therefore increased by more than 20 billion catty (Wu and Dong 2001: 752). In 1951, an extra few billion catties of real agricultural tax was gained on top of the expected budget.

These were the mechanisms of how the state, based on the urban–rural dual structure, made use of internal power to resolve urban crises by way of agricultural policy and investment, making villages the institutional facilitators and bearers of soft-landing.

Obviously, with a very tight fiscal budget, the key to the effectiveness of the various policies—whether concerning grassroots mobilization by land reform, irrigation infrastructure building, or sideline agricultural production—was the mobilization of the labour force, a resource very rich in China.

The reason the state benefited from it was that these workforces that answered the state's call to take part in building national infrastructure were paid according to the cost of rural labour reproduction under an urban–rural dual structure, which was obviously lower than the cost of urban labour. Therefore, China became the only developing country able to rely on a low-cost labour force for a long period of time.

4   New Crisis: Government Regulation Under a Weak Market and Political Movement

Very few have looked into the experience of dealing with a market crisis under private capital. Not many have understood the pattern of an economic crisis turning into a political contradiction, and taken the opportunity it affords to analyse the strategic adjustments a government has to make in such matters implicating national security.

The developmental strategy of New Democracy was set up by the state before the republic was born. This strategy approved market economics and encouraged private capital. However, urban hyperinflation and the subsequent speculation by private capital, which is inevitable under a free market economy, would generally lead to the collapse of the real economy in developing countries and the modernization trap.[47]

Earlier in the chapter, the new government's measures such as increasing market liquidity and creating demand by government purchasing were discussed. Admittedly, these market rescue policies were an effective counter-regulation to save urban private industry and commerce. However, the management and moral risk of urban private capital soon spread to the government. Numerous cases of corruption demonstrating the collusion between enterprises and officials occurred.

As Einstein said, 'Problems cannot be solved with the same mindset that created them.' In the same vein, we say that urban private capital crisis cannot be solved by strengthening urban capital. Therefore, China undertook socialist reform in 1953, which was a major strategic adjustment. That a new regime emerging from the Chinese peasant revolution could overcome the crisis may be attributed to two basic conditions of the rural regions.

---

[47]Since the expansion of European imperialism, many traditional societies faced the pressure of being invaded and colonized or surpassed in international competition. Taking the success (western societies) as model, they pushed forward modernization which consisted of building industry and modern social management system by implanting technologies and knowledge from the West. However modernization is a highly capital-intensive process. Managing industry and modern government system is very costly. Many developing countries, after dismantling traditional social structure fail to establish a sustainable social and economic model to support and further develop the modern system. They find themselves got stuck in between: no longer traditional organic societies, however not yet successful modern societies. Usually they face serious fiscal and trade deficit problems as well as recurring social and political instability. We call this "modernization trap".

First, the government suppressed inflation and speculation mainly by putting enormous amounts of essential supplies (mostly agricultural products) into the market. At the same time, these supplies were produced by a great number of peasants mobilized by land revolution.[48]

Second, official commercial institutes could collect enormous amounts of supplies from geographically highly scattered peasant households only because of the extensive mobilization of peasants by a powerful regime formed during a violent revolution.[49]

In the name of land revolution, the government as a political practice distributed land to 400 million of peasants based on the natural boundary of villages. On the one hand, the three agrarian sectors (*sannong*; peasants, villages and agriculture) became delinked from the high-risk urban economy, which lay a solid foundation for stabilizing the financial order. Hence, Mao repeatedly emphasized the political and economic function of land reform, which secured the victory of the financial struggle in cities (Bo 1991). On the other hand, this became a serious institutional path dependency, first on the traditional land system in villages (afterwards, any distribution of land must delineate boundary of property right within the natural village, latter transformed into production squad and economic cooperative), and second on the institutional cost transfer from urban capital to the *sannong*, which subsequently became the bearer of soft-landing in every economic crisis.

Background: Sluggish Urban and Rural Economies After Curbing Hyperinflation

It is a general law of cyclical crises that depression follows after the suppression of hyperinflation. Officially, it has been explained that the Chinese national economy was in a difficult period of transitioning

---

[48]Many contemporary discourses were unheard of in Chinese history, for example, politics, class, party, which were of foreign origin. However, land to the tillers has long been a politically acceptable idea. For peasants, it is not a modern revolutionary slogan, but rather a traditional mobilizing banner of thousands of years. What the peasants aspire to be are petit property owners having a small place to live on.

[49]Some scholars point out that the extent of violence of a revolution is determined by the backwardness, scarcity of capital, and the extent of foreign exploitation and suppression. See Gerschenkron (2009) and Cheng (1998).

from the old to the new order. However, the real reason was the law of cyclical crisis emphasized in this book. Under high inflation, the physical economy will decline and private capital will rush towards the speculative economy. A laissez-faire approach, as advocated by interest blocs, would eventually lead to the bursting of the bubble. However, harshly putting down speculation will inevitably lead to recession.

At that time, the new regime had yet to be influenced by interest blocs. It therefore took forceful measures to suppress speculation, which was then followed by recession. That is the reason we put the hyperinflation in 1949 and the recession after 1950 in the same economic cycle. A complete economic cycle usually consists of four phases: boom, recession, depression and recovery. The feature of the Chinese economic cycle was a bipolar oscillation between boom and depression, even if it was with relatively little government regulation. It had nothing to do with ideology. In the so-called free market economy, an economic trend is correlated with the form in which the cost of crisis is transferred outwards.

We may also look into other explanations. For example, some studies believe that apart from the destructive factor of the KMT regime retreating, there were problems with transforming a part of the old economic foundation, for instance, luxury goods, services sector, speculative sector, comprador import–export sector, etc. Further, some overreacting behaviours of squeezing out private industry and commerce also led to a certain increase in unemployment.

We believe that the trend towards regression after 1950 in urban industry and commerce was obviously related to the speculation on essential supplies in the phase of high inflation. As prices stabilized and declined, the opportunities or speculation and value protection shrank greatly. Industrial products started to overstock. Market turnover was much lower than commodities available.

In the second half of March 1950, 70 million catties of staple food was available in the market, only 14% of which (10 million) was sold. Of 280,000 sacks of flour, only 7% (20,000) was sold. In Chongqing, some of the major commodities transacted in private commerce decreased in April compared with March: edible oil and coal by 50%, cloth by 70%, cotton yarn by 92.5% and cotton by 93.5%. As for the wholesale market in Shanghai, taking the transaction volume in January as 100, in April, the transaction of cotton yarn was 53%, rice 17%, flour 56%, rolled tobacco only 5%. The sales turnover of six large departmental stores in Shanghai decreased by 50% in March compared with January, and by 90% in smaller stores.

As the market was weak and sales declined, production of private enterprises dropped drastically. The most difficult sectors were flour manufacturing and spinning, where speculation was previously most intensive.

In May 1950, compared with January, the production of cotton cloth decreased by 38%, silk fabric by 47%, wool by 20%, rolled tobacco by 59%, caustic soda by 41%, and paper by 31%. In eastern and coastal regions, where private industry and commerce were concentrated, the situation was more difficult. In Shanghai, the production of matches decreased in April compared with January by five-sixths, and flour, rolled tobacco, wool yarn, chemical glue, glass, etc. by 60–80%. Many factories were run at half capacity and many were closed down. The situation developed in stages. From January to February 1950, the number of private industry and commerce business start-ups was still higher than close-downs. Since March, however, the number of close-downs increased while start-ups dropped drastically. From January to April in Beijing, 1,043 shops were applying for starting a business, while 1,573 were shutting down, many of which were shops selling rice and flour, cloth and coal, as well as departmental stores. From January to April 1950, in 14 large cities, 2,945 factories went out of business. Urban private industry and commerce ran into trouble. In 16 big cities, 9,347 shops shut down (Wu and Dong 2001: 357–358). In April 1950, 2,600 employees in Tianjin were about to lose their jobs, most of whom were working in staple foods, coal and money exchange stores (Wu and Dong 2001: 654–655). The situation was bad in Shanghai, where industry and commerce were concentrated. In the second half of April, 1,000 factories closed down and 2,000 shops went out of business. The number of unemployed workers was more than 200,000 (Wu and Dong 2001: 866).

When spring was turning to summer in 1950, a 20% unemployment rate was recorded for the first time in the new republic. According to incomplete statistics, by the end of September 1950, the number of jobless workers in the nation amounted to 1,220,231 and unemployed intellectuals numbered 188,261, resulting in a total of 1,408,492. Moreover, semi-unemployed workers were 255,769, out of which 120,472 were about to lose their jobs. The unemployment rate peaked in July 1950. Registered unemployed persons were alone 1,664,288, which was about 21% of the total urban employees. The number would have been higher if it included unregistered unemployed persons (Wu and Dong 2001: 865–866). The increased unemployed population during the price stabilization was about 380,000–400,000.[50]

The crowding out effect of inflation-induced speculation over the real economy and depression following the curbing of speculation took place more than once after 1949. It is still relevant today.

Efforts in Promoting Urban–Rural Market Exchange and Their Limits

It is noteworthy that the economic difficulties mentioned earlier took place in modern cities where capital was concentrated, whereas villages, which were delinked from the modern urban economy after land reform, were more insulated. Under the dual urban–rural structure representing modernity and tradition respectively, the effect of depression over the cities and the villages showed remarkable difference. In the cities, it was general recession, while in the villages it was expressed as underdevelopment of agricultural sideline production, unmarketable local products, tax overburden, etc. In some grain-producing regions, the sale of staple grain was also a problem.

Confronted with depression, the government took two different types of measures. First, it acted as the regulator and conductor of the market economy, a policy of New Democracy. Second, it acted as an economic agent to transform private capitalism into state capitalism, also known as socialist reform.

In the actual process, the government was constantly adjusting its measures and policies. Fortunately, the leadership and management had

---

[50]He Guang, 当代中国的劳动力管理 (*Contemporary Chinese Labour Management*). Beijing: China Social Sciences Press, 1990, p. 4. Quoted in Wu and Dong (2001: 866).

yet to construct interest complementarity with domestic and foreign capital at the time. Therefore, the policy adjustment was a practical one of amending errors and diversification, confined neither to the revolutionary discourse nor bound by urban interest blocs. However, the enormous institutional benefit and the political energy gained by the extensive mobilization of peasants started to express itself as an institutional cost in relation to urban capital.

Agrarian reform had a dual impact on the urban–rural relationship. On the one hand, the political distance between rural areas and governments was reduced. On the other, the economic connection between rural sector and urban industry–commerce was severed.

Apropos the first aspect, land reform made peasants (at that time 88% of the population) highly dependent and loyal to the People's Republic of China under the leadership of the CPC, just as peasants in history were loyal to any dynasty that had realized land distribution and tax exemption. That means the new Chinese government had succeeded in the most extensive national mobilization in state building through land reform, which in terms of fundamental institutional condition was essentially different from many developing countries without complete land reform.

However, with regard to the second aspect, land reform involved even distribution of land to rural households according to the number of family members. As a result, what were simultaneously eliminated were two important traditional economic agents extracting surplus value from rural China at low cost for the accumulation of urban capital. First, rich and middle-income peasants, the agents of production of scale, who could rent land on a large scale, were gone. Second, landlords, the agents of commodity circulation of scale, who could turn agricultural products into commodities at low cost merely by real rent, were also gone.[51]

Along with the elimination of the two agents of the economy of scale, the previous economic setting was also altered. That is, gone too also was the phenomenon of industrial and commercial capital descending

---

[51]The author has elaborated on these views about the two agents of scale in 1999 and 2004. See Wen (2000: 95, 107; 2004: 77).

into rural areas with financial capital, while landlords running industry and commerce acted as loan sharks.

As agrarian reform was not favourable to capital, what arose as a result was the confrontation between the geographically scattered peasant economy and urban capital concentrated in cities. Henceforth, private capital would find it difficult to extract surplus value from the peasants for the sake of primitive accumulation.

It is as true today as it was then. So it was for China in the 1950s and for developing countries now as well.

Although land reform substantially reduced the degree of exploitation of peasants by external agents, it led to a contradiction between urban and rural sectors due to the economic disparity in the phase of New Democracy. In order to develop national capitalist industry in cities, rural surplus had to be extracted from a peasant economy comprised of geographically scattered peasants who also operated sideline production. The concern was that the transaction cost between the two sectors would become very high. Furthermore, the peasant economy had been under the impact of hyperinflation for more than a decade. It was expected that peasants would be risk-averse and opt for demonetarized behaviour. In other words, under market fluctuations, the peasants would generally save staple grain and cut their consumption of urban products.

The Achievement of Promoting Urban–Rural Market Exchange and Its Limit

From the point of view of managing the urban–rural market after hyper-inflation, industrial and commercial capital, whose chance of speculation had been curbed, had to leave cities to get out of the doldrums. The market had to be expanded to rural regions where 88% of the population lived so as to complete the primitive accumulation of capital. Therefore, as the first step towards dealing with post-inflation depression, it was logical and practical for the government to promote urban–rural exchange.

In November 1950, Chen Yun, who was in charge of economic and financial issues, pointed out in a speech on the Second National

Conference on Finance and Economy: 'The expansion of marketing of agricultural products is not only a rural issue but also a key to vitalizing China's economy. It is the first priority in the Chinese economy at present.'[52]

However, the contradictions of matching urban–rural markets under a dual structure started to unfold when the exchange between the two sectors was being promoted. As the issue of insufficient urban–rural exchange was raised, it was understood that the first step would have to involve the government paying peasants in advance by purchasing agricultural products. As money went into villages, the commodity exchange between urban industry commerce and peasants would be kick-started. After traditional urban–rural trade was banned or limited during and after the government's dealing with hyperinflation, there was still active demand in villages to exchange with cities and other regions.

According to surveys by local product companies, the value of special local products as well as handicrafts was 36% of the total staple food production in East China in 1950, about 1,500 billion yuan (in old RMB). In North China, local products except major cash crops were worth about 25% of the total production. In Central and South China, the value of local and special products accounted for about 30% of peasants' incomes. In Southwest China, it was about 30–40% of peasants' incomes. More than ten million people made a living through special local products. In Northeast China, the value of local products amounted to 26.2% of the total agricultural production in 1950. In Northwest China, it accounted for 30% of the total income. In Inner Mongolia, the value of special and local products was almost equal to other agricultural income. In Guizhou, the value of 46 major local products was equivalent to 2.7 billion catty of rice, about the same as the income from staple foods (Wu and Dong 2001: 388) (see Box 18).

---

[52]陈云文选 (1949–1952) (*Selected Writings of Chen Yun 1949–1952*). Beijing: People's Press, 1984, p. 113. Quoted in Wu and Dong (2001: 390).

Box 18: Economic Difficulties in Various Regions After Hyperinflation Was Controlled

In Northeast China, because of stagnation in the flow of goods between urban and rural regions, various provinces, cooperatives and peasants together had a grain inventory of around 540,000 tonnes. Out of this, the provinces had no more than 100,000 tonnes, cooperatives had around 80,000 tonnes, and the remaining 360,000 tonnes were in the hands of the people. In the north-western region, the economic crisis that had been hiding behind artificial prosperity was fully exposed. Speculators not only refrained from buying anything, they even sent their hoard of commodities to the market. With more supply than demand, the sale of commodities became difficult. In the southwest, 'local produce had no market so the countryside had no money. Therefore industrial goods in turn found it hard to go to the countryside. The three had exerted impact on one another resulting in the stagnation of the rural economy.' In the northern region, peasants had urgent need to sell agricultural produce in exchange for production material and daily life goods. Based on Chahaer Province's statistics on 14 kinds of agricultural produce, the quantity waiting to be traded out valued over 28 million yuan. For this winter, Shanxi needed to transport out 400 million catties of surplus grain, over 45 million catties of cotton wool, and 100 million catties of various items such as oil, hemp, herbal medicines etc.

In the central and southern regions, local produce valued more than 1 billion yuan, accounting for 20% of peasants' income. Yet, due to the blockade by the United States and the ongoing land reform among peasants, sales and delivery of local produce were significantly affected.

Source: Wu and Dong (2001: 384–385).

Faced with depressed urban industry and commerce, leaders in the central government who were experienced in rural issues came up with policies to expand commodities exchange among regions and promote industrial products in villages. These measures included restoring and developing transportation capacity, encouraging private merchants to take part in purchasing and transporting between cities, encouraging state-owned cooperatives to promote selling of special local products, holding supplies exchange fairs, developing rural market trades, increasing commercial loans, developing remittance and mort-gage services, enlarging the remittance network, bringing currency into villages by purchasing agricultural and sideline products, etc.

These measures of bringing currency into villages were effective. Statistics show that the value of agricultural and sideline products' purchasing increased to 129,730 billion yuan (in old RMB) in 1952 from 80,000 billion in 1950, a growth of 62.16%.[53]

However, taking a further look at this data, it is not hard to see that these improvements in fact owed largely to the rehabilitation of traditional local market exchange between peasants, irrespective of region. The commodification rate of peasant household production was only 30–40%. A self-sufficient peasant economy appeared to continue in this mode. It was unlikely that it would spontaneously become the market of urban industrial products. Even in the market of agricultural tools and means of production, where the expansion rate of the market scale was much higher than the growth rate of the peasant income, the deepening of capital was still inhibited (see Box 19).

Box 19: Industrial Goods in Support of Agriculture Found It Difficult to Go to the Countryside

Based on statistics, following an increase in peasants' income, the supply of agricultural production material nationwide increased from a total value of 7,300 billion yuan in 1950 to 14,100 billion in 1952, an increase of 93.15%. This was higher than the increase in peasants' purchasing power by 11 percentage points.[*]

After 1949, there was a story in China about an iron plough finding it difficult to go to the countryside, which demonstrated the contradiction in the dual urban–rural structure. Following the Soviet Union's advanced farming approach that relied on horse-drawn ploughs to raise the level of agricultural production facilities, the revived urban industry produced a type of two-wheel, two-spade plough whose power was double that of the wooden plough. It could dig two parallel ditches deeper than any

---

[53]National Bureau of Statistics, 商业统计资料汇编 (1950–1957) (*Compilation of Commercial Statistics Data 1950–1957*), 1958. Quoted in Wu and Dong (2001: 401).

common plough was able to. It was referred to by the rural folks as an iron plough in contrast to the wooden plough that was commonly used. The cost of the iron plough was only 29 yuan and the selling price was 39 yuan (new post-1955 monetary value).

For the city, it was supposed to be a major event marking the beginning of agriculture-supporting goods production by the national industry. A lot of newspapers publicized it. Many urban cadres excitedly named their newborns that year after the iron plough. However, in the countryside, no matter how much the government publicized it and pushed it, hardly any peasants bought the plough.

That was because the traditional peasant economy that was revived after land reform was still a type of 'lightly capitalized' economy: for one thing, a plough could simply be constructed with the help of a village carpenter who could build a frame and a blacksmith who could hammer out a spade and plough. After that, all it needed was an animal yoked to it to make it ready for the field. There was no need to go and purchase an iron plough. The other thing was that within the rural community many types of operations in industry and commerce did not use cash, hence, rural people were not in the habit of buying urban industrial goods.

Afterwards, this type of two-wheel, two-spade plough was distributed on a semi-mandatory basis and pushed into the countryside. However, this kind of one-size-fits-all command did not consider the vastly diverse geographical and geological characteristics of different places. While productivity had clearly increased in some places, in others the allotted ploughs were simply put aside unused since they were not appropriate for the local fields and animals. This outcome regarding the iron plough subsequent to the cooperative movement in the countryside also demonstrated that it was only with the establishment of the peasant cooperative system that urban industrial goods could be received by the countryside.

Note:

*Agricultural means of production data from State Statistics Bureau, 商业统计资料汇编 (1950–1957) (Commercial Statistics Compilation 1950–1957, General Volume 1), 1958; Peasants Purchasing Power data from: State Statistics Bureau, 中国商业历史资料汇编 (Compilation of Historical Data of Commerce in China), 1963; quoted in Wu and Dong (2001: 401, 403).

Source: This box has been compiled by the author based on personal experiences and materials.

Top photo: The two-wheel, two-spade plough being manufactured.

Bottom photo: Mao Zedong inspecting the two-wheel, two-spade plough; 人民画报 (People Pictorial), Issue 11, 1955.

Photo source: https://www.wzrb.com.cn/article299816show.html.

What has been discussed so far shows that whenever a developing country modernizes, it faces the difficulty of high-transaction-cost trading with geographically dispersed peasants and the problem of primitive accumulation of capital. This phenomenon of high-transactions cost is the institutional cost of modernization and is implicated irrespective of the official ideology a country maintains. In our case, regardless of the classic Marxist theory imported from the Soviet Union in the late 1940s or New Democracy by the CPC, China fell prey to the development trap as early as 1950. As it was difficult to promote exchange between industry and the rural sector by market transaction, the primitive accumulation of private capital necessary for industrialization became impossible.

We may look into statistics to understand the overall situation. The value of agricultural and sideline products purchasing increased to 129,730 billion yuan (old RMB) in 1952 from 80,000 billion in 1950, a growth of 62.16%. From 1949 to 1952, peasants' net money income increased to 127,900 billion yuan from 68,500 billion, a growth of 86.7%. The purchasing power of peasants was increased by 80%. The total volume of retail sales in cities and villages was 170,560, 208,840 and 246,880 billion yuan in 1950, 1951 and 1952 respectively.[54]

In 1951, the increment in value of agricultural and sideline products purchasing was 19,100 billion yuan. Meanwhile, the rise in expenditure of peasants buying industrial products due to price rise was 9,200 billion yuan. The benefits peasants gained were therefore 9,900 billion yuan. In 1952, the increment in the value of agricultural purchasing was 27,700 billion yuan, a slight drop but still higher than 1950. The benefits peasants gained were 18,000 billion yuan. In two years, it was 27,900 billion yuan.[55]

The supply of agricultural means of production increased to 14,100 billion yuan in 1952 from 7,300 in 1950, a growth of 91.15%.[56]

---

[54]National Bureau of Statistics, 中国商业历史资料汇编 (*Compilation of Historical Data of Commerce in China*), 1963. Quoted in Chen (1995a). To make the data consistent, here value given is in old RMB.

[55]National Bureau of Statistics, 解放后全国工农业商品价格剪刀差变化情况 (The Price Scissors between Industrial and Agricultural Products After Liberation), August 1957. Quoted in Chen (1995a).

[56]National Bureau of Statistics, 商业统计资料汇编 (1950–1957) (*Commercial Statistics Compilation 1950–1957*), 1958. Quoted in Wu and Dong (2001: 293).

At the end of 1952, RMB held by peasants because of habits of saving, ready for purchasing livestock or land, etc., was up to 11,000 billion yuan, about 40.4% of the total volume of currency in circulation.[57]

Admittedly, the above data was often quoted to represent the achievement of the government in increasing the income of peasants. Nevertheless, if viewed in the context of Chinese industrialization and from the perspective of the difficulty of industrial products going into the countryside, we can provide a new reading of this data.

First, the increment in the total amount of agricultural and sideline products was a result of raising the purchasing price. Peasant production showed no trend towards a higher extent of commodification. The total value of the increment was RMB 19,500 and 27,700 billion in 1951 and 1952, respectively. The sum was 47,200 billion yuan, about the same as the total amount of purchasing which was 49,700 billion (129,700 minus 80,000). Therefore, only RMB 2,500 billion (49,700 minus 47,200), about 5% of the increment, was gained because of the increase in the purchase volume of agricultural products.

Second, peasant production in general did not show a trend of capital deepening. In 1952, the commercial sector's supply of agricultural means of production to the countryside was RMB 14,100 billion, merely 10.87% of the total value of agricultural and sideline products, which was RMB 129,700 billion. If the RMB 110,000 billion held by peasants was deducted from this RMB 129,700, then the expenditure of peasants in rural and urban sectors was about RMB 118,700 billion in 1952, of which merely 11.88% was demand for agricultural means of production.

Third, the demand for industrial products by geographically scattered peasants did not change in proportion to the income level and relative price. The income and price elasticity of demand for industrial products by geographically dispersed peasant households were extremely low. In 1951, peasant income increased by 19,500 billion yuan after raising purchasing prices. However, less than half (47%, 9,200 billion) was rendered into increased demand for industrial products. In 1952, the value of purchasing was increased by RMB 277,000 billion. Still, only

---

[57]Data from People's Bank of China, 关于目前货币流通情况与一九五三年货币发行问题的报告(Report on Currency Circulation and Money Issuance in 1953), 18 March 1953; He (2008).

RMB 9,500 billion was rendered into increased demand for industrial products, the ratio further dropped to 34.3%. Therefore, as the price scissors between industrial and agricultural products was decreasing and peasant income was increasing at a higher rate than expenditure, the currency going into the countryside stayed there. Only a relatively small portion of it circulated back into the cities.

It is apparent that peasants held a large amount of cash, mainly for internal circulation within the traditional rural economy, including a small section of the rich peasants who saved money for buying houses and land. On the one hand, it helped to absorb the expansion in the money supply by the government and relieve the pressure of inflation. On the other hand, it showed that urban–rural economic exchange was difficult to establish. In managing inflation, the former aspect was positive. However, after inflation was curbed, its negative impact started to emerge. Though it did not represent a long-term trend, nevertheless, as industrial production was totally revived, the market of industrial products was hard to expand if the purchasing power of peasants did not release itself through buying urban industrial products.

The situation of different industrial sectors matched well with the above analysis. Industrial overproduction occurred mainly in light industries related with daily life, for example, in the sectors producing matches, rolled tobacco, soap, flour, silk fabric and soy sauce (Wu and Dong 2001: 361).

Primitive Accumulation of Capital and the Policy Paradox of Price Scissors

It is generally thought that primitive accumulation of capital came from the extraction of rural surplus. Only by enlarging the price gap between industrial and agricultural products could the industrial sector extract surplus from the agricultural. Many scholars in China have conducted research on how much surplus the urban industrial sector has extracted from the rural sector through the price gap between them (Cui 1988; Han 1993; Jiangsu 2003; Li and Li 2008; State Council 2006; Su 2006; Wen 2000; Yan et al. 1990). However, we argue that it was when the state coercively pushed rural collectivization that urban industrial capital was capable of extracting surplus from the rural sector, hence the importance of the state. Before that, it was almost impossible for the geographically scattered and mixed-business running peasants to accept industrial products produced on a large scale in cities.

We would like to point out that the self-sufficiency of the peasant economy is typical of peasant economic behaviour of deploying internal/domestic labour to diminish its exposure to external risk. This peasant household rationality sustained by the internalization of risk is the vital mechanism by which traditional peasant sponge society can remain self-sufficient and stable (Wen 2011). However, in modern society, where industry is prioritized in development, this mechanism becomes an obstacle for industrial products going into the rural market. This binary contradiction has nothing to do with ideology. It is common to all developing countries.

The difficulty and experience of China achieving primitive accumulation for industrialization in a prevailing peasant economy may help us to understand the difference between the development path of the West and the East. Macfarlane (1978) suggests that as early as 800 years ago in England, rural organization typical of traditional peasant society had disappeared. Economic activities and social relationships were highly individualized. England achieved primitive accumulation of capital through colonization. The colonies afforded England with the demand for industrial products. Therefore, we are not able to find similar mechanism internalizing external risk through a family portfolio of allocating labour force as in rural China. In other words, China has achieved primitive accumulation of capital through rural households internalizing the cost by self-exploitation while England achieved so through colonization.

It is well known that the textile industry was a pioneer of modern industry and an important sector of light industry. In the early 1950s, the volume of the urban market was limited. Unlike developed countries in the West, which had access to markets overseas, China could only rely on its rural regions as market outlets for its modern industrial products such as textiles. According to a survey in April 1951 of 18 cloth shops in Beijing, there was an increment in sales turnover. Sales to the countryside was increased by 120–130%, whereas merely 65% to Beijing. The former was two times the latter.[58] The problem was that in traditional rural society, weaving had long been the work of women. As land reform restored the long history of weaving, the competition faced by the Chinese urban textile industry was not the dumping of foreign products but rather the looms spinning in every house in villages.

Therefore, we had the policy paradox of price scissors between industrial and agricultural products.

The reality of the practice of New Democracy during 1949–1952 was as follows. The traditional peasant household in China had long been a mini composite economic cell in which production and consumption were highly internalized. When peasants' income did not increase substantially and the price scissors was too large, household weaving replaced machinery production. It became difficult to sell industrial products to the countryside. At the same time, faced with low grain prices, peasants would rather consume more grains than sell them. It became difficult to gather grain to supply the cities. Therefore, besides the transaction cost of peasants trading with the external market, peasant incomes also became an important factor for the textile industry to expand into the rural market. And until the 1980s, the textile industry remained China's major export sector capable of earning foreign exchange. In essence, there was a conflict of interest between urban and rural sectors, and also between industrial and agricultural sectors. It was not easy to come up with a balanced decision.

Even though peasants benefited from the urban–rural exchange as described earlier and peasant incomes did show a remarkable increase during 1949–1952, the income rate was still lagging behind that of industrial and commercial sectors.

During 1949–1952, total arable land was increased by 10.25% and grain production by 46.1%. However, the value of agricultural production only increased by 41.4%. The increment in value lagged behind the increment in volume. In terms of division within agriculture, the greatest

---

[58] 1949–1952 中华人民共和国经济档案资料选编·商业卷 (*Selection of People's Republic of China Economic Archives 1949–1952: Commerce*). Beijing: China Supplies Publishing House, 1995, pp. 338, 365. Quoted in Wu and Dong (2001: 656).

increase in production and income took place in cotton cultivation. However, the total farming area of cotton was small in ratio. It helped little in increasing peasant incomes (see Box 20). The largest income growth of peasants was recorded in production of local special products and sideline products based on a traditional mixed business mode, which is a feature of peasant livelihood diversity. As the traditional peasant economy was not monetized and commercialized to a great extent, the influence of cotton planting in increasing peasant income was limited.

Box 20: Revival and Growth of Agricultural Production After Land Reform

According to available data, total cultivated land area and total grain production quantity did not increase significantly after land reform.

China has always had the pressure of more people and less arable land. The population in the late Qing period already exceeded 300 million. Without any significant technological breakthrough, there was limited room for development and utilization of land. After the establishment of the PRC, with policies that encouraged the development of barren land, cultivated land area countrywide increased from 1.47 billion *mu* (15 *mu* = 1 hectare) in 1949 to 1.62 billion in 1952, an increase of 150.5 million or 10.25% (Wu and Dong 2001: 506).

In the early period of the PRC, the production of key agricultural produce had realized a large-scale increase. Comparing 1952 to 1949, total grain production increased from 112.18 million tonnes to 163.92 million tonnes, a growth of 46.1% (Wu and Dong 2001: 246). Given that the production in 1949 had been more seriously affected by natural disasters, a significant portion of the growth reflected the natural revival of production. Nevertheless, compared to the production of 150 million tonnes in 1936 (Wu and Dong 2010: 50), there was still an increase of 9.28%.

The highest growth was recorded in the cash crop, cotton. Total production of cotton increased from 444,000 tonnes in 1949 to 1.3 million tonnes in 1952, an increase of 193.69% in three years, and 153.6% of the historic high. The average per capita production increased from 1.6 catties in 1949 to 4.6 catties in 1952. The main reason was that in order to meet the demand in industrial raw material, the government had raised the purchase price of cotton. In April 1950, the Central Committee of Finance and Economy had set the price equivalent between cotton and grain as 1 catty of 7/8-inch medium grade ginned cotton for 8 catties of millet or 7 catties of wheat or 6.5 catties of rice. In March 1951, it was raised to 1 catty of 7/8-inch medium grade ginned cotton for 8.5–9 catties of millet, 8 catties of wheat or 8.5 catties of rice. By 1952, it was 1 catty of cotton for 8–9 catties or 8.5–9.5 catties of millet, 7.5–8.5 catties of wheat or 8–9 catties of rice (Wu and Dong 2001: 673). It should be noted that the increase of cotton purchase price subsequent to 1951 was implemented after the announcement of the government policy of unified purchase and marketing by the state on cotton yarn and material. That did not lend support to the general view that the state policy of unified purchase and marketing was for the purpose of procuring material from peasants at a low price. On the contrary, from the perspective of handling hyperinflation, that policy did have an obvious effect in curtailing speculation as well as hoarding by intermediaries.

Although 'to get rich, grow cotton' became the slogan of many peasants, yet given that the proportion of cotton relative to the total agricultural produce was insignificant, its contribution towards improving peasant income was limited. Furthermore, since cotton was using up land used to cultivate grain, the former could not be allowed to expand unchecked. From the table below it can be seen that in 1949, the cultivated area for cotton was about 2.2% that for grain. By 1952, it had gone up by 104.7% compared with 1949, yet as a percentage of cultivated area for grain it was still only 4.7%. Therefore, the impact of cotton on driving peasant income was generally limited.

1949–1952 Cultivated Land Area, Grain Cultivation Area and Cotton Cultivation

Area by Region (in million *mu*)

	Item	1949	1950	1951	1952
Northern China	Cultivated land	189.34	194.37	199.01	204.41
	Grain cultivation	179.10	184.24	181.24	197.33
	Cotton cultivation	10.691	14.706	20.595	19.573
Northeast China	Cultivated land	224.89	229.76	230.69	238.87
	Grain cultivation	208.18	216.99	208.68	219.16
	Cotton cultivation	1.916	3.647	7.127	6.164
Eastern China	Cultivated land	337.80	344.94	360.52	375.29
	Grain cultivation	433.39	454.23	482.62	500.84
	Cotton cultivation	12.124	16.578	23.867	24.71
Southern Central	Cultivated land	333.09	345.55	370.48	382.47
	Grain cultivation	447.28	468.33	483.80	517.52
	Cotton cultivation	11.042	14.681	21.110	22.803
Southwest	Cultivated land	166.02	166.86	169.24	176.82
	Grain cultivation	205.38	202.46	208.70	215.01
	Cotton cultivation	2.144	2.742	4.596	4.345
Total	Cultivated land	1,251.14	1,281.48	1,329.94	1,377.86
	Grain cultivation	1,473.33	1,526.25	1,565.04	1,649.86
	Cotton cultivation	37.917	52.354	77.295	77.601

Source: Wu and Dong (2001: 588–624).

Even though the new government sought to develop national capitalism as a state strategy, it failed to solve the problem of transaction cost between urban enterprises and the peasant economy. Limited by its dual feature of natural reproduction and economic reproduction, the development of the peasant economy usually lagged behind second and tertiary industries. It was the same for the New Democracy under the leadership of the CPC during 1949–1952. Compared with modern economic sectors such as industry, construction, transportation and commerce, agriculture recorded the lowest growth rate. Peasant income growth rate was also the lowest. Even including all incomes due to the sideline businesses, the purchasing power of peasants increased merely by 80% during the period, whereas national incomes in other sectors at least doubled.

Table 6 Production value growth rate in different sectors and national income growth index, 1950–1952 (Value in 1949 = 100)

Sector	1950		1951		1952	
	Production value	National income	Production value	National income	Production value	National income
Agriculture	117.8	117.1	128.8	128.9	141.4	138.7
Industry	136.4	133.3	188.6	186.6	249.3	255.5
Construction	325	500	600	900	1425	2100
Transportation	100	116.6	126.3	150	184.2	208.3
Commerce	111.8	109.1	129.4	127.2	166.2	160.0

Sources: Sectors growth rate: National Bureau of Statistics (1984: 20); National income growth index in different sectors: National Bureau of Statistics (1987)

Commerce grew by 60%, which was 22.3% higher than agriculture (See Table 6).

Aside from the low-price characteristics of agricultural products, policy has been decisive in determining peasant income.

For instance, the even distribution of land and tax exemption was a common practice at the beginning of most dynasties in history. In new China, however, the policy entailed the even distribution of land but without tax exemption.[59]

The way the CPC dealt with inflation at the beginning of the new republic was based on extracting agricultural surplus through the mobilization of peasants. At that time, peasants' burdens were not relieved but actually increased. Tax relief was supposed to have been implemented in 1951, but such planned tax exemption was rescinded due to the Korean War.

Second, the commercial gains in the countryside were taken by state-owned cooperatives as a result of the government collecting agricultural products to fight speculation in cities.

The major consequence of land reform was the redistribution of wealth inside villages. However, during the process, the landlord, the

---

[59]The household responsibility system in the 1980s of Deng Xiaoping's era was in effect the same as the land reform in the 1950s of Mao's era. Both involved even distribution of land without tax exemption. It was not until 2004–2006 that agricultural tax was abolished. After 57 years, even distribution of land and tax exemption was eventually completed.

agent of the circulation of scale, was also eliminated. Commercial organizations and businesses of different components were developed in the urban–rural exchange. Nevertheless, the gains of rapid growth in urban–rural trade were appropriated by state-owned commercial bodies and cooperatives.

From 1950 to 1952, state-owned commercial enterprises increased from 7,638 to 31,444, a growth of 312%. Profits and tax increased by 302%. Domestic commodities' sales volume increased from RMB 34,420 to 155,080 billion yuan, a growth of 350%. The number of supply and marketing cooperatives increased from 22,817 in 1949 to 335,096 in 1952. The value of purchase by cooperatives increased from 12,290 billion yuan in 1950 to 86,840 billion in 1952, a growth of 610%. In comparison, the number of private commerce and catering enterprises increased from 4,770,000 in 1950 to 5,150,000 in 1952, a growth of 8%. The total volume of retail sales by private commerce increased from 100,890 billion yuan in 1950 to 120,400 billion yuan in 1952, a growth of 19.3%.[60]

Third, the short-term measure of repressing inflation by price control over agricultural products in cities became a long-term policy.

The purchase prices of staple grain as essential commodities were maintained at a low level until the end of 1951. The prices of most of the other agricultural products were hard to increase as the prices of staple grain were low. As a result, the growth of agricultural production value lagged behind the growth of volumes. The rate of peasant income growth was accordingly low.

Apropos the problem of price scissors, the state had in fact tried many times to adjust policy. However, the difficulty can be summarized as two contradictions. The first was the opposition in the urban–rural dual economic structure. When the government attempted to enlarge the price scissors in the second half of 1950 and 1951, it faced the unconscious soft resistance of the peasant household economy of mixed

---

[60]Wu and Dong (2001: 402). To be consistent with the above text, the currency unit is used here is the old one.

business, which did not take labour cost into consideration. Then industrial products and consumer goods found it hard to get into the rural market.

The second contradiction was the fundamental change in China's development strategy in a sudden shift in the geopolitical setting. When the government started to narrow the price scissors between industrial and agricultural products and pushed industrial products going into villages, the condition of rural market exchange was improved. Nevertheless, the Korean War armistice in 1953 had fundamentally changed China's international situation. China started to receive strategic aid from the USSR. The aid of military-heavy industry from the USSR was rendered into state capital. Within a short period, state capitalism controlled by the central government became dominant.

Facing internal and external contradictions, China pushed for socialist transformation beginning in 1953, the substance of which was the reconstruction of private capital by state capitalism. The New Democracy strategy of promoting private capital by market economy became history. The process of expanding and narrowing of the price scissors by government policy can be summarized as occurring in three stages.

The first stage took place at the beginning of the new republic. Due to the destruction caused by war, industry recovered at a slower pace than agriculture. As industrial products were scarce, peasants could exchange lesser industrial products with the same amounts of grain and cotton. The price gap in 1950 increased by 31.8% compared with 1930–1936, and 45.3% compared with 1936. At the beginning of the regime, the priority was to stabilize prices and control inflation, the price-setting of industrial and agricultural products was subject to this task before any other considerations. As staple grain and cotton were the primary commodities of inflation and the policy in 1950 was to stabilize prices, the price scissors continued.

The second stage started in early 1951. The government attempted to develop urban industry and commerce by enlarging the price scissors between industrial and agricultural products so as to accelerate the primitive accumulation of capital by extracting surplus from the rural sector. However, in less than a year, this policy faced rural market resistance. As the prices of yarn and cotton were relatively high, the peasants increased local weaving. Cotton flowed into villages and the state found it hard to purchase. Besides, as the official staple grain price was relatively low, urban and rural consumption increased and the market price became higher than the list price. State-owned companies found it difficult to purchase grain from the peasants.

The third stage was the narrowing of the price scissors. To deal with the problem in the second stage, the state gradually increased grain prices in November 1951, and in February, September and December 1952. The prices of yarn and industrial products were lowered. Although the relative prices of industrial products were higher than agricultural products, the price scissors was narrowing. Compared with 1950, the purchase price of staple grain in 1952 increased by 7.4% and of cotton by 8.9%. The prices of other agricultural products also rose. The purchase price index of agricultural products rose at a higher rate than industrial products in the countryside (see Box 21 for details).[61]

Box 21: Adjustments in Comparative Prices Policy of Industrial and Agricultural Products in the Early Years of the PRC

In the early period of the PRC, the national economy was severely impaired by war. Since the revival of industry was slower than the rural economy under the peasant rural community system, industrial products were relatively scarce. Therefore, industrial products that peasants could barter with were fewer than in the pre-war period with the same quantity of grain and cotton. In 1950, the rate increased by 31.8% compared to the average level in the pre-war years of 1930–1936, and by 45.3% compared with the year 1936. At that time, the first priority of the CPC was to stabilize the price level and control inflation. Given that cotton yarn and grain were the key commodities of inflation, the policies in 1950 were mainly for maintaining price stability, which had the effect of extending the scissor differential in prices at the early days of the PRC.

In the second half of 1950, grain prices declined, while prices of industrial goods and cotton gauze rose. The peasants were very upset

---

[61]From   1949–1952   中华人民共和国经济档案资料选编·商业卷   (*Selection from People's Republic of China Economic Archives 1949–1952: Commerce*). Beijing: China Supplies Publishing House, 1995, pp. 549–636. Quoted in Wu and Dong (2001: 670–672).

about it. The central government's policy was: to prevent grain price from going down and allow appropriate rise; stabilize cotton gauze prices to prevent its further rise and to make suitable adjustments on the premise of ensuring a certain profit for producers and distributors.

In September 1950, the Central Committee of Finance and Economy suggested that the key task in preventing or reducing damage to peasants due to low grain price was not so much reducing the price of industrial goods but maintaining a certain level of grain price, hence the plan to procure grain in large quantities to establish a reserve of five billion catty. Yet, since the state had limited funds for procurement, some regions were forced to reduce or stop it, and the effect of that price stabilization was unfavourable.

In January 1951, in order to supplement revenue and to balance income and expense, the Central Committee of Finance and Economy agreed with the suggestion from the mid-southern regions to widen the price scissors and redirect it to other regions, with the thinking that it was necessary to plan and expand the differential to stabilize the price of local produce while suitably raising the price of industrial goods. In April, it was suggested by the second national price level working session that consideration must be given to ground reality; a simple-minded emphasis on reducing the scissors differential, while well-intended, would not work in practice; it would hurt the peasants while also affect industrial production. In terms of policy, during 1951, the state adjusted the price of cotton yarn upwards twice, in January and April. Simultaneously, it adjusted the prices of grain downwards, partially each time. On 4 January, the price of rice in Shanghai and in the urban areas of rice-producing regions in Eastern China was reduced by 5%. On 12 April, the price of coarse grain was reduced all around. The procurement price of millet was changed to become the selling price. In July, the Central Committee of Finance and Economy felt that according to the rising trend in prices over the recent two months of 1% daily, and further, given that the state's control over cotton yarn was not yet adequate, the purchasing power of peasants after the cotton harvest would increase by an estimated 40% compared to the previous year. The liquid fund in the hands of capitalists would increase over the previous year. Therefore, price levels were potentially at risk of massive fluctuations in the lead-up to autumn. Furthermore, with financial needs arising from the Korean

War, starting 1 August, at the time of raising the price of yarn, grain price was reduced. Starting from the mid-southern regions, the procurement price of new grain harvest was reduced by 10–15% relative to the current price for rice. The price of flour was also appropriately reduced everywhere.

These several price adjustments led to the widening of the price ratio between industrial and agricultural products. Therefore, while the short-term problem was resolved, it created new unreasonable relative prices. The relative prices of cotton gauze and cotton wool were too high, resulting in the expansion of local yarn weaving in rural regions. Cotton flowed to rural areas and the state had difficulty procuring it. Moreover, with the price of grain at a relatively low level, not only did it increase both urban and rural consumption, but it also resulted in a higher market price than the official price, making it difficult for the state to procure. The state was forced to gradually raise the price of grain and cotton while reducing the price of cotton gauze and industrial goods in November 1951 as well as in February, September and December in 1952. The impact of this was that although the prices ratio between industrial and agricultural goods was higher than the pre-war period, the price scissors became narrower.

Comparing 1952 to 1950, grain price rose by 7.4% and cotton by 8.9%. The price of other agricultural produce also increased. Further, with the return of higher prices in trading markets for agricultural produce, the overall price index for agricultural produce procurement exceeded that of the retail price of industrial goods in rural regions. With 1950 as base, the overall agricultural produce procurement price index for 1951 and 1952 was 119.6 and 121.6, respectively, while the general price index of industrial goods in rural regions was 110.2 and 109.7, respectively. The quantity of industrial goods that peasants could barter for with the same quantity of agricultural produce grew. The average index of industrial and agricultural products price ratio, with 1950 as base, was 90.3 in 1952. Out of this, the narrowing was less significant in coastal regions, and more in inland and remote regions. The net gain for peasants through bartering increased, from 0.99 billion yuan in 1951 to 1.8 billion in 1952.

Source: *1949–1952 中华人民共和国经济档案资料选编·商业卷*
(Selection of People's Republic of China Economic Archives 1949–
1952: Commerce). Beijing: China Supplies Publishing House, 1995,
pp. 549–636; quoted from Wu and Dong (2001: 670–672).

The price scissors between industrial and agricultural products during
1950–1952 are shown in Table 7.

The purchase price index of agricultural products was higher than the
rural retail price index of industrial products in 1951. However, as the
price scissors was relatively larger in the early period of the republic, the
rural retail price index of industrial products had a comparatively high
base figure. The rural sector was in a less favourable condition in the
market exchange with the urban sector.

In short, the predicament of limited rural market capacity for industrial products was yet to be solved during 1950–1952. Therefore, the
government intervened directly in the market during depression.

Dealing with the Crisis: Counter-Cycle Regulation and Political Movement

After the repression of hyperinflation during 1949–1950 and the
construction of the national fiscal and financial foundation, the physical

Table 7 Purchase price index of industrial and agricultural products and price ratio index, 1950–1952

Year	Purchase price index of agricultural products	Rural retail price index of industrial products	Composite prices ratio index of industrial and agricultural products
1950	100	100	100
1951	119.6	110.2	92.2
1952	121.6	109.7	90.3

Source: '解放后全国工农业商品价格剪刀差变化情况' (Variation of Price Scissors between Industrial and Agricultural Products after Liberation), 统计工作 (Statistics Work), Issue no. 17, 1957 economy with private capital as its chief agent was supposed to be in a relatively more stable condition for development. Accordingly, the primitive accumulation of capital for industry and commerce should have accelerated in China.

Nevertheless, apart from the problem of depression after crushing speculation, there was another seldom discussed problem. Developing national capitalism with private industry and commerce had been an urgent strategy of the state. However, primitive capital accumulation for industry and commerce is a process of exploitation everywhere in the world. No official Marxian theorist in China has ever openly discussed this problem. Even if it was represented as New Democracy, internal exploitation was the real process of this development model.

Private capital tended to maximize its gains on capitalizing resources. During this process, risks would accumulate. When this enormous institutional cost could not be directly transferred to urban and rural workers after revolution, internal economic disorder in cities where industrial and commercial capital was concentrated would become inevitable, implying that a hard economic landing would become a persistent occurrence. Even if the government directly intervened by taking counter-cycle regulation measures, it was impossible to reverse the deterioration of the business environment and economic behaviours. Furthermore, disorder spread to the government through market-saving measures such as government purchasing and orders, breeding corruption among some officials.

This situation, which was unexpected in the idea of New Democracy, was the background of political movements *sanfan* and *wufan*. During the primitive accumulation of national capital in 1949–1952 (also known as national economy rehabilitation), counterfeiting, speculation as well as corruption and favouritism among officials occurred in almost every major city. The contradiction became acute as the requirement of securing military supplies for the Korean War was imperative. Then the central government under the leadership and revolutionary authority of Mao Zedong ordered local governments, which had yet to take firm footing in cities but still controlled the distribution of supplies, to launch popular movements such as *sanfan* and *wufan* within the governments and against certain industrial and commercial capitalists.

The institutional transition experiment in Northeast China is more noteworthy. In the northeast regions, the outbreak of the Korean War and the strategic aid from the USSR elevated state capital, which justified its taking of more surplus than private capital. State and private capital were caught in opposition and competition, and a choice had to be made between them. Then the institutional transition of unified purchasing and selling by the state was implemented. After 1953, when aid from the USSR was at its peak, unified purchasing and selling was also implemented in the whole nation.[62]

The First Counter-Cycle Regulation

Faced with the problem of a weak market after price repression, the Central Government Committee used the Seventh Conference on 8 April 1950 to discuss the economic difficulties and find solutions. Mao pointed out that 'in the following months, the government should focus its fiscal and economic policy on adjusting public enterprises and private enterprises as well as the relationship between different sectors among public and private enterprises, and overcoming economic anarchy'.[63] It was the guiding principle of policy adjustment in the development of private capital in the New Democracy.

In April, after the value-anchored public bonds were issued and general prices were stabilized, the Central Committee of Finance and Economy decided to shift its focus from fiscal problems to revitalizing and developing the economy. The plan was to support the development of private industry and commerce by providing loans, a favourable tax policy, supply of raw materials, improving transportation, etc. In early May, the committee proposed concrete measures such as easing money supply, enlarging government order and purchase of agricultural

---

[62] In the 1950s China introduced technologies and facilities from the USSR. From 1950 to 1952, the completion rate of aid projects was 3.2%. From 1953 to 1957 it became 57.1%. From 1958 to 1959 it was 39.6%. During 1950–1952, the introduced investment was concentrated in the northeast.

[63] 中共中央文献研究室、中央档案馆，　共和国走过的路——建国以来重要文献专题选集(Selected Important Documents since the Founding of the Republic). Beijing:中央文献出版社(Central Literature Press), 1991, p. 120. Quoted in Wu and Dong (2010: 266).

products, increasing the purchasing power of peasants, facilitating the export of industrial products, increasing the turnover of industrial fund, unemployment relief and reducing the blindness of private industry only seeking profit.

In June, at the third plenary session of the Seventh Party Central Committee, Mao continued to emphasize developing capitalism:

> To improve our fiscal and economic situation, we need three conditions: first, the completion of land reform; second, reasonable adjustment of the present industry and commerce; third, heavy cuts in the budget of public institutions... Someone believes we can eliminate capitalism ahead of time and realize socialism. This is wrong and not suitable for the concrete situation of our country.[64]

This guiding principle was the foundation of the government's first counter-cycle policy adjustment in developing private industry and commerce.

There are three noteworthy points. First was the lack of a market economic agent. As discussed earlier, promoting urban–rural market exchange was the government's major measure of counter-cycle regulation. However, we also pointed out that as land was distributed evenly, the existing agents of production of scale as well as the agents of circulation of scale in villages were eliminated, whereas a new agent of the agricultural economy of scale was yet to emerge. The rural sector had limited demand for the agricultural tools that the industrial sector was producing. Therefore, the result of promoting industrial products in the countryside was not as expected by policy makers. The effect of this measure was limited to rehabilitating urban industry and commerce in 1952. In comparison, expanding fiscal expenditure to boost domestic demand was more effective.

---

[64] 毛泽东文集 (Selected Writings of Mao Zedong), vol. 6. Beijing: People's Press, 1999, pp. 71–73. Quoted in Wu and Dong (2010: 120).

Second, the government implemented 'targeted going-long' measures as opposed to general selling-short during economic downturns.[65] Only after successfully resolving hyperinflation and having complete financial sovereignty did the new government gain the legitimacy of counter-cycle regulation. Until 1998, fiscal and financial systems were unified in China. The new government could coordinate loose fiscal and monetary policies in counter-cyclical regulation. Apart from general monetary tools, such as increasing bank loans, a greater amount of money supply was targeted towards a specific sector. A large part of increased money supply was invested in the target sector through a direct financial tool. After the Korean War, the government became even more dominant in supplies distribution.

Third, political movements went hand in hand with economic regulation. Not long after the initiation of the first policy adjustment, the government had to face the challenge of a geopolitical shift. The demand for fiscal expansion for economic recovery and the rigid fiscal expenditure of war had exerted double pressure on the fiscal budget. It was the background of the production expansion and frugality movement, and the *sanfan* and *wufan* political movements. As politics is the focused expression of the economy, they were not contradictory. The greatest political issue was China's involvement in the Korean War. War had created great demand for industrial production and agricultural products. However, at the same time, these industrial and agricultural products were requested to be clear of the 'original sin' of primitive capital accumulation. Clearly, it conflicted with the spontaneous tendency of private capitalism.

Here, let us analyse the second point and move the third into the next section.

In 1950, the government started to expand expenditure. Practices such as commissioned production and unified purchase and selling had effectively changed, in Mao's words, 'the anarchy of private industry and commerce'.

Government purchasing began in December 1949 with the saving of Shanghai's industry and commerce that was in dire straits (see Box 22).

---

[65]We conceive that 'targeted going-long' is an effective tool in economic regulation. A comparison can be made between these practices of China in the early 1950s and the 'quantitative easing' policy taken by many governments in the world after the 2008 credit crunch.

Box 22: Helping Shanghai's Industry and Commerce, Setting a Precedent of Processing Order and Purchase by the Government

During the severe nationwide price fluctuations between 15 October and 25 November 1949, the Shanghai industrial and commercial sector, based on years of experience, overestimated the extent of the price fluctuation and believed that the renminbi would devalue continuously to a large extent. They thought the rise in interest rate would fall behind the price increase. Therefore, speculators borrowed to buy goods. Factory owners also preferred to borrow to pay for expenses (such as wages) than sell inventory. The interest on borrowing rose to a monthly rate of two yuan for every one yuan of loan. As it turned out, the situation was not what had been expected. Beginning on 25 November, the price level stabilized and then went on a decline, forcing the disposal of goods to repay loans. The outcome was increasing difficulties in selling goods even as prices fell. More and more people raised new debts in order to repay old ones. As a result, even though prices had dropped, liquidity was still tight and the interest rate remained high. Many factory owners suffered from liquidity problems.

On 3 December, the Shanghai Municipal Party Committee wired CPC Central and informed the latter that many large and medium-sized factories in Shanghai were in debt and could not maintain operations. They requested loans from the government to avoid a large-scale closing down. On 8 December, the Central Committee of Finance and Economy allotted RMB 50 billion to Eastern China. The larger portion of this was for procuring goods from factories in Shanghai and a smaller portion for lending to alleviate the imminent difficulty of industrialists and business people in the private sector.

During the time of his visit to the Soviet Union, Mao Zedong read the wire from the Shanghai Municipal Party Committee and asked Chen Yun: 'Do the factory owners in Shanghai actually have such serious difficulties? Has the government agreed to give a loan and how much? Is the outcry of the capitalists based on true circumstances or just on the intent to boycott the public debt offering?' Chen Yun reply was an analysis based on why Shanghai's factory owners were having such difficulties. He was of the view that 'the outcry… did in part reflect the intent to avoid buying the public debt. Still, tight liquidity and difficulty in financing were in fact the main reasons.' Chen Yun further told Mao Zedong that the 50 billion yuan allotted to Eastern China by the Central Committee of Finance and Economy on 8 December had already alleviated the crisis faced by the Shanghai industrial and commercial sector. After that, the plan was to provide a further 100 billion yuan to resolve their difficulties.

This resolution in the Shanghai business sector, while only within the scope of one city, set a precedent for the subsequent approach of processing order and purchase, whereby the state bought goods from factory owners.

Source: Jin and Chen (2005: 688–689).

The importance of demand from the government can be illustrated in the cotton yarn textile industry, which accounted for nearly one-third of the total production value of private industry in 1949. In the second half of 1950, the state's order amounted to 70% of the industry's production capacity (Wu and Dong 2001: 367). In 1949, the value of order, sale, and purchasing by and processing for the state accounted for 11.88% of the total value of private industry. In 1952, the figure rose to 56.04%. Accordingly, the ratio of independent production and sale declined from 88.12 to 43.96%. In 1950, the industrial value of the private sector grew merely by 6.59%, whereas order, sale and purchasing by and processing for the state increased by 158.6%, a 17% growth in total production value, up to 28.83%. The value of independent production and sale was decreased by 13.91%, a drop of 71.17%. The year 1951 was a boom year for the private sector. However, the government was still the dominant contributor to economic growth. Order, sale, and purchase by and processing for the state increased by 106%, representing 42.71% of the total production value. In comparison, independent production and sale increased by merely 11.9%, 57.29% of total value. In 1952, the value of order, sale, and purchase by and processing for the state increased by 36.49%. It went over 50% for the first time, whereas the absolute figure of independent production and sale dropped by 20.17% (See Table 8).[66]

---

[66] 1949–1952 中华人民共和国经济档案资料选编·工商体制卷 (*Selection from People's Republic of China Economic Archives 1949–1952: Industrial and Commercial Institutions*). Beijing: China Social Sciences Press,1993, p. 739. Quoted in Wu and Dong (2010: 192).

Table 8 Composition of production value of private industry sector 1949–1952 (1,000 yuan [old RMB])

Year	1949	1950	1951	1952
Total production value	6,828,160	7,278,260	10,118,360	10,526,109
State related order, sale and purchase and processing	811,410	2,098,310	4,321,459	5,898,365
Per cent of the above	11.88	28.83	42.71	56.04
Independent production and sale value	6,016,750	5,179,950	5,796,901	4,627,744
Per cent of independent production and sale	88.12	71.17	57.29	43.96

Source: *1949–1952* 中华人民共和国经济档案资料选编·工商体制卷 (Selection from People's Republic of China Economic Archives 1949–1952: Industrial and Commercial Institutions). Beijing China Social Sciences Press, 1993, p. 739. Quoted in Wu and Dong (2001: 572)

Under the government's policy adjustment, national capitalism underwent substantial development. In less than half a year, the business environment improved. In 10 big cities (Shanghai, Beijing, Tianjin, Wuhan, Guangzhou, Chongqing, Xian, Jinan, Wuxi and Zhangjiakou), the number of enterprises starting business was 32,674, whereas 7,451 went out of business. In the third and fourth quarters of 1950, tax revenues from private industry and commerce increased by 90 and 80%, respectively, compared with the first quarter. In August, September and October 1950, applications for business permit in industry increased 28 times compared with April, and 17 times in commerce. In that period, business closures were merely 12% of the number in April (Wu and Dong 2001: 371). See Table 9 for the variation of production index of major industrial products.

The statistics in Table 9 show that primary forms of state intervention, such as placing orders and purchasing were significant in resolving structural overproduction and the weak economy of national capitalism, especially when structural transformation was required and industrial products were hard to sell in the rural market because of the restoration of the traditional peasant economy in the early years of the republic.

The statistics also show that the new government was consolidating its understanding of the economic system and the ability of economic

Table 9 Variation of production index of major industrial products during April to December 1950 in Shanghai (production in January 1950 = 100)

Products	January	April	August	December
Cotton yarn	100	94	106	176
Wool yarn	100	75	104	319
Flour	100	19	98	127
Chemical glue	100	59	87	161
Paint and dye	100	61	160	113
Glass	100	60	221	292
Cement	100	113	247	413

Source: 上海社会主义经济建设发展简史 (1948–1985 年) (A Brief History of Socialist Construction and Development in Shanghai 1948–1985). Shanghai: People's Press, 1990, p. 64. Quoted in Xiao and Sui (2011: 59)

regulation when dealing with old and new crises. Therefore, the strategic shift during the beginning of the republic (socialist transition from New Democracy of private capital under trouble to state capitalism) was the final result of constant adaptive adjustments in the face of changing politico-economic circumstances. It was certainly not the product of a subjective wish based on a particular ideology of a particular leader. Accordingly, we can understand what Mao said in 1953 elaborating the general route of socialist transition: 'the socialist transformation in New China has been under way since 1949'.

The Korean War, and *Sanfan Wufan*

As described earlier, the counter-cyclical economic regulation by the government resolved the contradiction of primitive capital accumulation into economic growth. It is a general principle of development economics.

However, while the government was implementing counter-cyclical regulation, the Korean War broke out. In October, when industry and commerce had just stabilized, China decided to participate in the war. The fiscal and economic system that was getting rid of the burden of war returned once again to a state of war. Domestic resources and capital were concentrated into heavy and military industry necessary for war. The fiscal budget therefore became tight again. Resources supposed to

Table 10 Expenditure for economic building and national defence, and Ratios in Total Fiscal Expenditure 1950–1952

	Absolute number (1,000 billion yuan)			Ratio (%)		
	Expenditure	Economic building	National defence	Expenditure	Economic building	National defence
1950	68.1	17.36	28.01	100	25.4	41.1
1951	122.5	35.11	52.64	100	28.7	43.0
1952	176.0	73.23	57.84	100	41.6	32.8

Source: 中国统计年鉴 1992 (China Statistics Yearbook 1992). China Statistics Press, pp. 215, 220. Quoted in Dong (2009: 79). Converted into currency value of that time

be used for building the economy, culture and other sectors were transferred to national defence. And the budget for building the economy was reallocated to military expenditure. According to a rough estimate in the autumn of 1951, fiscal expenditure exceeded the original budget by 75%, 55% of which was military expenditure (Wu 2014: 24–25) (See Table 10).

Due to greatly increased military expenditure, and the need for heavy and military industry investment, the state had to take a series of measures to increase revenues and cut social expenditures in urban and rural sectors.

The measures to increase revenues in the countryside included: (i) cotton yarn sale tax and tax on cotton yarn and cotton cloth stock, both at 6%; (ii) agricultural tax revenues increased by one-tenth (the lowest tax rate rose from 3 to 5%; proportional tax system was maintained in the old liberated regions); and (iii) staple grain prices were suppressed to enlarge the price scissors between industrial and agricultural products. However, as stated earlier, the tax burden on villages was heavy enough. The space for extracting more rural surplus by increasing tax and purchase volume was limited. As for cutting expenditure, since the base was already small and villages were mostly self-sufficient, it did not work at all. Furthermore, these measures in fact constituted an institutional barrier for industrial products entering the rural market. The growth rate of peasants' income in cash was slower than the industrial production rate. The purchasing power of peasants lagged behind. Urban industrial and commercial products after structural adjustment found it hard to go into rural regions.[67]

In cities, as the war was marching on, the central government promoted the Patriotic Production Expansion and Frugality Movement to the whole nation, requesting the suppression of cost and increase in efficiency and production in different sectors. The main measure was to suppress and set a limit on expenditure. The cost of purchasing military supplies and materials for infrastructure had to be strictly controlled to suppress the profits of merchants. As the name given to the movement suggests, it was a full-scale national mobilization in the name of patriotism.

As the movement went on, some merchants thought that they were unfairly treated, as the difference between government purchasing and market prices were substantial. They had been under pressure due to the government's effort to suppress inflation (for example, it was hard to get loans and there was a limit on purchasing), and therefore had to bear high production costs. Then they had to face the double difficulty of pushing products into the countryside along with strict state price controls.

Experiences have shown that when enterprises face high business risks, they tend to engage in morally dubious activities. This tends to be the case irrespective of whether the enterprise is private or state-owned. If it were not content with government policy, the likelihood of such enterprises engaging in morally questionable activities would increase even further. Private enterprises did show a tendency towards misbehaviour. They were more prone to profit seeking by improper means. As a consequence, the institutional cost of primitive capital accumulation would intensify in cities. Commercial misbehaviour such as counterfeiting, adulteration and tax evasion prevailed, which converged with rent-seeking of some officials, leading to a negative impact on the conduct of the war.

Under general dispersive market demand, private industry and commerce could transfer their cost by various ways, for example, by

---

[67]Although some regions explored ways to increase agricultural production under the Patriotic Production Expansion and Frugality Movement, it was hard to promote the experiences extensively to other parts of the country.

suppressing customer rights or with bad money driving out good money. The institutional cost was thereby borne by society as a whole. The negative impact would not express itself immediately. Even if it were the government purchasing, the institutional cost would be spread among the people through government distribution. However, in the case of war, it was a different story. What the government purchased and ordered were industrial products to fulfil the needs of national defence. The information of quality was concentrated and transparent, and could be traced back to every single supplier. Counterfeiting and adulteration was instantly reported from the frontline to logistics departments.

When the institutional cost of primitive accumulation in national capitalism unfolded in national defence, its contradiction with national security became inevitable. That explains why even those top CPC leaders who were in favour of developing national capitalism also advocated the *sanfan* (literally "three-antis") and *wufan* (literally "five-antis") campaigns.

Although from the logic of capital, the targeted problems of *sanfan* and *wufan* emerged simultaneously, these movements took place one after another.

The *sanfan* movement began first, at the end of 1951. According to existing historical materials, during the Patriotic Production Expansion and Frugality Movement, there were many reports about misconducts such as corruption, lavishness and bureaucracy in local governments, state-owned enterprises and faculties. For this, Mao decided to launch the *sanfan* movement. On 1 December 1951, the CPC Central Committee announced the decision of mobilization.

Then, in early 1952, the *wufan* movement began. It was reported that during the investigation into corruption in the *sanfan* movement, many cases of misconduct were found to be related to unlawful capitalists. As early as on 1 November 1951, a report by the Northeast Bureau to the Central Committee pointed out that a common feature of many serious cases of corruption was collusion between merchants and corrupt officials to usurp state properties. Therefore, just after the *sanfan* campaign was launched, the CPC Central Committee initiated the *wufan* movement to eliminate misconduct in the economy (Wu and Dong 2001: 407–427).

An instruction drafted by Mao announced the *wufan* movement on 26 January 1952 (see Box 23).

Box 23: The *Sanfan* and *Wufan* Movements

Sanfan: A Struggle against Misconducts Known as the Three Kinds of Harm

The *sanfan* movement had arisen directly out of the Patriotic Production Expansion movement that was launched nationwide during the Korean War. In this movement, shocking problems of corruption, lavishness and bureaucracy were exposed everywhere. On 1 November 1951, the Chief Secretary Gao Gang of the CPC Northeast Bureau submitted a report to CPC Central titled 'A Report on Launching the Production Expansion and Frugality Movement, and Further Deepening of the Struggle against Corruption, Lavishness and Bureaucracy'. It captured the attention of Mao Zedong: 'The CPC Central upheld this report and requested all of you to pay attention to the various experiences described in this report to launch a·determined fight against corruption, lavishness and bureaucracy during this nationwide movement on production expansion and frugality....' On 29 November, Bo Yibo, Liu Lantao and others submitted a written report to Mao Zedong and the CPC with regard to the severe corruption and lavishness of the Tianjin Party Committee leader. This report attracted even more attention from Mao Zedong and the CPC, and on the following day it was redirected to the various regional bureaus. Mao Zedong had pointed out in his comments that 'it is essential to pay attention to the reality of party cadres being eroded by the bourgeoisie and engaging in severely corrupt behaviour. We should pay special attention to expose and punish the corrupt, and handle it as a major battle campaign.' On 1 December, the CPC presented the 'Decision on Implementation of Military Downsizing, Government Streamlining, Production Expansion, Frugality, Anti-corruption, Anti-lavishness and Anti-bureaucracy'. The curtain was officially drawn on the *sanfan* movement.

In January 1952, the focus on the *sanfan* movement was placed on investigating and striking seriously corrupt persons, known as the stage of fighting tigers. Those who had taken bribes of over RMB 100 million (old currency) were referred to as big tigers, while those between 10 and 100 million were small tigers.

After that, the *sanfan* movements roughly went through three stages: between January and February, it was the stage of reporting and exposing; between March and April, it was the stage of cases investigation; and in June, with the finalizing of cases, it went into the closing stage. On 25 October 1952, the CPC approved the Central Political Research Office's 'A Report on Terminating the *Sanfan* Movement'.

Based on relevant statistics, the number of people that were involved nationwide in the *sanfan* movement, from party and government organizations at the county level and above, were more than 3.83 million (not including the military). Over 100,000 people had received bribes of over 10 million, around 2.7% of the total involved. Of these, 9,942 people were given prison sentences and another 67 faced life imprisonment. Another 42 were given death sentences and 9 death sentences were suspended.

Wufan: A Struggle Against Misconducts Known as the Five Kinds of Venom

On 31 December 1951, Bo Yibo reported to Mao Zedong on the situation of *sanfan*. When he said that capitalists usually seek collusion with procuring personnel by giving rebates, Mao Zedong interrupted: 'This should be investigated not only in governmental organizations but also among business people. In the past during land reform, we had protected industries and commerce. Now we should differentiate between good and unlawful businessmen and fight with the latter.' On 26 January, Mao Zedong drafted on behalf of the CPC Central the 'Instructions Regarding the Launch of a Large-Scale, Determined and Thorough *Wufan* Movement in Cities within the Given Time-Frame'. The document requested:

> It is essential and timely now to launch in all cities nationwide, first in large- and medium-sized ones, a large-scale, determined and thorough movement against unlawful bourgeoisie to combat bribery, tax cheating and evasion, frauds on state assets, adulteration and poor quality, and stealing information about the economy (together referred to as the 'five venoms'), by relying on the proletariat and allying with the law-abiding bourgeoisie and citizens, and to collaborate with the internal struggle within the party, government and army against corruption, lavishness and bureaucratisation.

With that, the *wufan* movement was launched on all fronts. In early February, it was first launched in all the big cities, and soon after that spread to various medium and small cities, reaching the peak in fighting the five kinds of venom of capitalists.

Shanghai was the city where the national capitalists were concentrated, and the *wufan* movement there had been important to the overall situation. On 25 February 1952, before Bo Yibo arrived in Shanghai to preside over the Eastern Regional Bureau, the *wufan* movement had in fact already begun, with more than 200 people arrested. There were 48 attempted suicides and 34 deaths of capitalists. Given such radical actions, the CPC pushed back on launching the movement in Shanghai. In fact, besides Shanghai, other cities where commerce was relatively concentrated, such as Shenyang, Beijing, Tianjin, Chongqing, Wuhan and Guangzhou, also saw suicide incidents. In particular, the famous patriotic industrialist Lu Zuofu, who had recently led a fleet of ships returning to China, could not live with the insult and had taken sleeping pills to commit suicide in his home in Chongqing. It was a shock to the senior level in the CPC Central. On 5 March, Mao Zedong redirected the document 'Beijing Municipal Party Committee's Means and Standards for Classifying and Handling Industrialists and Merchants in the *Wufan* Movement' to various places, increasing the categories of private industrialists and merchants to five, the first three taking up about 95% (law-abiding, basically law-abiding and semi-law-abiding) and the latter two about 5% (seriously unlawful, completely unlawful) of the businessmen. The inspection of industrialists and merchants were tightly controlled at the municipal level. Other organizations did not have discretion to send inspectors and no authority to arrest people for trial. After revisiting the preparation work, the *wufan* movement was eventually launched on an official basis in Shanghai on 25 March.

On 25 October, the CPC Central circulated the report by the Political Research Office on the issue of ending the *wufan* movement. The report pointed out that: based on statistics from 67 cities in the five major regions of North China, Northeast, East, Northwest and Mid-South, as well as from the overall Southwest region, the number of industrialists and merchants involved in the *wufan* movement totalled 999,707 enterprises. Criminal sentences were given to 1,509 persons and 19 people got death or suspended death sentences.

Sources:
He Yunghong, '五反运动研究 (Research on the Wufan Movement). Chinese Communist Party History Publishing House, 2006.
Wang Shunseng, Li Jun, '三反运动研究 (Research on the Sanfan Movement). Chinese Communist Party History Publishing House, 2006.

The misconduct of capitalists—also known as the 'five types of venom'—revealed during the *wufan* movement were as follows: bribery, tax evasion, usurpation of state properties, shoddiness and spying on economic intelligence. Apropos of tax evasion, according to a survey, 99% of the 3,510 business taxpayers in Shanghai were involved. It was 82% among 1,807 business taxpayers in Tianjin. According to a survey in 1952, about 13,087 enterprises (26%) in Beijing were involved in bribery. In the first half of 1952, reports of *wufan* showed that in nine big cities (including Beijing, Tianjin and Shanghai) 340,000 among 450,000 private enterprises were involved to some extent (Wu and Dong 2010: 312) (see Box 24 for case examples).

The number of criminal penalties imposed on capitalists was much less than on officials. However, the crimes by the former were more serious.

Box 24: Major Expressions of the Institutional Cost of Primitive Accumulation for National Capital Prior to the Sanfan and Wufan Movements

1. Frauds and shoddiness in contracting state projects as well as in the manufacture and purchase for the government

For example, in the irrigation project for River Huai, the contracting companies disregarded the quality standard, using old or defective material in place of new and good material. In doing so, they stole large amounts of national wealth and assets that were meant for the project. In 1952, the total disbursement incurred by the Henan Province in Shanghai in procuring labour and equipment for the River Huai project amounted to over 50 billion yuan (old RMB). Of this, the amount cheated and stolen by vicious merchants in Shanghai had been up to a dozen billions yuan.*

In another example, after the start of the Korean War, the battlefront had urgent need for first-aid kits. The government assigned a large part of first-aid kit production to private merchants. The unlawful businessmen in Shanghai disregarded the life and death of the voluntary army and cadres, and put used cotton wool in the kits without even disinfecting it.

2. Widespread practice of tax cheating and evasion

Based on material provided in a typical survey conducted by the State Taxation Bureau in 1950, after the submission and first payment of business tax, out of the 3,510 business taxpayers in Shanghai, 99% showed tax evasion practices, while out of the 1,807 in Tianjin, 82% did so. Further, based on investigations in 1952 by Beijing, about 13,087 or 26% of industrial and commercial taxpayers showed bribery practices to varying extents.**

3. Exceptionally serious bribery and collusion between businesses and officers

In Wuhan, 109 business operations had been involved in bribing cadres to acquire over 130 billion yuan (old RMB) of state assets. Of these, 27 had used 400 million yuan to bribe more than 430 cadres. Of the latter, 22 became their insider informants. In Beijing, investigations in 1952 showed that more than 13,000 business operations in the city had had bribery actions, accounting for more than 26% of the total. Among them, there were 169 operations involved in bribery of over 100 million yuan. The unlawful capitalists in Tianjin had formulated a set of bribery experiences, which were: those who ask the time, give them watches; those who ask for a light, give them lighters; those who are interested in card games, give them the winnings and settle their losses; those who care about their image, give them gifts in secret; give wedding rings, clothes for children, eggs to celebrate a newborn, and even coffin material for parents of cadres; pay for prostitutes, dance girls, and even offer daughters and wives. Li Tinglin, the chief of bureau of medical affairs under the Ministry of Health in Northeast People's Government, colluded with Cong Zhifeng, manager of Guangming Pharmacy in the private sector, to cheat the government by selling at a high price to and buying at a low price from the latter. The cheating also occurred in speculations, forging checks, evading tax, faking accounting records and so on, resulting in a loss to the state of around 6.1 billion yuan (old RMB) (He 2006: 56–57).

Sources:
* 新华月报 (Xinhua Monthly) March, 1952, pp. 34, 39; quoted from Wu and Dong (2001: 428).
** 新华月报 (Xinhua Monthly) April, 1952, p. 20; quoted from Wu and Dong (2001: 428).

Not only did *sanfan* and *wufan* purge businesses involved in misconduct and official rent-seeking, it also had a remarkable effect on cutting lavishness and shoddiness.

Chen Yun affirmed the necessity of the *sanfan* and *wufan* movements by concrete examples when reporting to the Central People's Government Committee in April 1952. He concluded that 'after the movements, expenditure was cut by 20% in various departments, with the same task fulfilment'. He continued,

In the first season, the Ministry of Finance repaid 3,100 billion of old debt to banks. We still have 7,000 billion yuan, an increment of 1,000 billion. This is something big. Since the establishment of the Central People's Government two years ago, the Ministry of Finance has always had higher expenditure than revenue. We have spent too much last year. The Central Committee of Finance and Economy has reported this to Chairman Mao and Premier Zhou. If we continue like this, price stability would become impossible in March. However, now March is over. The situation is looking good. If you ask, 'Do you sleep well?' Yes, I sleep well because the Ministry of Finance has 7,000 billion yuan in hand. Therefore, *sanfan* and *wufan* have had a very positive effect on fiscal wellness.

There was a report about improvement in enterprise management in the movement. It was reported that an assistant of Tangshan Steel Factory invented a new way to decrease the consumption rate of pig iron, which saved 20.38 billion yuan annually.[68]

According to a report by the Central Committee of Finance and Economy on 29 November 1952, the direct benefits of the movements in 1952 were as follows. The total gains were 31,778.9 billion yuan (13,676.9 billion yuan of increased sale by the Ministry of Commerce not included), of which 11,660.8 billion yuan was increased production, with a profit of 2195.6 billion yuan (profit from the Mid-south and Inner Mongolia not included). Production costs saved were about 11,257.6 billion RMB. Infrastructure costs saved were about 2,454.4 billion RMB. They totalled 13,712 billion RMB. Saved capital flow due to an increased turnover rate and less excessive reserve amounted to 6,406.1 billion yuan. The result of the movement was proportionate to the scale of state-owned enterprises. In the north-eastern regions where state-owned enterprises were stronger, benefits contributed to 51.9% of the total gains (Wu and Dong 2001: 433–436).

Nevertheless, we should take note of the complication of social contradictions.

Admittedly, China at that time lacked the condition of class politics dominated by proletarians having a class consciousness. That made it impossible to achieve socialism defined by classic Marxism. A part of what rose along with these movements was the expression of partisanship formed in the war. A great part of what the movements unleashed was discontent among general urban citizens and enterprise staff, who were mostly petit bourgeois. Internal grudges that had accumulated among the people became over-aggression, which might be inevitable in any political system.[69]

From the perspective of social class features, the target groups were quite homogeneous in rural land reform and urban *sanfan* and *wufan* movements. They were elite groups relative to general people.

---

[68]*People's Daily*, 1/12/1952. Quoted in Wu and Dong (2001: 428).

[69]The author believes that this problem is inevitable in almost all left-wing and populist movements even today.

Whether in rural or urban society, over-aggression or even violence was commonly perpetrated by petit bourgeois in official political movements. This is the reason that one would not simply and uncritically approve a political movement. The experiences of popular involvement in politics show that in 'an ocean of petit bourgeois' (Mao Zedong), any petit bourgeois revolution transplanted from Western ideology would turn violent. Unfortunately, the subsequent political movements have proven this point of view.

However, the most regrettable aspects of these political movements, which were later heavily criticized, have never been discussed by castigators until it was too late. The problem the politicians and entrepreneurs failed to foresee was that it is impossible to absorb the institutional cost of primitive accumulation for national capitalism in the urban economy by way of an urban popular movement alone. That is the crux of why most developing countries have failed to achieve primitive accumulation for urban industrialization and have gone through one turmoil after another. Accordingly, it is no wonder that China fell into an economic depression again after the *wufan* movement.

The various measures the government took as a response can be called the second economic adjustment, which included providing reasonable profits for government orders and purchases, specifying the standard, adjusting interest rate and bank loans, adjusting tax and regulating the. At the end of 1952 and the beginning of 1953, the second adjustment became quite effective (Wu and Dong 2001).

We will not go into the details of the second counter-cycle adjustment as shortly after this, the socialist transformation followed, which commanded the attention of the world.

We would like to take this opportunity to remind the readers that the loop of a planned economy ('regulation results at stagnation and deregulation lead to chaos'), much criticized since the economic reform in the 1980s, had actually come in a full circle during the rehabilitation of the national economy (1949–1952), which then mainly comprised the market economy and private capital. An experience the government learnt in this process was counter-cyclical regulation. These two occasions of counter-cyclical regulation laid the foundation of socialist transformation in 1953, and it was applied again and again later in economic regulation.

Re-understanding the Shift from New Democracy to 'Socialist Transition'

We conceive that the determining major contradiction expressed in the transformation of urban economic institution in 1949–1952 was the institutional cost of primitive capital accumulation in two forms: state and private.

The bureaucratic monopoly capital in the old republic was directly transformed into state capital after the occupation of cities by the CPC. In addition, the Soviet strategic investment during the Korean War could only be rendered into state capital. During 1949–1952, what was growing the fastest in the national economy was state capital. The weight of industrial production in the state-owned sector rose from 34.7 to 56%, mixed ownership from 2 to 5%, whereas the private sector declined from 63 to 39% (Hu 1991: 339) (See Table 11).

During the period of Soviet aid after the Korean War, the divergence in trend between different sectors was obvious. However, these sectors were still complementary to a certain extent in the industrial structure. In 1949, industrial production in the private sector was 63% of the total

Table 11 Industrial production variation in different sectors 1949–1952

Type	Change in ratio (%)				Total value trend (1949 = 100)			
	1949	1950	1951	1952	1949	1950	1951	1952
State-owned	34.2	44.5	44.9	52.8	100	169.7	246.6	387.1
Cooperative	0.5	0.8	1.0	3.2	100	224.1	415.8	172.7
Mixed	2.0	2.9	4.0	5.0	100	188.7	367.2	622.5
Private	63.3	51.8	50.1	39.0	100	116.6	148.2	154.2
Total	100	100	100	100	100	130.4	187.5	250.6

Source: *1949–1952* 年中华人民共和国经济档案资料选编·工商体制卷 (Selection from PRC Economic Archives 1949–1952: Industrial and Commercial Institutions). China Social Sciences Press, 1993, p. 976. Quoted in Wu and Dong (2010: 182)

value, which was mainly light industry producing daily consumer goods. During 1949–1952, state-owned heavy industry was further consolidated. The transformation of private capital in 1953 took the path of 'acquisition', which allowed private capital to share benefits in the long term rather than revolutionary confiscation.

The weight of private and state-owned industry in various sectors is shown in Table 12 and Fig. 1.

Unlike the *sanfan* and *wufan* movements, which were launched by the government against the institutional cost of primitive accumulation of private capital, the structural expansion of state capitalism at its initial stage had a relatively low institutional cost. The cost of institutional transition it dominated was also relatively lower. There were five reasons for this:

1. *The revolution had covered the institutional cost.* After October 1949, the new regime confiscated the old bureaucratic capital and transnational enterprises in China, which became state capital. The sacrifice in the revolutionary war was not counted in the cost accounting of state capital. No payment to interest blocs or other sectors was required.
2. *The land reform had covered the organization cost.* Agrarian reform and the Korean War achieved total mobilization of the population through the 'reorganization' of society. This sort of organized mobilization hid the fact of state capital appropriating benefits behind the state's grand narratives. The transaction cost between the state and scattered individuals was thereby effectively reduced.
3. *Financial gains were generated from restoration at a lower cost than building new infrastructure.* Infrastructure was merely partially damaged, and the state had only to pay a part of the construction cost to gain all the benefits of the facilities. Lower cost contributed to fast growth of returns in economic accounting.
4. *Heavy and chemical industries had lower transaction cost.* State capital was concentrated in heavy and chemical industries, which manufactured intermediate products rather than consumer goods. Therefore, it did not have to pay the high transaction cost in trading with the rural market.

Table 12 Weight of industrial production in the state-owned Sector, 1949–1952 (%)

Year	Electricity	Crude coal	Steel	Pig iron	Rolled steel	Sulphuric acid	Cement	Electric motor	Metal-cutting machine
1949	57.66	68.18	97.27	91.74	82.79	70.84	68.14	20.42	75.34
1950	64.07	66.53	97.23	92.00	85.83	72.16	65.61	62.83	69.47
1951	83.25	66.08	95.25	91.44	84.33	67.75	55.47	68.82	37.08
1952	88.29	84.58	94.52	96.45	83.09	68.42	63.94	72.75	46.64

Note: Crude coal included production by cooperatives

Source: *1949–1952* 年中华人民共和国经济档案资料选编·工商体制卷 (Selection from PRC Economic Archives 1949–1952: Industrial and Commercial Institutions). China Social Sciences Press, 1993, pp. 977–979. Quoted in Wu and Dong (2010: 183)

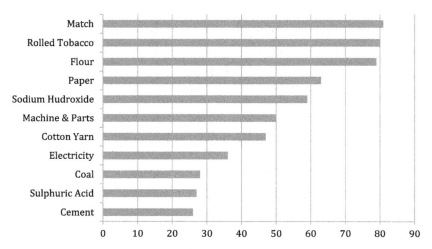

Fig. 1 Weight of the private sector in industrial production 1949 (%) (Source: Wu and Dong 2010: 265)

5. *State-owned enterprises offered better wage and welfare.* Employees in state-owned enterprises enjoyed better benefits than employees in the private sector. Conflicts between labour and employer (the state) were therefore milder.

In general, the primitive accumulation of state capital appeared to be milder than private capital. These factors can help us understand the socialist transformation of replacing private capital with state capital.

5   Conclusion: The Relevance of China's Experience to Developing Countries

At the early years of the new republic, the new government made use of various means (economic, political and even military) to curb the vicious circle of hyperinflation and speculation. This experience is relevant to present day situation where money supply expansion leads to speculation while very little money created by Quantitative Easing is eventually channelled into the physical economy.[70]

Mao Zedong said that we should take heed of historical experiences. The 13-year hyperinflation in China before 1950 was exogenous, a derivative that originated in the economic depression in the West which attempted to transfer the cost of crisis to other parts of the world. Under the pressure of war and inflation, the KMT government had to increase its dependency on the US dollar. The new regime born with the land revolution received no foreign aid and cut the nation's dependency on the US dollar. However it succeeded in controlling inflation by the power of the rural real economy. It can be seen as a significant victory of a sovereign nation in the long struggle of delinking from dependency.

Under long-term inflation, capital tends to leave the real economy and rush into the speculative sector, which is the invariable behaviour of private capital under a free market economy. Since 1947 the new regime advocated the development of a system of national capitalism with private capital as the major agent. It pushed the development strategy of New Democracy after crushing down speculation as a way to curb hyperinflation. As a result, recession in the real economy became inevitable.

At that time, the state was still not in the shackles of the interest bloc and could choose to 'go long' as a form of counter-cyclical regulation to tackle recession. The foundation of regulation was a combination of two apparently opposite elements: a dispersive peasant economy and a centralized state capital. The relevance of this experience of curbing the crisis of urban capitalism for other developing countries can never be overestimated.

Furthermore, the historical significance of China's victory over hyperinflation lay in the establishment of a sovereign currency system, a success finally achieved after the efforts of two regimes over decades. The UK,

---

[70]The same exogenous crisis appears again in China in the twenty-first century. However the CPC is no longer what it was. Incorporated into radical financial globalization, the government could no longer tackle the vested interest of financial sector by flexing muscle as it did in the early 1950s. The real estate bubble and financial speculation since 2008 marked the beginning of the new crisis.

USA and Japan had given up the gold standard in a short period of time. On the other hand, China under the double pressure of an exogenous crisis (originating from the West) and war, eventually succeeded in paper money reform.

This brought to an end the 500-year-old silver standard in China since the Ming dynasty. In a global economic system, where the history of currency is a history of devaluation, perhaps only by giving up the precious metal standard can a currency be competitive with others. This is not a simple matter of right or wrong.

The author has long emphasized that we should look into the development path of China objectively without using the lens of ideology. Institutions and thoughts taking shape in the modernization of advanced Western countries should not be regarded as absolutely correct standards that less developed countries must follow. If we are willing to put aside this lens, then we might understand that China in 1949 actually resolved the crisis of modernization by de-modernization. And we might be able to explain how China cured the plague of hyperinflation by a high degree of organization in villages. Accordingly, we might generalize some points in development economics.

First, the real economy with independent sovereignty is the foundation of currency sovereignty. For a sovereign nation facing sanctions and a blockade but with a traditional peasant economy as its major mode of production, the key to securing the fruit of the revolution lies in the state taking staple grain (the most important factor for livelihood) as the major standard of currency value. Sovereign currency is correlated with staple grain. Thus, a stable expectation of floating interest rate is also formed. From there, a steady growth in the rural real economy and a value anchored to basic agricultural products can prevent hyperinflation. Fiscal budget and finance are closely related with the distribution of supplies for livelihood. Given these factors, RMB became a widely accepted state credit tool both in cities and villages. All of these consolidated new China as an independent nation with its sovereignty fully intact.

Second, only by changing the mono-economic structure can developing countries get out of the colonial development trap. Many developing countries in the world are confined to being export zones of primary products. And they lose the power of pricing as logistics, trading and financial clearing are controlled by transnational corporations from (former) suzerains or master states. As a result, they do not have the foundation to correlate agricultural products with currency. Many developing countries born during the de-colonization movement after the Second World War have failed to achieve self-sufficiency with basic consumer goods (including industrial and traditional products) because of the mono-economic structure of agriculture. If they want to import these goods, regardless of factors like trade sanction or blockade, market prices at the destination is necessarily higher than in the place of origin. What is more, the goods have to be paid for with hard currency, which is generally scarce in developing countries. These countries might on some occasions take a ride on booming international trade to enjoy handsome short-term benefits. However, the boom is often ephemeral. If the countries fail to mobilize domestic production and initiate import substitution, they will repeatedly face a scarcity of staple grain and hard currency under the convention of the market economy.

Third, only under the dual rural–urban system can organized labour substitute capital in scarcity. Here, we come to the Gordian Knot of developing countries. Under conditions of capital scarcity, developing countries generally find it hard to effectively mobilize labour as a way of factor substitution for capital (Gerschenkron 2009).

The prelude to modernization in the West was colonization, which transplanted slavery prevalent in Ancient Greece and Rome to other continents. The primitive capital accumulation for industrialization in the West was achieved by drowning the colonies in blood and tears. Developing countries do not enjoy the same conditions for industrialization. Many development economists in the West, especially classical economists like W. Arthur Lewis, John C.H. Fei and Gustav Ranis, have attempted to elaborate on the industrialization of developing countries by the hypothesis of labour creating capital. For example, Lewis and others believe that under resource scarcity and when the foundation of capital accumulation is weak, people can mobilize their creativity as a way to substitute capital. For instance, people can be mobilized to build irrigation systems or dams with low or no payment.[71]

However, the foundation of these Western theories applies only to the history of colonization. These theorists hypothesize that under very hard conditions labour can take part in creating capital in the most primitive manner, which contributes to capital accumulation. But they do not give a reasonable explanation about how labour investment can be rendered into capital accumulation necessary for industrialization under scarcity of capital. In reality, Lewis' Labour Surplus Model under Dual Sector cannot be applied to the initial stage of industrialization where capital is scarce, nor to China in 1949 under hyperinflation.

In short, these models have yet to find success in developing countries. This is because if a country relies on importing basic goods for subsistence, then the price of labour in this country determined by the cost of labour reproduction must be higher than in the place of production of these goods. This implies that it is impossible to mobilize the labour force in this country at a low cost. Moreover, any way to organize the labour force through money will only lead to greater scarcity of capital.

Nevertheless, long before the birth of these Western models, China effectively mitigated the problem of capital scarcity by mobilizing a large amount of labour at a low cost into the construction of state projects. This is possible to do only in an urban–rural dual system where rural labour is priced according to agricultural factors.

To sum up, the agrarian reform in China created a mechanism of labour mobilization at low cost, which effectively helped to suppress

---

[71]'In the neo-classical model capital can be created only by withdrawing resources from producing consumer goods. In our model, however, there is surplus labour, and if (as we shall assume) its marginal productivity is zero, and if, also, capital can be created by labour without withdrawing scarce land and capital from other uses, then capital can be created without reducing the output of consumer goods. This second proviso is important, since if we need capital or land to make capital the results in our model are the same as the results in the neo-classical model, despite the fact that there is surplus labour. However, in practice the proviso is often fulfilled. Food cannot be grown without land, but roads, viaducts, irrigation channels and building can be created by human labour with hardly any capital to speak of— witness the Pyramids, or the marvellous railway tunnels built in the mid-nineteenth century almost with bare hands. Even in modern industrial countries constructional activity, which lends itself to hand labour, is as much as 50 or 60 per cent of gross fixed investment' (Lewis 1954: 160–161).

hyperinflation. Furthermore, it greatly contributed to China's successful industrialization through substituting capital with labour when capital was in extreme scarcity (Dong et al. 2011).

Apart from China, it is rare to find another developing economy in which one or two generations of people are willing to sacrifice themselves for the primitive accumulation of state capital. Moreover, for the millions of peasants mobilized during the land revolution, this sacrifice was not unconscious. Accordingly, to understand the subsequent institutional transition of state capital we must take large-scale labour force investment as a basic principle.

3

1958–1976: Three Rounds of Crises at the Initial Phase of Industrialization and the Background of Foreign Debts Due to Introducing Foreign Investment

After the Soviet Union withdrew its investment and technical support in the late 1950s, China's industrialization strategy could be summarized as follows:

1. Extracted surplus value from the agricultural sector through low purchasing price of agricultural products and high pricing of industrial products.
2. Forced the modernization of agriculture to absorb domestic industrial products through rural collectivization.
3. Mobilized intensive and massive labor input to substitute for capital under condition of extreme capital scarcity.
4. In case of economic crises, the transfer of unemployed labor force to rural sector through ideological mobilization. For example, intellectuals were sent to the countryside for "re-education" by the peasants and the youth were mobilized to build the rural sector.

© The Author(s) 2021
Wen Tiejun, *Ten Crises*, Global University for Sustainability Book Series,
https://doi.org/10.1007/978-981-16-0455-3_3

Unlike many developing countries, China had managed to build up a relatively complete industrial structure comprising of the primary, secondary and by then incomplete tertiary industries, which laid the foundation for development after 1978.

The year of 1978 is conventionally regarded as the point of departure of China's reform in spite of the fact that this was not the beginning of an economic cycle in that period. In reality, to understand the cyclicity of Chinese economy, a more appropriate approach is to delineate different periods in contemporary economic history by the years of outbreak of major crises. As per this principle, the first year of the Reform should be 1980.

Since the Reform and Opening Up, many official experts and scholars have conducted in-depth studies on the economic volatility in China. Admittedly the reality of economic volatility is recognized by all researchers. Nevertheless, the existence of cyclical economic crises remains controversial. The author's essay in 1988 was the first study which clearly elaborated the problem of cyclical crises in Chinese economy.[1] Before that, there was an unprinted manuscript circulating in Beijing's universities in 1979 with the title "Structural Economic Crisis in Socialism". It entailed striking ideological implication characteristic of the discussion during the late 1970s and early 1980s about whether economic cycles existed in socialist countries. This book tries to avoid this sort of ideological dispute. We identity and analyse the occurrence of crises from the functioning of the real economy. The discussion then covers the impact of crises on the rural sector under the dual structure of urban–rural dichotomy and the latter's role in mitigating against their detrimental consequences. The economic indicators quoted in this book include economic growth rate, fiscal deficits, the difference between financial stock and total loans, the growth rate in fixed asset investment, and CPI index etc. The reason for so doing is that there are two different

---

[1] Published in 经济学周报 (Economics Weekly Journal), 1988(5) and 新华文摘 (Xin Hua Digest), 1988(12).

industrial stages of economic development that may be thought of as being divided by the reform.

Unlike advanced industrialized nations, late developing countries could not transfer the cost of primitive accumulation of capital outward through colonization or war. The only option has been the internal transfer of costs through specific social institutions. We call this the "theory of cost transfer".[2]

It may be said that the social conflicts China experienced in the 1960s were the painful percussions of primitive accumulation of capital in the 1950s (two forms of capital: national capital and state capital). The costs were being transferred as the burdens of urban and rural citizens.

China's economic development, which has been mainly characterized by industrialization, can be divided into two different stages. Before the Reform, it was generally regarded as the initial stage of introverted industrialization, which can be known as the stage of primitive accumulation of capital according to classical theories. It is characterized by remarkable economic volatility, with clear features of economic cycle. During that period there were three major urban economic crises, approximately separated by 7–8 years. *The government's responses during these three crises had involved the transfer on a large scale surplus urban labour to highly organized people's communes and state-owned collective farms.* In three rounds of "Going to Mountains and Villages" movements (1960, 1968, 1975) there was a total of about 20 millions urban youth (mainly high school students known as *zhiqin*, young intellectuals) and approximately an equivalent number of youngsters returning to their rural origins. Meanwhile, the government intensified the extraction of agricultural surplus, which can be regarded as an "inward" transfer of the cost of crises caused by industrialization and urbanization. In other words, not only did the *sannong* bear the institutional costs of primitive accumulation

---

[2]The studies of China often miss the dimension of the world. The World System in which China is situated is a system of transferring cost from advanced/core nations to less developed/peripheral nations. Accordingly, the greater the external pressure, the greater domestic tension would become. Or internal tension is a reflection of external pressure. This holds true between countries as well as between social sectors. For example, when the extraction of *sannong*'s surplus becomes too much, social conflicts within rural community will also be intensified. Similarly, when the surplus of a country is being extracted too much by other, the tension between the state and the underprivileged groups will become exacerbated.

for industrialization; it also acted as the major carrier bearing the costs of economic crises.

Compared with the crises since the 1980s after the Reform and Opening Up, these earlier crises differed in terms of the regions toward which the costs were transferred. During the 30 years before the Reform, state-owned industrial capital concentrated in cities could transfer the costs of crises to the rural sector through highly organized rural collectives. Urban economy and its governmental system could therefore be maintained intact.

In the three "young intellectuals going to countryside" movements during the 1960–1970s, 20 million unemployed urban youth were sent to the 4 million production teams of 800 thousand brigades in 90 thousand people's communes. Besides, there were about the same number of rural students returning to the 200 million rural households in the communes, which were not included in the government's statistics of employment (Image 1).

The correlation between cyclical urban crises and the "Going to Mountains and Villages" movements can be shown as below. On every occasion of crisis, the numbers of urban youth ("zhiqin," literally young intellectuals) being mobilized to the rural regions would dramatically increase before decreasing again after the crisis passed. The political movement of Going to Mountain and Villages, isomorphic to the increasingly fortified urban–rural dual system, was the basic means by which the state transferred the costs of crises to the villages as large scale unemployment emerged in cities under crisis. The process continued until the completion of the primitive accumulation of capital for national industrialization (Fig. 1).

There has been little discussion about these social expenses or institutional costs of the primitive accumulation for state industrialization. The real unemployment rate was absent from official documents in that era. Comparing data in *China Statistics Yearbooks*, with urban employment number as 130 million in 1960 and 45.37 in 1962, the estimated unemployed labour might be around 85.36 million in the two years of recession. The number of urban employment was decreased by 65% (Fig. 2).

Image 1 In December 1967, 100 middle school students from Beijing were joining other thousands to volunteer to go to underdeveloped regions for the "Socialist Revolution and Construction". The picture shows the crowded Beijing Railway Station with the departing students and their parents

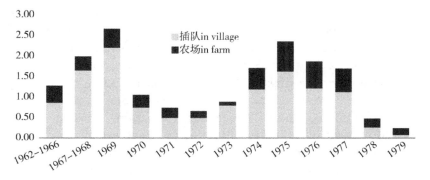

Fig. 1 Urban youth sent to rural regions during 1962–1979 (million) (Source: *China Statistics of Labour and Wage*)

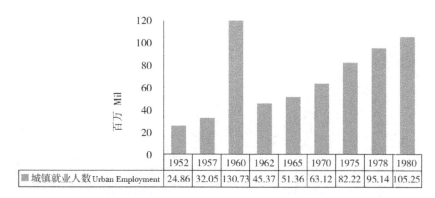

	1952	1957	1960	1962	1965	1970	1975	1978	1980
▨ 城镇就业人数 Urban Employment	24.86	32.05	130.73	45.37	51.36	63.12	82.22	95.14	105.25

Fig. 2 Number of urban employed population (Source: *China Statistical Yearbook 1996*)

Under general market economy, an unemployment rate of more than 10% in any country would lead to serious social problems. There was no serious social unrest in China during that period. However, in the name of "class struggle" the problem was expressed in a variety of political movements as a way to mitigate social tension in the urban sector, where capital was concentrated along with accumulated risk. Furthermore, during these economic crises the state could have the potential unemployed urban labour almost totally absorbed by the rural sector through highly stabilized collectivized organizations (people's communes).

During the 2 July to 16 September 1959, the ruling party held several important meetings in Lushan, Jiangxi including the outreach session of the Politbureau and the Eighth Plenary Session of the Eighth Central Committee. In these meetings, the lessons since the "Great Leap" Movement of 1958 were summed up. However, the leaders and politicians at that time were still confined by the ideological opposition of Left and Right, which in fact originated from the West. These Lushan Meetings had left us with much astonishment and puzzles. However, few have understood that the complication incurred by the crisis of fiscal deficit was a necessary consequence of China's making use of foreign capital for the primitive accumulation of industrialization. China, the biggest sovereignty in the world, was offered the chance because it got embarrassingly involved into the geo-political strategies of two superpowers.

Unlike their previous suzerains, developing countries generally could not transfer the cost of primitive accumulation externally. All they could do was to transfer the cost internally under certain institutional conditions. It is a regular pattern. Late industrializing countries are no exception.

The painful difficulties and social contradictions China suffered during the 1960s can be attributed to the transfer of cost incurred by the primitive accumulation of industrial capital that occurred under different names (national capital or state capital).

1   Background of the First Occasion of Industrialization Relying on Foreign Capital: The Reconstruction and Transformation of Geo-Political Strategy After WWII

In the previous chapter, we have discussed the experience of socialist China in dealing with chronic hyperinflation.

This serious economic crisis of hyperinflation and unemployment occurred mainly in the cities. Rural China was relatively stable at that time and benefited from an all-round agrarian reform which represented the fundamental appeal of peasants in China for a few thousand years. In the name of Land Revolution, the government distributed land to some 400 million peasants and property rights were defined by the natural boundaries of villages. This effectively "delinked" the *sannong* (peasants, rural communities and agriculture) from the urban economy, which was prone to risk. And in pioneering a rural institutional arrangement, this system of property rights created a "path dependence". Henceforth, all political redistribution of land would set the village boundary as the limit to which property rights in land would apply.

Industrialization and the Dilemma of Urban-Rural Dual Structure

Consequently, the peasants who comprised 88% of the population remained loyal to the new regime under the leadership of the ruling party. This was in accordance with a historical regularity in ancient China where the dynasty practising an equitable distribution of arable land and tax exemption would earn the loyalty of peasants. But what this particular historical instance amounted to was an exercise of mass mobilization for the nation-building of new China via a land revolution. This marks a fundamental institutional difference between China and other developing countries that have not undergone a similar popular land revolution.

However, this episode deepened a fundamental contradiction between the rural and the urban. The national capitalist industry had to face high transaction costs in trading with highly dispersed peasants in extracting the agricultural surplus. Under the threat of high inflation, peasants would become risk-averse and exhibit "non-monetized" behavior— generally the peasants would stockpile staple crops and purchase fewer urban industrial products.

Whenever entering into industrialization, all economic systems have to deal with the problem of transaction costs, which is a direct "institutional cost", no matter what kind of ideology a country claims to hold on to. If the costs cannot be transferred to the rural sector, it would be transferred to the urban milieu where industrial and commercial capitals are concentrated, the result of which would be a deteriorating business environment. In the primitive accumulation of national capital during 1949–1953, most of the cities in China witnessed the problems of counterfeit, speculation, corruption and favoritism. The new government, which did not yet have a firm footing in the cities, took advantage of its revolutionary prestige to mobilize the masses to deal with these problems by way of political movements. At that time, a class-based politics led by the working class having self-consciousness of proletarian class had yet to be formed and different classes including petit bourgeois, the majority of urban citizens and enterprise staffs, could vent their discontent through these movements, which functioned as pressure relief valve preventing the accumulated internal pressure from leading to radical social actions.

These political movements have been much criticized by latter generations. Nevertheless, the greatest pity of these historical experiences has not been discussed: the institutional costs incurred by the primitive accumulation of national capital in urban economy could not be dispensed with simply by mass mobilization in cities, which was a problem not presaged by the politicians of that time. The persistence of these "costs" may be considered to be the reason for the incomplete process of urban industrialization in most of the developing countries, notwithstanding the considerable social and political turmoil they have gone through.

These political movements should be contextualized into the initial development of urban capital and the urban–rural relationship. However, we have to take a further step to expand our perspective onto the international environment. International factors have always been decisive in China's different stages of development.

The Price of Soviet Union's Aid: The Socialist Restructuring of Economic Base and the "Sovietization" of Superstructure

After the victory in 1949, the new government attempted to accomplish the primitive accumulation of capital for national industrialization through developing the private sector (industry as well as commerce) and promoting urban–rural exchange. The idea was the government would lead the new small property owners emerging from the revolution and the entrepreneurs of urban private industry and commerce to gradually complete the primitive accumulation of national capital and to move into industrialization dominated by urban industry and commerce. During 1947–1950, it was expressed in official discourse as "New Democracy as National Capitalism under the Leadership of the CPC". The results of relatively autonomous development of local economies during 1950–1953 also testified this.

However, from the perspective of international geo-politics, China, like many late developing countries, was under the shackle of extreme capital scarcity and subject to unpredictable external tensions. After the establishment of the new socialist regime, the Chinese government adopted an overt pro-Soviet foreign policy. However, the Soviet Union did not immediately provide aid China desperately needed and asked for.

In December 1949, Mao Zedong on his first diplomatic mission flew to meet Stalin to negotiate a new treaty and various issues concerning their countries' bilateral interests. However, the process was not smooth. It was not until 14 February 1950 that the two leaders signed a series of agreements. The Soviet Union would help China to build 50 projects in coal, electricity, steel, nonferrous metal, chemical industry, machinery and military industry, which marked the beginning of three rounds of partnerships totalling 156 aid projects (see Box 1).

Compared with the difficult negotiations, the execution of these projects was highly efficient, with the reason being the Korean War. Only superpowers were capable of remaking the geo-political setting, which marked the great difference between them and other developing countries, including China, at that time.

The outbreak of Korean War in 1950 substantially changed the imperialist geo-political structure formed after the WWII. In October 1950, the Chinese People's Voluntary Army crossed the Yalu River. During the 3 year war, 1.34 million of armed persons were mobilized to confront an allied force of 1.11 million, 540 thousand of which was American. Paying a high cost, with a sacrifice of 140 thousand lives and 250 thousand injured, captured and missing in action, China managed to forge a strategic alliance with the Soviet Union, laying the foundation for the aid between 1950 and 1959, which was worth about 5.4 billion US dollars (including the military expenditures during the war).

With the strong pull of external investment accompanying the Korean War, China rapidly got out of the economic slump after 1950 and began the process of rapid primitive accumulation for industrialization. Because of the war, military purchases increased. Military and civil sectors competed for material supplies. The prices of industrial goods such as hardware, construction materials and general merchandises rose. For example, the price increase of construction materials was up by 82.9%. The prices of some industrial appliances even rocketed by ten times due to speculation.

Box 1: 1950–1953 Soviet Union's Aids to China's Economic Construction

New China's economic restoration was almost synchronized with the Korean War. During the war, China and the Soviet Union not only coordinated in military and diplomatic fields but also consolidated economic cooperation.

According to the report of the State Statistics Bureau on 11 March 1953, China and the USSR had signed contracts with the former agreeing to import facilities worth 683,940 thousand ruble during 1950–1953. The real accumulated imports were worth 469,740 thousand ruble, i.e. the completion rate of contracts was 68.7%.

Soviet aid focused on energy and fundamental industries. It was pivotal in China's modern industry infrastructure building during the 1950–1952 rehabilitation period.

	Project Number	Reconstruction & Expansion	New Projects	Regions	
				Northeast	Hinterland
1. Energy					
i. Coal	10	5	5	8	2
ii. Electricity	11	5	6	6	5
2. Raw Materials					
i. Steel	3	2	1	3	
ii. Non-ferrous Metals	3	1	2	3	
iii. Chemical	5		5	4	1
3. Civil Machinery	7	2	5	7	
4. Defence & Military	7	7		4	3
5. Paper Manufacturing	1		1	1	
Total	47	22	25	36	11

During 1950–1952 China's new increased fixed capital amounted to RMB 5.9 billion. Increment of productivity in energy and raw materials were as follows: electricity: 222 thousand kilowatt, coal extraction: 15,637 thousand tons/year, pig iron 764 thousand tons/year, steel ingot 558 thousand tons/year, rolled steel 336 thousand tons/year.

Projects	Construction Started at	Production Started at	Investment (RMB 10 thousand)	New Increased Productivity		
				Products	Unit	Amount
1. Coal						
Liaoyuan Central	1950	1955	5770	Coal Extraction	thousand tons	900
Fuxin Pingan	1952	1957	8334			1500
Fuxin Haizhou	1950	1957	19,472			3000
Hegang Dongsan	1950	1955	6512			900
Hegang Xingantai	1950	1956	7178			1500
2. Electricity						
Fuxin Thermal	1951	1958	7450	Capacity	thousand kilowatt	150
Fushun	1952	1957	8734			150
Fengman Hydroelectricity	1951	1959	9634			422.5
Hulan Ergi Thermal	1952	1955	6870			50
Zhengzhou Second Thermal	1952	1953	1971			12
Chongqing	1952	1953	3561			24
Xian Thermal	1952	1957	6449			48
Urumqi Thermal	1952	1959	3275			19
3. Steel						
Anshan Steel	1952	1960	268,500	Pig iron Steel Rolled Steel	thousand tons	2500 3200 2500
4. Nonferrous Metals						
Fushun Aluminium	1952	1957	15,619	Aluminium ingot Magnesium	thousand tons	39 1.2
Harbin Aluminium (Phrase I & II)	1952	1958	32,681	Rolled Aluminium		30
5. Machinery						
Shenyang Pneumatic	1952	1954	1893	Pneumatic tools	thousand/ ton	20/554

According to the table below, after the total completion of all aid projects, the new increased fixed assets were worth RMB 4.139 billion. The new increased productivity was as follows: electricity 875.5 thousand kilowatt, coal extraction 7800 thousand tons/year, pig iron 2500 thousand tons/year, steel ingot 3200 tons/year, rolled steel 2500 thousand tons/year.

The second batch of the 156 projects was executed along with the First Five Year Plan.

During August–September, 1952, Premier Zhou Enlai led a delegation to negotiate with the USSR government. The agreement involved the latter helping China to build and reconstruct 91 enterprises. Including the 50 projects already under construction, the 141 projects would greatly enhance China's industrial capacity by 1959. Production capacity would be doubled in ferrous metallurgy, nonferrous metals, coal, electricity, petroleum, machinery manufacturing and chemical industry. China would have an automobile and a tractor industry. Productivity of major products such as steel, coal, electricity and petroleum would be equivalent to that of the USSR in the First Five Year Plan, and close to or even surpassing Japan in 1937 (the year when Japan launched overall war against China).

The import of complete-set facilities from the USSR related with the First Five Year Plan was conducted in the form of trade. In return, China had to supply 160 thousand tons of tungsten concentrate, 110 thousand tons of tin, 30 thousand tons of stibium, 35 thousand tons of molybedenum, 90 thousand tons of rubber and a certain amount of agricultural products. In comparison, the major aid projects during 1950–1952 were provided through loans. As for necessary scientific and technological information, the USSR provided in two ways: library information exchange and contracts. During the period of strategic partnership, China enjoyed special favour. The cost was low and at times, even free. However, the remuneration of experts working in China became a matter of negotiation.

Relying on foreign facilities to push national industrialization, China faced the problem of "human capital" scarcity. For example, in the 1950s, merely a few of the cadres in Northeast region were educated. 70% of them were illiterate and semi-illiterate. Some received basic literacy training after taking part in the revolution. Scientists, technicians and administrative talents indispensable for industrialization were in extreme scarcity. Therefore, tens of thousands of USSR experts came to China along with the introduction of technology and facilities.

However, the negotiation concerning how they would be remunerated was not easy. When Liu Shaoqi visited the USSR, Stalin suggested that China could pay the USSR experts according to the remuneration level of top Chinese counterparts. The Soviet Union would subsidize the difference. Nevertheless, things became different afterward, especially after China insisted on maintaining its sovereignty on issues such as the Chinese Changchun railway, etc.

The Soviet Union proposed double payment, i.e. apart from paying the salary, Chinese government had to compensate 2000–4000 rubble for each expert to the enterprises or departments he or she worked in, payable to the USSR government. The US dollar value of this was equivalent to 10,000–18,000 *jin* of millets. At that time, the salary of chairman and vice-chairman in China was merely 3400 *jin* of millets, ministers only 2800. The Chinese government wished to pay by various staple foods and commodities, which was much easier than paying in US dollar, but the USSR insisted on payment by foreign exchange (in rubble according to US dollar exchange rate). It was finally agreed that Soviet experts be paid at the level of their top Chinese counterparts. In addition, China had to pay compensation for their absence from the Soviet economy, by 1500–3000 rubble per month. Moreover, the issue of remuneration and compensation of soviet military personnel in China also went through various negotiations.

Source: 沈志华 (Shen Zhihua), "新中国建立初期苏联对华经济援助的基本情况——来自中国和俄国的档案材料" (Basic Situations of USSR Aid to China—from the archives of China and Russia). *Russia Studies*, 2001(1–2).

China's industrialization was in fact dominated by foreign strategic investment made possible by the geo-political strategic competition between two super powers, the United States and the USSR.

The key projects during 1950–1952 were introduced as loans, totalling USD 300 million in value, to be repaid in 10 years, with annual interest rate of 1%. Later after the loan agreement, the Soviet Union requested precious strategic materials such as tungsten, tin and stibium to repay the loan. Despite the additional terms, the loan condition was generally favourable. However, on the second batch of aid projects, the Soviet Union requested to be conducted more in the form of trade, especially in those projects related with importing whole sets of equipment.

For example, China was requested to supply to the USSR 160 thousand tons of tungsten ores, 110 thousand tons of tin, and 30 thousand tons of stibium, 35 thousand tons of molybdenum ores and a substantial amount of agricultural products before 1959.

This put great pressure on China. As the central government was the agent of accepting these aid projects, it was also responsible for the financial liability. Right at the beginning, China had to face the dilemma of foreign investment bearing foreign debts, or no investment at all. The pressure on the central government was double. On the one hand, it had to provide accessories for the imported equipment and facilities. On the other, the government's fiscal budget had to be spared to purchase products for exchanging. At that time, the problem could not be resolved by increasing money supply, otherwise the hyperinflation that was just being tamed (see previous chapter) would be set loose again. Furthermore, with heavy industry requiring big investments, facing high-risk and a long returns cycle, it was impossible to be financially self-sufficient. Under this extreme scarcity of capital, how to resolve the problem?

Institutional Transition and New Ideology

The only option available seemed to be the Unified Purchase and Selling system, which was put into pilot experiment in 1951 and became well-known in 1952 as it was expanded to staple grain purchase. Only by unifying purchases in the rural sector and selling in the urban sector could price and supply become controllable. The central government's supplies and cash flow would not be broken. Therefore we suggest that the socialist transformation since 1953 was in fact an expanded version of the unified purchase and selling system China had explored.

Due to the problem of transaction cost, a full-scale unified purchase and selling system must be supplemented by new organizational innovation, the core of which was to reinforce cooperation to lead individual economic agents. It was embodied in three major aspects of socialist transformation: peasant households, urban artisan workers and capitalist industry as well as commerce.

It was called "socialist" transformation, the "general line of socialist transition".

Now, under full-scale orientation toward the USSR, China rapidly formed a Stalinist system to accommodate heavy and military industries imported from the former. A state capitalist industrial system took shape and was mainly located in large and medium cities. Then, according to the requirements in terms of investment, construction and repayment supporting state capital, the general line of socialist transition was pushed through. By the end of January 1956, all capitalist industry and commerce in large cities and more than 50 medium cities had become joint state-private ventures. Before long, the socialist transformation of industry and commerce, as well as peasant economy was completed.

Taking advantage of the centralized system led by a single party formed during the revolutionary war, three major factors of production were converted into state ownership under state capitalism: land, labour and capital.

1. Land—In February 1954, the central government promulgated the following: "state-owned enterprises, state institutions, army and schools can expropriate sub-urban land without paying fee or rent." This implied that land ownership which would have generated high yield by urban and industrial sectors was assumed by the government, which was then able to appropriate the added-value from the capitalization of land. (In 1956, rural land ownership was transferred to village collectives.) This condition may be called "government corporatism". The problem then became obvious. Expropriation without compensation had driven the first wave of land enclosure during the mid-1950s. According to a report in 1956, among 101 thousand *mu* of land expropriated in regions such as Beijing, Wuhan, Changsha, Hangzhou, Chengdu, etc., 41 thousand, around 40% was desolated or wasted. The situation was similar to the three rounds of land enclosure after the Reform since 1978.

2. Labour force—Since 1953, the government closed urban and rural labour markets to concentrate labour and intellectual resources into infrastructure building. All the surplus value of the labour force was appropriated by the government. In the three decades before the

Reform, urban citizens enjoyed social benefits from the cradle to the grave, which were subsidized by the state. On the one hand, the state extracted almost all of the surplus value of urban labour with "the promise of the future" and laid the foundation of the high-speed accomplishment of primitive accumulation of capital for national industrialization. On the other hand, peasants, comprising 80% of the population, who enjoyed little from the benefits of industrialization, contributed greatly to converting urban citizens, who were mainly staff working in state-owned enterprises, into a "middle-class" as a social force stabilizing society.

3. Capital—The government monopolized money supply and controlled the whole financial sector, appropriating seignorage and the added-value of monetization of economy.

The private ownership of the factors of production had existed only for less than seven years in New China before they were converted into state ownership to serve the primitive accumulation of national industrialization. Capital therefore became embedded in the government. This government corporatism with Chinese characteristics, under the condition of capital scarcity, proved to be effective in accelerating primitive accumulation for industrialization. It was an institution beneficial to the rapid expansion of industrial capital in cities. Nevertheless, it was also an institution which directly transferred the institutional costs of crises onto the peasants.

New Democracy (National Capitalism) existed only till 1953. Thereafter, the state as the recipient of foreign industrial investment, rapidly transformed national capitalism into state capitalism.[3] Within western ideological understandings, it was a "centralized system". This institution was set up upon the completion of socialist transformation in 1956 and continued until 1960 when a debt and deficit crisis broke out. Its essence was to introduce technologies and facilities from the USSR in the form of national debts. The central government then extracted surplus from

---

[3]National capitalism (New Democracy) meant developing capitalism with private capital as economic agents under the leadership of the state. State capitalism meant the state became the sole owner and agent of capital.

the *sannong* based on large-scale collectivization with village and town as units, repaying debts and accomplishing industrialization.

In order to implement an institutional transition, the ruling party had to construct a logical explanation with moral legitimacy, in turn turning it into an ideology to lessen the cost of institutional transition. It was reflected in the debate between Mao Zedong and the Confucian intellectual Liang Shuming. Here, socialism represented the public interest. Mao considered himself representing national interest in long run whereas Liang represented individualist kindness. In that particular era, Mao, when confronted by a more inclusive and native Confucian discourse, opted for a more radical western revolutionary discourse to construct his value logic.

During the First Five Year Plan, the USSR provided strategic aid and investment to China while the latter set up governments, schools, and research institutions complying with the Soviet management model. The superstructure had to be brought into conformity with the economic base. In order to comply with the industrial economic base formed by the Soviet investment, China's superstructure, including its ideology, was totally "sovietized" in that period. Russian experts coming to China not only worked as managers in factories and enterprises but also helped to overhaul the entire superstructure of China. The eight major industrial departments, the Planning Committee, Financial Committee, Economic Committee, Agricultural Committee, etc., were all set up according to Soviet model. The officials sent from the USSR were called "experts". They were everywhere in every department. Chinese governmental and university systems were copied from the Soviet Union. Only in this way could the governmental institutions adapt with the management of Soviet industrial economy. During the first half of the 1950s, the urban economy was managed by a Soviet system.

Nevertheless, the Chinese leadership, which had a long experience in anti-colonial and anti-imperialist struggle, was alert to the problem of complete "sovietisation" of the superstructure (including the army). Before the 20th Party Congress of the Communist Party of the Soviet Union (CPSU) in 1955, the Communist Party of China had already held internal discussion about the problems of complete sovietisation, which foreshadowed the breakup of the two parties.

The problem of complete sovietisation during the early 1950s became ingrained in Chinese government. Hierarchical soviet system fostered bureaucratism, dogmatism and formalism, which merged with the factionalism shaped during the guerrilla war. Not even massive popular mobilization in the Great Cultural Revolution could succeed in overthrowing this factionalism, to say nothing about the more gentle reforms subsequently.

The industrial economy led by state capital in cities stood in opposition to the traditional peasant economy rehabilitated in rural China after agrarian reform. Upon it thus rested an urban–rural dual system. The "path dependence" of this structure in the subsequent institutional transform in the next 50 years has been remarkable. Factionalism has become a pertinacious illness in contemporary China where politics is under the sway of interest blocs.

In summary, the Korean War afforded new China with the opportunity to introduce foreign investment for the first time. Transplanting Soviet production facilities along with its superstructure, China built an infrastructure of military-heavy industry and social institutions according to the Soviet model in order to accommodate the latter's mode of production. However, the price of fast industrialization was high. It was impossible to sell the obsolete industrial products overseas to cover the cost of industrialization in the cities. The foreign debt thus incurred had to be repaid by exporting produce and minerals not relatively abundant in supply in China while a domestic market had to be created to absorb these industrial products. For this reason, the state had to extract agricultural surplus from the agrarian sector through large-scale collectivization at village and township levels. Without taking these factors into consideration, it would be hard to depict a more objective picture of the turbulent 1960s of China unless we are content with those ideological perspectives prevalent in many researches.

2   The Second Crisis (1958–1960): What Happened in China After the USSR Aid was Interrupted?

The economic crisis of 1958–1960 was the first cyclical crisis since China began receiving foreign investment to initiate and spur its industrialization. The trigger was China's insistence on its territorial integrity and independent sovereignty. According to the agreement of 1956, the USSR had to return the Chinese Changchun railway and the Dalian Special Zone to China and retreat its military base in Northeast China. Dissatisfied with this, the USSR interrupted aid and investment in 1957. In 1958, it requested to forge a new military alliance by establishing a joint navel-air force command and unified radio communication system in China to better serve the former's military strategy in the Far East. Mao refused and responded in his characteristic fashion: "You may take China. I would go back to Jinggang Mountain [to fight a resistance war]."

For Chinese leaders, national sovereignty was not negotiable. However, without foreign aid, the heavy-industry-oriented government corporatism relying on external investment became unsustainable. The Second Five Year Plan, which was coordinated under the assistance of Russian experts, was also aborted.

Modern history has consistently demonstrated that if a developing country insisted on its sovereign integrity and refused too much concession in its national interest, foreign investment and aid would be interrupted. Many often, its economic reproduction and development would be disrupted, causing the collapse of its economic base. As a consequence, the corresponding superstructure (government, political system, etc.) modeled after the template of the advanced country would become unsustainable without the support of continuing investment. In many cases, this situation would result invariably in political turmoil.

In response, China's central government managed to secure follow-up investment on a few dozen projects as a way to maintain minimum diplomatic relationship with the USSR. Additionally, it had to adhere to certain unanticipated measures and make necessary institutional adjustments (not to be known as "reform" at that time). In 1958, the central government proposed to mobilize local governments into national industrial construction formerly monopolized by the central government. The mobilization of domestic and especially local public fund was barely able to support the national economy oriented mainly toward heavy industry. In 1958, the weight of local fiscal expenditures in national fiscal budget jumped from 29.0% (1957) to 55.7% (Fig. 3).

During 1957–1958 when there was a significant decrease of investment from the USSR, the central government decentralized the power of fiscal budget, planning and enterprise management. Local governments were mobilized to build "five small-scale industries".[4] However, the local governments which were granted such power for the first time had no time to learn how to proceed with industrialization. The only model they could imitate was the heavy-industry model the central government received from the USSR. As a result the fanatic industrialization initiative of local governments would eventuate in ridiculous practices such as the "Great Steel Forging" and the "Great Leap Forward".

Meanwhile, the central government, whose weight in total fiscal revenues dropped to 20% in 1958, accelerated the pace of accumulation by increasing money supply. Even though the shortage of agricultural products led to price fluctuations in small local markets, the official general price changed little due to the limited purchasing power of money notes under the voucher system. Furthermore, because of the control of unified purchase and selling, the quantity of commodities available for trade in the market was limited. Therefore, the increased money supply could be withdrawn from circulation into bank deposits to build funds to support accumulation and reproduction for the national economy. At the same time, budget deficits rose remarkably. Although the growth rate of fiscal revenues and investment decreased, their absolute values stayed at a high level during 1958–1960, until the full crisis of fiscal deficit broke out in 1960.

---

[4] 胡鞍钢 (Hu Angang) 中国政治经济史论 (On China's Political Economic History). Tsinghua University Press, 2008: 247–251.

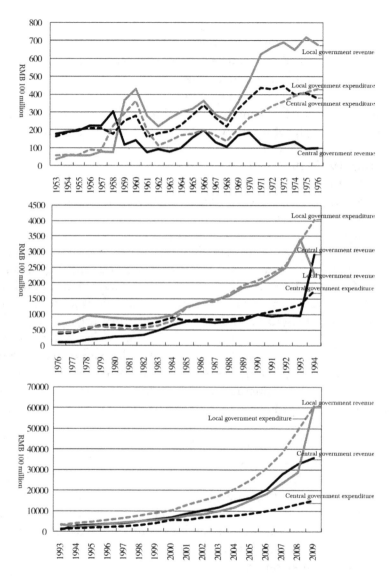

Fig. 3 Fiscal revenues of central and local governments 1953–2009 (Remark: since 1994, fiscal revenues no longer included domestic and foreign loan. Loan repayment and related costs were also excluded from fiscal expenditures. After 2000, loan repayment was once again included)

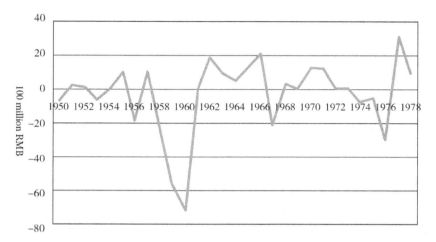

Fig. 4 China's fiscal balance before 1978 (Excluding Debt Balancing)

Figure 4 shows three stages. During 1953–1976, central and local annual fiscal revenues totalled less than RMB 100 billion. After the fiscal reform in 1980, local revenues increased rapidly, which amounted to 250 billion in 1992. In 1993, local revenues increased by 35%, mainly as a result of tax reform in that year, not normal growth. At the beginning of the twenty-first century, central and local revenues rose over RMB 1000 billion. In 2009, the fiscal revenues were up to more than 9600 billion.[5]

According to the fiscal report in 1958, the real revenues were RMB 41.89 billion, 126% of the budget (33.2 billion). It represented an annual increase of 35% (10.85 billion). Previously during the First Five Year Plan (1952–1957), average annual increase was only 12%, the highest 23% (1953). In 1958 the fiscal expenditures totalled 40.96 billion, 123.4% of the original budget (33.2 billion), representing an annual increase of 10.54 billion, also 35%. Most of the extra expenditures above budget were spent on infrastructure building, which amounted to 21.4 billion, a 70% increase compared with the previous

---

[5] 1953–2000 data from *China Statistics Yearbook 2001*. 2001–2008 from *China Statistics Yearbook 2009*.

year of 12.6 billion. The number did not include local governments raising fund outside budget for infrastructure building.[6]

Although high investment and growth rate was sustained in 1958 as the central government mobilized local initiatives to carry on autonomous industrialization, the trend abruptly turned downward when the USSR withdrew all investment and experts in 1960. The national economy slid by 21%. The government managed to maintain high fiscal revenues for three more years till 1961. Afterward, the economy tumbled into recession. In fact, discounting the means of balancing by debt, fiscal revenues had been actually declining since 1957 and hit the bottom in 1960.[7]

Figure 4 shows three fiscal deficit crises before the Reform. However, when the whole society bore the tremendous price of national industrialization, the weight of secondary industry in national economy surpassed 40% for the first time in history. The volume of industrial production jumped to a new level (Table 1).

In summary, since new China kicked started national industrialization, the decentralization of power during 1958–1960 was the first occasion, with the aim of mobilizing domestic local resources to substitute for disrupted foreign capital input. A relatively high level of accumulation for industrialization was thereby sustained.

In this period, mass mobilization became a relatively effective means to extract surplus from the labour force and to substitute for capital, which was in absolute scarcity. By some popularized version of "class struggle" and instrumental theory of "continuous revolution", almost the whole population (officials, intellectuals and general folk) were mobilized to contribute their labour into infrastructure building which was essential for state industrialization. The process of labor-based infrastructural building would in turn create demand for large equipment manufacturing. And both the infrastructure and manufacturing were owned by the state.

---

[6]Source: 关于 *1958 年财政收支决算和 1959 年财政收支预算草案的报告* (Report on 1958 Fiscal Revenue and Expenditure Settlement Account and 1959 Fiscal Budget Draft).
[7]Calculation according to data in China Economic Web Statistics Data Base.

Table 1 Major economic indicators in China 1957–1962

Indicator	1957	1958	1959	1960	1961	1962
GNP (100 million)	1069.3	1308.2	1440.4	1457.5	1220.9	1151.2
Second Industry (%)	29.6	37	42.7	44.5	31.9	31.2
Fiscal Revenues (100 m)	303.2	379.62	487.12	572.29	356.06	313.55
Growth (%)	8.2	25.2	28.3	17.5	−35.8	−11.9
Revenues/GNP (%)	28.4	29	33.8	39.3	29.2	27.2
Expenditures (100 m)	295.95	400.36	543.17	643.68	356.09	294.88
Annual Increase (%)	−0.9	35.3	35.7	18.5	−44.7	−17.2
Commodity Retail Price Index (last year = 100)	101.5	100.2	100.9	103.1	116.2	103.8
Urban–rural residents RMB Saving at Year End (100 m)	35.2	55.2	68.3	66.3	55.4	41.2
Financial Institution Cash Put into Circulation (100 m)	−4.5	15.0	7.3	20.8	29.8	−19.2
Raw Coal Production (100 million tons)	1.31	2.7	3.69	3.97	2.78	2.2
Electricity Generation (100 million Watt-hour)	193	275	423	594	480	458
Pig Iron (10,000 tons)	594	1369	2191	2716	1281	805
Crude Steel (10,000 tons)	535	800	1387	1866	870	667
Concrete Cement (10,000 tons)	686	930	1227	1565	621	600

Sources: *China Statistics Yearbook 2001*, 新中国60年 (New China 60 Years) (China Statistics Press, 2000). Data in table are slightly different from government reports

During the 1960s, China emphasized "self reliance". In a condition of capital scarcity, labour was the primary factor of substitution. And labour could be mobilized nationwide at a large scale as a legacy of long-term war and agrarian reform. Moreover, the communal cooperation in traditional rural community was also conductive to the formation of social capital. In the eyes of the west and its dominant ideology of individualism, this is represented as a form of totalitarianism suppressing individuality.

One aspect is noteworthy. During the "captialization of the labour force", staff democracy (as expressed by, for example, the Anshan Steel Constitution) took shape. It later went into conflict with management model when the capitalist mode of production was introduced from the West and Japan during the 1970s. The coexistence of these two essentially different models made state-owned enterprises seem inefficient and difficult to manage. Capitalist standards of measuring efficiency—capitalist rationality—made workers appear passive and slack in work. Serious fiscal deficits eventually led to crisis during 1978–1979. (In the next chapter, we will explain how the state-owned enterprises helped to resolve the crisis of the urban youth returning to cities and led to their "inefficiency".) As a response to the crisis, concessions of power and profit from the state to enterprises gave birth to state-owned enterprise reform during the mid-1980s when monetarization and the capitalization of economy was accelerating. As the dominance of the managers over enterprises, who acted as the personification of capital, was recognized, the ownership reform during the 1990s became inevitable. When profit-optimization became the guiding principle, large-scale layoffs and dismissal prevailed, along with corruption and cronyism. We will explore this further when discussing the 1978–1979 crisis.

Back to the 1960s. Without proper conditions to set up feasible learning mechanism for industrialization, the only experiences Chinese local governments could learn from when suddenly granted the power to capitalize resources were the USSR model and national mobilization during revolutionary war. As a consequence of "path dependence", local industrialization without technology and management experience mushroomed everywhere throughout the country. Admittedly, without technological support from the USSR, local officials knew little about developing the steel industry. Consequently, industrialization in that period was high-cost and wasteful. Yet there is more to be gleaned from this episode than just regarding it as a "learning cost".

During that period, a young and strong labour force that was sizeable in number was mobilized to leave agriculture behind and move into industrialization ("the Great Steel Forging"). According to the memoirs of Xue Muqiao, then the Deputy Director of National Planning Committee and Director General of National Bureau of Statistics, up to 90 million of workers were involved in the steel industry. Including assistants and supporters, the number was over 100 million. A drastic cut in the labour force had a great impact on peasant agricultural production replying on intensive labouring and household mixed sideline operations (such as husbandry and handicrafts).

Even though the economic and social cost was tremendous, national industrialization was at least salvaged from total disruption and the regime just taking a footing could avert being destabilized. The completion of socialist transformation in 1956 contributed a lot to the viability of mass mobilization for the primitive accumulation of national industrialization.

State capitalist industry along the lines of the Stalinist model of introducing heavy and military industries quickly took root in China. To accommodate this system, all private sectors and peasant household economy were converted by "the socialist transformation" in 1956. Social units composed of urban institutions and rural cooperatives were formed in the process. They later became the carrier of nation-wide mobilization. It was only with cooperatives that the government was able to fulfil a lot of tasks requiring a large extraction of surplus value from the countryside, for example, staple foods purchase, building agricultural infrastructure and pension for the families of deceased soldiers. However, the burden on cooperatives therefore became too heavy. Some peasant households would rather withdraw from the cooperatives[8] (Table 2).

In 1960, China had recorded the highest fiscal revenue since 1949 with RMB 57.229 billion. However, the economic growth dropped

---

[8]叶扬兵 (Ye Yangbing) "1956—1957 年合作化高潮后的农民退社风潮" (The Tide of Peasants Withdrawing from the Cooperatives after the 1956–1957), *Nanjing University Journal (Philosophy, Human Sciences and Social Sciences)*, 2003(6).

Table 2 Composition of different economic sectors (Unit: %)

Year	Public economy			Non-public	
	State-owned	Collective		Capitalist economy	Individual economy
		Cooperative	Private–public Joint-venture		
1952	19.1	1.5	0.7	6.9	71.8
1957	33.2	56.4	7.6	0.0	2.8
1978	56.2	42.9	0.9		
1997	41.9	33.9	24.2		
2005	31.0	8.0	61.0		

Data source: National Bureau of Statistics, 伟大的十年 (The Great Ten Years). Beijing: People's Press, 1959, p. 36; "数字看变化: 国有经济地位稳固非公经济比重上升" (State-owned Economy Steady, Non-public economy Rising) https://www.jia odong.net/news/system/2002/10/08/00532129.shtml; 李成瑞 (Li Chengrui), "关于我国目前公私经济比重的初步测算" (Preliminary Estimation of the Ratio of Public and Private Economies) https://www.wyzxsz.com/Article/Class4/200605/6832.html. Quoted from 王绍光 (Wang Shaoguang), "坚守方向、探索道路: 中国社会主义实践六十年" (Sixty Years of Socialist Practices in China), 中国社会科学 (China Social Science), 2009(5)

below zero with the situation described above. Furthermore, a huge fiscal deficit was also recorded due to over-investment into infrastructure by the state. Under government corporatism, the urban economy was mired in a recession as a result of the fiscal crisis. Urban employment crumbled from the peak of 130 million in 1960 to 45.37 in 1962, a deep cut of 80 million in two years.

As a response to the crisis, the government had to take a "recuperative policy" in 1961, mobilizing millions of urban citizens to countryside in order to release the unemployment pressure in the urban sector. By the expulsion of labour, state industrial capital in cities could achieve a "soft-landing" in the urban economy.

During the recession in 1961–1962, government's annual fiscal revenue further dropped from 57.23 to 31.36 billion, back to the level of 1957. At the same time, China had to face the problem of food scarcity. Since 1950, the national debt to the USSR had amounted to about US$ 5.4 billion, which were to be repaid by agricultural and pasture products, as well as precious minerals. The shortage of agricultural products within the country led to disastrous consequences.

The estimation of China's population change during 1960–1962 has been controversial and charged with political implication. According to the revised data published by the government in 1982, the population growth curve turned downwards during these three years. Some researchers estimate that population growth for this period had failed to reach estimated projections by some 20 million. Most of this was caused by declining fertility and infant mortality because of malnutrition. And part of the rising adult mortality could be directly attributed to starvation. In official documents, the economic crisis and depression during these years was known as "three years of natural disaster".

The economic recovery in 1962–1963 was in fact not due to growth in urban industrial sector and employment. The reason was instead the concession to the peasants. Under the pressure of crisis, the government had to adjust the policy of rural collectivization. Traditional peasant economy based on village community in Rural China was once again granted with permission. Peasant households were allowed to partly withdraw from the highly collectivized economy which served the state industrial capital. First, the all commanding economy based on people's communes was converted into village economy based on production brigades, which were formed based on natural village as the basic unit of accounting and administration. This meant that traditional village-based peasant economy was allowed to partly withdraw from the state-initiated collectivized economy at county level. Second, peasant households were permitted to independently cultivate some of the reserved lands within production brigade (natural village), which meant mixed-operation rural households were allowed to partly withdraw from the collectivized economy that was strictly controlled by the state.[9] In practice, the state capitalist government taking shape during the "complete sovietisation" in the 1950s relieved part of its control over the peasants. Because of it, agricultural production gradually recovered. Fiscal revenues increased thanks to continuous production growth. The weight of agricultural tax in national fiscal revenues rose from 8% in the 1950s during the first

---

[9]At that times, the lands peasant households could reserve for their disposal amounted to about 15% of total arable lands. Fifteen years later in 1977, a reform in rural economy similar to this practice was staged, known as "joint production responsibility contract system". In fact it was because the government retreated from agriculture which was no longer profitable.

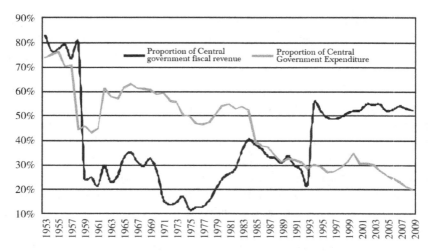

Fig. 5 The weight of central Government's fiscal revenues and expenditures 1953–2009

phase of national industrialization to 22%. The fiscal condition was ameliorated.[10]

The variation in policy was reflected on fiscal revenues and expenditures, as well as the weight of central government's share in the total fiscal budget. After 1961, the central government resumed its centralized management on national economy, taking back the power that had been decentralized a few years before. The central government's fiscal expenditures stayed above 50% and even 60% except a few years. It was until 1984 when the central and local governments had separate fiscal budgets did the power of the central government decrease (Fig. 5).

---

[10]Wen Tiejun, "周期性经济危险及对应政策分析" (Analysis on Cyclic Economic Crises and the Measures in Response), https://www.macrochina.com.cn/zhtg/20010608007807.shtml.

3   The Third Crisis (1968–1970): Strategic Adjustment of "Three Defence Lines Construction"[11] and Economic Crisis

During the late 1960s, a period which is now regarded as the "ultra-leftist age", the third crisis, also the second cyclic crisis since kick-starting the primitive accumulation for industrialization, broke out. Apart from general economic factors, it was characterized by the reaction of the super structure on the economic base.

At that time, China was under a total blockade and faced the pressure of an intense geo-political situation. At the same time, the governmental system built to accommodate the USSR model heavy-industry had been shown to be incompatible with the later "self-reliance and recalcitrant struggle" economic principle based on the mass mobilization. Both the external geo-politics and internal bureaucratism exerted reaction on the economic base shaped earlier by USSR investment. The latter had to adjust itself. In this complication, China suffered from another "deficits plus unemployment" crisis in the urban economy after repaying huge amount of foreign debt.

Before this crisis, there were debates on the guiding principle of the Third Five Year Plan and the abortion of the National Planning Committee. The Second Five Year Plan was aborted after the USSR withdrew strategic investment in 1957. In the early 1960s, chief officials responsible for economy, discussing the Third Five Year Plan, proposed to adjust the weight between agriculture, light and heavy industries, as a remedy to the Stalinist state capitalist structure which relied too much on heavy-military industry.

From the perspective of improving China's economic structure, it was definitely correct. Nevertheless, the most imminent problem then was the intensifying geo-political situation. China was up against with a series of regional "hot" confrontations: Kuomintang's attempt to strike back, China-India War and the Indochina wars. At the same time, American

---

[11]Translator's note: 三線建設 (*sanxian jianshe*) can also be understood as "three tiers" construction as nowadays people in China would say tier 1, tier 2, tier 3 cities, etc. Here we use "three defense lines" to emphasize its national defense background.

battleships and airplanes were constantly trespassing China's territorial waters (over 800 incidents according to official records). Furthermore, both the USSR and the USA were exploring the possibility of a nuclear attack on China. During the Cold War, China was actually on the brink of hot war.

Therefore, despite various arguments on the principle of economic building during the 1960s, Mao's opinion prevailed. On the one hand, all the technological capacity had to be invested into developing nuclear weapon. As Mao said, "Even a beggar must have a stick to drive off dogs." On the other, it was felt that parts of the industrial infrastructure along the coastal regions should be relocated in the hinterland to minimize the risks of military destruction. A brink-of-war economic model took shape. The overall layout of the national industry had to be restructured into three major layers of defense lines whereas regional industries comprised respectively three layers of minor frontlines of their own.

Meanwhile, the National Planning Committee responsible for the Third Five Year Plan was replaced. The idea of transplanting a foreign institution according to the planned economy model as conceived by experts trained in and returned from the USSR became futile. Moreover, without external investment and market demand as the country under a total blockade, and the economic system being incompatible with the "self-reliance" economic line, the reform of the Soviet superstructure became imperative.

Without taking into consideration the surrounding geo-political situation, researchers applying western micro-economic theory would come up with an absolutely negative assessment on the Chinese economy during the 1960s. Furthermore, the more negative an evaluation is, the more politically correct it seems to be in terms of economic rationality. According to the cost-efficiency analysis, China's three-layer industrial layout aiming at defence consolidation was extremely costly yet without economic returns. During 1965–1975 (including the Fourth Five Year Plan), nearly half of the national infrastructure investment was put into the construction of three layers of defence lines. It is estimated that from

1965 to the 1980s the total funds invested into the "three defence lines" amounted to RMB 205.2 billion.[12]

Admittedly, the three-layer construction was merely a spatial translocation of state industrial capital. It did not "vertically" upgrade the industrial structure. After the enterprises were transferred deep into the hinterland and mountainous regions, they became disperse geographically and hard to coordinate. The increment of the cost of industrial development in the 1960s was remarkable. It inevitably led to fiscal deficits. When crisis broke out as a result, the state once again relied on transferring the cost of the urban economy to the rural sector.

Box 2: Three Defence Lines Construction Since the 1960s

In the 1950s, Soviet economic advisors had suggested that China must concentrate on coastal regions and northeast to accelerate economic development. At the beginning, China accepted the advice. However, after giving a second thought, Chinese leaders found it risky. As the Korean War was raging on, if all the 156 projects located in the Northeast close to Korea and coastal regions were susceptible to bombing, China's industrial system especially the defence industry would be on a shaky ground. Therefore, Mao Zedong and other leaders proposed that some of the projects should be allocated in the western regions. At least half of the military defence projects should be located in west China. After consultation with the USSR, 21 of the 106 civil industrial projects and 21 of the 44 military defence projects were located in the western regions.

During the First and Second Five Years Plans, the production bases of jet planes, tanks, rockets and battle ships were located in west China. Western regions laid the industrial foundation for steel making, electricity generation, coal extraction, petroleum, nonferrous metals, weapons, aviation, construction materials and electronics, etc.

1. The International Background

---

[12]李彩华 (Li Caihua) & 姜大云 (Jiang Dayun), "我国大 '三线建设' 的历史经验和教训" (China's Three Defence Lines Construction: experiences and lessons), *Northeast Normal University Journals (Philosophy and Social Science)*, 2005(4):89.

In the early 1960s, China was surrounded by a very harsh international environment. The major threats were from two superpowers, the USA and the USSR which were armed with atomic weapons.

In 1964, the USSR deployed a million soldiers along the border with China and sent troop into Mongolia. Some of its strategic missiles targeted China's major cities and military facilities, and were aimed at China's atomic bomb construction site.

Meanwhile, the USA was surrounding China. Since 1960–1964, several countries in the region formed an anti-China alliance with the US. There were a few dozen US military bases in the regions. In August 1964, the USA started to bomb Northern Vietnam.

Moreover, Chiang Kai Shek in Taiwan, supported by the USA, was planning to strike back on the mainland. Spy infiltration and armed attacks were frequent in coastal regions near Taiwan. Chiang planned to create a "guerrilla corridor" in the southeast.

Mao thought that the whole heavy and military industries in northeast China was under the attack range of the USSR. Major coastal cities were also within the airstrike of Chiang's military power. Even if the enemies did not use atomic weapons, most of China's industrial infrastructure would be destroyed in case of war. Meanwhile the western hinterland was beyond the military impact of the USSR and Chiang.

Therefore, from the perspective of war preparation, the central government made two decisions. First, China had to build an atomic bomb. Second, China would launch Three Defence Lines Construction. The layout of China's industrial infrastructure would be spread out with one line in coastal regions, the second in mid-China, and the third in west and northwest China. Mao emphasized the strategic importance of Three Defence Lines Construction. The atomic bomb project was also located in the third defence line.

Since 1965, some industrial enterprises in the coastal regions were moved to west and northwest China. In that year, most of the new projects were allocated in the western regions.

In 1969, a minor military clash between the USSR and China occurred in border. To deal with the military threat from the Soviet Union, Mao further proposed "minor three defence lines". Each province had to set up their three defence lines system. The major three defence lines and other minor three defence lines would make a holistic system.

Since 1970, "three defence lines projects" were financially prioritized by the central government.

Furthermore, these projects had to make use of special terrain and geographical features for better protection. They had to be far away from major and medium cities and disperse so that in case of nuclear war, these factories and research centres would remain intact and continue to function to support the front lines.

In a word, economic efficiency was not a major concern of these projects.

2. Financial and Managerial Support to the Three Defence Lines Construction

Three Defence Lines Construction was a systematic project requiring fiscal support and complementary industrial layout.

To complement the project, heavy industry, especially the steel industry had to be robust to provide military industry with materials.

Major military personnel and scientific talents were sent to western regions for the atomic project. During the Cultural Revolution, Mao ordered military takeover of some major "Three Defence Lines" projects, with soldiers directly working at these sites.

The projects were commanded by Party's Secretariat of the Central Committee and the State Council. Regional committees were also set up, all led by local first party secretary.

The related financial investment was enormous. During 1965–1975, nearly half of the national infrastructure fund was allocated to the projects. In 1965–1971, the total investment had amounted to RMB 34.08 billion, not including local minor projects.

According to the Fourth Five Years Plan, the defence industry cost RMB 9.123 billion in 1970–1972, about 16% of total industrial infras-tructure investment,[13] the highest three-year record between 1949 and 1985. By estimation, from 1964 to the mid-1980s, the total investment by the central government into the projects amounted to RMB 205.2 billion.

3. Military-heavy industry in western regions was consolidated by the Three Defence Lines Construction

Over 1100 large and medium size industrial, transportation and defence technology enterprises, research centres and universities were built accordingly. A geographically disperse industrial system with coordinating sectors such as transportation, electricity, coal, chemical industry, petroleum, construction materials and steel making, was formed.

The decision to build six major railways in the regions was made in August 1964 by the central government. By the mid-1980s a complex railways system was functioning in these regions. In addition, complex highway systems were also constructed. Together they laid the foundation for mining, logistics, industrial and defence construction.

4. The strategic significance of Three Defence Lines Construction

Three Defence Lines system granted China a relatively safe home front. At the same time, China's military deterrence began to take shape. The projects were quite unprecedented in world economic and military history.

In 1973 when the US and China became strategically closer in the new global geopolitical situation, the system had reached a certain scale. Judging from the military and technological level at that time, China was equipped with quite an indestructible home front which could support long-term war. The problem of industrial overconcentration of industry in the coastal cities had been ameliorated.

When visiting western regions in the early 1990s, former president Jiang Zemin called for a better understanding of the significance of the Three Defence Lines Construction from the perspective of the international background.

In 1999, the central government put forth the Western Development Strategy. It was based on the historical experience of the Three Defence Lines Construction, with the view of the practical need of contemporary economic construction.

Source: Liaoning Party History Research Laboratory, "毛泽东在1964年的一个重大决策: 建设大三线" (Mao Zedong's major decision in 1964: Three Defence Lines Construction), 决策探索 (Policy Decision Exploration) (II), 2009(2); 彭成刚 (Peng Chenggang), "斯大林模式

在中国的历史考察" (Stalin Model in China: A Historical Survey), Wuhan Polytechnic University Master Thesis, 2006: 40–41.

In the 1960s, China's self-reliant national industrialization depended on increasing governmental investment. Moreover, the pressure of debt repayment primarily to the USSR also contributed to fiscal deficits. The situation was aggravated by the country's declining growth rate. The response to crisis was in line with what happened during 1958–1960. Millions of young unemployed urban citizens were mobilized to country sides. Apart from munitions factories and three defence lines related construction which employed limited numbers of new workers, most of the urban industrial economy in coastal regions just maintained a state of simple reproduction.

In a word, the second crisis caused by fiscal deficits achieved "soft-landing" once again through transferring the cost of crisis to rural communities.

The economic inefficiency of the Three Defence Lines Construction has drawn many criticisms from scholars on the grounds of its rationale and necessity. Here, we do not want to get involved into this sort of dispute with presupposed value judgement. However, readers should be reminded of the facts used to be covered up by factional disputation. China's response to western geo-political strategy during the 1960s-70 s should not be explained by "left or right" ideologies originating from the west.

We suggest one should reflect on this problem based on the real situation relevant to China at that time. In the 1960s–1970s, China had paid an enormous cost to sustain the state capitalist industry bequeathed from the age of total sovietisation in the 1950s. Then what was being consolidated was the bureaucratic superstructure having footing on this economic base.

---

13 当代中国的基本建设(上)(Contemporary China's Infrastructure Construction Book 1). Beijing: China Social Science Press, 1989: 161.

4   The Fourth Crisis (1974–1976): The Last "Going to Mountains and Villages" Movement

Background: Foreign Debt in the 1970s—the Second Round of Introducing Foreign Capital at a Larger Scale to Adjust Economic Structure.

Before the twenty-first century, China was constantly under pressure of fiscal deficits. Economic crisis would lead to increasingly serious fiscal and financial deficits. The fiscal budget and finance was the core of superstructure, government being its agent. Hence, whenever there was a major policy change, the background was always a fiscal and financial problem.

In fact, all of the economic crises in modern China, including major regime changes in the twentieth century, were closely related with its opening to the world. For example, the Foreign Affairs Movement in late Qing introduced foreign facilities and raw materials, leading to fiscal, foreign exchange and currency crises. The Qing dynasty had been doomed long before it officially ended in 1911. The result of Foreign Affairs Movement was the formation of scattered regional industries controlled by local military powers. Nevertheless, the foreign factor China faced was not unchanging. It was the international environment in which China was deeply entangled whereas the institutional benefits were acquired by core countries and the costs were being transferred to the semi-periphery and periphery.

China's opening up before the twenty-first century could be attributed to the measures in response to the domestic scarcity of capital. It was a process of improving the conditions for foreign capital as a quid pro quo for the benefits of national industrialization. Entering into the twenty-first century, it became an active strategic choice of domestic industrial capital facing the problems of excess capacity and insufficient domestic demand, while the gaps between the rural and urban, the poor and the rich, as well as the developed and less-developed regions have been widening. Opening was now a channel to release overcapacity into international market. Domestic excess industrial capacity seeks new opportunities in international market while internal capital coming under the pressure of a mounting financial bubble is seeking cheap factors of production in China.

New Geopolitical Condition in the 1970s

In the 1970s, the international and geopolitical condition in which China was situated changed once again. As technology was developing in the 1960s, the first post-war global industrial structural adjustment took place. It was dominated by the advanced countries where labour cost rose up and capital-labour confrontation intensified. Labour-intensive industries were transferred to developing countries while the advanced countries devoted themselves to upgrading their economic structure to capital and technology-intensive industries. Those countries and regions without institutional barrier accepted this first round of industry transfers. Korea, Taiwan, Singapore and Hong Kong belonged to the Confucian cultural circle without major institutional barriers and therefore received industry transfer from Japan. They adopted an export-oriented strategy aiming at labour-intensive manufacturing. These economies experienced economic booms in a short period of time and were called the Four Little Dragons of Asia.

Nevertheless, the Four Little Dragons were geographically small. Industry transfer rapidly re-priced the production factors of the recipients. In order to secure profitability, capital seeking after short-term returns had to move into countries or regions where land, resources and labour were even lower in price.

1972 was a year pivotal for both China and the world. After the disintegration of the Bretton Woods system, global capitalist system moved onto a new stage. The supply of US dollar as a global currency was sky-rocketing. The economic structure of advanced countries became hyper-modernized and increasingly financialized, with industrial capital flowing out seeking after cheap labour, land and resources. The astronomical expansion of US money supply catalyzed financial innovation drawing open the curtains of the age of financial globalization, in which unfettered speculation of derivatives was encouraged so as to absorb excessive liquidity as the supply of dollar was no longer limited.

Meanwhile, lifting two decades of economic blockade, the USA was reconciled with China which took the chance to. Mao accepted the judgement of his generals and military advisors that a world war would not take place in the next 20 years. Under the military pressure from the USSR along the borders, he directed the rapprochement with the West. China took advantage of the acute confrontation between the two superpowers to turn to the West including Japan to reform its economic structure. However, it also had to make concessions to the West by adjusting its geo-political relationship with peripheral countries. For example, China promised to give up supporting communist movements in the regions. This once again afforded China with the chance to take part in the international division of labour and exchange. By introducing industrial facilities, technology and management models from the US, Europe and Japan, China started to adjust its economic structure which comprised too high a ratio of heavy industry and endeavored to establish a balanced industrial system with diversified sectors.

The principle of economic structural adjustment of the second introduction of foreign facilities, technology and management model since 1972 was actually congruent with the general thought of the Third Five Year Plan, which in 1963 had to be aborted so as to construct the three-layer industrial layout.

Gripping the chance, Premier Zhou Enlai proposed the "43 Plan", introducing US$ 4.3 billion of industrial facilities from western countries. China's second round of relatively autonomous opening was thus initiated. The projects were generally concentrated in coastal major industrial cities.

However, the cost of introducing even more expensive western technologies in the 1970s was obvious. Before long, economic crisis once again broke out.

Since the late 1960s and early 1970s, China made use of foreign exchange reserve as well as deferred payment to import US$ 4.24 billion of machinery.[14] Then instantly, China faced the problem similar to the

---

[14]石林 (Shi Lin), 当代中国的对外经济合作 (Contemporary China's Economic Cooperation). China Academy of Social Science Press, 1989: 320. Quoted in 崔新健 (Cui Xinjing), 中国利用外资三十年 (China Making Use of Foreign Capital in 30 Years). China Financial and Economic Press, 2008: 6.

time after the First Five Year Plan was completed, when it "opened up" to the USSR: the state's lack of capability to sustain investment to enlarge reproduction. After 1974, fiscal deficits broke through RMB 10 billion whereas the total fiscal budget at that time was less than 80 billion.

Confronted with a serious fiscal crisis, the state, by path dependence, once again mobilized urban surplus labour to villages. Such was the third and last "Going to Mountains and Villages Movement". During 1974–1976, millions of capable labours not being absorbed by the urban economy were sent to rural collectives, as the direct cost-transfer of crisis from cities to the *sannong*. However, since the Cultural Revolution had ended and urban youngsters were no longer so enthusiastic to be mobilized, they were reluctant to leave cities. Furthermore, high level of investment had created some new employment opportunities in cities after 1972. As a result, the third movement did not run as smoothly as on previous occasions. Social discontent was mounting.

Then Mao Zedong, Zhou Enlai and Zhu De, the old generation of leaders who embodied revolutionary authority, passed away one after one. The appointed new leadership was more ambitious but less experienced. With rising fiscal deficits, the Hua Guofeng administration conceived an even bigger plan of introducing facilities and technologies. In 1978 alone, China signed contracts of 22 big projects up to US$ 7.8 billion in value and other letters of intent involving another US$ 5 billion with foreign parties. Meanwhile the fiscal revenue in 1978 was merely about RMB 113.2 billion. This round of economic adjustment by Mao's successor led to a fiscal deficit stock of more than RMB 30 billion in 1979–1980.

Consequently a typical stagflation crisis broke out. Counter-crisis measures later known as "reform" were put forth.

The "43 Plan" of Mao and Zhou in the 1970s and Hua's "82 Plan" differed only in amount. The contents were consistent. After the USA lifted the blockade in early 1970s, China had introduced large scale industrial facilities from the West and Japan. Therefore we would group them together as the "second foreign investment" in a continuous economic process. The second foreign investment differed from the previous in one aspect: the condition of the first investment in the 1950s was a strategic partnership. A number of Russian experts were sent from the USSR to help China. Therefore China could save a lot of technolog-ical and management cost. However, turning to the West and Japan since mid-1970s, China now had to pay expensive service cost (later known as the tertiary industry).

Similar to the first foreign investment from the USSR building China's national industrialization, this second occasion involved government corporatist behaviour at the central administration level. Furthermore, the state industry shaped by introducing the assembly line system from the USSR could not be effectively managed without the formation of a soviet superstructure. We may suggest the political unrest in the 1960s was the result of a painful attempt and failure to reshape the path dependence of the Soviet institution after the interruption of Russian aid. Likewise, the reform pushed by the central government since the late 1970s has been the reconstruction of superstructure corresponding to the economic base of the urban economy according to the western capitalist model. Now the government officials were obliged to painstak-ingly transform their mind and practices. They had to abandon the old mentality along with the whole obsolete institutions transplanted from the USSR. Otherwise, they would be incompatible with the new institu-tional requirements necessitated by the western model of production and management. Reforms in economic and political systems were gradually proposed by these officials in charge of the economy. In a sense, it is a passive form of institutional evolution.

Ironically, these two occasions of introducing strategic foreign invest-ment were later criticized by the CPC's second generation leadership in the early 1980s after the power transition. The first was denigrated as "ultra-leftist" impetuosity whereas the second a "foreign leap forward," echoing the Great Leap Forward in the early 1960s. Nonetheless, the administrations after the 1980s followed the path dependence sustaining government corporatism and directly introduced foreign capital.

Admittedly people of that generation could not understand their situ-ation as we can. But surprisingly, many researchers nowadays are not totally free from similar ideological judgment. Only by contextualizing these historical events into their real material conditions can we better understand the choices and actions of the social actors at a particular historical moment instead of putting simple ideological labels on them.

We wish the readers may grasp the historical continuity of this long process and, accordingly, have a better reflection on the Western-centric discourse in explaining China's Reform.

In conclusion, the state in Mao's age took advantage of the incomplete rural land ownership and intervened in heavy-handed fashion to organize the collectivized economy in the rural sector. It did not consider the development of agricultural productivity level or take care of the interests of the peasants. Nonetheless, it did play an unexpected function in the primitive accumulation for national industrialization. Collective and even distribution could not lead to a proper incentive mechanism. However, it was characterised by a traditional practice within small rural communities, namely resolving the risk of externality by internalizing it in the community. This may be called the peasant socialism with Chinese characteristics. Thanks to it, 40 million young unemployed urban citizens were accommodated into rural communities.[15] In 20 years, the *sannong* had, at least on three occasions, silently bore the cost of cyclic urban economic crisis caused by state capitalism.

After Mao's death in 1976, none of his successors had similar authority and charisma to mobilize unemployed urban citizens to villages in the event of urban economic crises. Afterward, most of the crises had to take "hard-landing" in cities, except the two occasions of 1979–1980 and 2008–2009.

---

[15]At personal level, many of these young urban citizens in retrospect may consider it a traumatized experience as they were being deprived of urban welfare and a normal youth. However, few of them would be grateful to the peasants who generously accepted the obligation to feed 40 millions without feeling being traumatized.

4

Three Endogenous Economic Crises since the Reform and Corresponding Resolutions 1978–1997

According to the authoritative and official phase-demarcation put forward by former President Hu Jintao, China has entered the "intermediate phase of industrialization" at the turn of the twenty-first century. The development path of industrial countries in general shows that the intermediate stage may be further divided into the stages of "industrial capital structural adjustment" and then "global industrial capital configuration adjustment as well as expansion". These are inevitable stages that follow the completion of primitive accumulation for industrialization. During this phase, the scope of flow and integration of production factors as well as the extent of institutional transition costs transfer would both expand significantly.

Within this intermediate phase of industrialization, that is, from 1978 when the Reform and Opening-Up started to 1997 when the Asian Financial Crisis broke out during which industrial capital structural adjustment occurred, China experienced three economic crises. Chronologically these would be the 5th, 6th and 7th crises in the seventy years of contemporary Chinese history since 1949. Furthermore, similar to the cyclical crises that took place during the "initial phase of

© The Author(s) 2021
Wen Tiejun, *Ten Crises*, Global University for Sustainability Book Series,
https://doi.org/10.1007/978-981-16-0455-3_4

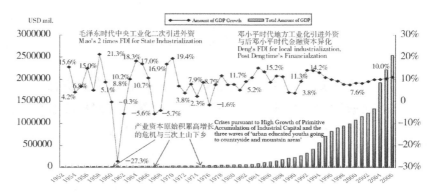

Fig. 1   China's Macro-economic growth and fluctuations 1952–2006

industrialization," the occurrence of all these three crises was mainly caused by domestic economic factors.

Under the constraints arising from the contradiction within the urban–rural dichotomy—the fundamental institution in China—a series of rural reforms, such as rural "de-organization" and marketization of produce, implied that it was no longer possible to make use of the organization of rural collectivization to absorb unemployed urban laborers, nor to extract more surplus from the *sannong*. As a result, except for the 5th crisis in early 1980s during which the launch of rural reforms had facilitated urban economic recovery, both the 6th in 1988–1989 and the 7th in 1993–1994 were forced to take hard-landing in urban sector, in turn causing significant negative impact on the *sannong*.

Another aspect was similar to the general experience of countries and regions that have already formed a complete industrial capital structure. The amplitudes of economic fluctuations in China during these three occasions that took place in the intermediate phase of industrialization had notably narrowed. China was still able to sustain a growth amid the institutional transition with "Chinese characteristics". (Fig. 1 shows year by year economic fluctuations since the establishment of New China.)

After mid-1990s, China was integrated into the international economic system. Its macro-economic fluctuations became increasingly aligned with the global macro-economic cycle. To some extent it led to the situation that since 1997, Chinese government had to face "imported" (exogenous) crises. The crisis in 1998 was induced by the

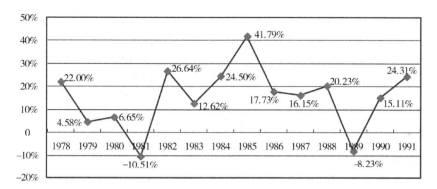

Fig. 2 Growth rate in total fixed investments by state-owned units 1978–1991 (Data source: *China Statistical Yearbooks*)

Asian financial crisis and the 2009 crisis was caused by the Wall Street financial crisis in 2008. Both of these led to drastic declines in overseas demand. Therefore, the "bailout" measures taken by the government responding to external factors were quite different from the austerity measures adopted during the previous six crises. We will discuss these two exogenous crises in Chapter 5.

The curve in the diagram showed that during the "intermediate phase of industrialization", the gap between the eruptions of the 5th (1980) and 6th (1988) crisis was 7–8 years. Back then the economy was still mainly state-owned/operated, and investments were largely government funded. In both cases the macro-regulation measures adopted by the government were similar, which meant cutting the scale of investments, hence the large declines in the investment growth rates—10.51% in 1981, 8.23% in 1989, in turn leading to faster decline of the macro-economy (Fig. 2).

However, the economic crisis led to the 1989 Tiananmen incident and what followed was the second blockade of China by the West (the first blockade had been lifted in 1971), accompanied by the clamors of "China collapse". After that, what happened in early 1990s was a strong push to accelerate economic reform, with deepening marketization and financialization, as well as Deng Xiaoping's "Southern Inspection Speech" which was in complete opposition to the previously effective austerity policy. The main contents of these policies were the concessions to local authorities to empower their autonomy to expand the scale of attracting investment and directly take the gains from local resource capitalization. It could be seen as a bargain for the political support from local governments to consolidate the second generation core collective leadership of the central. Compared to the formation of the first generation core collective leadership through revolution, this process eventually strengthened the authority and legitimacy of China's new centralized system. Its direct institutional costs might indeed have been reduced but people seldom raised the issue of indirect costs. Judging from what actually happened afterwards, one of the indirect costs might be a shorter gap between crises, from 7 to 8 years as was the case between 1988 and 1993–1994 to once every 5 years afterwards.

Among the economic activities launched in the name of "market economy" in 1992 on the 14th National Congress by the CPC Central Committee, the main and most substantive one showed in the form of local authorities' autonomy to drive forward government corporatism by drawing support from Deng's Southern Inspection Speech, which eventually gave rise to economic overheating and had the central government take the liabilities for foreign debt. The central government did not have a sufficient share of the fiscal revenues to bear that cost. Therefore it had no option but to accelerate monetization—money printing machines operated round the clock to increase money supply in large quantity. Simultaneously, three speculative markets: real estate, securities and futures, took the opportunity to liberalize, instantly attracting speculative funds from different walks of life in the society. Short-term investments grew aggressively and severe inflation emerged. Wherever speculative capital are building up within a short time span on a large scale, systematic economic risks intrinsic to it will intensify as a rule. China was no exemption. It rapidly triggered the economic crisis of 1993–1994, the substances of which were serious deficits in three major sectors directly controlled by the central government—fiscal, financial and balance of payments (Image 1).

With an economy overheating and at the same time encountering the three major deficits, the third plenary of the 14th Congress affirmed the line of "comprehensive reform". The Chinese government adopted in 1994 a stop-loss approach and introduced austerity measures that were

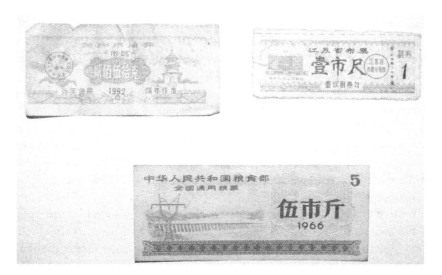

Image 1 In the 1950s to 1990s, China had issued various coupons for various consumer goods in specific periods. Back then, people had to have coupons in order to purchase corresponding goods. After the Reform and Opening-up, these coupons that witnessed the transformation of eras gradually faded out of people's lives

even broader and tougher than the ones later taken by the European Union in response to the European debt crisis. Major reforms in three realms were kick-started: the Renminbi devaluation, the marketization of foreign exchange by converging the official and market foreign exchange rates, and the Tax Division Reform between central and local governments. To supplement these, stringent macro-regulation measures were applied to tighten liquidity and land supply.

These three major measures were still limited to the regulation of resource flow. However, there were another two crucial and unprecedented measures related to the disposal of public assets: the government's retreat from two major aspects—from many state-owned enterprises (SOEs) and from public welfare provision. On the former, marketization reform of state-owned assets was launched. The government retreated from inefficient small and medium non-monopolized SOEs. Many SOEs would directly lay off workers, streamline operations and reduce headcounts to increase efficiency. On the latter, the SOEs introduced the marketization of staff housing accommodation (equivalent to the "public rental housing" in new pro-livelihood policy that has been a priority in recent years) as well as the commercialization of education, medical care and so on.

Eventually, after disposing of public assets stock at low prices in various ways, a large amount of non-performing debts were left on the books of banks and handed over to successors. After paying an enormous cost—tens of millions of workers laid off, tens of thousands of mass protest incidents, a decline in people's income resulting in weak domestic demands and so on—China finally achieved the so-called "soft-landing" in 1996.

Yet just when this successful soft-landing was announced by the media to the world, China had to face yet another setback due to the 1997–1998 Asian financial crisis which led to a decline in overseas demand. Instantly, with low demands both domestic and overseas, China became entrapped in a deflation lasting 3–4 years.

In the second half of the 1990s, given that China had already transformed to a growth model mainly relying on external demands and infra-structure investments, Chinese economy encountered the 8th economic crisis since its industrialization under the impact of external factors before it could fully recover from the previous one. That 8th crisis was also what this book refers to as the first imported (exogenous) economic crisis in contemporary China.

From the start of the Reform till the year 1997, the three crises (chronologically the 5th, 6th and 7th) had one thing in common, unlike the crises that had happened before—they could no longer directly transfer the costs to the *sannong* through government mobilizations and mandatory resettlement of surplus urban laborers on a large scale to the rural sector, which would then alleviate the unemployment pressure in cities. That was because after years of over-extracting agricultural surplus for urban industrialization, the *sannong* had become debilitated. Now as the urban sector became the state's main source of fiscal revenue, rural collectivization had completed its historical mission of serving the primitive accumulation of state capital. What followed was the government's retreat from the *sannong* that had no more surplus to extract from, with the household contract system. The state-organized rural collectivized economy then disintegrated and traditional peasant community that had been sustained for thousands of years now revived. The 200 million geographically and economically scattered peasant households could no longer accommodate surplus urban laborers on a large scale.

We attempt to point out the major differences between different policies in response to various crises. The rural reform which in fact constituted the retreat of the government from the non-profitable agricultural sector, brought institutional gains to the micro-economic realm with an active peasant economy and general increases in agricultural production. Yet in terms of the institutional costs in the macro-economy, it was manifested as "hard-landing" on urban sector whenever crisis took place hereafter.

In comparison, China begun to strengthen the investments into the debilitated *sannong* through the New Countryside Construction strategy since 2005. With the high profile "government re-entrance" into the agricultural sector, it was possible to again achieve a "soft-landing" in the 2008–2009 "imported" inflationary crisis, which relied on the rehabilitation of the *sannong*.

It is necessary to further point out that due to differences in their macroeconomic contexts and institutional orientation between the 1997 crisis and the three crises ending up at hard-landing in cities before that, the respective measures adopted were remarkably different. So were their impact on the *sannong*.

After the 5th crisis broke out in cities in 1980 many enterprises were closed down or merged, or transited to other operations. The consequence was the emergence of large numbers of unemployed youths, which gave rise to crimes and delinquency issues. To deal with the severe situation, the central government launched two major crack-down campaigns.

Yet the 5th crisis had precisely been the impetus for the rural reform, and had occurred in step with the rural reform. By making use of the *sannong* to develop county economy involving mainly rural industrialization and townization (an appropriate scale of urbanization in organic relation with the rural), it was possible to substantially boost domestic demand with the peasants as consumers. That in turn had kick-started the national economic recovery, and before long a high growth resumed. Regretfully, this self-initiated institutional experience embodying Chinese characteristics that had driven country-wide economic growth largely through domestic demands from rural sector have been interpreted through the ideology of vulgar economics, resulting in the failure to learn from this experience as a reference for analysis and comparison to deal with problems.

As for the 6th crisis in 1988, although it had still ended with a typical hard-landing in cities, under the dual structure of urban–rural dichotomy, the rural enterprises had been the first to take the impact of government macro regulation. The costs of the crisis were partially transferred to the *sannong*. The repercussions were wide-spread closing down of rural enterprises and an accelerating decline in non-agricultural employment as well as in peasant cash incomes for three consecutive years. What inevitably resulted was the decline of domestic demand, and that in turn led to the transformation of GDP growth driven by domestic demand to its partial reliance on external demands (export).

The 7th crisis in 1993–1994, if analysis is to be made based on its nature rather than simply as a cyclical phenomenon, it could be considered as an extension of the 1988–1989 crisis. The policy makers back then, lacking experience in handling this stagflation crisis thus adopting inappropriate measures, had created too high a cost which gave rise to the 1993–1994 crisis. If historical comparisons are made on a non-ideological manner, then this crisis would be comparable to the Great Depression that swept through the West in 1929–1933.

Based on an objective analysis, the major cause of the 7th crisis was economic overheating due to regional overinvestment across the country, stimulated by Deng's Southern Inspection speech that justified a greater autonomy to local authorities. Having to bear the full liabilities for foreign debts incurred by regional investments but taking little institutional gains from it, the central government initiated in emergency the 'monetization' reform, with its institutional gain completely belonging to the central government. That was accompanied by the bloom of three major high-risk markets—real estate, stocks and futures—with turbulent volatility. Eventually, by the end of 1993 serious deficits appeared in fiscal budget, state financial system and balance of payments along with the inflation surge. Next, the central government introduced in 1994 the tax division reform while expanding public debts and money supply on a large scale. Moreover, the RMB was devaluated by a staggering 52% at once. These macroeconomic reforms that aimed to secure the interests of the central government led to a surging CPI, reaching 24% in 1994, the highest record since the Reform.

Unfortunately, these lessons with Chinese characteristics concerning government corporatism as well as the central-local governments relationship have not been seriously discussed in an objective and non-ideological manner.

At that point, to alleviate fiscal pressure the government also implemented the policy of "offloading fiscal burden"', or the "government retreat" as some academicians have eulogized. The SOEs underwent a wide scope of reforms. The government, which should have encouraged employment, directly pushed ahead with the policy of layoffs, streamlining and reducing headcounts to improve SOE efficiency. As a result, tens of millions of workers in SOEs who had not been in time to enjoy mandatory social security plans set up by the government were forced to leave their workplaces with little compensation. Many were forced to cash in their tenure at a low rate, becoming a group of "three no's"—no jobs, no security and no housing.

This kind of practical experience of weathering serious crisis by "deepening reform" is not something that any country in the world would dare to learn from, not to mention the European countries in the midst of a debt crisis.

Nevertheless, for the *sannong*, the impact of this round of governmental policies was relatively positive. In order to control the impact of inflation on the peasants, the central government was raising the official price of staple grain consecutively by more than 100% for three years from 1993 to 1996. It in practice stabilized the peasants' agricultural income growth in that period. Furthermore, the reform in 1992 of completely abolishing the food coupons system had largely removed the main obstacle of rural to urban mobility. The tide of "migrant workers" took shape from there.

These cyclical crises occurring during the intermediate phase of industrialization are to be analyzed in more details in following pages.

1   1979–1980: The First Economic Crisis since the Reform and Economic Recovery with the Help of the *Sannong*

Up until now, when people talk about the marketization reform of Chinese economy, they would as a rule consider the CPC Third Plenary of the 11th Congress in 1978 as the starting point. Very few people however have seriously looked into the relevant documents from that meeting which is regarded as a historical milestone. The question is: was there any reference in those documents that clearly indicated the initiation of marketization by the CPC? If one could not find such reference, then one should simply resort to a patient examination of what actually happened at that time and how the government responded to it.

We have already pointed out in previous researches that China's economic institutional reforms usually originated from responsive measures taken by the government in times of economic crisis.[1] Nevertheless, people are generally bound by particular ideological inclinations and would not discuss it from that perspective.

The central government had started the dual-price system reform as early as 1979, allowing both central planning and market to set prices on targeted goods with the same value. In the same year, a decision was also made to transform the international trade system. Any projects that could help to ease the pressure of repaying foreign debts would be approved.

It is necessary to further point out that the over-investments in urban industries in late 1970s even under the pressure of foreign debts and budget deficits would inevitably lead to economic crisis and depression, and so they did come one after the other in 1979–1981. With the passing away of Mao in 1976, the government in a transition phase could no longer directly transfer the crisis costs to the *sannong* as it did in previous crises. Consequently the crisis had a hard-landing in cities, which then led to the rural reform, referred to as 'Household Contract' system,

---

[1]Wen Tiejun, '中国经验与比较优势 (Chinese Experience and Comparative Advantage)', 开放时代 (Open Era), 2008(2).

which in essence meant the government's retreat from the non-profitable agriculture sector.

Since certain important institutions in the rural economy previously carried by collective organizations (such as irrigation, rural credit unions, grain stations and various agriculture-related departments) had to bear the costs of the institutional transformation regarding the government's retreat, the institutional gains were also by and large left with the rural regions. Thus, almost simultaneous to the micro-economic reform of reviving peasant mixed operation on a household basis, the rural sector took the opportunity to develop autonomous industries, commerce and finance. Through this development, the rural economy rapidly stimulated China's economic recovery to another phase of high growth (Images 2 and 3).

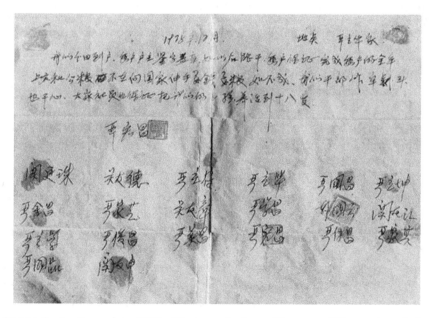

Image 2 In December 1978, 18 peasants from Xiaogang Village signed the household contract with their fingerprints in red. According to an interview with the then local party committee secretary, this contract kept in the museum is not the original, but a replicate

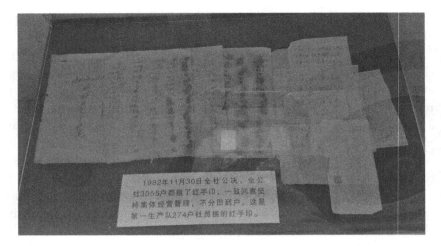

Image 3 In November 1982, members of the Zhoujiazhuang Commune signed with red fingerprints appealing to maintain the commune system (Source: Zhoujiazhuang People's Commune Exhibition Hall, Jinzhou, Hebei Province)

How the First Crisis Since the Reform Happened and the Characteristics It Displayed

If the year 1978 is to be regarded as the starting point of reform following mainstream ideology, then it was right at the first step of reform in the years 1979–1981 that an economic crisis took place.

After the surge of investments in 1978–1979, and given the strict austerity measures adopted, China tumbled into serious depression. Considering the fact that under a market economic system people would usually use the macro-economic growth rate as a measure to tell whether an economic crisis occur or not, we may look into the figures at that time. The economic growth recorded a decline from 11.7% in 1978 to 5.2% in 1981. The growth of fixed investments, represented mainly by fixed asset investments in SOEs, showed even more severe decline, from 22% in 1978 to barely 4.58% in 1979. It then went up to 6.65% in 1980 but a negative growth of −10.51% was recorded in 1981.

The economic crisis this time was mainly caused by the huge fiscal deficits that had emerged in the late 1970s. The reason was two-fold:

first the accumulation of over investments since the 1970s and second, the recuperative policy adopted by the government in a transition phase, with the consequence of a rapid increase of welfare and subsidy expenditures. In early 1970s Zhou Enlai personally formulated and directed the "43" project, importing western industrial equipment and facilities valued at US$ 4.3 billion, with the aim of making use of the technology, management and services by developed countries to adjust China's domestic industrial structure that was weighted toward military and heavy industries. From mid-1960s to the 1970s China imported mechanical equipment on a large scale through deferred payment and foreign currency deposits in the Bank of China, totaling US$ 4.24 billion.[2] That became a crucial reason of its fiscal deficits exceeding 10 billion yuan since 1974.

The accumulated fiscal deficits from the 4th Five-year Plan, drawn up in conjunction with the "43" project, was yet to be settled. Under such circumstances the new leadership made further attempts in 1976–1978 to expand the scale of introducing technology from the West. The proposal budget was US$ 8.2 billion while there was no assessment of project feasibility and domestic capability to accommodate these projects. In implementation, 22 mega project agreements were signed with foreign countries in 1978 alone, amounting to as much as US$ 7.8 billion. In addition there was another US$ 5 billion of projects from memorandums of intention that were yet to be signed. The total fiscal revenue that year in China was only 113.2 billion yuan.

The Chinese economy was then run differently from a market economy. When the Reform first started, China was still under a system in which the government centralized investments and played a dominant role in allocating resource. The government was the largest investment agent and actor. Therefore, over-investment would put an enormous pressure on the fiscal budget. Furthermore, prompted by the impetus arising from the endeavors by local governments and various authorities, over investment would often keep its momentum.

---

[2]Shi Lin (石林), 当代中国的对外经济合作 (Foreign Economic Cooperation in Contemporary China). China Social Science Press, 1989: 320. Quoted from Cui Xinjian (崔新健), 中国利用外资三十年 (China Making Use of Foreign Capitals for Thirty Years). China Financial & Economic Publishing House, 2008: 6.

Even though the central government had put forth the slogan of "fine-tune, rectify, reform, enhance" in 1979 and a key policy was to cut the scale of investment, it was not actually reduced in 1979–1980.

Box 1: Over-Investment in Industrialization 1978–1981

In November 1977, the National Planning Meeting proposed that by the end of 20th century, the production volume of major industrial products would come close, catch up and then overtake most developed capitalist countries. Key industrial production would become automated. Mass transit would be on high-speed to a large extent. And key production skills would be modernized. Various economic and technological benchmarks would also close up on, catch up and surpass the advanced level of the world. In the government report presented in February 1978, Hua Guofeng proposed to undertake around 120 major projects during 1978–1985, in the areas of fuel, power, steel, non-ferrous metals, chemical industry as well as railroad, ports and so on. Among these were 30 major power stations, 8 major coal mining bases, 10 major oil and natural gas fields, 10 major iron and steel factories and 9 major non-ferrous metal factories. In July 1978, the State Council Discussion Meeting further proposed a "Great Leap Forward" to make use of foreign capitals boldly and import advanced technology and equipment on a large scale.

In 1978 alone, agreements were signed with foreign countries to introduce 22 major projects from abroad. Adding to that the memorandums of intent, a total of US$ 13 billion, about RMB 39 billion would be needed. And adding the domestic matching ancillary projects of over 20 billion yuan, the total amount was more than 60 billion yuan.

Of the 22 projects to be imported in whole, about half in terms of the total transactional value were actually signed hurriedly during the last ten days of 1978, many of them previously not included in the original plan.

In terms of the actual implementation, the total investment on SOE fixed asset countrywide in 1978 was 66.9 billion yuan, an increase of 21.9% from the year before. Among this, infrastructure building totaled 50.1 billion yuan, higher than the previous year by 31.1%. Industrial infrastructure amounted to 27.3 billion yuan, an increase of 55.8%. At the end of 1978, projects-in-progress in enterprise under the Whole People Ownership numbered 65,000 with a total investment of 370 billion yuan. 8.3 million tons of steel was imported in 1978, higher than 1977 by 65%. The imported quantity had accounted for 37.6% of total domestic production but it was still insufficient to meet the demand.

Since the proportion of heavy to light industries was out of balance, the differential between the supply of market goods and the purchasing power was as high as 10 billion yuan.

Beginning in 1979, China undertook adjustments of the national economy. The State Planning Commission made major amendment to the original plan. The growth rate of total industrial production had been tuned to 8% from the original 10–12%. In actual, total industrial production value in1979 reached 468 billion yuan, higher than the prior year by 8.8%. It grew to 515.4 billion yuan in 1980, an annual growth of 9.3%. To cool down the overheating, 295 large and medium size projects were aborted or decelerated in 1979. Another 283 projects were further cut in 1980.

The regulation in 1979–1980 had been effective. Nevertheless it did not resolve one important problem that it should have, i.e. to suppress the scale of infrastructure investments. Infrastructure investments that were included in the 1979 state budget, after adjustment, was 36 billion yuan, lower than the previous year by 3.6 billion yuan. However, the actual number came to 39.5 billion yuan, only 0.1 billion yuan lower than 1978. For 1980, the budget was 24.1 billion yuan while in actual 28.1 billion. It did appear lower from the previous year by 28.9%. Yet, outside of the budget, various local authorities, sectors and enterprises had year over year increased in self-financed investments of 56.2%. As such, the total investments in 1980 actually came to 53.9 billion, higher than 1979 by 7.8% and the highest record in 30 years since 1949–1980. Among these, investments on industrial infrastructure (including those outside the budget) remained high as 29.2 billion, at par with the 1978 level and more than 1979 by 1.03 billion.

Source: Wang Haibo (汪海波) 中華人民共和國工業經濟史 (History of Industrial Economy in PRC). Shanxi Economic Publishing House: 1998, pp. 498–500, 506–507, 510–511.

In a country where the primitive accumulation happened endogenously, high level of investments during industrialization would mean a high degree of concentration and accumulation of social wealth. Yet looking at the actual situation, the accumulation rate in China had declined substantially in the period 1979–1982. A fast growth in various subsidies and welfare expenditures was one of the causes of fiscal difficulty. The policy makers back then had a consensus about this. The backdrop was that the industrial primitive accumulation from the 1950s to 1978 had relied mainly on excessive extraction of surplus from the society. As a result all the labor workers in the society—urban and rural—had been living at subsistence level during that period. Before the Third Plenary of the CPC 11th Congress in December 1978, the new administration put forward a new policy directive to build a moderately well-off society, with a series of recuperative measures: in cities, increasing the subsidies to SOEs to award bonuses to workers, improving workers housing condition, promoting employment and so on; in rural areas, raising the prices of agricultural produce, exempting taxes in poor regions, increasing agricultural support and so on. Given the political background at that time, these policies also had the political consideration of maintaining social stability during the transition from the first generation leadership to the second, i.e. by lowering the primitive accumulation in the society to exchange for majority support. In May 1978, the State Council made the decision that enterprises which had gone through a clean-up process and were in good operating conditions could experiment on bonus system and limited piecework wage. The proportion of bonus would in general not exceed 10% of an enterprise standard salary.[3]

---

[3] 中華人民共和國工業經濟史 (History of Industrial Economy in PRC: October 1949 to 1998), p. 497.

Box 2: Government Work Report Regarding Subsidies and Welfare Expenditures

Based on the 1980 Report on the Work of the Government, peasants' income in 1979 had increased by 10.8 billion yuan thanks to the development of agricultural production and a higher purchase prices of produce. Furthermore, with the exemption and reduction of taxes on agriculture and rural enterprises, peasants' tax burden was cut by 2 billion yuan. The income that was allocated to the peasants by the collectives had reached 83.4 yuan per person, higher than 1978 by 9.4 yuan, compared with an increase of 10.5 yuan only during the entire 11-year period from 1965 to 1976. In 1979, over 9 million people were given employment in cities. 40% of workers had salary rank promotion. Wage categories were adjusted in some regions. Subsidies for non-staple food were given to employees and bonus system was generally adopted in enterprises. The total salary paid to enterprise employees under the Whole People Ownership, including bonuses, had increased by 6 billion yuan from the prior year. Annual salary on average reached 705 yuan, higher than the year before by 61 yuan. New housing accommodation for the workers built in 1979 totaled 62.5 million square meters, higher than the previous year by 66% and highest since 1949. In the first half of 1980, the total accommodation space built came to 73.7 million sq. m. (*Source*: Report on the Work of the Government 1980 delivered by Vice Premier Yao Yilin on 30 August, 1980 at the Third Session of the Fifth National People's Congress: 'Report on 1980-1981 National Economic Plan Implementation'.)

Based on the 1981 Government Report, with higher purchasing prices for agricultural products paid by the state and the tax exemption on certain rural regions, the fiscal revenues recorded a total decrease of 52 billion yuan in 1979–1981. Moreover, with employments provided to over 20 million people, rural and urban combined, as well as rises in salary and adoption of bonus schemes, the total impact on the fiscal budget was 40.5 billion yuan. These two items totaling 92.5 billion exceeded the budget by more than 54%. Furthermore, state subsidies on agriculture-related use of fuel, electricity and fertilizers as well as on import of grain, cotton, sugar etc. amounted to 23.4 billion yuan. The weight of consumption in national income increased from 63.5% in

1978 to around 70% in 1981 while the proportion of capital accumulation went down correspondingly from 36.5% to 30%. (*Source*: Report on the Work of the Government 1981 delivered by then Premier Zhao Ziyang on 30 November and 1 December 1981 at the Fourth Session of the Fifth National People's Congress: 'Current Economic Situation and Direction of Economic Construction in Future'.)

The 1982 Report presented more details: from 1979 to 1981, 44.2 billion yuan was spent on raising the purchase prices of produce, 30 billion yuan on raising salary and bonus scheme, 10.5 billion yuan on providing employment for 26 million people in cities and towns, 15.2 billion yuan on increasing worker housing. In addition, rural tax exemption, increased subsidy on imported commodities and so on added up to a total expenditure of more than 140 billion yuan. (*Source*: Report on the Work of the Government 1982 by then Premier Zhao Ziyang on 30 November 1982 at the Fifth Session of the Fifth National People's Congress: 'Report on the Sixth Five-Year Plan'.)

The 1983 report summarized the living standard improvement for the people during the five years 1978–1982: average net income per capita for peasants reached 270 yuan in 1982, doubling that of 1978. During the five years, newly built accommodation in rural regions totaled 2.2 billion sq. m., with tens of millions of peasants moving into new homes. In cities and towns, employment was arranged for more than 38 million people. Furthermore, with wage increases and bonus scheme, the livelihood of workers also saw notable improvements. In 1982, workers in cities on average had disposable income of 500 yuan. Discounting the inflation factor, the growth was 38.3% from 1978. During the five years, state expenditures on urban worker accommodations came to 448 billion yuan with an area of 350 million sq. m., equaling the total area built in the 19 years before 1977.

Source: Report on the Work of the Government 1983 by then Premier Zhao Ziyang on 6 June 1983 at the First Session of the Sixth National People's Congress.

Considering the above two aspects in combination, the cause of the 1979–1981 fiscal crisis could be summarized as follows. With limited fiscal revenues, the government nevertheless wanted on one hand to strengthen industrial infrastructures by higher investment, and on the other hand prioritize the improvement on people's living standard. Both were beneficial to consolidating the new administration's legitimacy. Yet the generous outlays spent simultaneously on these two fronts were in competition with each other for the limited fiscal revenues. A society that had no resources coming from outside could hardly have high accumulation as well as high consumption at the same time. Whatever political system it adopts, relying on fiscal deficits and over-drawing government credit, a government would eventually result in severe fiscal difficulties.

In reality, the contradiction between consumption and accumulation had been concomitant with the primitive accumulation for industrialization in the first 30 years of the socialist China. Coming to 1979–1981 at the early days after the passing away of the first generation core leadership and with the coming on stage of the second generation, the choices the latter made were implicitly in line with the changes in the political situation at that particular moment. On the surface, welfare expenditures were non-elastic. A deeper reason was the rendering of social resources into social capital required particular historical condition and social background.

Quoting from the Report on the Work of the Government 1981, "[s]ince 1979, various expenditures for improving people's livelihood have increased substantially. Although the pace might be somewhat fast, yet overall it has been done right. At the same time, the reduction on infrastructure investments that was planned in the budget was not sufficiently met, and administration expenses have also continued to rise. That has resulted in total expenditures exceeding total fiscal revenues. Very large fiscal deficits have appeared in 1979 and 1980 consecutively. Money supply has been too high and general price is rising." Based on this report, the budget deficits in 1979 and 1980 were 17 and 12.7 billon yuan respectively.[4]

Yet in subsequent policy documents, the "over investment" took the "main responsibility" for the fiscal crisis and economic crisis.

In fact, whether the new administration had focused on investment or consumption, the transition of power that was completed in late 1970s to early 1980s ultimately had to pay the price in the form of an economic

---

[4]Quoted from *History of Industrial Economy in PRC October 1949 to 1998*, p. 497.

crisis. Furthermore, there was a causal relationship between that crisis and the economic reform.

Box 3: Contents in the Report on the Work of the Government Relevant to the Recognition of Fiscal Deficits as a Cause of the Crisis and Its Measures

With regard to the possible repercussions of large fiscal deficits, the central government was obviously well-aware. "If effective measures are not taken to resolve the problem, there will be another deficit of 11 billion yuan in 1981. In that case, the improvements that people had in the past few years would be lost. The situation of imbalance would further deteriorate. Serious disorder would occur in the national economy. The stable and cohesive political situation could hardly be consolidated and developed. (*Source*: Report on the Work of the Government presented at the Fourth Session of the Fifth National People's Congress: 'Current Economic Situation and Direction of Economic Construction in Future').

The government had made pertinacious effort since the winter of 1980 to cut the budget deficit. The deficit was cut to 2.5 billion yuan in 1981, a decrease of more than 10 billion. The fiscal expenditure in 1981 was lower than the 1979 level by around 25 billion yuan. Most of this was realized by suppressing infrastructure projects in state-owned units and sectors.

Sources: Reports on the Work of the Government 1981, 1982, 1983.

Economic crises had always been accompanied by high unemployment, not to mention a large number of youths returning from countryside to cities since 1978 that drastically added to the employment pressure in cities. From 31 October to 10 December 1978, the second "National Working Meeting on Intellectual Youths Going to Mountains and Villages" was convened in Beijing. Two important documents came out: the meeting minutes and the State Council document on temporary measures regarding the matter. The key point was that while the "going to mountains and to village" should persevere yet the conditions for another mobilization were not suitable. Its scope was to be gradually reduced. Cities that could accommodate the youths with employment needed not engage in such mobilization. Towns and cities should actively explore new realms and create new occupation and employment opportunity. This meeting and its documents signaled the historical turning point on intellectual youths' deployment to mountains and villages in China. There were still 1.7 million of them in 1977. By 1978 the number sharply dropped to 480 thousand and further went down to 247.7 thousand in 1979, most of them staying in suburb farms and factories. Entering mid 1980s, there was no more mobilization in most regions.

A large number of youths returning to cities instantly turned into an employment problem. Adding to the growing labor force and those still seeking employment, the total number of urban citizens waiting to be employed reached a peak of 15 million. That was just the official statistics. Different sources indicated that the unemployed population in cities during 1980–1982 was much higher. Some estimated that it might be as high as 40 million. Still, compared to 1960–1962 when the employment in cities and towns was cut down by 80 million, the situation was not as severe. However, given that it was not possible to transfer the surplus labor to villages as before, a large number of unemployed urban population in cities directly led to a deterioration of social order. The crime and delinquency rate was almost as high as in 1950 right after the establishment of the new regime.

In response to the delinquency problem in cities, a conference was convened in the winter of 1979, followed by a meeting by the CPC Central Political and Legal Affairs Commission in Beijing focusing on the situations in five major cities. Two strong Crack-down Campaigns were then launched.

The 1980 Economic Crisis Hard-Landing in Cities; Revival with the Help of the *Sannong*

Given that this economic crisis had arisen due to the fiscal deficit crisis in late 1970s, anything that could help alleviate the fiscal pressure would be accepted by the state for policy consideration.

It could be seen that while the crisis had a hard-landing in cities it was the *sannong* that helped to stimulate the revival and growth of the economy.

Reforms on Two Aspects in Rural Policy

a. Comprehensive reform of basic rural operating system:

The Household Contract System was launched whereby the production-operation entitlements of agrarian land was allocated to rural households based on headcount. At the same time government's financial support of agriculture was largely cut. In effect the government had retreated from the non-profitable collectivized agriculture in order to alleviate part of its fiscal deficit pressure.

To revive the economy and improve employment, the central government officials in-charge of planning had proposed "offloading some fiscal burdens both in industrial and agricultural sectors," "in [poorer] provinces like Gansu, Inner Mongolia, Guizhou and Yunnan. The central government had to allocate to them a large quantity of staple grain; they are heavy burdens to the state". "[Is it possible to consider] adopting Household Contract or some such schemes in sparsely populated regions with backward and poor economic condition? Let them find ways to look after themselves and reduce the burden on the state." According to Mr. Du Runsang, he had proposed to the then Vice Premier and Director of State Planning Commission Yao Yilin "adopting household contract system in poor regions. Let the peasants contract on production, which would be beneficial to both sides." When Yao reported to Deng Xiaoping, he had mentioned offloading burdens in industrial and agricultural sectors.[5] The rural reform that was launched in full-blown fashion on 1 January 1982 coincided with the urban economic crisis. It could be seen that the rural household contract system was beneficial to the government quickly emerging out of the fiscal crisis.

---

[5]Du Runsang (杜润生), 杜润生自述: 中国农村体制变革重大决策纪实 (Du Runsang's Narrative: Documentary on Major Decisions regarding Rural Reform in China). People's Publishing House, 2005:114–115.

Agriculture was by nature not as profitable as urban industries. The reason why agricultural production in China had been even more unprofitable could be attributed to the impact of external factors. From 1972 onwards China gradually resumed diplomatic relationship with Western countries as well as Japan, and began to launch new projects involving the import of industrial equipment from these countries for light industries, petrochemical industries and those supportive to agriculture. The production of industrial goods such as chemical fertilizers and farming machineries grew up and the products were sold to rural regions through the "unified sale system". As a result, agricultural production costs went up significantly yet the "unified purchase" prices of produce remained unchanged. Therefore, even though staple grain production increased, People's Communes operated at low-efficiency and under high indebtedness. By the end of the 1970s, rural communes with heavy financial losses due to years of surplus extraction, had become "burdens" to the state budget.

In any case, the rural reform with the household contract system should be categorized in theory as a 'government retreat'. Alternatively it could be regarded as a 'deal' in which the government conceded to rural collectives and the peasants the ownership of land and other agricultural means of production, in order to shrug off its responsibilities of welfare and public management in the rural regions, and ultimately became an institutional "transaction".

In the five consecutive "Documents No. 1" since 1982 that the central government issued once a year, people would see many instances of "approval" and "allowing", an indication that the government had expressed unprecedented concessions to the peasants.

Yet due to conservative, institutional and ideological constraints, it had not been possible for the new scene to sweep the country in one go. Certain provinces and regions (for example Heilongjiang Province and Yantai in Shandong) where there were relatively sizeable farming areas with mechanized cultivation even refused to adopt the Household Contract system. Therefore the central government pushed forward the new system in 1984 with a political approach. Since then, the rural ownership was completely transformed, with the result that the actors of rural interest changed from the previous 700 thousand production brigades and 4.8 million production teams to 200 million peasant households.

On one hand, the implementation of Household Contract system fundamentally dismantled the collectivization system established in early 1960s to serve urban industrial primitive accumulation. The model of "three-tier ownership with brigade as the basic unit" in scale agricultural operation was changed to a two-tier mechanism, in which scattered peasant households with their multi-occupational operations became the main agents, while rural collectives were retained to perform certain service and management functions. The rural collective ownership generally had production teams (natural village) as the basic unit. Certain regions had brigades (administrative village) as the basic unit. And in isolated cases the commune (township) was kept as the unit. As such, while acknowledging the communal collectives having the fundamental land ownership, accompanied by the right of land adjustment and rent collection (as a sort of contract fee), the peasants themselves were entitled with the household contract right—the autonomy of production and the right to operational profits.

On the other hand, since 1979 the government had raised the purchase price of staple grain as part of the rural "recuperation" policy. The price increases of six major kinds of grain were as much as 20.8% in 1979. Since then, the unified purchase price had been further raised while the unified purchase volume was lowered accordingly. With the dual price mechanism, state controls were gradually reduced over the pricing and distribution of produce, as well as over the prices of key production factors. The scope for adjustments by the market was expanded. The price surge on agricultural products as a result of these marketization-oriented policy adjustments had reached 49%. The peasants had more profits and therefore pursued higher production. It was breaking through the welfare-type allocation based on headcounts back in the period of collectivization, necessitated by the high level of agricultural surplus being extracted by the state, with little remaining for the collectives to allocate. It was a realization of the "higher pay for more work" type allocation, not possible in the past while the state appropriated the larger part of the surplus at a low or even no cost.

The previous ten years of collectivization did have the positive effect of large-scale input of labor into infrastructure building such as irrigation system. That was also one fundamental reason why agricultural production could substantially increase after the reform. The common explanation back then of the exceptionally high agricultural production increment was that each of the above three factors—household contract system, price adjustment and infrastructure building—had contributed one-third towards the result.

b. "Self-capitalization of Rural Resources" in the form of rural industrialization and townization

The government had, since the start of People's Commune system in 1958, encouraged rural collectives to develop five mini-industries locally. Later, with the onset of a vicious economic crisis in 1960, rural industries had been restrained. In the late 1970s, the government again allowed the peasants to employ workers or to become self-employed in industries and commerce previously monopolized by the state. At that time it already initiated a *sannong* development path with Chinese characteristics, which promoted peasants' non-agricultural employment and incomes through rural autonomous industrialization and townization.[6] The policy that encouraged rural industrialization, simultaneous with the household contract system, suited the institutional needs of micro primitive accumulation of capital for the numerous and widely-scattered rural industrial and commercial enterprises. On one hand the rural reform of early 1980s nurtured the development of rural enterprises and townization in rural regions, which in turn became the effective factors stimulating domestic demands that drove economic growth. On the other hand, however, because of the large quantity of resources and industrial goods taken up in the process, the inflation that emerged in 1988, exacerbated by the attempt of price reform, cumulated in the next economic crisis—the sixth in the 60 years of industrialization in China, or the second since the Reform and Opening Up.

---

[6]According to the *2008 China Statistical Yearbook*, the number of workers in rural enterprises was 30 million in 1980, 70 million in 1985 and 150 million in 2007.

During the 1979–1984 rural reform, the government retreated from the realms where it previously had fiscal responsibilities. In addition to giving the peasants the right to profits from agricultural surplus, the government also returned to the peasants the right to "capitalize" key local production factors (rural land, labor and so on) and to profit from it. Since then, rural industries operated at the brigade level were viewed as the important means of subsidizing the agricultural sector, hence given policy favors to some extent. On 3 July 1979 the State Council promulgated the "Trial Draft on Regulations Regarding Certain Issues Relating to the Development of Brigade Enterprises" which explained the significance of brigade enterprises: "the development of brigade enterprise would first of all serve to improve agricultural production, strengthen the collective economy at both the commune and the brigade levels and finance the necessary funds for agricultural mechanization; and secondly open up production opportunities for the labor force that became surplus by agricultural mechanization, thereby fully utilizing local resources to develop diversified operations, increase income for the collectives and raise members' living standard." It also pointed out that "the development of commune enterprises on a large scale could provide a large supply of raw materials and industrial products to the society, expediting national industrialization, while at the same time avoid the pitfall of over concentration of industrialization in mega and medium cities, an important means for narrowing over time the gaps between industry and agriculture as well as the urban and the rural". There were clear regulations on the deployment of brigade enterprise profits, "other than investing in the expansion, reproduction and setting up of new enterprises, it should be used in agricultural infrastructure building, mechanization and supporting brigades in poverty." Since the 1980s, the utilization was further transformed, with part of the profits directly allocated to members in accordance with headcounts or acreage to subsidize their incomes. After the Joint Production Responsibilities Contract system, the productions of staple grain and cottons were subsidized to fulfill the state's purchase target. In some cases, subsidies were given to supplementary operations such as raising livestock, aiming to stimulate the peasants' incentive. Thus, rural enterprise became the main agents for the capitalization of rural land and labor resources.

With rural industries and commerce rapidly taking up land, labor and other rural resources, a large number of peasants left agriculture to rural enterprises or went to towns. The rural economy therefore realized a comprehensive development relying on autonomous industrialization and townization.

Yet there were unfavorable institutional factors—whenever a government, under any political system, had to respond to an inflation-type economic crisis, it would adopt austerity measures that hurt small and medium businesses first and foremost. Faced with the 1979–1981 economic crisis, brigade enterprises still at the primitive accumulation phase bore the brunt of being constrained. Some major industries in cities went into a quagmire due to lack of raw materials, and appealed to the government to adjust the policy orientation. As a result, there were debates around whether brigade enterprises were crowding out the bigger and more advanced urban enterprises.

Relevant research showed that this situation was not really caused by the growth of brigade enterprises. Surveys organized by the State Machinery Commission found that "brigade mechanical industrial products had both crowding out and ancillary effects on large state-owned factories. At this time the ancillary effect is larger than the crowding out." Afterwards, the report was submitted to the CPC Central Committee and the State Council and terminated the debate.[7] Yet the document "Certain regulations by the State Council to adjust Policies regarding Brigade Enterprises" that came out in May 1981 still regarded brigade enterprises as having crowding out the raw materials that should have gone to large urban enterprises. On that basis rural enterprises were to be regulated. It further re-emphasized that brigade enterprises would only be allowed to operate on the premise that they did not impact major urban industries, which meant mainly the processing of local produce. Under permissible conditions they might also engage in the supply of parts and components to facilitate the development of urban industries.

Following that, other policies were also put forth, such as higher taxation targeting brigade enterprises, tightening credits to them, and so on. Nevertheless, given that the primitive capital accumulation for

---

[7]See: *Chinese Rural Enterprise Yearbook (1978–1987)*, China Agriculture Press, 1989.

rural industries and commerce had relied mainly on the mechanism of internalization in rural communities or households, i.e. large scale and intensive input of labor regardless of costs, a form of self-exploitation, unlike state-owned industrial sectors that relied on state revenues and debts for support. Furthermore, given that the consumer goods market in China in mid-1980s was in general supply shortage, rural enterprises still had sufficient room to develop. The comprehensive development of rural economy not only led to rapid income growth among peasants but also spurred a rapid revival of the national economy.

To summarize, in the economic crisis that broke out in 1981, on one side the government no longer had the conditions to mobilize surplus urban labors "going to mountains and villages" as in the 1960s-1970s. Not only that, they had to accommodate the tens of millions of youths returning from villages. That meant the crisis could only have a hard-landing in cities. On the other side, the rural policies, with historical particularities, were practical to the situation, releasing rural productivity and generating a positive institutional reform for the rural economy. As a result, rural economic growth accelerated after 1982, especially for rural enterprises. Not only were the latter not constrained by the unfavorable policies advocated by the vested-interests in urban sector, they even formed a strong new force by 1984 that stimulated the recovery and the subsequent growth of Chinese economy overall.

Three Factors by Which Rural Industrialization Facilitated the Recovery of National Economy

The acceleration of rural industrialization may be attributed to the three following factors with typical Chinese characteristics.

The first factor was the peasantry. Rural population accounted for 80% of the total population in the 1980s. Given that peasantry incentive was the first essential factor of productivity, with the release of their initiative over a short span, an opportunity return thus emerged. The "recuperation" policies in early 1980s had enabled the peasants to retain their labor force used to be appropriated and the agricultural surplus that was extracted by the government at no cost. Furthermore, the peasants attained higher cash income level with the policy of raising the unified purchase price of produce to promote productivity. With regard to the national economy, the peasants with their higher cash income hence higher purchasing power filled the gaps in demand that had been affected by the over-tightening of urban industries. Besides, with the anticipation of sharing in the opportunity return of rural industrialization and town-ization, the peasants had the initiation to increase investment, boosting the demand on industrial goods. In turn they provided large quantities of low-quality yet low-cost consumer goods to the society, leading to higher turnover of tangible goods on the market and thereby absorbing the possible risks of inflation due to higher fiscal deficits and money supply expansion by the government.

The second factor was the rural communities. In the 1980s there were 780,000 brigade-level administrative villages and 3.8 million team-level natural villages around the country that still practiced common collective ownership. Around two-third of the rural communities still had collective assets and revenues to be distributed to members. There-fore, the traditional rural communal rationality mechanism was able to function in the process of rural industrialization—rural collectives, making use of the newly-released production factors (collective funds, highly-disciplined labor force and land resources), took on the primitive accumulation for industrialization at a low cost, and dealt with the risk of externality by internalizing it.

The third factor was the market. The Reform's market-orientation and the initial opening up of the market for consumer goods resulted in a rocketing demand of general low-quality consumables. At that period urban state industry was still mainly comprised of military and heavy industries, yet to be transformed to satisfy the demand on general consumables. However, rural industrialization was by nature oriented towards consumable goods production and therefore able to fill the huge low-price consumable market with almost no competition.

It could be seen from statistical data that brigade industries, even while disadvantaged by macro-economic regulation oriented to the interests of urban industries, still displayed an institutional advantage of that self-initiated rural development with Chinese characteristics. From the start of rural industrialization to the year 1988, the production of rural enterprises had an average annual growth of over 30%, higher than that of state-run industries in the same period by more than 10% points, and also higher than the total production volume by a similar margin. With its primitive capital accumulation being completed internally over a short span of time, it became a main force capable of supporting the rural as well as the entire national economy.

Experience and Lessons from Handling of the 1979–1981 Crisis

In response to this crisis that happened in the early days of the Reform, the government, having great difficulties in applying macro-regulation, decided to retreat from the collectivized agriculture that was recording heavy losses. On one side, the Household Contract system had returned to the peasants almost all land and labor force. On the other side, the controls over rural markets and essential production factors were relaxed in order to stimulate the peasants' initiative to develop production. Such was the essential substance of the five successive Central Documents Number One issued annually in the 1980s.

What followed after 1983 was a period of high growth for five to six years. The development of rural small and medium enterprises had brought about rural townization and raised peasants' income level at a rapid pace for four successive years, until 1988 when inflation recurred. During that period the gap between urban and rural income narrowed at a fast pace; rural consumption grew by a large extent, at one point accounting for over 60% of total retail value. China therefore had a period of 'golden growth' in the 1980s that was driven by domestic consumption. This experience of golden growth should have been an important content of the "Scientific Outlook on Development" latterly proposed by the central government in 2003. Unfortunately it had been largely neglected by mainstream opinion during the 1990s under deliberate suppression by interest blocs at the time.

The government had attempted to suppress brigade industries to help the urban sector in the quagmire of insufficient investments during the economic crisis. As a rule small and medium rural enterprises bore the brunt of impact first and foremost under the austerity policies. For two reasons it was no longer possible to transfer the bulk of the costs from the urban sector to the *sannong*: first the disintegration of People's Communes making it impossible to repeat the campaigns of "going up to mountains and villages" as a way of directly transferring urban surplus labor, hence the costs of the crisis to the *sannong*. Second, the government rural policy research departments at that time could still play a role in the decision-making process, protecting the interests of the *sannong*. Therefore, the policies that aimed at transferring the costs to the *sannong* had not made real impact.[8]

From the above, it can be seen that China had a decade of reasonable development in the 1980s. It provided an important historical experience for the central government to adjust its strategic orientation in the twenty-first century—strengthening input into the *sannong* to foster its self-initiated development would build a solid base with Chinese characteristics that could help alleviate the impact of economic crises.

The Profound Impact of the Institutional Costs Brought About by the Reform

It is generally agreed that China's Reform and Opening Up in the 1980s was different from the Soviet Union's "shock therapy". The former was gradual while the latter was radical. Justin Lin Yifu et el (1984) summarized the characteristics of China's reform as "making the cake bigger", "incremental reform", "experiments then generalization" and "non-radical", and provided corresponding theoretical explanations. The view that the reform in the first half of the 1980s was of the incremental adjustment type is worthy of further discussions. Looking at the actual process, whether it was the adjustment in the fundamental land ownership, or the adjustment of the national income distribution

---

[8]A series of policies favorable to the *sannong* in the above-mentioned Documents were suggested by two departments, the Rural Policy Research Office of the CPC Central Committee and the State Council Rural Development Research Center. However, they were dismissed in 1989 and 1990 respectively.

structure, it was in essence a structural sea change in the distribution of the assets stock. The reform at that time was essentially of the stock-adjustment type, undertaken under the pressure of crisis. If any increment was generated, it would only be the result of rural industries with much higher marginal return as compared to urban sectors. When the rural sector was given a chance of investment and funds support, the marginal returns thus generated were no doubt higher than urban industries backed up by fiscal expenditures.

Nevertheless, the theoretical interpretation of the Reform did have practical value in politics. Chinese politicians, under the pressure of further opening up to introduce foreign capital and forced into the urgent need to have dialogues with the West, accepted the discourses of the Reform, and the latter then became the mainstream. Furthermore, with China's continuous high-speed economic growth, Chinese economists who were trained by the Western system continued to sum up the experience in accordance with that discourse, and that was in turn absorbed into the analyses of Western scholars over time. In the early twenty-first century, the international media and academic mainstream's concern and assessment of China's Reform and future development gradually shifted from "China's collapse" to "China's experience" (yet it tended to be more about "China's threat"). As an attempt, see Ramo (2004), the American China expert summed up the three aspects of the development path that China went through since the Reform: "innovation and experimentation", "defense of national borders and interests" and "increasingly thoughtful accumulation of tools". In keeping with the Western convention, he coined the phrase "Beijing Consensus". During the Sub-prime Crisis that started in the U.S. in 2008 and subsequently spread to the world in the form of the financial meltdown, China's ability to maintain growth once again called the attention of the international mainstream. At that point, the concept of the "China Model", interpreted and accepted within the academia long before, became an object for sensationalism in Western society.

These studies on China's Reform and development by domestic and overseas mainstream intellectuals and media, whether they are sorting through the experiences or theorizing the process, are not irrelevant for us today to rethink the path that has been taken since the Reform and to maintain the mobilization mechanism endogenous in ideologies. However, today when we look into those events at the early and middle period of the Reform, it is quite difficult to have the same clear thinking that was embodied in the experience studies or theoretical evaluation described above. Much of what we find today is ideologically entrenched interpretation and ambiguous conclusions drawn by theorists taking benefits from varied interest groups. That is not to negate the effort of domestic and overseas researchers on the study of 'Chinese experience' or 'China model'. In fact not everyone would agree with the so-called 'Chinese experience' or 'China model'. Otherwise it would be hard to explain why such discourse would surface only at times of apparent success, whereas during the moments of crises in the reform the key-words were usually "collapse," "failures" and so on.

Looking at it objectively, indeed those many policies formulated and launched by the central government during the Reform and the subsequent fast growth could hardly be "a priori" innovative. Choices and decisions could only be made as a response to the situation in conformity with people's basic understanding. The targets of regulation were mostly pragmatic, unlike the conclusion deduced today from studying that experience, which is with clear foresight or scientific definitiveness and orderliness. On the contrary, back then if any point of view in relation to the superstructure or ideologies would interfere with the introduction of particular regulation, it would generally be put aside in accordance with the instruction of "no debates" and allowed to remain vague. With regard to the export-oriented economy that was strongly promoted in line with the "coastal economic development strategy", theoretical and academic discussions today are somehow superficial and often off-the-mark due to the complicated context in which such macroeconomic policies were deliberated.

Actually, as long as people are willing to go back to the economic and political situation around the time of 1978, even in a simplistic manner, it would not be difficult to attribute that round of opening to China's macro-economic conditions and institutions at that time.

During the fiscal crises in Mao's era, the mobilization of youths to "mountains and villages" by the central government to transfer the costs of crisis to rural regions was relatively effective to achieve "soft-landing" for the industrial capital concentrated in cities (most governments would find it hard to transfer the costs of crises to society). These three rounds of transfers in this era did incur an enormous price to be paid by both the peasants and urban residents.

Yet in the late 1970s after the death of Mao, when the new government had to deal with fiscal crisis, those in power could no longer undertake the same approach, not having the charisma of Mao. Therefore, they were obliged to adopt the approach to deal with the problems, which later were dubbed as the reform, including three famous major reforms in the 1980s—fiscal responsibility was decentralized to different administrative tiers; the funds provided to state-owned enterprises were no longer budget allocation but became loans; the enterprises did not turn over all the profits but pay tax to the government—and other institutional changes such as the factory contract system and bonus system in enterprise reforms that were replicas of the rural household contract system.

And with regard to the foreign trading system, it was also impossible not to make ground-breaking reform unprecedented in the prior thirty years. In face of the climbing fiscal deficits and a serious shortage of funds for major national industrial structure transformation that had already begun, Li Xiannian, in September 1978 in the State Council Discussion Meeting, proposed to engage in more supplementary trades so as to reduce the burden of domestic investment in relevant projects. Moreover, Deng Xiaoping's speech on "Raising the banner of Mao Zedong's thoughts, persevere in the principles of practicality and being realistic" broke through two traditional forbidden zones relating to foreign capital—foreign loans and joint ventures. In December that year, the Foreign Trade Minister announced that China would accept loans from foreign governments and allow foreign companies to make investments in China. In effect, any commonly employed practices in international trade would be permitted.

Yet such a large extent of opening to the outside of course had its institutional costs—breaking through these two forbidden zones meant that national debts would substantially increase and eventually be taken up by central government's budget. At that time, the fiscal system was unified but there were no clarification on sharing liability, power and benefits among various tiers of government, departments and persons in charge in regard of the large scale debt increment. This issue which has not been thoroughly discussed back then still plagues China today.

Due to lack of clarification on how to share liability, power and benefits between the central and local governments, an essential institutional problem was created wherein "the central government takes up the liability while the local takes the benefits". On that basis it inevitably led to the frenzy in coastal regions competing to open up and requesting the concession of power to set up special development zones.

The foregoing was the essential context behind the central's approval to open four special economic zones (Shenzhen, Zhuhai, Shantou and Xiamen), as well as the subsequent opening up of fourteen coastal cities.

In these two breakthroughs, the institutional costs thus incurred due to lack of clear delineation on liability, power and benefits, given with the centralized fiscal system, had no other way of being transferred but within the system itself. Impossible to transfer the cost to the *sannong*, a hard-landing within the urban system became inevitable, and that in turn led to an endogenous reform.

With the above elaboration, we agree with the prevalent statement that "Opening up came before the Reform and Opening up has in turn driven the Reform".

2   The 6th Crisis (1988–1990): The Second Economic Crisis since the Reform and the Response of the *Sannong*

In 1988 China experienced hyperinflation with annual CPI reaching 18.6% (the highest monthly rate after the introduction of "price reform" had been 26.7%). What happened next was a production stagnation in 1989, with the "chain debts" among enterprises as a symptom. The combination of these two was a typical stagflation crisis. Following that was a depression in 1990. During the same period, the economic relationship had become increasingly tensed during the time of high growth. Social contradictions accumulated and eventually exploded under the pressure of crisis, resulting in the 1989 Tiananmen Square Event. One of the repercussions was the blockade on China by the West as well as the international clamors of "China Collapse".

Characteristics and Intrinsic Mechanism of the 1988–1990 Economic Crisis

It was the 6th economic crisis in 60 years of China's industrialization, the second since the Reform. Judging from its basic characteristics, it belonged to the category of stagnation, due to the expansion of industrial capital driving large investment increment. On that basis it was consistent with classical political economic theory.

During this crisis, economic growth declined from 11.6% in 1987 to 4.1% in 1989, dropping further to 3.8% in 1990. Moreover, it was accompanied by the serious 1989 Tiananmen event. Similar to the previous crisis, as economic growth declined, the growth of fixed asset investments, represented mainly by the fixed asset investments of SOEs, also showed a continuous declining trend, from 41.79% in 1985 to -8.23% in 1989.

In an essay, we have analyzed the process and the dynamics of this crisis.[9] Here, we would simply expand on the characteristics of this crisis from a comparative perspective.

Looking at the price levels, high inflation was an important characteristic of this economic crisis. The rise in price level was already notable in the second half of 1987. Entering into 1988, the rise in January was 9.5%, and from then on it rose up month by month, with an average of 1.4% point in the first half of the year. The government then adopted the suggestion to force through price-marketization reform, and the decision was announced by government media. It gave rise to a wave of panic shopping countrywide, led by profiteer companies related to government officials, with the result that the monthly price levels in July and August

---

[9]Dong Xiaodan & Wen Tiejun "宏观经济波动与农村治理危机——关于改革以来 '三农' 与 '三治' 问题相关性的实证分析" (Macro-Economic Fluctuations and Rural Governance Crisis – Empirical Analysis Regarding the Correlation of the 'sannong' and the 'sanzhi' [Governance in Three aspects] since the Reform), 管理世界 (Management World), 2008(9).

rose by 3% points (Fig. 3). In September the central government, in the third plenary meeting of the 13th National Congress, decided to launch rectification measures, implementing a series of austerity measures to tackle the inflation, such as price control, suppression of investment, tightening of credits, interest rate adjustments and so on. By September the price rise began to slow down but the economy still remained at a state of hyperinflation of 26.7% (Fig. 3). The retail price index for the year went up to 18.5% while the purchase price of basic commodities such as industrial raw materials and fuels rose by 19%, the industrial product output price by 20.7%, urban general consumption index by 20.7%. In that year of inflation surge, the quantity of money put into circulation by the state-owned banks reached 67.95 billion yuan, compared to 23.61 billion in 1987, and just 1.66 billion in 1978 soon after the reform.

Coming hand in hand with inflation, another characteristic in line with classical political economy was a stagnation in production. The main reason was the emergence of chain debts at the end of 1988 caused by rigid austerity measures, with rising interest rates aimed at tackling inflation. The serious debt problem of "triangular debts" emerged. The old causes of "triangular debts" formation were three-fold: first, infrastructure projects had been running substantially over budget while the financial input was insufficient and the financing target was

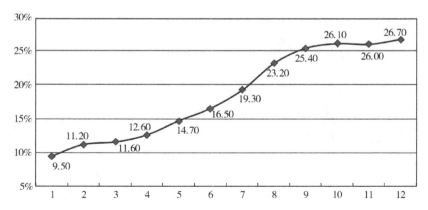

Fig. 3 Monthly rise in price level 1988

not met. The result were serious shortfalls in fixed asset investments, causing overdue payments to manufacturers and engineering companies; second, the enterprises had serious losses, depleting their capital funds and loans from banks, exacerbating the situation of debt defaults among one another; third, slow sales of products resulted in more funds being tied up in unsold inventory. The overall result was a vicious cycle: input—output goods—high inventories—arrears—more input—more output—more inventories (Image 4).

A new reason for the triangular debts was the behavior distortion of enterprises under severe scarcity of funds: under the pressure of sudden interest rate surge hence a higher cost of capital, the commercial and retail enterprises that took up most of the liquid funds on one hand protected their own profits by monopolies on wholesale and retailing; on the other hand they put products on consignment and tied up the manufacturers' operating funds. The manufacturers in turn made the same practices on up-stream suppliers of parts and components. At the end, the long-term potential conflict of interests among various state-owned economic sectors rapidly broke the surface and led to the prevalent debts chains around the country.

Image 4 Failure of Forcing through Price Reform—People jostling for panic shopping (Source: https://www.21ccom.net/articles/1sjd/ts1s/articks_2001052636 245.html)

However, the officials involved in policy making back then had lacked experience and knowledge. Official documents simply expressed that what exacerbated the problem of triangular debts had been trade disorders, undisciplined clearing and weak creditability.

Overall, while this crisis had many similarities to the previous one, the fundamental difference lay in the emergence of high inflation as indicated by the annual price index of 18.5%, due to a large expansion in money supply as well as the production stagnation that followed. These characteristics had also been absent in pre-reform economic crises.

In terms of the monetary input structure, the government, under pressure of crisis, had taken from early 1980s the reform of separating the fiscal sector and financial sector with measures such as changing the fund provision to state-owned enterprises from fiscal allocation to loans. After that, given with the overheated economy and high demands of investment and consumption in 1986–1989, the M2 money supply sharply increased with an average annual expansion of 150 billion yuan. The money stock cumulated to 1.2 trillion in 1989. However the expansion was concentrated relatively in M0 supply. In 1988, the growth of M0 supply reached 46.7% whereas M1 and M2 increases were only 13.13% and 22.38% respectively (Figs. 4 and 5). That meant the new money

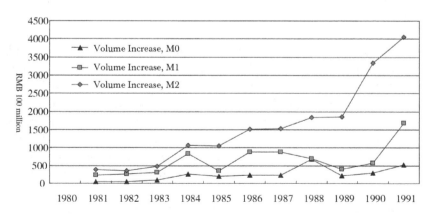

Fig. 4 Money supply volume at various levels 1981–1991 (Source: *China Financial Yearbook* 1992; *China Statistical Yearbook* 1992; *China Statistical Abstracts* 1993)

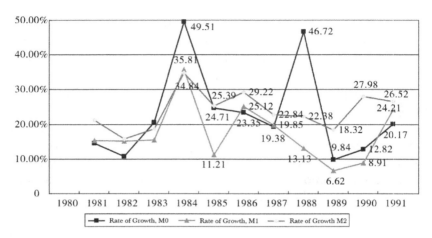

Fig. 5 Money supply growth rate at various levels 1981–1991 (Source: Same as above)

supply in 1988 was mostly in the form of cash. The portion that went into production was relatively small. It added to the inflationary pressure as the demand of goods was higher than supply. The overall demand structure that year provided further evidence on this—the demand for investments grew in 1988 by 16.1% while consumption demand by 26.5%.

Before the crisis broke out in 1988, not only did the money supply increase faster than the overall economic growth, the input of fiscal funds had also expanded strongly. In 1986, even though the book amount of budget deficit was less than 10 billion yuan, the total deficit on a comprehensive basis, i.e. including those areas within the fiscal system where revenue was less than expenditures (including domestic debts, foreign debts and fiscal deficit on the book), already reached 20 billion, amounting to 9.8% of fiscal revenues. The comprehensive deficit rose in 1988 to 30 billion yuan, 14.8% of fiscal revenues. The fiscal capacity for economic regulation was far from adequate. By 1989, the ratio of comprehensive base deficits-to-revenues reached 25.1%. That means one-fifth of the total fiscal expenditures did not have corresponding revenues.

If people are willing to analyze China's cyclical economic crisis free of ideology, the 1988–1989 crisis was not essentially different from pre-reform occasions, whether from the perspective of cyclicality or the weight of fiscal deficits.

In summary, the major reasons for this crisis were as follows:

First, under the condition of a "shortage economy", given that the rural industrialization had brought about fast growth in consumption and investment which gave rise to money over-supply, serious inflation was inevitable (Fig. 6).

Second, it had much to do with the radical reform measures adopted by the government, the crucial one being the dual price system reform and subsequently a whole series of pricing marketization reform in 1988, which exposed the enormous hidden institutional costs.

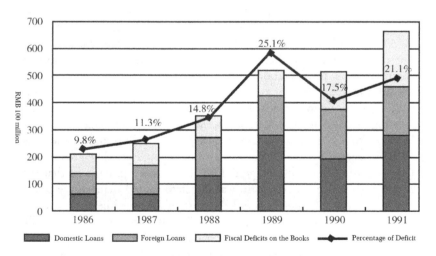

Fig. 6 Budget deficits 1986–1991. Formula: (Book Amount + Domestic Debts + Foreign Debts)/Final Account of Revenues other than lending X 100%

Box 4: Decision-Making Process Regarding the Price Reform in 1988
Going into 1988, several acute contradictions simultaneously exposed indicated the inevitability and urgency of reforming the unreasonable pricing system and price-control. With the State Council's approval, the State Bureau of Commodity Prices and the Ministry of Commerce had decided, starting from 1 April, to adjust the purchase price of certain kinds of grain and edible oil. On 5 April, the State Council promulgated the "Notice Regarding the Trial Implementation of Proper Subsidies to Workers for Major Non-staple Food Price Fluctuation". The subsidies on non-staple food items (meat, eggs, vegetables and sugar) were then changed from hidden to open. After May, the price of color television was allowed to fluctuate and domestic manufactured models generally rose up by 20–30%. With the State Council's approval, starting from 28 July the prices of cigarettes and liquor with famous brands were fully opened and the prices of certain medium rank cigarettes and liquor were raised. At the same time, a systematic scheme to design a price reform was put on the agenda. From 30 May to 1 June, the CPC Central Political Bureau convened the 9th plenary session in Beijing to discuss nationwide economic reform and the economic situation. The meeting indicated that the price and wage system reform required comprehensive consideration and a systematic plan. While it should smooth their relationships and stimulate production, it should also gradually raise the living standard of the majority of the population. The meeting resolved to formulate a systematic reform on price and wage. From 15 to 17 August, the CPC Central Political Bureau convened the 10th plenary meeting in Beidahe and eventually passed "The Preliminary Plan Regarding Price and Wage Reform". The meeting believed that the overall direction of price reform was the state should manage the prices of the few key commodities and the cost of labor, while the prices of most commodities would be open to variations in the market, gradually to realize the objective of "the state regulating the market, the market directing the business". The overall requirement of wage reform was that through raising and adjusting wages and increasing appropriate subsidies to ensure that most workers' living standard would not go down, but instead would gradually improve in line with production development. Furthermore, the principle of income according to work would be carried out to resolve certain unreasonable issues in the allocation of

wage. This meeting further emphasized that the country's economy was in a period of lively and vigorous development. It would be a favorable time to launch price reform and wage reform. Although problems would be expected yet there would be ample potential and leeway to overcome difficulties. Nevertheless, what happened in reality was far from what was concluded at this meeting.

Now that people could finally free themselves from the old shackle of ideological debates between the "Reformists" and the "Conservatives" and are able to realistically discuss issues that people in that era did not sufficiently understand. The analysis we put forward here would have the originality of going "beyond the left and the right". The government, in an attempt to shrug off the hidden institutional costs of the "dual price mechanism", had pushed ahead the radical price reform. What detonated were two institutional costs previously hidden by the internalized mechanism of the dual-price system: first, the costs relating to rent setting and rent seeking that arose from the collaboration of government departments with bureaucrat profiteering companies; second, the costs relating to marketization giving rise to speculative profits under the conditions of a temporary shortage of goods. Both costs would inevitably have led to high inflation. (In this regard, those who went through the process at the time should have the courage to admit. No one had the foresight back then to foresee what was ahead.)

Thus, when the government was forced to tighten credits in implementing macro-regulation measures, referring to past experiences, it in effect prompted a rift among the interest blocs during the marketization, exposing their contradictions. That in turn led to further deterioration of the chain debts among enterprises.

Even though the government's marketization reform during this period did attain certain result, the national finance was still under a high degree of monopolies by various tiers of governments. The central government, other than reducing money supply and raising interest rates, did not have other financial tools that could regulate local economies (after the tax division reform in 1994, there were even fewer measures that could possibly and effectively regulate local governments.) As a result, during this crisis the central government could only exert regulation by reducing fiscal investment to the state-owned industrial enterprises, similar to the approach adopted in the previous case. However, a contraction in investment directly led to depression, characterized by declining economic growth.

The Transferal of the Economic Crisis and the Costs to the *Sannong*

The economic crisis that broke out due to the severe inflation arising from the expansion of government credit driven by the expansion of industrial capital, would as a matter of course take place in cities where industrial capital was concentrated. Furthermore, the government responded by the path-dependency of transferring the institutional costs to the *sannong*. Moreover, the form of transferal was substantially the same as that of the 1979–1980 crisis.

The target of transferal remained the same—the rural enterprises. In execution, the state in the name of the "coastal economic development strategy" requested the rural enterprises to "orient themselves towards overseas markets at both ends of the supply chains", conceding domestic raw material supply and finished product markets to urban enterprises. In addition, the state cut fiscal support to local governments and party organizations, as well as rural public services such as education, health care and so on. Both aspects resulted in peasant incomes declining, hence their consumption. At the same time, the inelastic expenditures of local governments and their affiliated organizations also had to be transferred to the peasants, further adding to their burden. Social tension in rural regions became intensified and the number of mass incidents such as protests and public conflicts increased substantially as a result.

There was yet another outcome with the most significant historical consequence: given that the macro regulation was urban interests-orientated, the rising rural economy and peasant consumptions were to a large extent suppressed. As the peasants comprised the majority of the population, domestic consumption became weak, increasingly intensifying the contradiction within the economic structure. As a consequence, it dictated the transformation of the national economy from being domestic demand driven to increasingly export-dependent. This transformation may also partly explain why, upon entering the 1990s, China was so anxious to get incorporated into the globalization dominated by international financial capital.

It should be pointed out that, as compared to previous cases, this time the transferal of the crisis to the *sannong* brought a notably more adverse impact. As early as in November 1987 when putting forward the coastal economic development strategy, the then Premier had requested the coastal regions to make the best use of their advantages, namely an ample labor supply and the flexibility of rural enterprises, to develop labor intensive industries with the approach of "orienting towards overseas markets at both ends". (That implied making use of foreign capital fund as well as importing raw materials and production facilities. China focused on processing manufacturing.) He believed that Chinese rural enterprises "had the ability to participate in international competition, and should undoubtedly step up to join the export economies." In December that year, the Working Conference of CPC Central pointed out further that in future it would be entirely possible for the rural enterprises to take a share of the international market, as the main form of business operations in China's coastal regions, relying on low-cost labor to produce labor-intensive goods for export. In January 1988, the CPC Central Committee formally published the document expressing this view.[10]

If there had been concrete complementary policies, it might have been considered a proactive policy orientation. Yet most of the politicians and theorists back then could not have possibly realized that under the constraint of the fundamental institutional contradiction in China's rural–urban dichotomy, rural and urban agents each had their own respective predicament, and needed representatives for their respective interests inside the government. The problem was simply that those who represented the urban interest blocs always had much greater influence

---

[10] See: 江苏省志·乡镇工业志 (Chronicles of Jiangsu Province—Chronicles of Rural Industries).

on the urban-based governments and their policy decisions than those representing rural interests.[11]

Based on that, the essential context of the urban–rural contradiction in the 1980s during the industrial capital expansion phase was still that same old problem that had emerged ever since the brigade enterprises came into being in the 1970s. The urban enterprises, comprised mainly of state-owned capital and seriously indebted, had attempted to avoid competition with the emerging rural enterprises that had nearly no burden of social cost. Just at the starting point and not yet having accomplished the primitive accumulation of capital, the rural enterprises were facing an array of difficulties in their path of development.

---

[11]During the same period, the State Council Rural Development Research Center and the CPC Central Rural Policy Research Office, the two official faculties representing rural interests at the central decision making level and responsible for issuing the annual Central Document Number 1 on rural policies, had been disbanded upon reorganizations. The agriculture ministry itself could only issue policies within its own scope, not able to coordinate and align relevant policies among other areas such as fiscal, financial, taxation, trade, utilities, and so on. Therefore they could only focus on technicality around agricultural input and structural regulation. In 1991, Fan Xiao Jian, the then head of Collective Economy Directing Department under the Ministry of Agriculture, had personally surveyed around 20 counties on incidents of peasant resistance against excessive levy burden. Yet not only was his report rejected, he had to step aside for nearly ten years without promotion, even though he had been one of the youngest department heads back then. Another person who had spoken up on behalf of Fan about the worsening situation of the *sannong* was Liao Zhongyi, the Minister of Agriculture. He was criticized and transferred to a lesser post. Without *sannong* policies and the Document Number 1 that symbolically expressed the central government's intention of guarding peasant interests, the consequence was increasing decline of peasant incomes over 1989–1991, while peasants' cash tax payments kept rising. The number of rural mass protest incidents and violent conflicts grew and the problem of the *sannong* broke the surface. The author joined in 1993 a survey at a base in Anhui, organized by the Rural Reform Pilot Scheme Zone Office under the Ministry of Agriculture. Most of our team's discussions had revealed that the macro regulation's biased interest orientation was the key factor impacting the *sannong*. Afterwards, the author published an article in May in *Economic Daily*, "Support to Agriculture Need to be done Outside of Agriculture", emphasizing that the interests of various departments outside the agriculture realm, such as fiscal, taxation, finance, foreign trade and so on, had impacted the issues of peasants and agriculture. From then on, the author has increasingly focused on the fluctuation and measures in macro-economy and their impact on the *sannong*.

Box 5: Rural Enterprise's Predicament during the 1980s

1. Backward Equipments

The proposition of brigade enterprise great development was put forward in the Third Plenary of the 11th CPC National Congress in 1978. Ten years later in 1988 the coastal economic development strategy was put forth. During that short span of 10 years, the rural enterprises, especially those in coastal regions, had already made remarkable strides. However, although there were a number of enterprises with advanced technology and state of the art equipments, most of the other were generally backward in technology. In the early days of their development most of them had started by acquiring obsolete machinery from urban industries. For example, more than 85% of the rural enterprises in Jiangsu Province had pre-1960s equipment. Even in Wuxi where rural enterprises were most developed, only 28% had equipment made in the 1970s–1980s (1). The backwardness in technology and equipment directly impacted their product quality, and in turn the ability to export, particularly for machinery processing industry which required higher technological standard. For example, the quality inspection of Wuxi's bicycle export in 1988 showed that almost all batches being inspected had problems. In January to May, 3,700 bicycles did not pass the quality control, accounting for 90% of its total export (2).

2. Insufficient Funds and Foreign Exchange

The rural enterprises had been short of funding right from the start. In its early stage, this problem was resolved through the collective economy with the mechanism of "using large scale labor as a substitute for capital". In the later stage it was resolved through financing by the local financial sector with support and direct intervention from the local governments. Even so, the rural enterprise still found it difficult to solve the problem of capital shortage. In particular, the problem worsened at the end of 1988 when the central government started macro-regulation to tackle the economic overheating, so much so that many enterprises went into "triangular debts". Under the circumstances, it was unrealistic for most rural enterprises to solve the problem through domestic financing. The central government had already put forward relevant policies for the enterprises to retain part of the foreign exchange that they earned from export. However, since most of their scales were relatively small, it was hard to have sufficient foreign exchange to purchase advanced equipment. Moreover, the reality was that being short of funds the central government would frequently hold back some of the foreign exchange that should go to local regions.

3. Shortage in Foreign Trade Talent

Most rural enterprise staff were comprised by peasants from rural regions, with relatively low education level and technology proficiency. With Wuxi as an example, according to 1988 statistics, out of the 11,000 rural enterprises there were only around 600 employees having corresponding technical education and officially certificated as technicians, representing only 0.75% of total rural enterprise workers (ibid.). Even fewer were versed both in the business and foreign languages. Such conditions were very unfavorable to the development of an export-oriented economy.

It went without saying that the decision-makers on relevant policies were well-aware of these widely known practical problems. Yet in putting forward the policies, they faced the similar problems as in early 1980s—that the economic crisis tightened the supply of raw materials and financing to urban industrial sector, being crowded out by its smaller and more backward rural counterpart. The decision makers again granted priority to the urban sector; the rural enterprises, formerly brigade enterprises were once again confronted with the exclusive policies. Being the direct bearer of the institutional costs arising from the economic crisis, the rural enterprises suffered severe impact on their development, with the outcome of many bankruptcies or closing down.

In any case, the setback in rural enterprise development during this time not only significantly impaired their capacity to absorb rural labor, resulting in the sharp increase of surplus rural labor, depressing peasants' income level, but also depleted the factor of "industry subsidizing agriculture" because of large-scale closing down, resulting at lower agricultural investment and shrinking rural welfare.

References:
(1) Bao Youti (鲍有悌), "三省市乡镇企业发展外向型经济调查" (Survey on the Development of Export-Oriented Economy among

Rural Enterprises in Three Provinces and Municipality), 宏观经济
管理 (Macro-Economic Management), 1988(9).
(2) Ji Yongming (季永明), "关于江阴市乡镇企业发展外向型经济
调查之系列报告 (续)" (Survey on the Rural Enterprise in Export-
oriented Economy Development in Jiangyang Township (cont'd)), 现
代金融 (Modern Finance), 1988(10).
Source: Article published by the author's research team.

Another consequence arising out of this policy was that from 1989
onwards, the growth rate in peasant annual cash income declined for
three consecutive years, forcing rural labor to go to cities in search of
employment, hence the phenomenon of "migrant worker tide" in the
early 1990s. In response, the state began to relax various constraints on
the peasants so they could go to cities to work. Since 1988, the state
began to allow the peasants to set up service industries and provide
various services. The cities were requested to give them favorable terms
in providing land and servicing facilities. Urban enterprises were allowed
to employ rural workers with permission. The export of labor became
a major source of revenues for impoverished regions. Coastal regions
with better developed economies as well as large and medium cities were
requested to absorb the labor force from impoverished regions in an
orderly fashion.

Although in 1989, with a new round of economic austerity measures,
the restrictions on the outflow of rural labor force were again tightened,
given that the policy of allowing the peasants to go into cities to provide
labor and service had been in place for 4 years starting from 1985, it was
not possible to stop the flow with just one policy, as in the old days of
planned economy. As such, the only feasible measure was to strengthen
the management of rural labor migrating.

In the spring of 1992, Deng Xiaoping's Southern Inspection speech
prompted the reviving Chinese economy to a rapid surge. At that point,
the government further released the regulation on the flow of rural labor.
The basic position was to acknowledge, accept and encourage the flow
of rural labor towards manufacturing. However, disorderly and unregulated flow would not be acceptable. Various departments were asked to

work together, adopting multi-facet measures to guide and control the flows. The aim was to direct them to the same or proximal regions and migration to local towns.

The most important measure that collaborated with the relaxation of labor force flow was the cancellation of food vouchers, starting from 1 April, 1992 as a way of alleviating fiscal pressure due to subsidies. With this measure, the peasants were able to procure food as long as they had income. Thereupon the number of migrant workers sharply increased in 1993 to more than 40 million, directly compensating for the declining peasant income due to the close down of rural enterprises.

Very few people have realized that the cancellation of food vouchers due to fiscal pressure had given rise to an even more paradoxical outcome, which was that the Chinese currency resumed its function as a general equivalent for commodities. From then on China entered the era of monetization.

3   Third Round of Foreign Capital and Debts: Background and Rationale Change—1988–1994: "It is Crucial to Develop Exports to Earn Foreign Exchange"

In the 30 years from 1949 till 1978 when the economic reform took place, China in Mao's era had gone through two rounds of "opening up": first to the socialist countries led by the USSR in the 1950s; and then to Western capitalist countries in the 1970s following the rapprochement between China and the U.S.A. (The "opening up" in 1977 during the joint leadership of Hua Guofeng and Deng Xiaoping should only be considered an extension and expansion of Mao's policy. However, that round of opening up had to be abandoned due to the 1979–1980 economic crisis, hence not a complete round.) The central government, upon the eruption of crisis caused by heavy debts, was obligated to make major adjustments; having in both cases transferred the costs to the *sannong*. That was the reason why the *sannong* had been in continuous hardship.

Since the 1980s, Deng Xiaoping, as the core leader of the second generation collective leadership, launched another round of "opening up" with breakthroughs—bringing in foreign capital gradually to coastal special economic zones and development zones, which then transformed into various export-oriented regions. Since the costs of crisis could not be now simply transferred to the *sannong*, the contradiction between the centralized state system and various regional interest groups became intensified. Hence, it triggered major structural adjustments in fields from the economy to the politics.

During the early wave of urban economic reform in 1985, urban interest blocs having entrenched vested interests in the accumulation of industrial capital increasingly dominated the design of the Reform and Opening Up policies. Furthermore, they directly prompted the coastal economic development strategy in 1988, driving China into the path of an export-oriented economy.

Box 6: The Central Government's Coastal Economic Development Strategy

In March 1987, the 5th Session of the 6th National People's Congress officially proposed to gradually shape an export-oriented economy in special economic zones and opened cities and regions along the coast. In the 13th National Congress convened in the same year that direction was further affirmed. Next, in November 1987, the then Premier and Acting General Secretary Zhao Ziyang, during his inspection trip to Jiangsu, Zhejiang and Shanghai, provided a guideline for this new strategy:

> "The coastal regions had advantages in climate and geography, and adding to that the support of inland resources. They would definitely be able to develop an export-oriented economy by developing export trade to enter the international market and competition. In doing so, they could stimulate the development of the coastal regions while allowing inland regions to have more of the domestic market share, thereby also stimulating the inland development." (1)

It could be viewed as the core thinking of the "coastal economic development strategy' formally put forth in the Political Bureau meeting on 6 February, 1988. To implement the strategy, the State Council convened a meeting in Shanghai on 4 March regarding the opening of coastal regions, making concrete plans on execution. It was agreed in the meeting that the key was to promote exports in order to earn foreign exchange. The focus would be on processing manufacturing on a large scale, with raw materials coming from outside and finished products going to the outside. The exports would sustain the imports while imports would nurture exports, hence the integration of imports and exports. According to Tian Jiyun's memoirs, Zhao Ziyang submitted in January 1988 to Deng Xiaoping the report "Regarding the Strategic Issues on Economic Development of Coastal Regions". Deng gave his feedback on January 23: "in complete agreement. Move boldly. Accelerate the pace. Do not procrastinate and miss the opportunity" (ibid.).

Reference:
Tian Jiyun (田纪云), 改革开放的伟大实践 (The Great Praxis of the Reform and Opening Up). Xinhua Publishing, 2009.

There have been numerous discussions among scholars regarding the formation of the concept and substance of "export-oriented economy" in the coastal economic development strategy. Yet up to this day, there is no uniform definition. Different definitions have been given under different contexts and in different historical stages during the formation of China's industrial capital. Tang Jianyu (1988) summarized the theories into three major categories:

- the economic structure theory—export-oriented economy being a state of economic structure, signified by relatively high dependence on exports;
- the operational mechanism theory—a form of economic operation mechanism, denoted by market economy's extent of development;
- the dominant strategy theory—a dominant strategy of an economy with an "export orientation".

Tang himself believed that the export-oriented economy was an economic development model, a systematic economic whole integrating factors such as economic structure, economic operational mechanism and economic development strategy. With regard to that kind of theoretical controversies and conceptual ambiguities, we could consider it as an inevitable outcome of China's "groping on boulders to cross the river". Yet it was only opaqueness at the surface. If the strategy was contextualized to the background of the era, the rationale discussed earlier for the Reform and Opening up was clear—the strategy of opening up in 1988 was put forth as a tactic for stimulating economic development and alleviating domestic economic problems.

If the substance of the policy was examined in itself, the main purpose would be to promote exports in order to build up foreign exchange reserves, in turn to alleviate the foreign debts pressure. That was because simultaneous to the eruption of the cumulative fiscal deficit crisis in early 1980s, the foreign exchange reserve balance had also turned into deficit, forcing the central government to take urgent measures in response. The shrinkage of foreign exchange reserve was caused by expanding import and rising debts. China's import volume once again surged following the all-round urban economic reform and a greater extent of opening up, as well as the high initiation among regional governments to develop local economy, with the outcome of continuous trade deficits since 1984. A direct consequence was a sharp decline in China's foreign exchange reserve, from US$ 8.9 billion in 1983 to US$ 2.9 in 1987 (Fig. 7). And in the same period China's foreign debt ratio[12] jumped from 56% in 1985 to 77.1% in 1987 (Fig. 8).

That was to say, in mid to late 1980s, for every US$ that China could make from exports, more than a half, even three quarters had to be spent by the state on debt repayments.

It was the two sides of a coin: in a period of capital shortage, under the situation of continuous fiscal deficits and lack of investment capacity, the state could only bring in foreign capital. Yet the increase in foreign debts and decline in foreign exchange reserve would inevitably further add

---

[12]The ratio of net foreign debts to revenues from export; when a debtor nation does not have foreign exchange reserve or the latter is not taken into consideration, this is a key indicator for measuring debt burden and the risk of foreign debts.

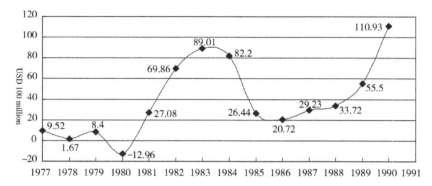

Fig. 7 China's foreign exchange reserve 1977–1991 (Source: State Administration of Foreign Exchange)

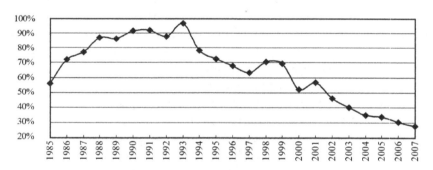

Fig. 8 China's foreign debt ratio 1985–2007 (Source: State Administration of Foreign Exchange)

to the country's fiscal pressure. From this, one would understand why in carrying out the coastal economic development strategy and driving forward the development of an export-oriented economy, the central government emphasized repeatedly that the key was to promote export to earn foreign exchange.

Why this policy was mainly oriented toward the rural enterprises just having started up in coastal regions, far from their completion of capital primitive accumulation? Part of the reasons was due to the needs to protect the state industrial capital. Under the urban–rural dichotomy, it would innately oriented itself towards urban interest blocs.

Box 7: Wang Jian's Economic Development Strategy Conception of "International Great Circulation"

Almost simultaneous to the central government proposing the coastal economic development strategy, on 1 November 1987 Wang Jiang, Assistant Researcher of the Economic Research Institute of the State Planning Commission published an essay in Xinhua News Agency's internal reference journal 动态清样 (Dongtai Qingyang [Dynamic Fair Copies]), titled "走国际大循环经济发展战略的可能性及其要求" (Possibility and Requirements of the Economic Development Strategy of International Great Circulation). It was highly consistent with the state's coastal economic development strategy, so much so that when it was published later in the Economic Daily on 5 January, 1988 with the title "选择正确的长期发展战略——关于国际大循环经济发展战略的构想" (Choosing the Correct Long-term Development Strategy—Regarding the conception of International Great Circle Economic Development Strategy), many people thought that the central government's decision had much to do with that paper. Although Wang Jian himself denied that, his paper nevertheless provided a theoretical basis for the strategy.

Wang Jian pointed out that China's overall goal in the next economic development phase should be to move towards a mature industrialized society. To realize this goal, it was necessary to choose the right development strategy; and the basis to consider should be the macro context and the principal contradiction. The macro context for China to move towards a matured industrialized society was that under the condition of a very low per capita income level, and with the situation that China's evolution of industrial structure had skipped the phase of light industries. Even though a relatively developed base of heavy industry had been formed, considering the proportion of agricultural labor, China was nevertheless still underdeveloped.

This highly solidified dichotomy had brought to the strategic choice for the next stage of development a major contradiction of fund allocation between industrial structure upgrade and diversion of rural labor force. It was impossible to continue with the mandatory prohibition over the diversion of rural labor force that had in the past served to accumulate funds for industrial development. In any case, if the problem of directing 800 million peasants towards industrialization was not resolved then China could not have truly accomplished industrialization. However, allowing a large number of peasants into non-agricultural sector would reduce the latter's organic constitution, causing the industrial structure to tilt towards light industries, hindering industrial upgrade.

In order to resolve the dilemma brought on by the dichotomy, Wang Jian listed four strategic options: first, give priority to agriculture and light industries in order to fulfill the phase of rural labor diversion; second, make use of foreign funds by lending to fulfill domestic accumulation; third, develop electrical manufacturing for export so that the heavy industries could accumulate for itself through international exchange; fourth, divert the rural labor force into the great international circle by developing labor-intensive manufacturing for export, on one hand resolving the issue of surplus rural labor and on the other hand gaining foreign exchange from the international market.

After analyzing the four strategies, Wang Jian believed that the fourth would be the best choice. To develop with this strategy, he believed there would be three phases.

In the first phase, the effort should focus on developing labor-intensive products for export, such as textiles, food and beverage, household electrical appliances, light industrial goods and so on. The priority should be put on coastal regions given their relatively better conditions. In this phase the development of heavy industry itself would have to be temporarily sacrificed; and the mission of heavy industry at this time would simply be to support the export of light industrial goods. The foreign exchange generated would partly be used to strengthen the servicing capacity of heavy industry and partly for bringing in technologies and raw materials abroad, so as to further develop exports. There would also be a need to improve the infrastructure for transportation and communication, particularly in inland regions, thus creating conditions for export industries to expand to central and western regions. While goods from coastal regions would be exported, goods produced inland would fill the local and domestic markets, laying the ground for exporting in future by upgrading quality. This phase would take 5–7 years.

In the second phase, inland products would begin exporting to the international market. The capability to earn foreign exchange through labor intensive goods became stronger. A larger portion of the foreign exchange would be used to support the development of basic industries and infrastructure. This phase would take another 5–7 years.

In the third phase, the foreign exchange generated would be applied to develop heavy processing industries that had high added-value. Capital and technology-intensive products would begin to enter the international market. The proportion of labor-intensive goods would decline. The pressure from labor diversion would also decline. Employment would begin to shift to heavy processing industries. All these would signify the arrival of China's industrial structure upgrade as well as high-speed growth. This phase would probably begin only towards the end of the ninth Five-Year Plan.

Wang Jian's analysis at that time had been very objective with foresight. Its impact on the central government policies had also been quite direct.

However, would the coastal economic development work out in real life the way it was conceived to forge an export-oriented economy through rural enterprises? In this regard most analyses from theoretical studies thought it was unrealistic. Nevertheless very few people had directly expressed dissenting opinions on the central government's strategic goal. Instead, most had expressed their views through direct responses to Wang Jian's idea of "international great circle".

Based on the contents of the discussions back then, people had valued highly Wang Jian's exploration of China's future economic development. Yet most researchers had doubts about the feasibility of the "international great circle" (Yang Peixin (1988), Wei Dakang, Gao Liang (1988), Liang Guiquan (1988), Yan Jinmin (1988), Min Jianshu (1988), Cai Wenxiang (1989)).

The focus was mainly on a whole series of difficulties that existed in rural enterprises: could labor intensive products, being low-end goods, be able to exchange into the international market for sufficient foreign currencies to support the development of heavy industries? How would the rural enterprises, most of them with backward technology and equipment, as well as little foreign trade experience, realize the strategy as prescribed? Under continuous inflation, how could the rural enterprises gain the impetus on export-oriented development?

Furthermore, from the perspective of enterprise echelons, the main force to develop export-oriented economy should be the urban large and medium enterprises and foreign trade enterprises. That was because compared with the rural counterparts, the urban enterprises were superior in terms of management quality, organization, technological know-how, resources efficiency, scale of economy, industrial-chain effect, risk-bearing and so on. If the urban large and medium enterprises were given more autonomy in their operations and the right to export, they would be able to become the leaders driving rural enterprises to form conglomerates and organizing the export-oriented processing manufacturing.

It goes without saying that such obvious, commonly known real life issues were well perceived in the minds of decision-makers. Still, when the policy was introduced, the main intention became a realistic resolution about the contradiction between coastal and inland regions over raw materials and domestic market. The coastal regions were requested to develop an export oriented economy with "both suppliers and markets abroad".

Source: Wang Jian "Choosing the Right Long-term Development Strategy—Regarding the conception of International Great Circle Economic Development Strategy".

Actually, since 1958 when the urban–rural dual structure was formerly established, internal contradictions of this sort in policy making had never ceased. The problems facing Chinese decision-makers in 1988 were similar to those in early 1980s with controversies such as "the small crowding out the big" and "the backward crowding out the advanced". The crux was still the urban industries once again got in a bind in the supply of raw materials and funds. Looking at the policy that finally came out, one found the same consideration of prioritizing urban industries. As a result rural enterprises (formerly brigade enterprises) were being discriminated once again. The argument that "coastal regions and inland regions had fought over raw materials and market" was no more than a pretext hiding the fact that urban interest blocs dominated the reform policies making.

The various issues around export-oriented coastal economy and the national development strategy were well worth of further reflection. But no matter what, the promulgation of the strategy to focus on export-oriented processing manufacturing on a large scale, trumpeted the commencement of the export-oriented economic development with Chinese characteristics by non-state-owned enterprises.

What came next was another important year, 1994, when there was a large devaluation of the Renminbi in one shot, accomplished by converging the official and the market exchange rates in the name of marketization.

Since the time of the Opium War in the nineteenth century, China recorded its last instance of major trade deficit in 1993, with the outbreak of major deficits in two other sectors. What helped ending the large trade deficit of US$ 12.2 billion in 1993 was partly the decision in 1992 to open up more selected cities around the country after the economic crisis in 1988–1991. Another more direct reason was the 1994 foreign exchange reform which was executed under the pressure of balance of payments deficit with a one-time devaluation of the Renminbi to USD exchange rate by more than 50% (Fig. 9).

The substantial devaluation amounted to artificially creating a huge basin for the global capital liquidity. It meant that Chinese enterprises, then not yet competitive in the international market and still under

Changes in China's Foreign Exchange Rate since 1979 (100 USD to Rmb)

Fig. 9 Renminbi exchange rate since 1979

a blockade imposed by the West due to the June Fourth Incident in 1989, were abruptly and unexpectedly given an enormous cost advantage. Moreover, with the expansion of financial capitalism and another round of international industrial structure upgrading towards the end of the 1990s, China's export trade situation underwent an immense change within a few years.

In 1994, China's trade turned from deficit to surplus, and since then trade surplus has gone up year after year.

4   The 7th Crisis: 1993–1994, the Third Economic Crisis since the Reform, and the Transformation to Export-Oriented Model

In 1992–1993, the central government, in an attempt to accelerate the monetization and the opening up of the capital market, was obliged to take full liability for the high level of foreign debts arising from the overheated economy. Because of that, the 1993–1994 economic crisis soon broke out—major deficits simultaneously in three aspects: fiscal, financial and balance of payments, which wreaked serious damage. It had not been long since the 1988–1990 crisis. The external situation was also harsh, with the blockade by the West still in effect and the recent disintegration of the USSR. The idea of the coming "China's collapse" became a fad in the international media. At this time, the third generation collective leadership just formed a relatively centralized leadership system, and needed to put a curb on the reactions in the society by resorting to an iron-fist approach, with enormous costs to both urban and rural sectors. Only then was China able to stumble out of the shadow of crisis.

Such was the objective context of that era when people blamed everything about crisis on the "old system" and advocated radical marketization reform. After that, given that the radical reform had resulted in an even higher degree of external dependency for China's economy, the third generation leadership core then went along with the trend and decided to accelerate China's integration into globalization.

Internal Mechanism and Characteristics of the 7th Economic Crisis in 60 Years of Industrialization, the Third since the Reform

Unlike the previous two crises generated due to a surge in domestic demand, the 7th economic crisis in 1993–1994, in which the three major deficits occurring simultaneously with the large expansion in money supply giving rise to a staggering CPI of 24.1% in 1994, was not only closely linked to the deepened reforms as a response to the depression caused by previous regulation, but also the first instance of economic crisis caused by speculative demands since the reform.

When China was in depression in 1990–1991, there were controversies around the Reform. Some who did not have sufficient understanding on the cyclical pattern of economic crises blamed the Reform, while others with specific purposes in mind, mainly those supporting Deng's Southern Inspection Speech, advocated deepening the reform. Such controversies seemed similar to past ones regarding the "left" and "right" line struggles. Perhaps they had diverted people's attention from seriously learning the experience and lessons from the failed attempt of forcing through the "price reform". When economic revival emerged in 1991–1992, people swiftly started to take part into the newly established speculative markets of stocks, futures and real estates. The further liberalization of these speculative markets which had higher capacity to absorb funds than general goods and production factor markets stimulated a surge in China's GDP. The Chinese economy seemed to have jumped through the stage of recovery directly into a boom.

This coincided with the affirmation in 1992 by the CPC 14th National Congress that the goal of the Reform would be a new market economy. Thereupon all kinds of interest blocs, including bureaucrat profiteering companies (profit-making companies previously set up by various government units to provide employments to the adult children of the officials) that had made their first bucket of gold taking advantage of the dual-price mechanism, jostled into the bonanza in the name of the Reform with political correctness, but in fact aimed at reaping personal gains and wealth. Within a short span of time, the aggressive expansion in fixed asset investments nationwide as well as the continuous disorder in the financial sector steered the Chinese economy towards high growth, as measured by GDP.

If people would leap beyond the binary ideological framework of reformist versus conservative, they could easily identify two systemic characteristics of China in the 1990s similar to those before the Reform—first, the institutional malady of economic regulation still lay at the dilemma confronting the old model in 1958 when the state conceding power and interests tier by tier: either economic disorder as a result of concessions or immediate recession if power was once again centralized; second, the dominating mechanism for fast economic growth during industrial capital expansion was still the urge towards crude and extensive growth.

Two intrinsic contexts should be noted about the investment frenzy of early 1990s that took place under such institution and mechanism:

First, in 1992 the new system of market economy was set as a goal and Premier Li Peng signed a document, "Regulation on the Transformation of Industrial Enterprises Operation owned by the Whole People". It clearly required the orderly moves of those enterprises into the market. Then the policy of "separating the government and the enterprises" promulgated by the central government further gave rise to the frenzy among official departments to set up their affiliated businesses. In 1992 alone, more than 200,000 companies were set up. As soon as these new capital interest blocs came into being, with their intricate connections to the government, they strengthened the process of primitive capital accumulation through rent-setting and rent-seeking. The institutional costs intrinsic to that abuse of power, transferred smoothly to the whole society by their privilege, was a powerful factor that drove the 1993–1994 economic crisis. This kind of institutional transformation, as Justin Lin Yifu said, resulted simply at turning government departments into companies. Apart from changing the titles of management personnel and removing government restrictions on their remuneration, the fact that their survival relied on administrative monopoly and favorable government policies basically remained unchanged.[13]

---

[13]Justin Lin Yifu, "企业自生能力与改革的深层次问题" (Enterprises' Ability of Self-reliance and the Profound Issues of the Reform), 国研网 (National Research Network), 2002-03-28.

Second, after Deng Xiaoping's Southern Inspection Speech, there was large scale expansion in investments around the country, in the name of "development is the hard-core truth". The real estate frenzy, the development zone frenzy and the development project frenzy that prevailed everywhere all drove the frenzy in investment and financing. The concession by the authorities gave birth to diversified agents, multi-level decisions on projects, and myriad sources of funding. However corresponding standards and regulating mechanisms were yet to be established. The outcome was increasing difficulty in suppressing the drastically expanding investment desire. Money was needed to expand investments, hence the mass financing activities as well as the fights for funding through high interest rates. All kinds of bonds, cash coupons and self-made stocks were on offer at increasingly high interest rates, generally as high as 20–40%. Yet the rate of growth in savings was slowing down and even became negative in many regions.

Under such a chaotic situation due to local authorities' autonomous pursuits of "development", the central government, in an attempt to sustain the operation of the financial system, could only increase money supply by an excessive amount. The volume of new money supply in 1993 was 152.87 billion yuan and in 1994 142.39 billion (Source: *China Financial Yearbooks*).

Even with the large expansion in money supply by the central government, many regions still had cases of payment troubles. More than ten provinces had called the Party Central Committee or the State Council to report that they were short of fund. Inland banks had the worst problem. Therefore, various kinds of notes in lieu of cash payments were commonly used.

At this point, most of the financial institutions nationwide recorded "financial deficits"—loans more than deposits—which in turn prompted higher supply of money and exacerbated the prospect of inflation.

A severe shortage of funds had led to abnormally high price to start with. The deep differential between official and market interest rates added to the problem. Rent-seeking activities therefore became increasingly rampant. Consequently, the operations of financial institutions were in a state of chaos. The state-owned banks set up numerous companies in securities, real estates and various investment trusts with myriad titles. Large amount of funds were diverted from the banks to those companies. Most of the banks also participated in real estate development projects, security trading and so on, taking up the funds available for turnover. Furthermore, there were the bureaucrat profiteering companies that wielded havocs in the markets, speculating on stocks and bonds, using state's money to reap private gains.

Box 8: Stock Markets Resumed in China

As symbolized by the opening of the Shanghai and Shenzhen stock exchanges in 1990 and 1991 respectively, China's stock markets officially resumed and gradually became an indispensable part of China's economic system. Some people said it was China's "greatest revolution" in the financial sector in the last decade of the twentieth century. The establishment of the securities market set up a larger arena for China's financial capital. The flow of funds into stock markets through varied channels became an obvious trend. It marked the beginning of the new era in which China's financial capital was alienated from industrial capital. The expansion of the financial market begun with China's currency becoming capital and its generation through credit-creation.

At the end of 1999, Qin Xiao, General Manager of CITIC, talked about the process in his speech at Beijing University Economic Research Center, "The Alienation of Financial Industry and the 'Virtual Economy' in the Financial Market". Following the appearance of stocks and bonds, currency became a kind of financial investment vehicle, i.e. the capitalization of currency. That was also when money was being generated through credit-creation. The creation of money through credit-creation and its transformation of into capital was the early state of a virtual economy. It no longer had a correlating relationship with the physical economy, but instead was an outcome of credit expansion.

During this period when financial capital gradually became alienated from the real economy, those companies having government connections were able to enter the primitive capital accumulation phase and in turn made an impact on the related government departments causing chaos in economic management.

Ever since the tax division reform that started in the 1980s and altered the allocation of tax revenues between the central government and local governments, local recklessness had emerged in three areas—levy-fees, fines, and fund-raising. The years 1983–1984 saw the first wave of government employees going into business. Then the second wave was in 1986–1987 and the third round started in 1992 with Deng Xiaoping's Southern Inspection speech. Yet since the third round with the simultaneous opening of the three speculative markets, the "recklessness" now turned into disorder– reckless financing, reckless (short-term) lending, and reckless setting-up of economic entities.

Back then people summarized this phase of economic overheating vividly as the "four fevers" (real estate fever, development zone fever, funding fever, stocks fever), the "four highs" (high investment expansion, high industrial growth, high monetary expansion and lending, high inflation), "four crunches" (transportation, energy, raw materials supply, funds supply) and finally "one chaos" (chaos in economic order, especially in financial order). Such chaotic phenomena in the local economies that happened after 1992 were similar to those during the "Great Leap Forward," a result of the central government conceding power to the local governments as an attempt to stimulate the latter's initiative in carrying on industrialization. The institutional costs of the 1958 chaos had transformed into the 1960 crisis which had to be borne by the entire society. Similarly, the institutional costs of the 1992 economic disorders also transformed into the crisis of 1994. A high inflation of over 24%, widespread lay-offs of SOE employees, large-scale expropriation of land from the peasants, sharp increase in mass incidents and so on—all that had been caused by the primitive accumulation of capital by interest blocs, giving rise to disorder in the economy, and the enormous institutional costs of which were inevitably transferred to the whole society.

The successive fiscal deficits and abnormally high money supply immediately detonated the inflation crisis. Furthermore, because of overheated investments, China's external economic relations were also being seriously challenged. In the 170 years counting from the Opium War of

1840 to the year 2010, the last instance of a severe foreign trade deficit emerged in the year 1993 when there were major deficits simultaneously in three realms. The accumulated balance of payments deficits handicapped China's foreign exchange reserve system. At the end of 1993, China's foreign exchange reserve was US$ 21.119 billion. Taking out the short-term liabilities of US$ 13.55 billion, the balance was US$ 7.65 billion, not even sufficient to cover the trade deficit in that year (US$ 12.2 billion), not to mention the accumulated trade deficits since the 1980s (totaling US$ 38.46 billion by the end of 1993) as well as long term liabilities of US$ 70.027 billion). Total foreign debts accounted for 13.9% of GDP in 1993, compared to the proportion for fiscal budget of 12.56%!

Based on the foregoing, people should deduce de-ideologically from China's essential experience as a developing country—Deng Xiaoping, by path-dependency, had inherited the 1970s' experience of bringing in foreign funds under Mao Zedong and Zhou Enlai. This third round of foreign investments in the 1980s, mostly brought in by local governments without having to bear the associated risks, resulted in an accumulation of foreign debts, which became the central government's liabilities. The foreign debt volume in 1993 reached a historical high since the establishment of New China.

The "three major deficits", other than the balance of payments deficit, also included the fiscal deficit that was directly borne by the central government, as well as the "banking deficit" i.e. minus capital funds in the state-owned financial sector, with serious negative differentials between deposit and loan (Fig. 10).

The simultaneous deterioration of the three major deficits gave no choice to the central government other than launching macro-regulation again in the summer of 1993.

On 24 June 1993, the CPC Central Committee and State Council promulgated the document "Regarding Current Economic Situation and Strengthening Macro-regulation", with important directives on "grasping the opportunities in economic management, speeding up the development; at the same time emphasizing reliability, avoiding loss, especially

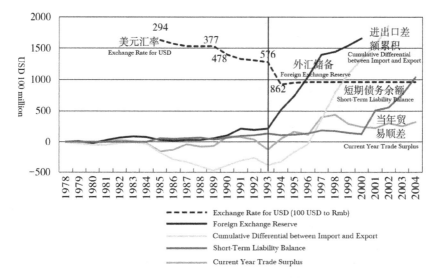

Fig. 10 Background of China's foreign exchange reform in 1994

big loss". The focus on speeding up development would involve deepening the reform, transforming the mechanisms, optimizing the structures and raising effectiveness. Furthermore, it put forth sixteen measures on strengthening and improving macro-regulation, with strict control on monetary expansion and stabilization of the financial situation.

The wordings of these documents that went into the official record were somehow gentle and proper. Yet back then they were referred to as the "sixteen iron-and-blood articles". That was because these macro-regulative measures aiming at accelerating marketization reform would "draw blood like a knife".

Indeed, 1994 was generally recognized as the "reform year". During this year, the government, in the name of Reform, put forth three major macro-economic measures to deal with three respective major deficits:

First, foreign exchange reform:

Accomplished exchange rate adjustment at one stroke by one-time 57% devaluation of the nominal exchange rate of the RMB. The exchange rate of Renminbi against USD was dropped from 1: 5.64

to 1: 8.27 as a way to stimulate exports and alleviate the quagmire of international payments.

Second, expansion of credit:

With successive years of fiscal deficits, the state financial sector was severely overdrawn, to the extent that the capital funds of state-owned banks were completely depleted and even part of the deposit funds were used up. In addition, there was enormous domestic demand during this stage arising from the investment frenzy. There was no other option but to substantially increase public debts and expand money supply.

Third, taxation system reform:

To alleviate the central government's fiscal difficulty, the system of fiscal responsibility by various tiers of local government established in 1984 was further transformed into the tax-division system. This reform altered the proportion of fiscal revenues division between the central and regional governments, from more than 70% to local governments down to 50%, a substantial cut. The consequence was local governments taking to generate revenues from selling land in a frenzied manner in order to compensate for the shortfall in fiscal revenues (Figs. 11, 12, and 13).

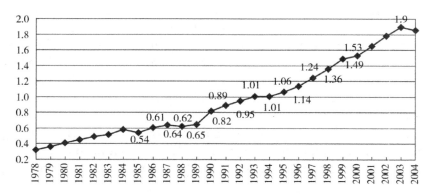

Fig. 11 Real M2/GDP 1978–2004 (Source: Han Ping (韩平), Li Bin (李斌) & Cui Yong (崔永) "我国 M2/GDP 的动态增长路径、货币供应量与政策选择" (M2/ GDP Dynamic Growth Path, Money Supply and Policy Options in China), 经济研究 (Economic Research), 2005[10])

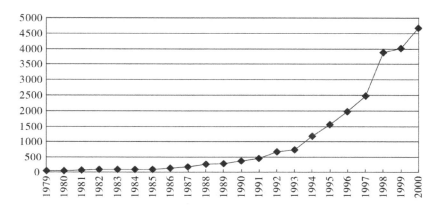

Fig. 12 Volume of national debt issued 1979–2000. Unit: 0.1 billion (Source: Li Biao (李彪) & Lu Zhihong (卢志红) "我国国债发行规模中的协整和 ECM 实证分析" (A Co-integration Analysis and ECM Empirical Analysis on China's Debt Issuance Scale), *Journal of Anhui Agricultural University (Social Science)*, 2004[4])

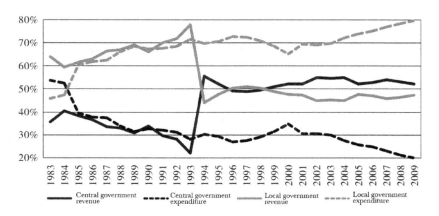

Central government revenue Central government expenditure Local government revenue Local government expenditure

Fig. 13 Proportion of fiscal revenues and expenditures between the central and local governments 1983–2009 (Source: *China Financial Yearbook 2002*)

In addition to these three major macro reforms, the decision makers further launched the state-owned-enterprise reform, with the consequence of China's social structural contradiction becoming increasingly accentuated. Given that the total fiscal revenues of the central and local governments declined to a historic low level of 11–13% of GDP

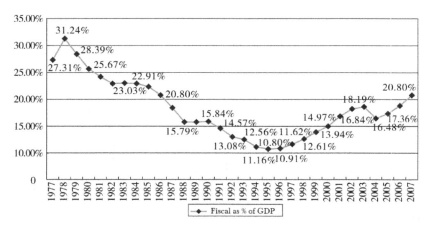

Fig. 14 National fiscal revenue as percentage of GDP 1997–2007 (Source of data: *China Statistical Yearbooks*)

(Fig. 14), local governments high-handedly forced through this reform mainly by selling off state-owned enterprises. The result was large scale lay-off and dismissal of SOE employees in tens of millions with little compensation for their tenure. And most of them had not been in time to be included in the social security and medical care coverage. There was a reduction during 1995–2000 in staff of 48 million just in state-owned sector and township collective units.[14]

The central government had already proposed macro regulation in 1993 amid the overheating. Nevertheless, the formal launching of the tax division reform in 1994, while well-intended, objectively made it hard to effectively implement the macro regulation.

Within the new taxation system, the local governments only had two main sources of revenues under their control—the profits realized from cashing in land and the increase in tax revenues from expanding foreign investments and urbanization, leading to higher income tax, business tax from construction and real estates. These tax categories were entitled to

---

[14]Wang Shaoguang (王绍光), Hu Angang (胡鞍钢), Ding Yuanzhu (丁元竹) "最严重的警告: 经济繁荣背后的社会不稳定" (The Most Serious Warning: the Social Disability behind Economic Prosperity), 战略与管理 (Strategy and Management), 2002(4).

local governments.[15] Under the pressure of inelastic fiscal expenditures, land became the main source of revenues that could be realized in the shortest period of time. "Generating money with land" thus became a widespread local government practice subsequent to the tax division system reform.

Another aspect was that as a part of the reform, the tax revenues collected by local governments in 1993 would be taken as the benchmark for the central's fiscal allocation to the local in future years. Using 1993 as the benchmark year, the year before the new system was actually launched, was a "deal" with local governments in exchange for their support. What happened was that in the few months after it was announced, there were abnormal surges in the amount of tax collected by local governments countrywide, including ad hoc impositions, collection of long-overdue taxes, even taxes owed by enterprises that were already closed down. The increment in local tax revenues in 1993 was 96.66 billion yuan or a 40.2% growth, out of which 75.7 billion were collected from September to December, with a growth of 51.8, 62.5, 86.1 and 121.3% respectively compared with the same month last year.[16]

It became a key factor determining the success of the new system, which depended on whether the local governments could keep up the high growth in tax revenues in 1994. If the macro-regulation measures were strictly executed, they would definitely be handicapped. Hence, much had been said but little was actually done. In this regard, the then Minister of Finance Xiang Huaicheng commented that "a strong support from local governments is essential to drive major taxation reform. Compromise was inevitable. The price had to be paid. The concession has won over the people, united their minds and assured the smooth launching of the tax division reform" (ibid.).

---

[15]Jiang Xingsan (蒋省三), Liu Shouying (刘守英), Li Qing (李青) "土地制度改革与国民经济成长" (Land System Reform and the Growth of National Economy), 管理世界 (Management World), 2007(9).

[16]*Source*: Xiang Huaicheng (项怀诚) & Ma Guochuan (马国川) "改革是共和国财政六十年的主线 (上)" (Reform was the Main Line for Fiscal Finance over Sixty Years of the People's Republic [Part 1]), 读书 *(Doushu)*, 2009(9).

In this way, amid the repeated game playing between the central and local governments, the former announced in 1997 that a "soft-landing" had been successfully accomplished.

On 23 January 1997, the State Statistics Bureau published the article "Macro-regulation achievements have been notable and structural optimization is imperative—economic situation of 1996 and prospect for 1997", pointing out that with dedicated effort by all sectors, the national economy was operating well now; the "soft-landing" was basically successful; economic growth had gradually and smoothly declined from the peak of 14.2% in 1992 to 9.7% in 1996, on average around one-percent drop every year; price level increase had dropped from the high of 21.7% in 1994 to around 6% in 1996, a total drop of 15.7 percentage point.[17]

These macro-regulation measures also resulted at a much higher dependency of China's economy on export. In 1994 when the Renminbi was devalued at one stroke by over 50%, China attained the historical record of US$ 121.01 billion in export, a growth of 31.9% from previous year. If the growth rate was calculated on Renminbi basis, it was even more staggering at 97.3%.

Indeed, these measures also led to weak domestic consumption and a rapid decline in domestic demand. On one aspect it motivated various local governments to eagerly bring in outside investors, thereby stimulating the momentum for internal structural adjustments. Objectively it was also a response to the transnational corporation's needs amid their structural upgrade in terms of financial capital to acquire strategic industries in developing countries. On another aspect, it was also one of the main reasons that impelled the mainstream policy makers and researchers in China to embrace economic globalization with enthusiasm, thereby speeding up the pace of China's negotiation with the WTO. The foreign economic and trade sector formally proposed in their documents "the strategy of going global". In 1994, China's oil industry went abroad for the first time—the Sinopec Group signed agreements with six countries to participate in their oil and gas projects, including Iran, Saudi Arabia,

---

[17]Liu Guoguang (刘国光) & Liu Shucheng (刘树成) "论软着陆" (On Soft-landing), *People's Daily*, 7 January 1997, page 9.

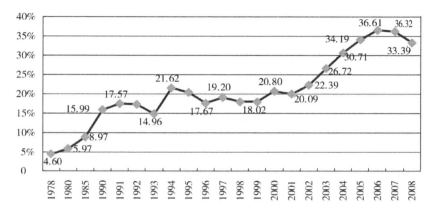

Fig. 15 Export as % of GDP in China 1978–2008

Gabon, Kazakhstan, Yemen and Ecuador, as well as an agreement with Saudi Aramco and the Ministry of Energy of Saudi Arabia on natural gas prospecting and extraction in Block B area of the Rub al-khali Basin.

The reliance on export trade (export trade as % of GDP) in 1991, 1992 and 1993 was 17.57%, 17.37% and 14.96% respectively. After the exchange rate reform n 1994 it sharply went up to 21.62%, and then20.48%, 17.67% and 19.2% in 1995, 96, 97 respectively. Even with the onslaught of the Asian financial crisis when China's export trade contracted substantially, with a growth rate lower than that of the GDP, yet the reliance remained at a high level (Fig. 15).

Becoming increasingly dependent on export trade, China further internationalized its economic development. However, it also intensified the global economic cycle's impact on its economy. Since then the economic crises in China have become increasingly correlated to external factors.

The Urban and Rural Sectors Jointly Shared the Costs of 1993–1994 Crisis

The reason that this 7th crisis was regarded as ending at a "soft-landing" by the mainstream was mainly based on two benchmarks—GDP and

CPI. It did seem reliable. Yet, What accompanying the "soft-landing" were a whole series of unprecedented enormous costs: a huge number of layoffs of SOE employees, the withdrawal of the government from public services leaving the latter to the private sector, the deterioration in rural governance, the *sannong* issues, and so on. It would not be objective to neglect the enormous social costs behind the "soft landing".

We believe that the costs of this crisis had been transferred to and shared by both the urban and rural sectors. In particular, this macro-economic crisis impacted rural economy and peasants' income in many respects. They were not merely the bearer of the crisis costs.

Urban Workers Laid off on Large Scale

The eruption of this crisis was different from previous ones in that it was not manifested in variations in fixed asset investment level or rate of employment in the society. Rather, it was expressed as a sudden jump into the overheating of regional economies agitated by the Southern Inspection speech by the supreme leader, pushing further the Reform and Opening Up. That was simultaneous to the central government's opening of the three major capital markets as well as the large-scale expansion of money supply. The consequence was a crisis symptomized by three major deficits giving rise to hyperinflation. And under pressure, the policy makers kept their mouths shut regarding the reason for the over-staffing and inefficiency in SOEs: ten years ago the SOEs were given the instruction to absorb young people seeking employments, with the approach of "hiring ten persons with the wages of five", as a measure to deal with the crisis back then. On the contrary, they now reproached the SOEs for low efficiency. From the vantage point of capitalist interests, the government mandated the SOEs to improve efficiency by means of lay-off and down-sizing (Image 5).

This crisis and its handling took place during China's eighth five-year plan. Based on statistics, we can find a striking phenomenon during 1991–95—the emergence of unprecedented high economic and investment growth rates along with an unprecedented low employment

Image 5 In Beijing, close to ten thousand female state-owned enterprise workers over age 35, who had been laid off or in a semi-unemployed state, participated in the recruitment of a commercial group. Two thousand of them would be hired as salespeople in the group's 100 chain stores. The re-employment of China's older laid-off female workers was raising the concern of the whole society

growth rate. According to Hu Angang's research, during the eighth five-year period, the average GDP growth was 11.9%, the highest record up to that point. At the same time, the total investment in fixed assets had an annual growth of 36.1% on average. Even taking out the impact of CPI, the average yearly growth was still 20.6%. Yet during this period, the annual employment growth was merely 1.3%, much lower than that of all the former five-year plan periods.[18]

In particular, during 1994–1995, there was almost no employment growth in the SOE sector. The other side of the low employment growth was the widespread lay-offs of urban workers. Compared to previous

---

[18]Hu Angang (胡鞍钢) "就业: 中国发展的第二号任务" (Employment: The Number 2 Mission of China's Development), 改革内参 (Internal Reference on Reform), 1997(12).

crises before the Reform and Opening Up, the state now did not have the possibility to send surplus labor to the countryside as a means to alleviate the unemployment pressure in cities. Moreover, due to serious fiscal deficits, the government retreated from its commitments to the public services such as health care and education, not even providing basic social security. The urban residents painfully bid farewell to the traditional system that had provided social welfare from cradle to grave, similar to those Scandinavian welfare states. They lost their largest social identity advantage compared to their rural counterparts.

In the name of SOE reform, the massive lay-offs, bankruptcies and mergers being forced through during the 1993 crisis marked a new era in the urban sector. The urban workers, used to be members of the urban vested interest blocs, this time had to directly bear the costs of economic crisis caused by a series of events—the expansion of state industrial capital, the concession to local governments and the subsequent frenzied introduction of foreign investments. Since then, the urban interest blocs became diversified. Most importantly, capital has taken absolute dominance over labor.

Since the introduction of the Bankruptcy Law in 1988 till 1993 before the crisis, there had been 940 cases of enterprise bankruptcies. Most of these were small to medium enterprises and collective enterprises. In the year 1994 when the crisis broke out, China finally established in a formal way the status of "capital" in the sense of classical economics. The State Commission for Economics and Trade proposed pilot scheme zones for "optimizing capital structure", and raised the issue of re-settling workers from bankrupt enterprises in Document Number 59 [1994].

By 1997, out of 111 cities that were pilot scheme zones, a total of 16.87 million staff was being "diverted", actually through mergers, bankruptcy and down-sizing. In January 1997, the State Council convened a working meeting in Beijing on the nationwide re-employment of SOE workers. During this year, the State Council and other related departments as well as organizations like All-China Federation of Trade Unions promulgated many documents relating to

SOE bankruptcy and merger, as well as projects on staff re-employment, boldly and resolutely forcing through this task.[19]

According to a survey on Mianyang Township in Sichuan conducted by the Ministry of Labor, Mianyang, being a national pilot scheme site for "optimizing capital structure" as well as the provincial "two transformations" project [modern enterprise system and flexible market mechanism], had 62 cases of SOE bankruptcy since 1996, with 21,000 workers being laid off, accounting for 7% of SOE workers in the township.[20] Another example was a survey conducted by Chinese Textile Trade Union in 1996 on six cities in three provinces. Just under the Xian Textile System there had been 8,940 laid-off workers, 55% of the staff. Of them, 70% had no income. In Zhangjiakou, the laid off workers under the textile system had reached 10,500, 61.7% of the total. Some factories even let workers take woolen material from the inventory in lieu of compensation.[21]

When all these became twentieth century history, different theorists gave different assessments. One young scholar pointed out that it was a polarized and exclusive growth while another reputed reform theorist expressed in an implicit way: what China practiced was a "non-populist growth". Although the latter was more widely accepted by the mainstream in the West, the contents of these two formulations were not essentially different.

Marketization and Privatization of Public and Social Services

Provision of services by public sector usually has the characteristic of "information asymmetry". Among these, medical care and education even have absolute "information asymmetry". They are liable to

---

[19]https://www.wyzxsx.com/Article/Class4/201008/172397.html.

[20]Liu Xiahui (刘霞辉) & Mo Rong (莫荣) "国有企业改革与职工再就业问题研究" (On SOE Reform and Workers Re-employment), Working Paper.

[21]China Textile Union "救救纺织行业困难职工" (Rescue the Textile Industry Workers in Difficulties), 改革内参 (Internal Reference on Reform), 1996(21).

monopoly by individuals for profiteering if they become commercialized and privatized.

Whichever the political system, so long as the state allows the commercialization of medical care and education where absolute information asymmetry exists, it is inevitable that hospitals, schools and individuals in the related professions would make use of their absolute information-monopoly positions to reap super profits from clients in disadvantaged positions. Therefore, any normal state would have to provide basic inclusive social services in public sector with a stable fiscal budget support. It should also strictly scrutinize the sources as well as motives of non-public investment in order to protect public interests by maintaining a relatively high ratio of public services.

The simultaneous major deficits in fiscal budget, balance of payments and financial sector in 1993 resulted in the comprehensive marketization reform in 1994. During this time the government, under the pressure of increasing fiscal deficits arising from the accumulation of foreign debts, was forced to cut budget support to medical care and education (in rural regions in fact a full retreat), thereby prompting the completion of commercialization in these realms. Accompanying this institutional change were a series of problems including unaffordable medical charges and high sales commission on drugs, unregulated education fees, unregulated financing, etc. Moreover, the serious corruption of relevant intellectual groups (medical doctors and teachers) became a chronic ailment.

The problem of the unspoken rule behind these phenomena, generally regarded as social corruption, became even more severe. Many professional practitioners in these fields took abnormally high profit as a matter of course, based on their monopoly on information, and deliberately constructed an open system with intrinsic mechanisms to protect their vested interests. Those officials in the authorities responsible for the institutional provision had intricate connections and relationships among themselves, leaving little room for institutional improvement. Therefore, even though they continued to take up and devour a large portion of public resources, low-cost and inclusive public services became almost impossible.

Before the reform most of the public services had been provided by workplace units. They were public institutions affiliated to various tiers of the government, including schools, hospitals, agricultural technology stations, cultural centers and so on. In the first few years of reform, the government at one time had increased expenditures on public services, putting education, medical care, poverty alleviation, environmental protection and social welfares as priorities. The proportion of budget expenditure on education as a percentage of GDP was raised from 1.8% in 1978 to 2.2% in 1982. As for medical care, it was raised from 1 to 1.3%.[22]

However, with fiscal deficits rising, the state adopted a "shrugging off burden" measure similar to reforms in other realms. It shrank the functions it should have been performed, even fully withdrawing from some social services. In addition, both the government departments and workplace units had to increasingly rely on off-budget sources of funds, with the result that it became a common practice for government departments to set up companies, while public faculties would hasten to provide fee-charging services. Hence, urban residents and the peasants had to take increasingly the costs of public services.

The state's target for education expenditure as percentage of GDP was supposed to reach 4% by the end of the twentieth century. In 1990, the number was 3.04%, then down to 2.73% in 1992, 2.54% in 1993 and 2.46% in 1996 on a declining trend. It was not until 1997 that the decline stopped and it went up slightly to 2.5% in 1998.[23]

According to regulations, local governments should be responsible for obligatory primary education. Yet when local fiscal capacity failed to pay for the cost, primary education that should have been a public good had to be paid for by the people in the name of reform, with the slogan "people's education run by the people".

The medical care expenses in 1990 had taken up only 2.79% of GDP in China. By 1997 it declined to 2.45%. Yet according to the

---

[22]Wang Peihua (黄佩华) "中国能用渐进方式改革公共部门吗?" (Can China Reform the Public Sector with a Gradual Approach?), 社会学研究 (Sociological Research), 2009(2).

[23]Wang Xiaohui (王晓辉) "教育财政体制改革应有新思路" (There should be New Ways of Thinking in Reforming Education Expenditures), 改革内参 (Internal Reference on Reform), 1999(22).

minimum standard set up by the state—"everyone enjoys health care"-
the percentage should not have been lower than 8%.[24] The proportion of
health care expenditure paid by the citizens relative to total health care
expenditure was 23% in 1980. By 1990 it went up to 37%, a rise of
14 percentage points in the first decade of reform. By 1999 the proportion became 59%, a rise of 22 percentage points in the second decade.
It was a process of state expenditure contraction, while the citizens had
to pay more and more. The medical care insurance reform was launched
in 1996. However whether in cities or rural regions, the coverage was
reduced and the proportion of medical fees to be paid by individuals rose
up. There had been doubts and comments from international special-
ists and international trade unions regarding the design of individual
accounts in medical insurance, similar to the pension fund system.[25]

Local Government Transferred the Governance Costs to Villages; Serious Social Contradictions

Since the beginning of the Reform and Opening Up in the 1980s, China
had undergone two fiscal system reforms, first the 1984 "fiscal responsibility by tiers" in 1984 and second the "tax division" in 1994. Both
of these reforms which embodied the policy principle of "shrugging off
burden" resulted in adverse impacts on rural governance.

At the same time as the central government and various tiers of local
governments implemented the fiscal responsibility in 1984, the policy
of "self-financing" among the two-tier rural administration—county and
village—was launched as part of the reform. The people's communes
were disbanded to set up counties while the production brigades became
villages. As a result, the administration costs to be paid by the villages to
maintain the two tiers of superstructure substantially increased. In addition, the funding for public services in rural regions had to be provided
by the grass-root (mostly the peasants).

---

[24]Zhou Yanling (周雁翎), "差异悬殊: 中国卫生保健事业面临严峻挑战" (Wide Differential:
China's Medical Care Profession Facing Severe Challenge), 中国改革 (China Reform), 2002(4).
[25]Liu Haiying (刘海英) "我们到底能做什么" (What In Fact Can We Do?), 中国改革 (China
Reform), 2002(4).

By the time of the 1994 tax division reform, every tier of government attempted to shrug off its responsibility of building local infrastructure and providing public services to the next tier below. Most of the local budgets were spent on infrastructure and public administrations.[26] At the levels of county and village, particularly in central and western regions, the problem of asymmetry between financial power and administrative power emerged. Most local governments had only sufficient financial power to maintain the very basic administration, with no capacity to make improvements to the society, thus deviating from the principle of public finance.[27] The central government exerted tighter grip on regional finance. Locally disposable financial capacity rapidly contracted. A governmental organization would in nature tend to protect its self-interest by "taking the financial power from lower tiers while pushing down the expenditures". After tier by tier holdbacks, the grass-root level public bodies at counties and villages, the lowest end of the administrative hierarchy, got trapped in financial quagmire.

Under normal circumstances, the consequence of fiscal system reform with tier-by-tier "offloading burden downward" would not be visible. However, when there was crisis giving rise to austerity measures, the costly superstructure designed according to the imagination of political modernization and built over a peasant economy with little extractable surplus to support it would inevitably result in additional burden on the peasants scattered in rural regions. Hence, the rural regions became the hotspots throughout the entire 1990s with increasing cases of mass protests at larger and larger scale, mostly against excessive tax and levies, illegal expropriation of land, disruption to the land responsibility contracts etc.[28]

---

[26]Li Chenjie (李晨婕) & Wen Tiejun (温铁军) "宏观经济波动与我国集体林权制度改革" (Macro-economic Fluctuations and China's Collective Forestry Rights System Reform), 中国软科学 (China Soft Science), 2009(6).

[27]Chen Xiwen (陈锡文), Han Jun (韩俊) & Zhao Yang (赵阳) "中国农村公共财政制度研究" (Study on Rural Public Finance System in China), 宏观经济研究 (Macro-economic Research), 2005(5).

[28]Dong Xiaodan 董筱丹 & Wen Tiejun "宏观经济波动与农村治理危机" (Macro-economic Fluctuations and the Crisis of Rural Governance), 管理世界(Management World), 2008(9).

Financial Capital Alienated from Physical Industries

Of the so called "sixteen iron and blood articles," the central government macro-regulation measures in response to the crisis in 1993, more than a half were concerned with financial policies. The ailment of economic overheating created by bureaucrat profiteering companies and related government bodies had to be cured with the medication of nationwide austerity measures. The overall credit-tightening damaged the overall balance in credit. Restricted credits among some regions largely reduced the money circulation rate. It hurt to a large extent mostly the small and medium non-SOE enterprises, while the impact on large SOEs was insignificant. The most striking phenomenon was the big differential between the official and market interest rates. In the summer of 1993, bank loan interest rates along the coast were between 10 and 16% (annual rate up to 20%) while the market rates reached 20–35%.[29] Long-term financial capital scarcity would naturally push up the interest rate. Economic overheating was like adding fuel to the fire. Yet under macro-regulation it took a twist. Financial capital became alienated from real industries—the allocation of financial resource in the 1990s increasingly drifted away from the real economy, swarming the stock market and real estate market in seeking profits. Virtue capital started to take shape in China. It transmuted into a means to share the allocation of profits, rather than creating real profit. Financial capital would depart from realms with lower liquidity and lesser odds for speculative profitability. The consequence is the trend of "financial exclusion" that developing countries in general would experience in their course of development.

During this period, it was precisely because of the trend of financial exclusion that the natural environment suffered disastrous consequences. The situation of forestry in mountainous regions was a typical example.

---

[29] https://zhidao.baidu.com/question/41628982.html?si=9.

Box 9: Predicament of Forestry in the 1990s

Since forestry has a long production cycle, implying a slow turnover of funds, long investment maturity and high risks, the macro-economic institutional changes had a dampening effect on forestry as well as the reform and development of forestry districts. Given the structural adjustments in national economy, industrial capital was set to transmute into financial capital seeking higher profitability. Eventually it would be drawn to the monopolized financial sector. Whether the forestry ownership was scattered or concentrated would not be a matter of concern to financial capital. Therefore forestry found it hard to draw investments from financial capital in this period. In 1993, in the loess plateau regions like Shanxi and Shaanxi where even the local governments were entrapped in extreme poverty, there were cases where usage rights of barren land had been auctioned off at a negligible price. Then in August 1995, the Ministry of Forestry in conjunction with the National Reform Commission promulgated the document "林业经济体制改革总体纲要" (Comprehensive Outline of Forestry Economic Reform), consolidating the direction of forestry rights marketization as mandated by the central policy. It clearly specified the goal of creating a market for the living stumpage in forest plantation. Forest assets should be liquidated through various means such as biding, auction, renting, mortgage or consignment.

The pilot scheme sites started with auctioning barren land suitable for reforestation and transferring forestry resource and further developed into the circulation of forestry usage right.

In view of the fact that China was at the industrial expansion phase back then, the capacity for capital to integrate with other essential factors of production was strengthened. Therefore this marketization of forestry rights, referred to as "the second forestry reform," resulted in the resources of the mountain regions being concentrated in the hands of well off households and cadres to form economies of scale. The goal was to attract external funds to realize the capitalization of local resources in order to stimulate economic growth in the mountain regions.

After the second forestry reform the facts from different places stated clearly that the related benefits were mainly taken by well-off households, cadres or tycoons that were already quite well-endowed in capital whereas the resource owners could attain the social average return for production factors by their participation in the social division of labor. However the negative externality arising from this institutional reform was embodied in higher social contradictions and the worsening predicament of the country's forestry, indirectly causing environmental disasters.

The social contradictions became intensified because the outcomes of the reform were not consistent with the intention of promoting the development of collective forestry land to increase peasant incomes. No matter how the property right was transformed, the concentration of resources led to the deprivation of a part of the right of mountain people to make a living from the resources proximal to their settlement.

The worsening predicament for forestry was expressed as follows:

On one hand China had to pay other countries to import large quantity of wood and other forestry products (Zhang Daohui 2001). Yet on the other hand the collective forestry regions had large areas of barren land. After the tax division system reform in mid-1990s, forestry tax was raised further and the total levy of tax and charges in forestry operation amounted to more than 51% of the selling price of timber. In addition there were all kinds of fees collected by various tiers of governments and various tiers of forestry departments during the production and distribution. The higher the overall tax and charges the lower the purchase price became. Furthermore, there were widespread cases of sabotage, illegal logging as well as bribery and corruptions, indirectly causing destruction to the environment. The high levies were ultimately transferred to the peasants as producers of forestry products. As a result, large areas of forestry land were deserted.

Source: materials collected by the author's research team

Fundamental Change in the Mechanism for Capitalization of Land Resource

In the first round of "land enclosures", arable land had been recklessly appropriated mainly by rural enterprises, disrupting the overall plan of national construction. On 21 March 1986, the document issued by CPC Central Committee and the State Council "Notice on Strengthening Land Management and Stopping Misappropriation of Arable Land" clearly pointed out that: "the phenomena of rural enterprises and residential properties in rural regions recklessly occupying arable land is conspicuous. If the situation continues it would lead to serious bad consequence to national construction and the livelihood of the people, endangering future generations." One aspect that should be noted was that the profits generated from appropriating arable land for industrial use within rural communities had mainly gone to the collectives while the government could barely take a share. Yet the latter had to take the responsibility for "food security". In late 1980s the central government started to request a stricter control on converting arable land to non-agricultural purposes, and gradually took back the power to approve converting arable land for industrial and commercial use. That notice issued on 21 March 1986 had requested regional governments to comprehensively investigate illegal use of arable land and not to grant lower-tier administrative bodies the approval authority. In the same year the "Land Management Law" was also introduced to confirm the state's authority on converting land use to non-agricultural purposes. In 1988, the State Bureau of Land Administration was set up to exercise full authority in this regard.

However, at the same time when this authority on approving land use was taken by the government which was characterized by corporatism, the nature of land as a commodity was also been gradually established. In 1988, the Amendment to the Constitution of the People's Republic of China stipulated that the land use right would be transferrable in accordance with legal regulations, thus officially ushering in the compensable use of land in China. On 19 May, 1990, the State Council announced the implementation of "Provisional Regulations on the Transfer and Conveyance of the Right to the Use of State-owned Land in Township", providing clear regulations on the transfer, renting and mortgage of land usage right. Land was in practice endowed with the attribute of commodity. That fundamentally changed the nature and mechanism of land capitalization. In the 1980s land was used for productive purpose by the self-initiated development of grass-root rural enterprises i.e. "building enterprise with land". In the 1990s, however, land became a means for local governments to generate fiscal revenues to cover the inelastic expenditures, i.e. "cashing in land". Its nature changed from productive to consumptive. Cashing in land became the fastest way to make money for the local governments.

Box 10: Real Estate Development and Regional Expropriation of Land in the "Second Land Enclosure"

In 1992, the liberalization of real estate pricing instantly prompted a boom. The growth in completed real estate investment in 1992 was 117.42% and the profit growth was 140.39%. In 1993, these two indicators were 164.98% and 145.47% respectively. The local governments and real estate development related sectors all enjoyed a hefty share of profit from this booming. The enormous monetary capital of state-owned monopoly banks was instrumental to the formation of capital land rent and differential rent since 1994 by way of real estate development through the transfers of state-owned land use rights and ownership. With the financial sector acting as an agent of capital oversupply, the land rent was embodied in the high return rate from real estate investments, the profits of which were devoured by the developers. Through this movement of stripping off the state ownership of land (the essence of the frenzy in granting such permissions), giving rise to the real estate investment craze, by which the nouveau riche class in China made their second bucket of gold.

Yet, it was precisely these high profits generated by real estate development (in essence land rent) that stimulated the economic prosperity in China during 1993–1995. The total operating incomes from real estate development in 1992 and 1993 reached 52.86 and 113.59 billion yuan respectively, higher than the previous year by 86.1% and 114.9%, while the revenues from providing construction land reached 4.27 and 8.39 billion yuan, higher than the previous year by 177.9% and 96.4% respectively.

The development zone craze and real estate craze in early 1990s brought on the second peak of land enclosure. Since 1992, the total constructed area skyrocketed to the peak of 271,000 hectares by 1993. In 1992 and 1993, the total area of real estate developments grew by 174.96% and 96.61% respectively from the previous year (Source: *China Real Estate Market Yearbook* 1996).

Excerpts from: Yang Shuai (杨帅) & Wen Tiejun "宏观经济波动、财税体制变迁与三次圈地运动" (Macro-economics, Taxation Institutional Transition and Three Rounds of Land Enclosure), 管理世界 (Management World), 2010(4).

The second round of land enclosure that was initiated by the local governments was very unlike the first as it involved different agents and lasted longer. During 1994–1998, with year-over-year decline in the economic growth rate and the central government sparing no efforts to suppress land enclosure, the arable land reduction per year still averaged at 215,000 hectares (since the data for 1996 was not available, the computation was based on the average of 1994, 95, 97 and 98).

The peak of land enclosure during 1992–1995 may generally be interpreted as the institutional costs of implementing institutional transitions in order to resolve the 1989–1991 economic crisis. During this period, the large amount of expanded money supply was able to be absorbed within a short span of time by large scale capitalization of land. That in turn helped revive a high economic growth. The central government under the burden of taking the ultimate liabilities for domestic and foreign debts was able to leap out of the predicament of 1993 in which the volume of three major deficits had been larger than China's total GDP.

It was somewhat similar to the situation in the 1980s in which large scale land enclosure had prompted high economic growth. Yet the actual mechanism and channels of capitalization were very different. In the 1980s it was because of the rise of rural enterprises that land was appropriated. Land required an integration with other physical assets of enterprises to become a material "asset" in industry or commerce. The added value of land was realized through business operations. Yet by early 1990s, land itself became the object of business. Simply by means of land development or entitlement transfer, it was possible to attain much higher profits than in the stage of "building enterprises with land" in the 1980s. For example, in Xietang township in Suzhou, thanks to the Suzhou Industrial Park, the local government cashed in 98.8687 million yuan in land leasing during 1992–1999. Taking out 8.866 million submitted to the state and 266.1 thousand as balance, the rest was all spent as public expenditures in the town. 11.1671 million yuan was allotted to the villages at lower tier, 2.3816 million for agricultural expenses, 4.9189 million for culture and health care, 6.8261 million for administration, 13.881 million for public services, 4.4929 million for hygiene, 20.569 million for development, 20.25 million to external investments, 5 million others.[30]

It also meant that the interests-structure inside government corporatism underwent changes. Alienated from localized industrial capital, the local governments generally relied less and less on sharing the added value of localized industrial capital, but instead welcomed investments from outside that did not have to take the responsibilities for local community welfare.

Given that the mechanism of land capitalization and the agents of land capitalization had both undergone changes, the allocation of added value generated from converting arable land to non-agricultural purposes also showed corresponding changes.

First, the village collectives no longer played a leading role in land capitalization. Also, after the change of land use, the revenues generated were no longer relevant to the collective accumulation for local members. Instead, after a one-time compensation for expropriation, the peasants lost connection to their land.

On one hand, when the local governments exercised its monopoly power granted by the state over arable land conversion, they obtained the monopoly gains generated from the added value of the land. During the process of land expropriation, given that the collective economy was in reality no longer the property right owner, the government was able to exercise direct control over the administrative and party organizations at the village level to largely reduce the transaction costs in acquiring the land. According to a survey by Wen Tiejun and Zhu Shouyin in 1996, the peasants would only get 5–10% of the revenues; village collective economic organizations would have 25–30%; and 60–70% would go to the government and various authorities. And the portion that went to the village collective organizations would usually be controlled by the village cadres.[31]

---

[30]Xietong Town Chronicle Editing Committee, 斜塘镇志 (Xietong Town Chronicle). Beijing Local History Publishing, 2001.

[31]WenTiejun & Zhu Shouyin (朱守银) "政府资本原始积累与土地'农转非'" (Government Primitive Accumulation of Capital and Converting Land from cultivation to non-agricultural purposes), 管理世界 (Management World), 1996(5).

On the other hand, the separation of government and enterprise starting in 1992 and the rural enterprises ownership reform in mid and late 1990s in effect transformed the rural enterprise from being the vehicles responsible for communal welfares and maximum employment in the collective into industrial entities simply seeking profit maximization. The collective enterprises had relied on the collective resources to complete the capital accumulation. Then by means of institutional changes the enterprises became the sole and exclusive owners of the assets generated. It was highly similar to the process in which the enterprises under whole people ownership had completed the accumulation relying on state power and then during its reform the ownership was gradually altered and these enterprises became the sole owners of the assets. Moreover, the industrial capital brought in by local governments to various development zones has never established any direct connection to local welfare as collective rural enterprises once did.

Second, the one-time compensation was being deducted tier by tier before it finally arrived at the hands of peasants. Moreover, the sharing of profits from land development was also extremely uneven. As a comparison, in the 1980s when villages initiated land appropriation on their own to establish productive enterprises, the profits generated from land capitalization had stayed within the village to a large extent, and been spent on community welfare and agricultural expenses. At the same time it had stimulated non-agricultural employment and raised cash income for the peasants. In the 1990s, however, the profits generated from cashing in the land were mainly shared between the local governments as well as the industrial capital. In the 1990s, some local governments proposed the slogan of "generating wealth and making the towns prosperous through land". However, in practice, some surveys showed that in some counties the local governments relied on land leasing for 20–30% of their finance. In some towns, more than 80% of off-budget revenues came from land leasing. While land and capital, two scarce factors, were both leaving agriculture, the proportion of agricultural population moving to towns was consistently declining as the land price was rising (ibid.).

The growth rates of peasant income and consumption in the 1990s were significantly lower than in the 1980s when domestic demand was the main thrust of economic growth. From a long-term perspective, it gradually led to a serious shortfall in general domestic demand during the 1990s since the peasants comprised the majority of the population. Therefore the national economy shifted towards a greater dependence on export. This important shift did not suit the strategic needs of the time when China's industrial capital was in a phase of rapid expansion. However, the short-sightedness created by the symbiosis of government corporatism and localized industrial capital resulted in their blindly going along with the economic cycle into the next phase that entailed even higher institutional risks.

The Positive and Negative Impacts of Crisis Management on the *Sannong*

On the positive side, at the same time when urban and rural sectors both had to bear the costs of this crisis, the rising staple grain prices did contribute to raising peasants' income level. Also, since the peasants could now buy staple food with cash in cities, they left their home villages and swarmed the urban sector to seek employment with the rapid expansion of land development.

Because of the higher demand on coarse grain due to the rising population of migrant peasant workers, there had been a shortage of low quality grain in 1993. The policy makers became worried that inflation might be incurred in case of inadequate grain supply. To secure the supply, the government launched various projects during 1994–1996 with a larger financial support to agriculture. The purchase prices of grain were twice raised by a large amount, with an accumulated increase of 105%. The agricultural income was consistently growing. And China was able to realize its target of 1 trillion catties production in 1996, four years ahead of the scheduled year 2000.[32]

Yet there was also negative impact. With the eruption of the 1997 Asian financial crisis, the economy went on a downward cycle. The urban demand for grain declined while total population growth remained at the

---

[32]Wen Tiejun "中国粮食供给周期与价格比较分析" (Comparative Analysis of China's Food Grain Supply Cycle and Prices), 中国农村观察 (Rural China Survey), 2003(3).

expected rate. That meant, in terms of population number and demographic structure, the consumption of grain could not possibly expand to the 2000 level four years ahead of time. The problem of grain oversupply emerged. As the economy fell into depression, the prices of grain and the cost-effectiveness of grain production both declined.

Chinese agriculture increasingly showed signs of degeneration in the late 1990s.

In summary, Chinese economy started in 1992 to change from being industry-oriented to capital-oriented. It led to economic revival, immediately followed by a surge. With this stimulation, an increasing number of peasants went to the cities for employment. Their labor and service incomes went up (even though the financial crisis later in 1997 would lead to a new cycle of agricultural employment growth with the reverse-urbanization). A survey found that since the 1990s China has a clear cyclical expansion and contraction in the primary industry. The first cycle lasted from 1991 to 1996, with the agricultural employment of 390.98 million in 1991 down to 348.2 million in 1996, a reduction by almost 10.94%.[33]

In any case, this crisis marked the transition and watershed from endogenous economic crisis to exogenous (imported) crisis in China. It was a time in which the industrial capital in China was approaching a state of overcapacity while the financial capital was expanding rapidly and increasingly alienated from the former. Moreover, it was a time when China began to transform into an export-driven economy, thus becoming increasingly susceptible to international economic cycles.

The costs of this crisis were borne by both the rural and urban sectors. The institutional condition of collectivization was no longer available for a complete transfer of the costs to the rural sector. Despite the official announcement of a "soft-landing," both the urban and rural residents suffered hard from it. In the urban sector, an astronomical number of workers were laid off while the villages saw an intensifying social contradiction expressed as protests against heavy tax and levies as well

---

[33]Xie Maoshi (谢茂拾), Cai Zexiang (蔡则祥) & Wang Haiyan (黄海艳) "金融危机影响下农业就业的困境与新出路" (Predicaments and Solutions of Agricultural Employment under the Impact of Financial Crisis), 中国发展观察(China Development Observation), 2009(11).

as rampant land expropriation. In both cases the costs of the crisis were expressed as an increasing number of mass protest incidents. At the same time, attempting to resolve the fiscal crisis, the government continued to retreat from the public services provision. As a consequence, urban citizens and the peasants had to bear most of the costs and pay a higher price for the services.

5

Two Exogenous Crises in 1997 and 2008: Occurrence, Response and Impact

In the mid and late 1990s, the Chinese government had adopted radical reforms in response to crises, effectively taking a further step of "retreat" from non-profitable small and medium state-owned enterprises through sell-offs. After that, Chinese economic growth went from a model that relied predominately on domestic demand and government investments, to one mainly dependent on overseas markets. International economic circumstances therefore began to have an increasing impact on China's economy. China was inevitably being incorporated into globalization dominated by transnational capital.

We refer to this process of China's absorption into globalization as "the 4th wave of foreign capital introduction" over the 70 years of contemporary Chinese history.

The process manifested two key characteristics: first, foreign capital played an increasingly dominant role in the Chinese economy amidst the structural adjustment brought on by Chinese industrial capital's overseas expansion. Entering the twenty-first century, transnational companies almost completely controlled China's high value-added industries, taking most of the profit; second, China became the recipient of outward cost transfer from countries that dominated globalization. Hence the

© The Author(s) 2021
Wen Tiejun, *Ten Crises*, Global University for Sustainability Book Series,
https://doi.org/10.1007/978-981-16-0455-3_5

economic crises it had to deal with were also predominately exogenous. Faced with this kind of crises created by external factors, the Chinese government lacked the necessary rights to participate in international negotiations and in setting institutional arrangements. Domestic regulatory measures were generally far from effective. As a result, even before the "government retreat [from the economy]" reform was completed, there emerged the "government advance" reform.

These two were new characteristics of economic reform and development that were brought on by globalization, dominating China's direction in history. Although China had adopted three rounds of opening up in different forms in the past, their impact on the domestic and world economy was on a different scale compared to this 'opening up' in the new century after the country's integration into globalization.[1]

1   Four Rounds of 'Foreign Capital Introductions' Over Sixty Years, Each Accompanied by Emergence of Two Crises

During the 60 years from 1949 to 2009, China had experienced four rounds of foreign capital introduction. On each occasion, the contents as well as results were similar, involving the introduction of foreign equipment and technology, followed by two economic crises.

The first of such crises took place in the 1950s. During the ten years between 1950 and 1960, the USSR had first heavily invested and then abruptly halted the investment, thus leading first to an economic surge then a sharp decline, resulting in two deficit and unemployment crises in 1960 and 1968 respectively.

The second round happened in the 1970s, notably from 1972 to 1979. The high costs of Western equipment, technology and services as well as the debts incurred gave rise to two deficits and unemployment crises. These occurred in 1974–1976 and 1979–1981 respectively.

---

[1]Wen Tiejun et el: 解读苏南 (Interpreting South Suzhou). Suzhou University Press, 2011.

The third round of "foreign capital introduction" into China took place in the 1980s, simultaneous with the central government's policy of conceding power and interest to local governments. Given the excessive debt repayment pressure the central government had to bear, local authorities were given the right to expand the scale of "opening up". That gave rise to the stagflation crisis of 1988–1989 as well as the economic crisis in 1993–1994 in which three simultaneous major deficits were accompanied by high inflation and high unemployment.

Although these six crises were closely related to "introducing foreign capital" or "opening up", the triggering key factors were mainly deficits in the fiscal budget, the current account and in the financial sector. Essentially they constituted an "endogenous crisis" in the economy.

Yet in the mid-1990s, under the effect of the reform that had urban and rural populations both bearing the costs of the crisis, as well as the effect of the subsequent decline in domestic demand, China had accelerated its pace into joining globalization. Consequently, the two crises that occurred in 1997–1998 and in 2008–2009 were related to external circumstances.

On this basis, we believe that the latter two crises were quite different from the previous six, and belonged to the "exogenous crisis" category, brought about by the "fourth round of foreign capital introduction", under the conditions of globalization.

China's fourth introduction of foreign capital took place in a situation in which the national economy was already under the determining impact of overseas demand and followed the trend of being taken up in global capitalization. Garnering the common points between the two exogenous crises, we can hardly find any dissimilarity.

First, the cause of the crisis. Before it happened, the domestic economy had to a large extent been driven by exports. As such when foreign financial crisis broke out, causing significant decline in export, domestic economic growth also suffered. Another outcome was increased unemployment.

Second, measures in response: In contrast to the austerity measures that the government had adopted in the past when endogenous crises occurred, the government undertook large-scale expansionary fiscal policy to increase investments and provide a stimulus for domestic demands, preventing a sharp decline in economic growth.

The biggest difference in the central government's measures in response to these two crises lay in higher investments after 2008 to the *sannong*, which was effectively an extension of the new policy supporting the *sannong* by the central government since 2003. Because of that, not only did capital and labor, two of the three essential factors of production, flow back to rural regions on a large scale, partially restoring the regulating function of the countryside as a 'labor pool', it also facilitated the construction of a 'second asset pool' in the county economy.

That may have been the most notable favorable experience out of the measures in response to the crisis of 2008–2009, with outcomes beneficial both to urban and rural sectors.

Yet, on the adverse side, the social contradiction that was of concern also became intensified alongside these bail-out measures. While the bail-out investment of 1997–1998, in which urban interests were the prime focus, did bring economic revival, it brought excessive institutional costs to the rural sector due to the excessive use of rural resources, to the extent that a large number of social conflicts arose. Coincidentally, in the even larger bailout investment of 2008–2010, that past approach of transferring the crisis to rural regions—appropriating scarce rural resources and accelerating resource capitalization—became even more blatant. Local governments around the country adopted pro-capital policies with little restraint. Therefore social conflicts, referred to as "mass incidents", increased sharply. The more vociferous the domestic and overseas opinions were, the more difficult "stability maintenance" became.

Very few have presented objective analyses integrating politics and economics to explain a confrontation like this, which is the outcome of institutional cost transfer as a response to crisis. Many scholars would do no more than echo ideologues overseas, taking such social conflicts as the ground for "political self-deprecation." For example, they would claim that these conflicts signal political or social failure. By doing so, these scholars have mostly benefited themselves. Without proper explanations it would not be possible to come up with solutions. Hence the kinds of contradictions accompanying bail out measures simply continued. The mass incidents spread and sharply increased year over year, so much so that even though the political direction of 'constructing a harmonious socialist society' was put forward in the fourth plenary of the 16th National Congress, formally mobilizing all positive factors for that purpose, local governments and authorities around the country that were already thoroughly corporatized simply dismissed it, and continued to give priority to cashing in land for attracting business and investments.

Since reform and opening up, the developmentalist outlook—the essence of which was to push forward the capitalization of resources—marched on and the allocation of institutional costs and gains became increasingly imbalanced. That constituted the biggest obstacle to carrying out the CPC's governing ideas of 'scientific development outlook', 'building a harmonious society' and 'ecological civilization'.

2   The Eighth Crisis: Measures to Deal with 1997 Asian Financial Crisis and the Impact

In the same year that financial storms erupted in various East Asian countries whose economies based mainly on manufacturing and trade, the CPC proposed in the 15th National Congress report (1997) to continue the development of various markets, focusing on markets for essential production factors including capital, labor and technology, as well as improving price formation mechanisms for these factors. Furthermore, the commercialization reform of state-owned banks and of the People's Insurance Company of China would be quickened, to enhance the policy-oriented financial system.

It was the first time that the CPC, in its transition from a revolutionary party to governing party, clearly affirmed the status of "capital" in a political report of the National Congress, putting forward the notion of "capital (as production factor) market".

On one side, although this official confirmation of capital came five years later than the actual opening of the capital market in 1992, it nevertheless implied that "capital" had already secured a sense of 'political correctness' in the ideology of Chinese economic system.

Yet we should not ignore the other side of this major institutional transition—the force of circumstances. In fact, no sooner had the Chinese leadership confirmed the status of "capital" than the East Asian Crisis occurred, demystifying the East Asia industrial expansion model that Chinese intellectuals held their belief in. It sounded the alarm for China's monopolized financial sector, where non-performing debts were mounting. Closely following that, just one month after the 15th National Congress, in the national financial working session the central government made the decision to launch marketization reform of state-owned financial institutions on all fronts, as a response to the challenge of the South-east Asian financial crisis. From then on, Chinese financial institutions went along the path of "securitization and market offering". Given their nature of pursuing liquidity for profit, they inevitably became alienated from the real economy over time, forming an independent interest bloc. Right after commercialization, they dived into the brave new world of mixing investment banking with general commercial banking, replicating Wall Street's "too big to fail" scale, in an attempt to join the global competition of financial capitalism.

Change in Origin of the Crisis: Why Was It an "Imported" Crisis?

China encountered an "imported (exogenous)" crisis in 1997–1998 and then economic depression in 1999–2001, which was signified by deflation. That was the outcome of two factors, first the macro-economic regulation that started in the second half of 1994 and cumulated in a "soft landing" in 1997, then the East Asian financial crisis in 1997, with the former being a prelude of the latter.

The central government's macro-regulation over three consecutive years from 1994 to 1997 had brought about the major structural change of declining domestic demand and rising dependence on oversea markets.

Even though the guiding principle of macro-regulation was introduced in 1993, it was not until 1996 that economic overheating, driven by the capital markets of stocks, futures and real estate was cooled down by economic and political measures, hence the declared "soft landing".

This could be reflected in fixed investment growth rate. Based on monthly statistics, it could be seen that in early 1996 the growth rate of fixed investment fell below 10% for the first time, with the rate for the full year falling below 20%. In the first half of 1997 the investment growth rate was controlled and kept within 15%, indicating that the macro-economy had generally passed the overheating phase. Based on annual statistics, the full year fixed investment growth rate during the 1993 peak was 61.8% while in 1997 it came down to 8.9%, below 10% for the first time. The pull of investment on GDP was 11 percentage points in 1993 while the contribution rate was 78.6%. In 1997 the figure dropped to 2.1% and 18.6% (Figs. 1 and 2).

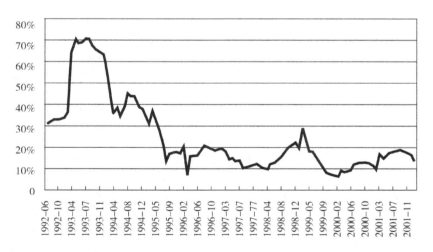

Fig. 1 Monthly fixed investment growth rate in China 1992–2001 (Data source: *China Statistics Yearbook 2009*)

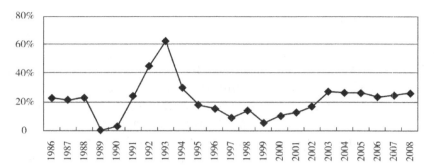

Fig. 2 Annual fixed investment growth rate in China 1986–2008 (Data source: *China Statistics Yearbook 2009*)

At the same time as the investment demand declined, export was growing year over year. Under the double stimulation of macro-regulation and foreign exchange reform since 1994, export replaced investment to become the primary impetus to China's economic growth. "The net export of goods and services reached 99.85, 145.93 and 274.5 billion yuan in 1995, 1996 and 1997 respectively, higher than the preceding year by 57.5%, 46.1% and 88.1%, and accounted for 1.68%, 2.1% and 3.6% of GDP".[2] In 1997 when the East Asian financial crisis erupted, the pull rate of full year exports on the national economy was 4.2 percentage points, a contribution reaching 44.4%. The pull rate of current year investment on economic growth was 34.3%.

In other words, before China put forward a strategy to narrow the "three major gaps" (the rich and the poor, urban and rural, coastal regions and inland), and had there not been the large-scale diversion of excess industrial capital towards the international market, the domestic supply and demand would have been seriously unbalanced.

Unexpectedly, when mainstream Chinese academics were passionately talking about "the inevitable trend towards global unification through marketization and political liberation," closely following the "World Bank consensus" transition path prevalent in the 1990s, the East Asian crisis broke out abruptly in the second half of 1997. The economic crisis

---

[2]Ma Hong (马洪) & Lu Baipu (陆百甫), 中国宏观经济政策报告 (China Macro-economic Policy Report). Beijing: China Fiscal and Economic Press, 1999.

that it induced in China happened right at that essential moment of its historical transition, from bidding farewell to the age of scarcity to entering that of oversupply. China was then caught in a dilemma. The strategy just formed by the central government to foster globalization was struck by a sudden decline in overseas demand (Fig. 3).

With regard to "over production" in the general sense that classical Marxism had analyzed, not only were the Chinese economists at the time not aphasiac like contemporary Chinese economists are, they were able to point out its correlation to macro-regulation with Chinese characteristics. Experienced experts in the policy advisory section of the government had made assessment in 1998 that China started to move from an economy of scarcity to the phase of excess production capacity, which was in essence more in accord with other industrialized countries:

"From the perspective of the economic growth environment, externally there is the onslaught of the Southeast Asian financial crisis and domestically there have been severe disasters of flooding. From the perspective of economic development, (China) is situated at an important turning point, beginning to move into a new phase. The characteristic of scarcity is fading out and the characteristics of buyer's market are gradually showing up. The change in the overall relationship of supply and demand volumes as well as the structural contradictions that are exposed would exacerbate market competition and difficulties in businesses would stand

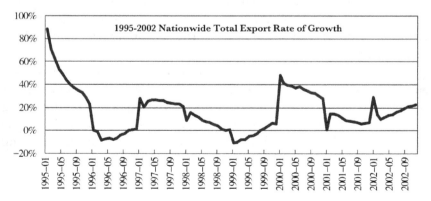

Fig. 3 Export trade monthly growth rate in China 1995–2002

out. From the perspective of the economic cycle, the economic policies since 1993 to curb inflation have gradually lowered the demand growth rate. Economic growth will enter a relatively obvious self-contracting state as a result. The sum impact of the various factors above will make it unprecedentedly difficult to maintain stable economic growth in 1998.

The change in the economic institution and development phase actually began in the mid-1990s. That they have not quickly appeared in the overall supply and demand capacity relationship is mainly because growth in net export had, to a certain extent, hidden the changes there ...... The growth in external demand has to some extent alleviated the domestic contradiction of higher supply than demand, hence diluting the changes in the economic model in that supply and demand capacity relationship aspect. The East Asian crisis that began in July 1997 had a major impact on China's export growth. The rate of export growth abruptly fell to 0.5% in 1998. The rapid contraction of external demand is bound to reveal the change in supply and demand capacity relationship caused by changes in domestic economic model."[3]

On this aspect, another influential economist in Chinese policy-making, Justin Yifu Lin, proposed unambiguously at the end of 1999 in an internal conference that to target the problem of overcapacity it would be essential to initiate the New Rural Construction investment strategy. He felt that the Chinese economy had already fallen into the "vicious cycle under the condition of a double excess". Although that strategic adjustment proposal was not adopted then, he persisted in raising it and ultimately in late 2001 it came within the scope of vision of central leadership. In 2005 it was affirmed to be the top priority in China's 11th Five-year Plan.

Actually, as early as in 1978 China's industrial goods export had already accounted for 45.2% of total exports. By 1997 the total export volume was US$ 182.697 billion with industrial goods export totaling US$ 158.767 billion, accounting for 86.9% of total exports. Out of the export goods, electrical goods had reached US$ 59.32 billion, reaching

---

[3] Ibid.

32.5% of total export in that year, exceeding textile goods for three consecutive years to become the largest export goods category in China.[4]

It can be seen that even before the Reform and Opening Up, China had already transformed the structure of purely primary goods export in a period of thirty years. Then in less than twenty years after the Reform and Opening Up, the country completed industrial capital's domestic expansion and its adjustment on export structure.

And yet, this milestone change in the economic structure that happened at the end of the twentieth century would inevitably make Chinese economy more vulnerable to external economic volatility. In particular, ever since the West entered into the stage of financial capitalism, it has introduced measures to deepen financialization in developing countries. This has had a great impact on China.

From the perspective of changes in the international political-economic order, after Nixon announced in 1971 the abrogation of the USD gold standard, and in 1973 adopted the monetary policy of a "floating exchange rate", European countries and America had resolved in the Brussels conference to follow the approach of increasing the net capital flow rate to sustain real consumption. The relocation of industrial production outwards and the inflow of capital gains induced a fundamental transformation in the nature and characteristics of crises happening in the West, different from those that previously took place during the phase of industrial capitalism. The outcome was that the exploitation of developing countries by Europe and America far exceeded that occurring in the 1950–1960s.

Furthermore, under the "free market" mechanism of complete opening up, developing countries entering the industrialization phase but facing severe capital scarcity accelerated the inflows of foreign capital, which sought to capitalize and take ownership of these countries' resources. And the financial capital that aimed to make quick profits by market liquidity was the least constrained by national frontiers. Once those financial investments made profits, they could escape anytime.

---

[4]Li Jingzhi (李景治) & Pu Guoliang (蒲国良), 社会主义建设理论与实践 (Theory and Practice of Socialism Construction). Beijing: China Renmin University Press, 2003.

Like Northeast and Southeast Asia before them, the disintegrated Soviet Union, Eastern Europe as well as China that was expanding its industrial capital, were one after another absorbed into the Western monetary system In the 1990s. This was in fact a system sick to the core with inflationary bubbles. Then in accordance with the pattern, a whole series of changes were brought about by the inflows and outflows of foreign capital.

We may take a look at the impact of crisis on China's export structure. Before the 1997 crisis, export growth had an obvious effect in pulling up China's economy. Part of that effect also included the devaluation of Renminbi in 1994 and 1995, giving rise to sharp export growth, which then slowed down in 1996. The annual export growth was 31.9% in 1994 and 22.9% in 1995 while only 1.5% in 1996. In 1997 it had revived to 20.9%. The form of trade had also seen significant changes. In January 1995, the growth in general trade was 98.1%, higher than total export growth in the same period by almost 10 percentage points. However, from the second half of 1995 onward, growth in general trade export rapidly fell behind total growth and declined in the overall proportion. In all of 1995, general trade export growth was 15.9%, lower than that of total export by 7 percentage points. In 1996 it fell down to 11.9%, and the gap with total export growth widened to 13.4 percentage points. In 1997 the growth in general trade was higher than total by 3.2 percentage points. In 1998, with the impact of the Asian financial crisis, growth in export fell on all fronts rapidly and the full year total growth was only 0.5%. From the perspective of ownership, state-owned enterprises' general exports recorded lower growth, well behind the overall growth rate. Enterprises under collectives had notably higher growth in general export than the rest of the country. From 1996 onward, general trade export by foreign enterprises were on the rise notably. As a whole, China's export as an impetus on economic growth fell from 4.2 percentage points in 1997 to 1.3 percentage points in 1998.

In a nutshell, given the trend of modest investment growth as a result of macro-regulation, the decline in overseas demand directly led to a domestic economic crisis characterized by depression and deflation.

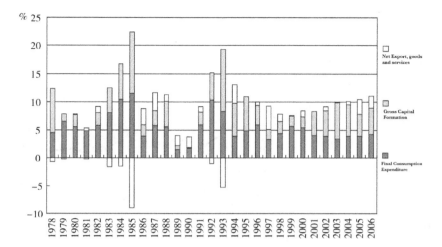

Fig. 4 Volatility and key drivers for China's macro-economic growth, 1978–2006

If in 1994 the key word that would send a chill down people'
spine was "inflation"–the price index up to 24.1%—then in the five
years 1998–2002 with the impact of the Asian financial crisis the key
word that would describe China's macro-economic trend changed in a
quiet manner to one that common folks could no longer understand:
"deflation" (Fig. 4).

"From October 1997 to December 1998, the price index recorded
decline in absolute number for 15 consecutive months. That is a
phenomenon that has never happened since the Reform and Opening
Up. The change in price level index is an important reflection of the
change in supply and demand relationship of goods and services. To a
certain extent it reflects the level of development of the supply-more-
than-demand relationship pattern"[5] (Fig. 5).

After the official Chinese media announced in 1997 that the national
economy had accomplished a "soft landing", it should have resumed a
period of modest growth. Yet with the onslaught of the East Asian financial crisis, exports were severely affected. The entire Chinese economy

---

[5]Ma Hong & Lu Baipu, *China Macro-Economic Policy Report*. Beijing: China Fiscal and
Economic Press, 1999.

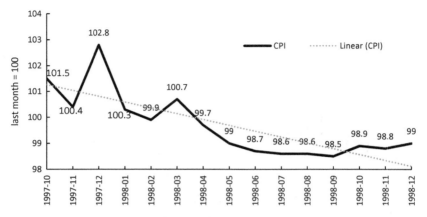

Fig. 5 Monthly CPI in China 1997 (October)–1998 (Data source: China National Bureau of Statistics website)

that was overly reliant on exports was hit hard. Therefore, the economic depression in China towards the end of the 1990s as characterized by deflation was an "imported" crisis brought on by the East Asian financial crisis.

China's Key Experience in Responding to Imported Crisis: "Government Intervention"

Facing that typical imported crisis brought on by the external financial storm, the central government's measures were mainly applied in the areas below: first, reforming the financial sector with resolve to prevent risks; second, issuing public debts on a large scale to invest in infrastructure construction and to expand domestic demand; third, simultaneously launching industrialization reforms in various sectors such as housing, education and health to spur on the growth of market consumption of domestic public goods through deepened monetization. Further, the central government raised the tax rebate rates on export to strengthen the price advantage of Chinese goods in the international market.

Although these measures entailed extremely high social costs, they did prevent the economy from a downward slide. In relation to the policy target for GDP, simplified as slogan of "ensuring 7, striving for 8," the measures were indeed effective.

Financial System Reform—Financial Capital Controlled by Central Government Transformed into Monopolistic Capital Independent of Localized Real Industry

One might say that it was only in 1992 when the government abandoned the coupon system that Chinese people used paper currency entirely for trades in the market. It signaled the start of monetization of the Chinese economy on all fronts. By 2002, the Chinese were able to complete the market reforms of finance, separating banking from the fiscal sector so that banks would no longer be subordinate to the latter. It signified the fact that from then onwards China had commercial banks that operated independently.

The East Asian financial crisis brought the issue of financial security to the attention of countries around the world. Under increasing pressure of bad debts in the domestic financial sector and with the financial crisis on the brink of eruption, the central government convened in November 1997 the National Financial Working Meeting. After that, the marketization reform of state-owned financial institutions was initiated in 1998 on all fronts, eventually making it possible for China's banking sector to develop into a relatively independent capital bloc, the most profitable one indeed.

Before the commercialization reform of banking in 1998, the fiscal and financial sectors were both used by the government as functional bodies to regulate the economy. During the transformation of China's modern financial system, the roles for each sector had undergone many major changes, in step with the progress of China's industrialization.

Generally speaking, in the first forty years of socialist China, fiscal measures played a more obviously dominant role in resources allocation. While the Renminbi was China's legal currency, and given that people's individual consumptions were largely rationed by the coupon system, money functioned mostly as a value measure of allocated goods, not circulated as an independent means of payment. That was the reason why before and in the early stage of the Reform, when consumable goods were in extreme scarcity, China was still able to avoid the hyper-inflation that many developing countries generally suffered.

On that basis we could say that the deepening of monetization in China's economy and the general monetization of Chinese society, had its beginning in the 1980s in step with the Reform, adopting the approach of "shrugging off burden" from the fiscal budget, then launched on all fronts in the year 1992 when the government completely abolished the coupon system.

Looking back at China's modern financial history, during the ten-year "golden" era that started in 1920s in the Republic era and ended in 1937, the annual average national economy growth rate between 1928 and 1936 had been as high as 8.4%.[6] However, it had ultimately crumbled due to the "silver crisis" which was exogenous, as discussed in Chapter 1. The West had to abandon the Gold Standard due to the 1929–1933 Great Depression; further the U.S. propped up the silver price under domestic political pressure. These two factors led to the drainage of China's silver, in turn the collapse of the Silver Standard that had been in place for more than 400 years. The Republic government was faced with serious deflation due to substantial outflow of silver and in 1935 made the change to a fiat money system. At the beginning it was sustainable but soon after, with invasion by imperialist Japan first into Northern China in 1935 then all out in 1937, the supply shortage due to the war led to continuous high deficits and inflation. Ultimately, the U.S. stopped their aids in 1948, with the outcome of total collapse of the Republic's fiscal and financial systems. The Kuomintang regime was ousted in the revolutionary war.

Compared to the ill consequence that the Republic had suffered in abandoning the Silver Standard and fiat-monetization for 14 years which ultimately failed, the monetization that started in China in the 1980s in company with marketization had for the first time in contemporary history successfully established a financial system with paper money as the principal exchange medium.

---

[6]Sun Jian (孙健), 中国经济通史·中卷 (General Economic History of China second volume). China Renmin University Press, 2000–2001.

Before the reform, because of Soviet Union's abrupt termination of strategic economic aids in 1958, China was forced to initiate localized industrialization supported by investments mostly from local government fiscal revenues (see Chapter 2). That had given rise to the division of power between the central and local governments over the fiscal and finance sectors, as well as the "Great Leap Forward" driven by local investments. Being in the hands of local governments, the "Great Leap Forward" had little restraint, and the expansions were too ambitious to be suppressed. By 1960 the accumulated fiscal deficit became too high, which then detonated an all-out economic crisis.

Similar to the localized industrialization in 1958, in early 1980s with the fiscal system being decentralized to localized Contract Responsibility System, as well as the reform of banks to convert funding to state-owned enterprises "from fiscal allocations to loans," and adding to these the diversified vested interests among governmental bodies, the tens of thousands of local governments—controlled fiscal and financial systems had ignited a new round of rough, uncoordinated expansion. That was the substance of China's entrance into high growth mode by means of localized industrialization.

Within a short span of less than 20 years, China rapidly entered into the phase of overcapacity, which caught people by surprise. In particular, beginning with the accelerated development of speculative capital markets in early 1990s, the Chinese people, who had been inured to the government slogans of "fight for export, fight for foreign reserves" ringing in their ears as they woke up from the nightmare of extreme capital scarcity, were quickly finding themselves in a situation of excess industrial capital.

Box 1: Chinese Financial Capital in Modern History—Formation and Expansion

Whether in China or other countries, fiscal crises often become the juncture for innovation of the financial institutions. Yet the Chinese road of development of modern finance is not the same as that in the West.

Even if in Sung and Ming dynasties China was able to take in an enormous quantity of precious metals from the West through overseas trade and, hence, alleviated the scarcity of currency, financial capital integrated with state credit had yet to take shape. The main reason had been that the formation of the state and the formation of capital did not take place in the same historical period, thus the power structure and relationship between them was fundamentally different from that in the West. Private capital had never become an independent agent that the ruling power could rely on. On the contrary, since the state had matured earlier than financial capital, when the monarchical system collapsed and China was passively absorbed into the world economy since Late Qing, the accumulation and expansion of industrial capital had more readily become dominated by bureaucratic capital and state capital. In this process, the bureaucratic capital found it easier to transform into national finance that held monopolistic status as compared to private finance. It had reached a peak for the first time during Chiang Kai Shek's rule, at which time domestic fiscal and financial systems mainly relied on American aid for support.

Since the late 1990s, China's finance became more concentrated and monopolistic. Later on, the Chinese banking sector replicated the Western financial system on all fronts. Combined directly with the state apparatus it was further integrated in the global financial regime, in the global competition dominated by financial capital.

Historically, it appeared inevitable that the state and bureaucratic capital instead of private capital played a dominant role in the century of modernization in China.

Source: Quoted from Liu Haiying's doctoral thesis, Chinese Renmin University.

The decentralization of power and concession of interests to local governments in the 1980s had given rise to subsequent reform involving the division of fiscal and financial systems as well as the uncoordinated expansion of localized industrialization. Yet very few people mentioned the biggest externality resulting from the Reform: given the need to secure the centralized political system, the central government was obligated to bear the debt responsibility that arose from the endeavors of local governments and enterprises (mostly state-owned) bringing in capital. That power division reform with its delineation of rights, obligations and interests would inevitably further complicate the relationship between the central and local governments.

It is obvious that financial reform was of paramount importance and relevant to the state political system.

To the central government, fiscal deficits would directly or indirectly become bank overdrafts although in 1993 it was announced that fiscal budget could no longer be overdrawn from the central bank. Under the pressure of deficits the central bank would increase money supply to purchase national debts, which was no more than shifting debts between pockets and bound to giving rise to mild or serious inflation. Since the Chinese fiscal and financial systems could still be regarded as an alternative form of state capitalism, the credibility of Renminbi during this period was still derived from "institutional credit" rather than "commercial credit". Fiscal and financial institutions were not separable in function in the Chinese economic system before the early 1990s. As long as there was no subversive political crisis and the government stayed intact, the state-owned banks would not need to secure ample capital funds as required in Western private capital financial system. Not only were the non-performing debts in banking sector underwritten by the central government using foreign reserves from the treasury, even the serious differential between deposit and loan that had emerged in the entire banking system was ultimately guaranteed by state credit and settled with increased issuance of money as the last-resort repayment.

Besides, given that the power division reform had been started by the central government in the attempt to shrug off its fiscal burden to local governments, the local fiscal and financial deficits would eventually have to be borne entirely by the central government nominally centralizing power in its hands. Thereupon that particular system gave rise to another aspect of government corporatization under the condition of a monopolistic economy: high speed expansion of state financial capital, the rights and obligations of which could not possibly be synchronized.[7]

---

[7]Wen Tie-jun & Ji Han (计晗), 'Risk Borne by the Central Government and Competition among Local Governments'.

After the fiscal system reform in the 1980s (since then local governments have had their own fiscal systems and budgets), local financial systems gradually became the main tool for accumulation and expansion of local resource capitalization driven by the corporatized local governments. Thereupon multi levels of banking systems and financial institutions took shape in China. Spurred on by local government-controlled funds, all kinds of localized banks and financial institutions flourished. For example, the setting up of Mercantile Bank, Shenzhen Development Bank, Guangdong Development Bank, Fujian Industrial Bank and Hainan Development Bank was for the purpose of motivating economic development in coastal provinces and special zones. The setting up of Shanghai Pudong Development Bank was for driving economic development in Pudong. The Huaxa Bank was a product of the Shougang Group comprehensive reform pilot scheme. Various trust companies also became financing channels for local regions. With these, local governments and departments could usually avoid policy intervention by the central government, getting around the objective of controlling the scale of credit loans.

The economist Fan Gang pointed out: "Local governments' impulse and actions to control financial resources, i.e. funds, have effectively resulted in local financial institutions being subordinated to local governments. It was through this channel that the government's power became integrated with the market."[8] The on-going deposit and loan differentials in banks around the country had continued to strengthen local real economies. The more a local government and enterprises dared to make use of the externality of this system to create high leverage, the faster the economy would grow! One could randomly select cases for analysis from the "good models" of the 1980–1990s, regardless of the ideologies in which they were packaged, and discover similar factors. It may be seen as the outcome of the continuous deepening of the power division reform since 1979 between the central and the local over fiscal and financial systems, which intrinsically characterized by the effort of shrugging off fiscal burden from top down. It was also the institutional gain brought

---

[8]Quoted from: Liu Haiying (刘海英), '话说金融"故"事 (Old Stories of Finance)', 中国改革(综合版) (China Reform (General)), 2003(3).

about by the 1984 policy of "contract responsibility by tier", and the 1994 policy of "tax division system".

Nevertheless, since the various "good models" under ideological packaging were all "politically correct", very few people realized that the agents which took the most of the institutional gains and those who bore the most of the institutional cost were not the same. The success and failure of such reforms did not depend merely on who took most of the gain but, more importantly, on how vested interest groups that reaped the benefits could successfully transfer the costs to others.

If one would stand on this base to analyze the misalignment and disorder among various levels of the Chinese bureaucracy, a clear view would instantly open up. The biggest chunk of institutional costs from back then was the non-performing bank loans that were ultimately settled by the central government. It was the aftermath of the speculative bubble emerging since 1992, as well as a large number of unfinished real estate development projects due to illegal 'land grabbing craze' between 1993 and 1996 by local governments attempting to generate revenues from land. They later became bad debts within the banking sector under regulation and austerity by the central government. Yet those responsible for these "good models" were either being promoted to higher positions or got rich fast. The end result was simply that the central government had to settle the bad debts, and then in the name of various reforms transfer the costs to society.

Given the contradiction in the relationship between the central and the local that continued to defy alignment, two things occurred. First, the local financial sector, under the local government corporatism system, participated in local primitive accumulation and the coarse expansion of industrial capital, would often go hand in hand with industrial capital in times that were good but not when bad. The sunk cost became too much to retrieve, hence snow-balling into non-performing debts. It would indeed be unrealistic to expect the local financial sector to resolve them by itself. Second, along with the rising extent of monetization in the Chinese economy as well as the mounting deposit and loan differential within the financial sector since the mid-1990s, the banking sector controlled more and more resources and gradually replaced the fiscal sector to become one of the most important resource allocation institutions of the central government (Fig. 6).

It can be seen that the enormous non-performing debts in local banks had become a non-transferrable institutional cost of the financial sector, which then in turn forced the central government to launch

Red line – deposit loan differential   Blue line – fiscal deficit   Unit – Hundred Million Yuan

a.   1952-1979

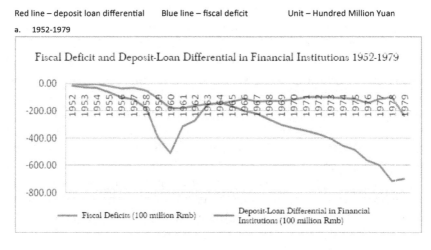

b.   1980 – 1999

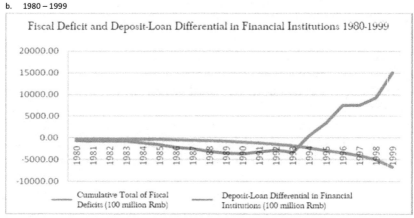

Fig. 6 Changes in China's fiscal deficits and deposit/Loan differentials in financial institutions 1952–2006

c.   1994 – 2006 (1994-1999 overlapped with fig. 4.6 b but at different scale)

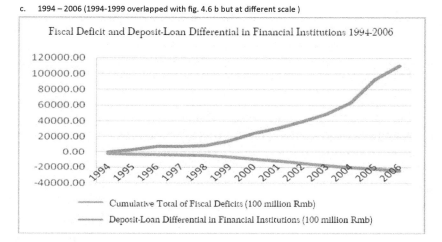

Fig. 6 (continued)

the Banking Commercialization Reform—a further step of 'burden-shirking', this time by the financial sector, after the comprehensive Tax Division Reform in mid 1990s absolving fiscal burden.

Banking Commercialization Reform

In 1995, the "Commercial Banking Law" was put forward with which state-owned banks were officially named as wholly-state-owned commercial banks, providing a legal basis for the banks to peel off their non-performing debts in the name of "commercialization".

The East Asia financial crisis in 1997 provided an opportunity for the central government to peel off that institutional risk. The crisis made the state realize the risk of the high number of non-performing debts in the banking sector. Thereupon a national financial working meeting was convened in November. The target was to strive, over a three-year period, to build a system of financial institutions, financial markets as well as monitoring and regulatory institutions that would suit the development of the socialist market economy.

As the proportion of non-performing debts in banking sector after the 1997 East Asian crisis had been too high, the central government launched in 1998 an urgent marketization reform of the state-monopolized banking industry. Yet given the dominant authority over banks in the hands of the central government, the situation bifurcated at two levels. The reliance on external financial market was mainly found at the state level, while at local and regional level the Opening Up mostly resulted in dependency on foreign capitals and oversea markets. This outcome was perhaps not an exception to the "law of financial exclusion" that global financialization would generally show, with polarization as a rule. As a consequence, on the one hand, excessive liquidity appeared in the monopolized financial sector controlled by the central government, manifested at the surface as deposits and loans differentials and in substance the alienation of financial capital from industrial capital; on the other, in industrial sector local governments relied on for tax revenues and in agricultural sector peasants relied on for survival there was generally deficiency of liquidity, manifested as difficulties in obtaining loans.

At that time, the People Bank of China provided a refinancing of 20 billion yuan to different provinces, and undertook strict rectification on various investment trusts. These were mostly private as well as city credit unions and rural cooperative funds below county level, which were popular among the grass roots. This was done in order to sever the encumbrances that these local organizations might create on the state-owned financial system.

Nevertheless, given that the banking commercialization reform involved many complicated processes, there had indeed been many undesirable outcomes. One of the significantly representative cases was the 1998 Grain System Reform that had given rise to much discussion. The central government attempted to adopt a coordinated reform approach that would integrate closely with 'food finance', to have the society pay the bills for the food system as well as for its capital cost. However, it was not successful.

Box 2: "1998 Grain System Reform" for Facilitating Bank of Agriculture Reform

In order to relieve the financial burden of the Bank of Agriculture which had the highest proportion of non-performing loans among the state-owned banks, the central government had launched a reform in 1998 that anchored staple grain purchase and distribution directly with agricultural finance. The idea was to clarify and separate the obligation and operation in the system. Grain enterprises were separated from the governments. The responsibilities of the central and local governments were clarified and separated. Grain reserve and business operations were divided into two systems. Old and new financial accounts were also separated. Finally the grain price mechanism would be improved. The State Council further issued a supplementary memorandum on improving grain purchase and distribution, as well as price management, emphasizing that the key to implementing the grain distribution system reform was resolute execution of three policies, namely, 'open purchase', 'selling at above cost price' and 'purchase funds operating in the closed system'. The goal was to speed up state-owned food enterprises reform and raise competitiveness. The core was comprised of the three polices—using the government's traditional approach of nationwide unified purchase of grain to ensure bank's funds would be secured within a 'closed operation' with 'selling at above cost price'. In addition, it was hoped that selling grain at above cost price to the society would cover the costs of grain distribution system and bank capital providing loans.

The policy design of this reform was logically correct. However, the transaction cost between the government and the widely scattered peasants had been too high. So was the cost of the relevant execution systems around the country, which had already completed marketization (including privatization of most ground level shops). Ultimately, not only did it fail, it had added further to fiscal subsidies and unsettled account.

On another front, the central government had injected 270 billion yuan to the four major state-owned banks to complement their capital funds, while simultaneously set up four asset management companies (as well as the China Development Bank) to peel off the 1.3 trillion non-performing loans from them. Finally the big four were pulled out of the quagmire of bad debts and washed clean by central government's fiscal budget.

Box 3: State-owned Bank Commercialization Reform

During the local industrialization that began in China in the 1980s,* local governments held the power to appoint, dismiss and manage personnel in state-owned banks around the country. The drawback of such decentralized management was that local government could directly intervene in bank investment decisions, making it hard for the banks to ensure the viability of specific investment projects. Many projects were launched simply in attempts to follow the trend. Once these projects failed they incurred non-performing loans in banks. That is to say, the state-owned banks had become the sites where risks of local industrialization would concentrate. That risk could hardly be handled by the bank's reserve.**

Therefore, when the central government initiated mandatory institutional transition—the commercialization of banking—in face of the enormous risks brought on by the 1997 financial crisis, the huge non-performing debts that the state had to bear were in fact the results of the institutional cost of industrialization that state-owned banks had carried for local governments.

At that time, the proportion of non-performing assets in China's banking sector had far exceeded the counterpart in the Southeast Asian countries before the eve of 1997 crisis—in Malaysian commercial banks the non-performing asset proportion was 6.4%, in Thailand 7.9% and even in Indonesia where the proportion was the highest it was merely 17%.*** Yet at end of 2000, China's state-wholly-owned banks had non-performing loans reaching 29.18% of total loans. Although the proportion had declined in 2001, it was still high at 25.37%.

And because of that, the disposition of non-performing assets became the top priority in the institutional reform of the banking industry. At the end of 1997 a national financial working meeting was convened. In 1998 a special issuance of national debt amounting to 270 billion yuan was made to supplement state-owned banks capital fund. At the same time the loans were classified. In 1999, four financial asset management enterprises CINDA, Great Wall, Oriental and Huarong, corresponding respectively to Construction Bank, Agricultural Bank, Bank of China as well as Industrial and Commercial Bank, were set up to acquire and dispose of each bank's non-performing assets, thereby segregating the bad assets from the big four.

In 2002, a swift handling of non-performing assets had taken place. According to the request of People's Bank of China the four major state-owned banks had to lower their non-performing asset rate to 15% before 2005, which meant 3–5 percentage points every year. It was not an easy task. In the first half of the year, the Bank of China had recovered cash of 15.7 Billion Yuan through auctioning, reducing the non-performing rate by 2.28 percentage points. According to statistics provided by the central bank, by the end of 2002 total loans in the four state—wholly-owned banks had amounted to 7 trillion yuan, out of which 1.7656 trillion was non-performing, a proportion of 25.37%. Of this, more than 600 billion yuan was actual loss. And these numbers were after 1.4 trillion yuan of bad assets**** had been already taken out and handled to the four asset management companies.*****

Notes:

*Wen Tiejun, "Hundred Year in China—Four Twists and Turns", *Dushu*, 2001 (3); Wen Tiejun et el., 'Special Topic Report 2: From "Central Government Corporatism" to "Local Government Corporatism",' in *Interpreting Southern Suzhou*, Suzhou University Press, 2011.

**Roland (1998) believed that before government functions realize successful transition, the fiscal system of local governments usually lacks the capacity to act in the role of supporting body to state-owned enterprises' soft budget-constraint. Further local governments would not have sufficient ability to provide construction funding to supplement local infrastructures and public services that were seriously lacking during the era of planned economy. Ba Shusong (2005) believed that in the aspect of local governance and banking reform, local governments had, during different stages of their own reforms, started out from their own self-interests and made use of system flaws in the banking reform to fight for financial resources, continuously changing the ways in doing so. From direct administrative intervention to exerting influence over banking policies, there had been profound impact on the effective transmission of monetary policy and the operation of micro financial agents. Reference: Liu Mou Yi Yang, 'Commercialization Reform of State-owned Banks and Future Trends,' Master Thesis, University of International Business and Economics, May 2012. http://www.doc88.com/p-4827071198102.html.

***Wang Liya, 'Reflections On State-owned Commercial Bank Reform Model,' *Finance and Insurance*, 2001 (11).
****Zhang Jie, *Analysis of China's State-owned Financial System Transformation*. Economic Science Press, 1998.
*****Source of information: Xu Tao, 'Studies on China's State-owned Banks Commercialization Reform', Master Thesis, Liaoning Normal University.

If the financial supports from the Central Bank and the Ministry of Finance were added together, since 1998 the state had invested 2.9 trillion yuan in total on state-owned banks reform. Overall, between 1998 and 2005, to maintain financial stability around 3.24 trillion yuan had been invested to support financial enterprises reform and alleviate financial risks. And the fiscal revenue of China in 2004 was only 2.63 trillion yuan. Even after that there had been further follow-up investments from the state.[9]

In this regard, the ratio of debt stock in China's financial system relative to fiscal revenue had exceeded 120%.

If one looks at this process simply from a theoretical perspective, it would amount to an embedded transaction in institutional transition: the central government had made use of the state's economic sovereignty in the realms of national debt and money to pay for part of the institutional costs of transition. In this transaction of power division reform, the central government paid the quantifiable part of the accumulated costs incurred in local primitive accumulation for industrialization. At the same time it enjoyed the institutional gain. The central government took control of the financial capital profiting from monetization, which in turn took the opportunity to transform into a mega monopolistic financial conglomerate that was alienated from local industrial capital.

By 2002, the monopolistic state-owned financial capital that had different interests and visions from local governments and industrial capital was finally able to free itself from the intricacy with the latter,

---

[9]Financial Stability Analysis Group of the People's Bank of China, 中国金融稳定报告 (China Financial Stability Report). China Financial Publishing House, 2005.

acquiring a relatively independent position in dominating and enjoying a share of the profit from capitalization of local resource around the country, thereby drawing open China's curtain on "financialization-deepening". That of course had a profound impact on China's economy.

On one side, financial capital controlled by the central government became a capital force taking the tide to join in the global competition. That was consistent with the development orientation that the core nation was leading in globalization. The other side was that it had resulted in debilitating local government's ability to acquire funds and worsening the financing environment of small/medium enterprises under diluted profitability.

At the same time, following large scale closing and merging of financial institutions at below county level, state-owned monopoly financial sector also withdrew from peasant agriculture and scattered non-agricultural industries in rural regions, which were plagued by exceptionally high transaction costs and liquidity deficiency.

This institutional transition wherein China's financial capital was alienated from industrial capital had been completed in 2002, coincident with China's accession to the WTO. What followed was the third wave of "land enclosure" campaign since the Reform, initiated by the local governments as a way of acquiring financial capital through cashing in land.

Actually, our understanding of the 'institutional costs transfer' could not possibly have been a priori. It was only after such transaction costs had been increasingly expressed as large scale social confrontations, threatening political stability, that the central government would, as the principal fund provider, request financial institutions to execute a series of interventional relief policies by the will of the state. Among these, the one that had typical significance was State Council's entrustment to the Agricultural Bank the mission of 'serving the *sannong*'. The Agricultural Bank was listed on the stock market in 2008, the last of the major four state-owned banks to complete commercialization reform. That mission was an important reason why China has the biggest number of agricultural financial institutions and the highest proportions of peasant credit needs to be met among developing countries.

A Review of the Evolving Relationship Between Financial Capital and Real Industry in China

Here, we may give a brief review of the changing relationship between financial capital and real industry from the early 1980s till 2002.

The 1980s: Local Financialization Propelled Local Industrialization

In the name of marketization, there had been several rounds of financial reform in China. However, few have ever conducted comparative research on the contents of "market" referred to in different periods.

According to common discourse, China's "economic and financial market system" emerged in the 1980s. To illuminate the contexts of these changes, we must, however, jump out of the banking sector.

During the state-dominated industrialization before 1980s, investment plans were mainly made by the national planning system. The fiscal budget then allocated funds to these projects. Insufficiently financed sectors were funded by public bonds or increasing money supply. Financing by the private sector was nearly absent. Hence, the financial system by that time was a unified regime in which the People's Bank of China was in charge of all financial business. PBoC managed balancing regulation at macro level and provided commercial service at the same time. In the words of Mao Zedong speaking to Chen Yun, fiscal faculty and the banking sector were no more than two pockets of the man in charge of economic and financial affairs.

The reform of separating finance from fiscal faculty was not motivated by endogenous drive within the financial system itself. In our previous discussion on the 1978–1981 crisis, we have shown that it was the result of attempts to shrug off fiscal budget constraints by the central government facing serious economic crisis. One of the three major reforms in the early 1980s was the shift from fiscal allocation to loans to state-owned enterprises as the state's fiscal revenues were not enough to support the investments. These enterprises had to gain loans from banks instead of getting funds from the fiscal budget. Therefore, the business of loaning, along with the risk, had to be separated from PBoC and managed according to financial logic. A double-decked banking system thereby took shape: the commercial finance and the PBoC turned into the central bank. In this system, the central bank focuses on macro-regulation, monitoring and providing services to banks, such as inter-bank settlements and clearance while commercial financial institutions provide services to businesses and citizens.

Under the "government corporatism" regime in which the state directly performed the function of capital accumulation, it was impossible for nominally commercial banks established by the government not to carry the policy responsibility commanded by the state. For example, if a state-owned enterprise was short of funds to pay the employees, then the big four banks might have to support it. Each of these big four had its own policy-oriented business. It's worth noting that many of these demands for policy support came from local governments.

Many researchers may selectively forget the fact that what emerged at almost the same time with the reform from fiscal allocation to loaning to enterprises was the influential "Central and Local Stratified Fiscal Responsibility System" in 1984 which resulted in two consequences.

1. Under the previous "central government corporatism" responsible for state industrialization, there was only one centralized ledger. However, there were subsequently nearly 70 thousands fiscal ledgers in the whole country after the reform with 65,000 county and township units. Here came the era of local industrialization dominated by local government corporatism.
2. The fiscal autonomy enjoyed by local governments had promoted local tax revenues. By that time, local authorities could share 70% of their total revenues. Merely 30% went to the central government. Under this arrangement, the central government found it very hard to carry its macro-regulation policy. Eventually, under the severe condition of serious fiscal deficits later in early 1990s, all the interested parties were impacted. After negotiation, the Tax Revenues Division Reform in favour of the central government was put forward in 1993 (see previous chapter).

Box 4: Local Fiscal Budget Soft Constraint and Financial Deepening
Fan Gan points out that under the power division system, local governments and enterprises had the right to approve projects on their own. The fight among these local units to get more resources was expressed as competition for capital fund. Under a "soft budget constraint," the more capital fund one got, the more revenues it would generate and the more advantages it could have. Therefore, in the soft constraint competition among various local governments and enterprises under state-owned economy power division system, the demand for capital fund tended to be unlimited. This competition for capital might be fiercer than market competition in some aspects.

A financial market system built against this context would only serve the characteristics of local government corporatism, providing capital fund to the primitive accumulation for local industrialization. Otherwise, the institutional transition of shrugging off fiscal budget would never be successful.

Understandably, the right to appoint and manage personnel in local state-owned banks was granted to local governments in the 1980s. During this period, the operation of bank branches tended to prioritize local interests. To compete for capital fund, local governments and state-owned enterprises joined hand in hand to force the central government to expand credit scale, thus having de facto power to create money supply. The right of investment planning was decentralized to the local. The local branches of the central bank operated according to local interests. The interests of the central bank, the specialized banks and local branches worked in accordance with local governments, local economy and local enterprises. As a result, a "reverse mechanism" in which local bodies were pushing the expansion of credit loans and money supply took shape. Local governments and enterprises found it easier than before to satisfy their desire to expand investment.

It could be seen in the fact that the actual money supply generally exceeded the planned figure by the central government (see below table).

Table: Actual and Planned Money Supply 1983–1992

	Loan increment (100 million)			Cash increment (100 million)		
	Planned (1)	Actual (2)	(2)/(1)	Planned (3)	Actual (4)	(4)/(3)
1983	354	378	1.07	80	90.7	1.51
1984	423	988	2.34	80	262.3	3.28
1985	715	1486	2.08	150	195.7	1.30
1986	950	1685	1.77	200	230.5	1.15
1987	1225	1442	1.77	230	236.1	1.03
1988		1518		200	679.5	3.40
1989		1851		400	210	0.53
1990	1700	2757	1.60	400	300	0.75
1991	2100	2878	1.37	500	533	1.07
1992	2800	3864	1.38	600	1158	1.93

Source: Fan Gan, 'Soft Constraint Competition and Inflation of China in Recent Years,' 金融研究 (Financial Research), 1994(3).

The local soft budget constraint with subsequent reverse forced credit expansion explains high speed local industrialization after the power division reform as the concession by the central government. Compared with the Planned Economy Era 30 years ago, the financial deepening after 1980s moved ahead at extremely high speed. It helped the economic development (the substance of which had been the capitalization of resources) out of the 1978–1981 cyclic crisis. However, it also sowed the seed of deflation in the late 1980s. By estimate, China's financial asset expanded by 12.4 times from 1978 to 1991 while the ratio of total financial asset value to GNP jumped from 95.2% to 233.8% (see Table 1).

It is commonly agreed that China has achieved high speed economic growth and local government corporatism played an important role. However, few are aware of the function of localized financial tools to the growth. It followed a chain reaction. Local official promotion was determined by local economic growth which was achieved by investment growth. Therefore local governments fought for financial resources, which involved competition among financial institutions. Under this low cost-effective circle, the much admired high speed growth during local

Table 1 China's financial assets 1978 and 1991 (Unit: RMB 100 millions)

	Items	1978	1978*	1991	1991*
1	Cash	212	5.9	3177.8	16.2
2	Saving Deposits[1]	210.6	5.9	9110.3	46.5
3	Enterprise Deposits	902.5	25.2	7061.7	36.1
4	Treasury Deposits	187.4	5.2	504.3	2.6
5	Securities	0	0	114.2	0.6
6	Deposits in Non-banking Financial Institutions[2]	0	0	1421.1	7.3
7	Reserve in Insurance Sector[3]	15	0.4	190.8	1.0**
8	Total Credit's Rights in Financial Institution (1–7)	1527.5	42.6	21,580.2	110.2
9	Total Bank Loans	1850	51.6	18,061.4	92.2
10	Urban and Township Credit Union Loans	40	1.1	2124.9	10.9
11	Trust Institutional Loans	0	0	1211	6.2
12	Government Bonds	0	0	1168.2	6
13	Enterprise Bonds	0	0	386.8	2.1
14	Total Credit's Rights in Non-financial Sector (9–13)	1890	52.7	22,952.3	117.2
15	Bank Loans to Governments	0	0	1174.5***	6
16	Stocks	0	0	75.1	0.4
17	Total Financial Assets	3417.5	95.2	45,782	233.8

Notes
[1]Included postal savings and savings in Urban and township credit Unions
[2]Included various financial trust investment institutions and urban credit unions. Individual savings in these institutes not included
[3]Sum of responsibility reserve, life insurance reserve and property insurance reserve
*Ration to GNP in 1978 and 1991
**Originally '9.7'. According to other data, it should be 0.97, approximately 1.0
***Originally 1074.5. According to other data, it should be 1174.5
Source Xie Ping (谢平), '中国金融资产结构分析' (Analysis on China's Financial Asset Structure), 经济研究 (Economic Studies), 1992(11)

industrialization was in fact pushed up by even higher financial growth (see Table 2).

Take rural enterprises as an example. Much research has shown the importance of credit creation in the formation and expansion of rural enterprises. The State Council Rural Development Research Centre and National Bureau of Statistics Rural Sampling Survey Team conducted in

Table 2 Financial assets/GNP ratio in China, 1978–1991

	Financial assets balance (100 millions)	GNP (100 millions)	Ratio (%)
1978	3417.5	3588.1	95.2
1979	4000	3988.1	100.3
1980	4945.8	4470	110.6
1981	5782.7	4773	121.1
1982	6906.3	5193	133
1983	7759	5809	133.6
1984	10,543	6962	151.4
1985	12,808.7	8557.6	149.7
1986	16,868.3	9696.3	174
1987	20,932	11,301	185.2
1988	25,127	14,018	178.1
1989	30,117	15,916	189.2
1990	37,233	17,686	210.5
1991	45,782	19,580	233.8

Source: Xie Ping (谢平), '中国金融资产结构分析' (Analysis on China's Financial Asset Structure), 经济研究 (Economic Studies), 1992(11)

1986 a systematic research in 10 provinces. 200 samples were selected from 319 large rural enterprises. The result showed that of the initial capital in the sample enterprises, 4.02% came from the state's disbursement, 29% from the Agriculture Bank loans, 5/16% from credit unions loans, 4% from the Industrial and Commercial Bank, 5.84% from low-interest revolving fund by the government, 23.6% from collective's accumulation, 5.43% from factory workers fund-raising, 2.9% from pre-paid sale, 7.89% by manufacture processing, 0.69% from joint-venture investment, 1.06% from group or personal sponsorship, other 8.88%. Furthermore, the annual investment of the sample enterprises far exceeded the retained profit and even the total profit that year. In 1984, the average investment amounted to 416.3 thousand yuan, 109% of total profit and 276.0% of retained profit; in 1985, that became 115.6% and 267.5%. On average, of the newly increased total fixed assets, new bank loans and other debts in that year amounted to 58.6% in 1984, 48% in 1985, 64.7% in 1986.

According to a study by Lu Yang, during the 1980s, of the total 327.3 billion yuan investment in rural enterprises, 53.65% came from bank loans or inter-companies loans. Self capital investment amounted to merely 33.86%.

Even among South Suzhou rural enterprises during the early rural industrialization where internal community capital accumulation was significant source of investment fund, debts had replaced collective accumulation as the major means of asset formation. In 1984, the growth of loan was up to 83.52% among Suzhou rural enterprises, nearly 60 percentage points higher than the 24.64% growth rate of self capital. Instantly in that year, the total debt to asset ratio of rural enterprises in Suzhou rose to 51%. Total debts for the first time surpassed owners' equity.

There are two more noteworthy points. First, some researchers suggested that even though credit was essential in the rapid economic development of outside-state-apparatus rural enterprises, its weight in the total financial provision was less than 10% (see Table 3), which indicated the scale of loans by financial institutions to the state-owned sector.

Second, the large-scale financial expansion in the 1980s was different from the times of newly born Renminbi when money supply increase was the only means to deal with fiscal deficits. Now financial expansion took place at local level. It had little effect on relieving fiscal deficits.

1994–2002: The Re-Centralization of Finance and Its Alienation from Local Industries

The cost of financial localization as an institutional change was emphasized by researchers in later financial reform. Bad loans were mounting in the financial system as local governments sought rapid development. Confronted with economic overheating, the government started in 1993 to take regulative measures in different sectors: fiscal budget, finance, trade and balance of payments etc. Then in 1997, just after the government announced economic 'soft-landing,' the Asian Financial Crisis raised the alarm of systemic risk to the Chinese economy. Financial reform was necessary to face the challenge of globalization. The cancers of bad loans were cut off from banking sector as described earlier.

Table 3 Loans to non state-owned sector from financial institution 1985–1996 (Unit: %)

Year	Urban collective	Urban individual	Rural enterprises	Three types of foreign-funded enterprises	Agriculture	All non-state sector
1985	4.95	0.17	5.63	–	6.85	17.60
1986	5.11	0.13	6.82	–	6.68	18.94
1987	5.47	0.16	7.25	–	7.28	20.16
1988	5.58	0.17	7.59	–	7.19	20.53
1989	5.15	0.11	7.39	–	7.12	19.97
1990	4.93	0.09	7.42	–	7.17	19.61
1991	4.74	0.08	7.63	–	7.39	19.84
1992	5.77	0.26	7.16	–	7.54	20.73
1993	5.96	0.33	8.22	–	6.47	20.98
1994	5.08	0.38	–	1.94	11.38	18.78
1995	4.26	0.39	–	1.98	5.99	12.62
1996	4.31	0.46	–	2.20	11.65	18.62

Sources: Tao Shigui (陶士贵), '地方政府控股下的地方银行制度变迁逻辑与风险防范' (Institutional Change of Local Banking System with Local Governments as Stock-Holders: Logic and Risk Prevention), Nanjing Normal University Journal (Social Sciences), 2013(5). 1985–1991 data from Mai Jingnong (麦金农), 经济市场化的次序——向市场经济过渡中的金融控制 (Order of Economic Marketization: financial control during transition to market economy), Table 13. Shanghai Joint Publishing House and Shanghai People Press, 1997; 1992–1996 data calculated according to 中国金融展望 (China Finance Outlook 1994–1997)

1993–1996: Background of Contractionary Financial Policy

After the fiscal division in 1984, factional local governments competed out of their own interests. Local authorities at various levels used their power to intervene in bank investment decision-making. However, since many of these investment projects were based on irrational exuberance and trend-following, they ended up as bad loans in banks. However, the financial risks encountered during this period would be dwarfed in comparison with the situation after 1992.

After Deng Xiaoping's inspection trip to South China in 1992, the three speculative markets (stocks, futures and real estate) were liberated. The autonomy of local governments in economic development was further expanded, especially in terms of their financing and financial power.

Fan Gang pointed out that the following two were of utmost importance.

First, local governments had total power in decision-making related to investment projects. At the municipal level, the limit of autonomous investment project was raised to 30 million yuan, and at provincial level, 50 million. As a result, fixed asset investments rocketed. During January to May 1993, fixed asset investments in state-owned sector increased by 70.7% compared with the same period in previous year.

Second, autonomy in financing was the most important right granted to local governments and state-owned enterprises. It was used to evade central government's credit control and monetary policy. Direct financing allowed them to get the funds required at interest rates much higher than the general saving interest rate. In 1992, the total marketable securities in China amounted to 128 billion yuan, including 41 billion of public bonds, 12.7 billion of investment bonds by the National Investment Company, enterprises bonds 37.9 billion, financial debts 25.5 billion, stocks 10.9 billion, which were formal securities shown in statistics. According to the estimate by the People's Bank of China, the total value of "informal securities" such as enterprises internal stocks, planned financing, etc., might be up to 220 billion yuan, of which, besides 25.5 billion of financial bonds, 194.5 billion was direct financing, amounting to 54.6% of new bank loans in that year and 46% of total new debts in financial institution (including state-run banks, trust investment and urban-township credit unions).

The combination of these two autonomies led to expansion of money supply and investment. In 1992, currency in circulation increased annually by 36.4% and in 1993, 35.3%. In 1985, the total fixed asset investment amounted to 254.3 billion. In 1990, it had raised to 445.1 billion. It rocketed to 1182.9 billion in 1993 and 1600 billion in 1994!

Just a step out of contraction, the economy bumped into high inflation. It was estimated that the real inflation rate was rising from 1993 to 1995. The official statistical number peaked at 24.1% in 1994. Take two indexed bonds with 3 and 5 years maturity (000093 and 000193) as example. They were valued at 100 yuan when issued in 1993 and redeemed at 171.99 yuan three years later in 1996. That implied an annual inflation rate of up to 24%.

Each occasion of high inflation would impact the real economy. In 1993, the entire society had to bear the institutional cost of increased money supply.

There was remarkable change in enterprise cost structure. Enterprise capital deepening and industry upgrade were thereby inhibited. It facilitated rent-seeking by interest blocs while non-state-owned sectors had to bear greater institutional costs. For example, because of interest blocs in state-run sectors, loan interest was suppressed at a very low level. Loan interest was actually negative, lower than the inflation rate and became the most serious distortion in the Chinese economy. By that time, the non-state-run economy had accounted for over 60% of GDP and 30% of investment. However, 80% of bank loans went into the state-owned sector. At the same time, the state was developing the speculative capital market. Financial capital, by essence, seeks liquidity for profit-making, which could not be suppressed by administrative means. Unauthorized lending or speculation was unstoppable in the financial sector. Capital gray markets were pervasive. A large amount of low-interest rate loans became the source of rent-seeking by banks, government officials or state-owned enterprises. Domestic capital market interest rate constantly stayed at about 20% per month. Loan-sharks were rampant in the whole country. Small and medium enterprises were being squeezed out from normal lending.

The local sector fought for financial resources in order to internalize the gain of resource capitalization while striving to externalize the cost of financial risk, which expressed itself in a banking crisis and in inflation. To deal with economic overheating, the central government released signals of tough regulative measures. However, the signal of imminent regulation in turn increased the urgency of local about-to-be-launched projects. Overheating was intensified during 1993–1994. The central government was then forced to take stringent instead of mild measures. The game of interest and power between the central and local governments had once again led to economic fluctuation in China.

The Impact of Financial Austerity Policy During 1993–1996

Central regulative measures were put forth amid the tide of enterprises expansion and capital deepening through loans. Even though the target was speculative overheating, the real economy at county level, especially township enterprises were hit hard, as the central government, out of information asymmetry, cut all loan scale by rigid uniformity and tightened the right to approve lending. Banks then suppressed lending scale at and below county level. The intimate relationship between local financial localization and local industrialization started to change.

After 1994, state-run banks strengthened vertical leadership system and internal control. Financial institutions, especially banks would contract credit as systematic risks increased. Regarding the recipients of credit, the governments however did not relinquish policy favouritism towards state-owned large and medium enterprises and continued to subsidize unprofitable state-owned enterprises. Under credit rationing management, the opportunity cost of non state-run economy to get financial support became higher. Furthermore, the assets structure of many small and medium enterprises was not recognized by banks. They found it hard to get financing from formal financial market.

From the perspective of a complete economic cycle, whether during the credit expansion period of 1992–1993 or the contraction of 1994–1996, the financing condition of the real economy was structurally unfavourable. In the previous period, enterprises in the real economy were being squeezed out because financial capital was seeking after high-risk, high-return speculative realms. In the later period, they had to bear un-proportionally the institutional cost of economic regulation.

Regarding credit loans to rural enterprises from formal finance, the values amounted to 151.79 and 196.28 billion yuen in 1992 and 1993, a growth of 36 and 44.5 billion compared with previous year while the total national credit volume increased by 498.51 and 662.02 billion respectively. After austerity policies were implemented in 1994, total credit loans to rural enterprises were cut substantially, from 7 to 8% of total national credit volume to 3–4%. In 1994, credit loans to rural enterprises valued at 200.24 billion, with an increase of merely 4 billion compared with previous year while the total new credit loans in the whole nation amounted to 703.29 billion.

In 1996, the ratio of credit loans from financial institutes to rural enterprises fixed assets investment declined to 24.56%, a drop of 3.66 percentage points. Moreover, the credit structure in that period also had significant change. Short-term loans in financial institutes grew by 17.2% while long-term merely 6.66%. It was remarkable compared with the figure of 87.9% and 24.2% in 1994 as well as 35.25% and 20.71% in 1995.

During 1986–1991, bank loans to rural enterprises grew annually on average 31.85%, 1992–1995, 30.88%. And during 1996–1997, the average annual growth rate was merely 9.35%.

In retrospect, the macro-regulation during 1993–1996 was instrumental in stabilizing the national economy and its finances. China successfully took precautions before the Asian Financial Crisis in 1997.However, the institutional cost, the price of soft-landing, was unevenly shared between different types of enterprises, between urban and rural sectors as it was in previous reforms, the remarkable asymmetry of costs and benefits.

1997–2002: Banking Commercialization Reform and Its Aftermath

After the 1993–1996 regulation, we witnessed the banking reforms during 1998–2002 in which local financial resources were further constrained. This was also conventionally dubbed as marketization since the 1980s. A slight difference is the clarification of the commercial goal of banking reform. From then on, the banks have become independent entities of interest and profit seeking for even higher profitability.

After the 1997 crisis, the central leadership was resolved to push banking reform (see above column: State-owned Banks Commercialization Reform).

As the central government took over the historical bad debts in the local financial sector and, hence, regained its control on banking, state-run commercial banks replaced the 'administrative logic' with 'market logic'. The allocation of financial resources was strictly conducted according to market principle. The age of 'Three Eyes of Local Branches' (being inspected by the headquarter, local government and regulation authority) had gone.

As stated above, the bad debts in banking system accumulated along with speeding local industrialization. They may be regarded as the side products of financial localization in support of local industrial expansion. Furthermore, rural enterprises that thrived under a particular institutional arrangement of peasant community may not be well served by Anglo-Saxon banking model (generally seeking after profit through liquidity) as the former's assets (such as land and natural as well as cultural resources) are not as explicit as in their urban counterparts. Therefore, they usually record higher debt asset ratios. Whether Anglo-Saxon risk rating system suits the particular situation of China deserves further exploration. No matter what, the institutional transition set in motion by the central government to reduce systematic financial risk did take the responsibility to deal with the risk generated in previous round of local industrialization. However, it did not provide an alternative institutional solution to local financial provision. The formal channel of local access to financial resources was blocked. As a result, the benign symbiosis between financial capital and real industry was debilitated.

In the twenty-first century, Chinese financial capital turned to the speculative sector such as real estate and derivatives market to seek monopolistic returns. Industries with lesser liquidity or profitability were increasingly being alienated by capital. It did improve the risk of investment loss because of the alliance between local governments and finance. However the policy jumped from one extreme to the other. Under deficiency of new financial tools to support local industry, the institution transition to promote profitability and reduce risk in financial system would necessarily pass the institutional cost to real industry, especially numerous small enterprises failing to get credit guarantees from the state or local governments. Consequently, we have on the one side the local deindustrialization all over the nation, and on the other, the 'embarrassingly fat profitability' (as uttered by a state-owned bank CEO) in the state-owned banking sector.

From 1984 to 2003, Chinese finance took 20 years to complete the circle from a 'centralized system' to 'localization' and to 'recentralization'. Under the free market doctrine, speculation-rush is regarded as normal market behaviour. Macro regulation for the sake of constraining speculative bubble at the end threw the baby out with the bathwater. The real economy suffered a three-fold hard blow: the squeeze-out effect of speculative capital, the austerity of economic regulation and financial alienation after banking reform.

It is noteworthy that what is described above is more than a phenomenon with Chinese characteristics. Instead, it is a syndrome pervasive in the Anglo-Saxon-American model of finance. Before the 2008 Financial Tsunami swept the world, China had suffered from the structural imbalance between financial capital and real economy. If we jump ahead a bit here, we may see that the seeds of the 'new normal' of economic deceleration after 2013 were actually sowed twenty years ago in 1993.

Proactive Fiscal Policies—Infrastructure Construction Investments Mainly by the Central Government

In response to the change in domestic supply and demand relationship as well as the impact of Southeast Asian financial crisis on exports, the Central government promulgated in 1998 Document No. 3 and No. 12, proposing domestic demand expansion and adopting a series of relevant measures. That in fact marked a change in keynote policy orientation, from moderate suppression of domestic demand since 1993 to active expansion.

In early March of 1998 when the new administration took office, the proposal for "proactive financial policies" to relax bank investments was put forward. However, the marketization reform to insulate the banking sector from local government intervention had already been on track. Bank branches at county level had handed over most of their financial power to higher provincial counterparts. They could now only approve loan no more than 200,000 yuan. Therefore, it was not possibly for local administrations to expand bank investments on a large scale to comply with the new instruction from the central government.

Therefore, starting from the summer of 1998, the central government went on to implement an expansionary fiscal policy. That policy adjustment which began in early 1998 had originated with a report from Li Nanqing, Vice Premier in charge of foreign trade, to the Chief Party Secretary, Jiang Zemin on January 6, about the proportion of GDP growth attributable to export would likely decline from around 4 percentage points in 1997 to less than 1 due to the impact of the Southeast Asian financial crisis. On that basis he requested the central government to make policy adjustment in time to expand domestic demand and reduce over-reliance on exports. Jiang approved the report and the Premier Zhu Rongji, who just announced in 1997 the 'soft landing' of the previous crisis with completion of macro-regulation, was put in charge of the proactive fiscal policy of issuing large scale national bonds to expand investments.[10] These public debts were mainly invested towards infrastructure constructions.

From the aspect of economic operation, the effect of driving demand growth by government-led investments in 1998 was very obvious. Investments in state-owned sector recorded a growth of 19.5% as compared to 6.1% in urban/rural individuals and a decline of 3.5% in urban/rural collectives. Among the investments in state-run sector, the largest proportion was infrastructure, accounting for 56%, a growth as high as 20%. Renovation and reconstruction had accounted for 21%, with a growth of 13.9%; and real estate development 17%, 12.6%. It can be seen that the economic growth in 1998 was mostly driven by state investments. In conjunction with other analyses it can be concluded that the economic growth rate in 1998 was prevented from further falling because of state investments to expand domestic demands.[11]

---

[10]From 1998 to 2000, 360 billion yuan of long-term national building bond was issued. Xu Hongyuan (徐宏源), 2000年中国宏观经济形式分析与2001年展望 (Analysis of China's Macro Economic Form in 2000 and 2001 Outlook), Economic Forecast Department, National Information Center. http://www.cei.gov.cn/template/economist/yth_source/zgjj20010 10203.htm.

[11]Ma Hong and Lu Baifu (马洪,陆百甫), 中国宏观经济政策报告 (Report on China's Macro Economic Policy), China Financial and Economic Publishing House, January 1999.

It was not only in the year of implementation of proactive fiscal policy that the Chinese economy was able to counter much of the harmful impact on growth due to substantial export contraction. In the following 1998–2000, 3 years of relative depression, the national economy had been able to sustain a growth rate "below 8 and above 7". In addition, the constraint of inadequate infrastructure investments in the past had to a large extent been improved. For example, the construction of the first highway in China—Hu-Jia Expressway from Shanghai to Jiading—had ushered in a wave of expressway construction. By 2003 when the next administration took office, the mileage of China's expressway was second in the world, after the United States.

"Government's Entrance" as the Fundamental Experience for China in Response to Imported Crises

There is a saying "great luck amidst misfortune". It was an apt description for China in its first encounter with the imported crisis in 1997–1998 pursuant to the East Asian financial crisis. In fact, 1998 should be a year worth noting in history because the government has since then adopted the approach of directly using public debts to expand investments on a large scale to "turn crisis into opportunities". After that, China had enlarged government bond issuance for twelve consecutive years, initiating investments of around 10 trillion yuan. During this period, a whole series of major national strategies to adjust regional and urban-rural disparities were successively put forward.

Urban-rural, regional and rich-poor disparities subsisted in China due to factors such as geographic vastness and three-tier terrace topographic structure as well as market selection. These gaps had been widening continuously and become a subject of criticism. And under the pressure of crisis with export contraction and over-production, the under-developed regions and rural areas in China became the state's principal targets to expand investments!

For example, the Western Region Development strategy was put forward in 1999. It included large scale ecological improvement projects such as natural forests protection, forestation and grass-planting to revert ecological destruction in dry grassland and mountainous forestry regions due to funding deficiency in the past. In 2001 the strategy to revive the old industrial regions in northeast was proposed. President Jiang Zemin stressed in particular "supporting Northeastern region to accelerate rebuilding as well as adjustments of old industrial cities, and resource-extraction cities to develop sustainable industries". It effectively alleviated social disorder and the emergence of slums and shacks in old industrial cities in those areas. And in 2003 when the new administration took office, the strategy of central region development was proposed. In 2005 another major strategy in the name of "building socialist new countryside" was put forward to continuously increase rural infrastructure investments.

This direct government intervention into the economy, propelling the real economy through public debt expansion and increasing money supply to stimulate economic growth, could be regarded as the "reentrance" of government (after the state had retreated from social provisions in different realms since the 1980s). Having effectively dealt with the imported crisis of 1997, "government entrance" became the fundamental experience for countering economic crisis caused mainly by external factors.

A particularly noteworthy point was that this region-balancing development strategy through direct investments by the government to alleviate the "market malfunctioning" had not stopped with the change to the new administration. On the contrary it continued for more than twelve years starting from 1998. The total investment supported by public bonds was valued at more than 10 trillion yuan. There were also regional financing platforms below provincial level. The total investment from various levels of governments amounted to around 20 trillion yuan. The large scale increase of investments not only improved the situation of deficiency in infrastructure investments in the past, it became the principal measure that China used unwaveringly to sustain high growth in the first decade of this century.

Nevertheless, any proactive measures would have passive impact as well as criticisms from different vested interest groups. At the same time when public bond-sponsored projects had stimulated the economy and reduced regional disparity, the situation of "state advances and private sector retreats" arose, given that the mega projects were mostly executed by state-owned enterprises. That ignited heated public criticisms both domestically and externally that the government had intervened too much and caused a regression of privatization reforms. On another front, it also gave rise to a 'rough growth' inertia, simply using more investments to attain growth but also creating more over-production, which amounted to "making use of greater over-capacity in the future to cover today's over-capacity", leading to greater potential risks over time. In case an unexpected factor blocked this economic process of 'high investment + high consumption + high dependency', the entire national economy would be thrown into chaos.

Regarding the situation of "state advances, private sector retreats" that has emerged objectively, given that Western countries had adopted similar tactics of nationalization in dealing with the 2008–2011 financial crisis, the domestic pro-Western public opinions became somewhat mute. As for the over-reliance on foreign energy sources and raw materials, while it was regrettable it was nevertheless inevitable, since the domestic facilities developed over the past few decades were indeed insufficient to alleviate the difficulty. The Chinese, on the one-way road of investment-driven growth, could only rely on the international order maintained by the U.S. with its allies. In order to acquire the right to development in a global regime under effective US control of the global resource markets and logistic channels, China had to pay tribute of 'dual export' to the U.S. (exporting goods at low price and channeling the hard-earned dollar back to the US to support the US treasury bond market).

Admittedly, certain measures taken by Chinese government to strengthen strategic security have been relatively effective. For example, since 2003 subsidies have been granted to staple crops production and in 2004 agricultural tax was abolished. A whole series of proactive measures have given rise to grain production increases for nine consecutive years, reaching more than 550 trillion kilogram in 2011. During this period, although China was listed in 2008 by international organizations among the 37 "hungry countries" vulnerable to high food price caused by the financial crisis, China was the only one among these countries that did not actually have hunger. In other aspects, however, the measures were not so effective. For example, China began in 2005 to increase strategic oil reserves to strengthen energy security, yet it was no more than a drop in the bucket. China's predicament of over-reliance on imported energy and raw material has become increasingly severe.

Impact of Crisis on the *Sannong* and Rural Governance

The *Sannong* Became the Vehicle to Achieve "Crisis Soft-Landing"

First, the rural sector under the urban-rural dual system once again played a regulative role as a "labor force reservoir", so that urban unemployment would not flare up to a social crisis. After the 1997 crisis, agricultural employment began to increase year after year, from 348.8 million in 1997 to 368.7 million in 2002, a rise of 5.83%. This portion of "new" agricultural employment might be regarded as the unemployed urban laborers pursuant to onslaught on urban economy, given the urban-rural dichotomy.

Besides, given that the expansionary fiscal policy mainly aimed at urban infrastructure constructions, there was a need for large scale utilization of scarce land resource. Unlike in the past wherein the peak of the economy would coincide with the peak of land enclosure effort, the situation in 1998 was that substantial increase in appropriation of arable land took place during relatively serious economic decline. Overall, while large scale infrastructure construction did indeed build up asset pools in cities, it nevertheless could not avoid the pitfall of the cost of appropriating large areas of arable land. And every time resources were being re-allocated under the condition of worsening governance, there would be possibility of confrontation. From a long term perspective, the compensation policy on land appropriation had not been comprehensive regarding the functions of arable land, and it was not fair either. During 2008–2013, arable land in China shrank by 110.37 million hectare annually. Another problem was that rapid low-cost enclosure of land in the countryside led to serious wastage. Between 1998 and 2002 the total urban built-up area in 660 cities across the country had annual growth of 5%, yet population growth in the same period was only 1.3%. By 2005, average urban land use per capita was 133 sq. meters, 33 sq. m. higher than that stipulated by state urban planning regulations, and far higher than the level of 82.4 sq. meters in some developed countries. The urban floor area ratio in China was only 0.33, while it was up to 2.0 in some foreign countries (Jiang Shengsan & Liu Shouying et el, 2007).

It intensified the scarcity of land resource in a populous country like China. Moreover, the capitalization of land resource also gave rise to large number of confrontations and even mass incidents in rural society due to conflicts in profit allocation.

Impact on Rural Economy and Peasant Income

This round of depression in the macro-economic cycle was contextualized against a time when China was increasingly integrated into economic globalization dominated by international capital, while domestic over-capacity was emerging on all fronts. It was also a time when the dominant political orientation tended to "ideologize market measures".[12] All of these had multi-facet impact on the rural economy, peasant income and rural governance.

During the 1994–1996 economic overheating the state had raised the official purchase prices of staple grain, effectively stimulating essential produce production. Then the downward economic cycle in 1997 took effect and urban demand declined. As the economy sank into depression, the problem of over-supply surfaced, with grain price and agricultural effectiveness both falling. The Chinese rural economy became increasingly debilitated since mid—and late 1990s.

Under the combined impact of over-capacity in manufacturing as well as austerity policies, the business environment of rural small-medium enterprises once again deteriorated. Yet rural government's expenditures were mostly inelastic as community welfare, rural authority and

---

[12]The intellectuals and dominant sectors in China all have a tendency to ideologize economic system in order to safe-guard "discourse correctness", whether emphasis on planned economy in the past or on market economy nowadays.

enterprises were interwoven. Hence the loans that rural enterprises had borrowed to finance production were largely diverted to cover local government expenses. Rural enterprises indebtedness went even higher. Local authorities, in attempt to shrug off the debt burden just as their superiors were doing, adopted the policy of privatization with the transfer of indebtedness as a condition. After such reforms rural enterprises no longer had affinity with the local community and the mission to optimize community employment or to take responsibility over community welfare. Given the capitalist mechanism of 'capital intensification excludes labor', rural employment started to decline.[13]

Empirical research showed that in the fifteen years between 1991 and 2006, the growth rate of China's economy had strong correlation with the growth in rural enterprise employment, with Pearson Correlation Coefficient of 0.642. Considering the problem of statistic scale inconsistency since 2003, we conducted correlation analysis between GDP growth rate and rural enterprise employment growth rate using 1990–2002 data. The Pearson Correlation Coefficient was 0.648, supporting the conclusion (Fig. 7).

In response to crises in urban sector, a series of reforms were conducted since 1990, including rural financial reform launched in 1998, the main objective of which was to lower the risk in banking sector, and commercialization in education and health care that had the purpose of driving domestic demands, and so on. They had all become financial pumps drawing out scarce funds and resources from rural regions to cities.

Take rural financial reform as an example. Following the progress of the banking commercialization reform, the out flow of funds from the illiquid agricultural realm to non-agricultural and urban sectors had accelerated. The quota of financing that agriculture and rural regions were given by the state banking system had dwindled. By 2002 when the banking commercialization reform was completed, the loans utilized by

---

[13] As early as in 1986, a reputed young scholar Du Ying (later the Deputy Director of National Development and Reform Committee) and Zhou Qiren et el had published a survey report on 200 large rural enterprises, pointing out that the latter's mission of establishment was not the optimization of profit but optimization of community employment. The mechanism of capital excluding labor was put forward by Chen Xiwen (later the Director of Central Rural Affairs Leading Team).

Fig. 7 Rural enterprises employment and contribution to rural community 1990–2006; statistics after 1997 were rural collective enterprises; 2003 and 2004 were large rural enterprises (Source of data: China Statistical Yearbooks and China Rural Enterprise Statistical Yearbooks)

rural regions accounted for only 10.4% of total loans in the whole society (Chen Xiwen, 2004). The gap between supply and demand of funds in rural sector continued to increase, from 462.3 billion yuan in 1991 to 10.332 trillion in 2004 (Wu Cuifang 2007). Consequentially, rural development was faced with the predicament of fund shortage, thereby spurring the emergence of wide-spread rural usury since late 1990s. In addition, from our field studies performed in Northern Anwei and Northern China, we time and again heard that even grass-root officers would sometimes seek recourse to usury in order to fulfill the taxation requirements. As peasants were generally plagued by heavy levy, there was difficulty in tax collection. The grass-root taxation departments often had to borrow from usury to fill the gap. The heavy interest obligation was then passed onto peasants, resulting in a vicious cycle.

Impact on Rural Governance: The Model of "Self-Financing" for Rural Governance was Again at Danger

During this period the inelastic government expenditure relating to rural super-structure did not decrease alongside the downward economic cycle but on the contrary continued to expand. On one hand it was due to the closing down and bankruptcy of rural enterprises which reduced non-agricultural employment opportunities, thereby increasing the number of people that the grass root fiscal budgets had to provide for. On the other hand, ever since the tax-division system reform in 1994 various upper level governments essentially adopted the approach of "taking up fiscal power but pushing down responsibilities". The provision responsibilities of basic public goods that could not be readily "shrugged off" through simple marketization, such as obligatory education, medical and health care and so on were being pushed down level by level. The peasants, as China's biggest under-privileged group, eventually became the principal agent supplying fiscal funds needed for rural public goods during the 1990s reform (for example, education funding accounted for a large portion of peasant levy). Therefore, from late 1990s till 2004 when the central government announced the abolishment of agricultural tax, the frequent official documents directing that "peasants' burden should not be increased" were a reflection of the fact the load on peasants had continued to increase.

Box 5: Central Government Documents regarding Peasants' Burden in the 1990s

Sociological studies have indicated that during a particular period of time, the frequency of policies propagation on a certain subject would to some extent be proportional to the severity of that subject in society. After analyzing the material on policy regulations published in the *People's Daily* since its inauguration in 1946, we found that the issue of peasants being overburdened was first mentioned in the 1990 'Report on the Work of the Government' and since then it had been referred to every year with varying emphasis and frequency. In the 1993 report it was pointed out very clearly that "peasants in many regions had higher production but not higher income; the situation of haphazard fund-raising and apportioning to peasants, adding to their burden, was quite glaring."

In the document 'Report regarding the Situation of Increasing Peasants' income and Reducing Peasants' Burden' presented on 30 October

1999 by the then Agricultural Minister Chen Yaobang, the content quoted below reflects the seriousness of peasants' increasing affliction in late 1990s:

> Following the document 'Decisions of CPC Central and State Council regarding Faithful Execution of the Work on Reducing Peasants' Load' in 1996, further policy regulations were launched since last year. Last July, the CPC Central Office and State Council Office sent out the document 'Notice Regarding Faithful Execution of the Work on Reducing Peasants' Load,' clearly indicating that the total absolute amounts to be imposed on peasants in 1998 should not exceed the amount in 1997. The third plenary of the 15th CPC Central Committee affirmed the reduction of peasants' load as one of the fundamental goals in rural work, clearly stipulating that the reasonable amount to be borne by peasants should remain unchanged for three years. This year, the State Council Office forwarded various documents from the Agriculture Ministry, 'Report on Enforcement Inspections Regarding Peasants' Load for 1998' in March, then the document 'Opinions on Executing Well the Work of Reducing Peasants' Burden" in July. In mid-October, State Council convened the national phone and video conference on reducing peasants' load in which vice-Premier Wen Jiabao put forward the clear requirement to further reduce peasants' burden.

In fact, the tension in economy from macro to micro levels at that time led to tension in rural social relationship that was more serious than ever before. A series of reforms since the 1990s had resulted in extreme scarcity of funds at the grass root. The subsequent burden on peasants' shoulders led to wide spread confrontations between peasants and local officers at the turn of the century.[14]

When normal means of levying could not fulfill the target, grass root authorities would generally adopt unusual tactics such as mobilizing the mass to help collect, making loans, collective financing, even employing gangsters to coerce the peasants. Other levying means in disguise—e.g. appropriating land for contracting, levying compensation, fraudulently diverting compensations for relocations or for repatriation of forest and farm land—had also happened in large numbers.

Furthermore, in the Grain Circulation System Reform launched in 1999 for the purpose of facilitating rural financial reform and 'digesting' the funds of Agricultural Bank held up by grain system, various policies

---

[14]Dong Xiaodan & Wen Tiejun, 'Macro Economic Volatility and Rural Governance Crisis,' *Management World*, 2008 (9).

in favoritism of state sector's monopolization of grain supply included one that required 'collection of peasants' surplus household by household in cash', a change from the past approach of having the grain station handle it collectively. The approach originally had the good intention of protecting the interest of peasants. Yet during execution it became a mechanism causing incidents of mass confrontation. Rural society had become de-organized politically after the reform in 1980s. The marketization of grain system since 1998 further modified the relationship between local authorities and peasants. Peasant households were geographically, socially and politically scattered. It was difficult for village cadres to collect levy without using coercive means. The administrational, political and social costs of village cadres having to collect levy household by household were obviously very high. This high transaction costs between grass root authorities and scattered peasant households intensified the confrontation sharply. Looking from this perspective, the contradiction was the outcome of government's over-mobilization of peasant households for resources in the peasant economy, without being able to resolve the problem of high transaction costs with scattered peasant households (Wen Tiejun 2003).

Because of state involution (Duara 1995), some of its rural grass root personnel reverted to villainous gentry that had existed repeatedly over history in the past. Alliances of 'villainous gentry + elite' were formed with local governing authorities. For example, the Organization Department of the CPC Central Committee promulgated on March 22, 1999 the document 'Opinions Regarding the Strengthening of Building the Rank of Rural Grass Root Cadres' and the *People's Daily* published on February 9th, 2000 an article about certain typical cases of rural grass root cadres violently handling the mass in Fujian, Hunan, Shandong, Jiangsu and Hainan, which were respectively obverse and reverse reflections of the trend of grass root cadres degenerating into villainous gentry. It then developed further into situation of 'elite capture' and 'clientelism' in rural governance.[15]

---

[15]The World Bank's *World Development Report 2005*, regarding government's rent-seeking behaviors, used the terms 'capture' and 'patron-clientelism' to refer to 'the skewing of policies towards certain groups while damaging the interest of other groups due to uneven access to information and their impact on policy-making'. Xie Yue (2005), refers clientelism to 'protector politics' in

Large number of peasant petition as well as mass incidents happened at that time. Certain local governments, in some circumstances, made use of state apparatus or even gangsters to suppress mass incidents, thereby causing escalation of confrontation and even injuries and fatalities, which then further worsened the rural governance crisis. Kan Xiaoguang et el (2002) believed that Chinese society had since 1990s seen the formation of an elite alliance including political, economic and intellectual elites. They would skew the allocation of interests in the society towards elite groups while forming a stable base for the governing power of the state as a whole. The conflicts in rural regions were 'partial' opposition by the mass under exploitation. Elite alliance was endogenous and highly stable, and once formed were very difficult to break down. Yang Pan (2005) further believed that it was the era of double conflict, the conflict among elites and the conflict between elites and the mass. Although they had different assessments on the situation of competition among elites, yet regarding mass incidents both concluded that they were conflicts between elites (or elite alliance) and the exploited mass.

The direct manifestation of confrontation was mass incidents begun to rise sharply since 1997 (totally over 15,000 in that year) and then more than doubled in two years to 32,000 in 1999. Based on statistics from the police department, the number of incidents was 60,000 in 2003, 74,000 in 2004 and 86,000 in 2005. Although there were no further publicly available statistics after that, from on-line information search the number was more than 200,000 in 2009. About one third of those cases were related to peasants defending their rights. As for petitions, the frequency and causes were basically consistent with the changes in mass incidents, also escalating after 1997. For example, surveys conducted by a joint team of the Henan Academy of Social Science and Henan Provincial Petition Bureau found that people's sentiment was unstable in some rural

China rural society. During the transition under the authoritarian system, the use of public power for self-interest emerged within the interest-exchange network of 'protector-the protected' relationship. The expansion of this kind of network of self-interest had to a certain extent obstructed the normal operation of peasants' self-governance and the development of community self-administration, resulting in the marginalization of legitimate authority. 'Protectors' in the name of executing state authority provided the 'protected' with exclusive services, acquiring economic and political rewards in doing so. In many cases, public resources were appropriated to serve the interests of a handful of persons.

regions in Henan. Many had mounting distrust towards the county and village authorities. Large scale group petition cases increased year over year, with 187 groups, a total of 24,203 people in first half of 1998, an increases of 33.6% and 449.7% respectively over the same period in 1997.[16]

In summary, this imported crisis did not directly transform into depression due to a series of strong intervention initiated by the government in 1998. GDP growth was sustained at 7.8% in 1997 and 7.6% in 1998, thus maintaining economic growth and relative social stability. However it gave rise to an unprecedented situation of peasant incomes declining for four consecutive years, which led to insufficient domestic demand and 'deflation'. Furthermore, as the stimulating measures were oriented towards urban sector, the negative impact on the *sannong* and rural governance was quite severe.

3   Contextualizing the Fourth Round of Foreign Investments and Foreign Debts in 1997–2008: Collision of External and Domestic Over-Capacities

At the time before the 1997 crisis, export sector annually contributed over 3 percentage points to GDP growth. A noteworthy factor was the issue of 'maintaining social stability,' which was directly related to GDP growth. There had not been much attention paid to this issue in the discussions around the aforementioned macro-economic policies. In the 1980s hundreds of millions of excess rural labor had been released into market by the reform. Then in the 1990s as many as 30 million state-owned employees were laid-off on a large scale by another round of reform. Adding to that, population growth would bring about 10 million new labors every year, which put an enormous pressure on employment market. In case annual GDP growth was lower than 7% in China,

---

[16]Joint Survey Team of Henan Academy of Social Science and Henan Petition Bureau, '关于当前农村社会稳定问题的调查 (Survey Regarding the Present Rural Social Stability)' 调研世界 (The World of Survey and Research), 1999(1).

there would be less than 8 million new employment opportunities. And the contradiction arising from the pressure of workers seeking employment with a shortfall new job supply would become dangerous. During the 1990s, mass incidents in the society sharply increased to a scale of tens of thousands every year. The situation for social stability overall was extremely severe. At that time, the idea of China Collapse became popular in the West.[17] However, Bill Clinton who became U.S. president in 1993 adopted the 'China engagement' policy that was quite different from that kind of discourse.

But that buzzword did not last long. With a decade of growth driven by public debt since 1998 as well as its accession to the WTO in 2001 that brought in foreign investments, China had by 2008 when the financial crisis happened in U.S.A. already become the world's top country in foreign exchange reserve and second largest holder of U.S. Treasury bonds. During that same period, those western politicians and mainstream media who prophesized the collapse of China in the 1990s now changed their tune to the 'China Threat' hype.

It was in 2008 when the Wall Street financial tsunami gave rise to a global crisis that many Chinese began to realize China had already reached the monumental turning point ten years ago in 1997–1998 from over demand to oversupply. It was a decade of bidding farewell to shortfall and saying hello to excess in supply. It would be hard not to associate this ten-year period with the former after the 1988 economic crisis wherein the condition was that of a severe shortfall.

The word that scared the people in 1988–1998 was 'inflation'. Five years afterwards what described China's macro-economic trend had quietly switched to a term common folks would be hard put to it to understand: deflation.

During the economic trough from 1998 to 2002, the troika pulling the economy run out of steam, exposing with unprecedented clarity the contradiction between supply and demand. The first of the troika was domestic demand. Sale of general consumer goods became sluggish. (The wave of high-priced consumer goods such as cars and real

---

[17]When 'China collapse' was a buzzword in the West, a Chinese writer Wang Lixiong wrote a political fantasy fiction *The Yellow Peril*, which became a best-seller in early 1990s in the U.S.A., with 11 reprints.

estate was yet to arrive.) Moreover, the industrialization reforms of education, health care and housing that were intended to drive domestic demand had the reverse effect of increasing people's level of savings with anticipation of future expenditures, hence further suppressing the consumption at the present. The second in the troika was investment. Indeed investments had stimulated rapid economic growth since 1992. Yet with tougher economic regulation in 1996 it became dampened. The third was foreign demand. China's manufactured goods export in 1978 had already accounted for 45.2% of total export. In a period of thirty years since 1949, China was already able to export more than primary products. By 1997, that percentage increased to 86.9%. In that year the total export amounted to US$ 182.7 billion, 158.8 billion of which were manufactured goods.[18] That meant it took China just another 20 years to complete the domestic expansion of capital and the preliminary adjustment of its export structure.

Yet this monumental structural change of the economy would inevitably bring corresponding structural change in economic crises. Not only was China's economy more vulnerable to external economic volatility, it also became increasingly affected by financial globalization.

Justin Lin Yifu proposed in 1999 the notion of a 'vicious cycle under the condition of double over-capacity' based on neoclassical economic theories. It well explained the swift absorption of China under pressure of over-capacity into globalization in a world which was already troubled by over-capacity in a very 'classical' sense.

Wang Jian, who put forward in 1988 the strategic formulation of 'great international circle', summarized China's opening to the world over the previous 30 years into three phases in an essay (see below column). The first phase was the 1980s during which China relied on foreign funds. The second was the 1990s during which the reliance switched from foreign funds to overseas markets. The third was the period after 2000 wherein the reliance turned towards international financial market under the context of globalization.

---

[18]Li Jingzhi (李景治) & Pu Guoliang (蒲国良), 社会主义建设理论与实践 (Socialist Construction: Theory and Practice). China Renmin University Press, 2003.

Given that the central government was the dominating power in financial capital, the above-mentioned reliance on international finance was manifested mostly at the state level. At regional level, it still relied on foreign funds and the overseas market.

Box 6: Three Phases in China's Opening to the World over Thirty Years

From the perspective of the motivation to open to outside, China's Reform and Opening Up in the last thirty years went through three phases. The first phase was the 1980s in which China had to rely on foreign funds. That was the reason why I had envisaged the economic development strategy of 'the Great International Cycle', which meant taking the opportunity of industrial upgrade in Japan and Asia's Four Little Dragons, and making use of foreign capital to develop labor-intensive products export in coastal regions. Then with the foreign reserves earned we exchanged for capital goods from the international market so as to look after at the same time the relocation of rural labor and the reconstruction/upgrading of heavy industries.

The second phase was the 1990s. Following the progress of China's reform and the in-take of large amounts of foreign capital, industrial capability and savings were both gradually consolidated. In 1991 a positive deposit differential in the banking system had appeared for the first time. The overall savings rate grew from 33% on average in the 1980s to more than 40% in early 1990s. By mid 1990s, the reform had entered into the property rights stage, followed by a widening income gap. A fundamental change took place in the domestic supply and demand structure. Over-supply began to appear. Economic growth became increasingly reliant on export demand. As a result, the needs in opening up changed from reliance on foreign funds to reliance on overseas markets. Since the turn of the new century, under the context of globalization, export expanded rapidly and the scale of foreign capital being utilized continued to increase. Adding to that, the inflow of international hot money expanded the foreign currency reserves rapidly. Over the last 7 years the annual increase was on average US$ 200 billion. By the end of 2007 it had reached US$ 1.53 trillion, and firmly stayed in top position worldwide since 2005. Given that China's capital market was not opened and the Renminbi was not internationalized, that enormous foreign reserve asset could only be invested in foreign markets. Therefore the need in opening to the outside changed again, from reliance on overseas markets to reliance on the international financial market.

From reliance on funds to reliance on markets then to finance, it reflected the transformation of China's mode of articulation with the global economy. At present, we have reliance on all three realms, with the focus shifting somewhat at different stages of economic development.

Source: Wang Jian, '关于设立"珠三角金融特区"的构想 (The Conception of Setting Up the 'Pearl River Delta Special Financial Zone')' 中国宏观经济信息网 (China Macro-economic Information), 4-8-2008. http://www.macrochina.com.cn/zhtg/200808040 91350.shtml.

By the twenty-first century, China's opening up took a step deeper into the new circle of international economy dominated by U.S. financial capital, namely, financial globalization.

As discussed in previous chapter, China had implemented the exchange rate reform in 1994 under serious pressure of current account deficit with a one-time currency depreciation of more than 50%, as a means to raise export competitiveness and attract foreign funds inflow. With rapid growth in export and controlled capital account, mounting stock of foreign currency reserve was rendered into expansion of domestic money supply. With this kind of 'hedging', China was able to be sheltered to some extent from international financial risk.

Generally speaking, in this round of international transfer of industries led by transnational companies under the pressure of global overcapacity, those being transferred outward from developed countries like the U.S. included not only labor intensive industries but also capital-intensive or technology-intensive industries, a key feature unseen in previous rounds. Capital and technology-intensive industries had more stringent requirements on capital, cost of external financing as well as efficiency. Therefore those developing countries received industry transfer became more dependent on foreign financing. When these industries began to move out, most Asian countries experienced financial crisis. Even though China's financial development level was much lower than the U.S, it emerged as the most stable financial market in the Asia at that time. Besides, Renminbi exchange rate was appreciating consistently and therefore there was positive anticipation that China might gradually open up foreign exchange control. As a result, not only the U.S.A. transferred industries to China, other Asian countries also followed. China gradually rose as the main receptor of global industrial transfer.[19]

Nevertheless, to have a more comprehensive understanding on a phenomenon, it is preferable to make references to different evaluations.

From the perspective of Samir Amin's "dependency theory", what China's economy had completed in the 1990s, under the pressure of serious domestic and foreign debt crises, was a historical transformation from "de-linking" to "re-linking". The policies being adopted and the economic phenomena that had stemmed from it were also similar to those in other developing countries in general. Among the policies in response to the 1990s crises, the financial policy of 'raising interest rate and lowering exchange rate' had indeed transformed the economic development environment. On one side the high capital cost within the country was squeezing the profit margin of enterprises oriented towards domestic demand. What it facilitated was China's export economy that generated foreign reserves. On the other side, it matched precisely with the strategy of transnational corporations seeking profit by making use of "low interest rate + high currency value" combination. In the stage of so-called financial deepening, transnational corporations were motivated by the gains through this international capital circulation. What followed then was a new round of international industrial capital at the turn of the new century. That was also the reason why China all of a sudden became the number one recipient country worldwide of foreign direct investments (FDI) during 1998–2008 between the two imported crises. It was in this decade that many of the Fortune 500 companies made their presence in China. US transnational companies took the lead in almost all of the strategic industries. Thanks to these investments in

---

[19]Li Xingong (李新功), '美元霸权、金融发展差异与货币体系错配下中美经济失衡及调整 (Dollar Hegemony, Financial Development Differences and Monetary Systems Mismatch: Economic Imbalance and Adjustments in China and the U.S.A.)' 现代经济探讨 (Modern Economy Inquiry), 2009(9).

China their average annual rate of return went from under 20% to more than 30%. The industrial transfer out of the U.S. was detrimental to US industrial workers. Yet the rise in overseas capital returns stimulated Wall Street's prosperity to a large extent as the Dow Jones Industrial Average Index was breaking historical record year after year.

The above discussion of the transformation of China's domestic and foreign policies since the 1990s is an objective and factual description. However, it may help to unveil a part of the true face behind the so-called 'G2' or 'Chimerica', as some have put forward.

Under the impact of the above factors in the 1990s, China's principal momentum in opening up changed at the turn of the century from the force of domestic over-capacity to the pull of external demand. During the same period, the substance of the export economy mostly located in coastal regions also underwent transformation—from traditional general trade of manufacturing processing where profits came mainly from internal allocation inside localized industries, to a new type of processing trade where profits of branding and selling were mostly realized in foreign markets and high-tech industrial processing where both raw material supply and final market were outside of China.

Thereupon, Chinese enterprises and labors in general could only share a very small part of the total profits realized in the whole industrial chain. Worse still, the right of pricing in raw material markets and the power of institutional arrangement in international trade were not in China's hands. That effectively constituted the condition by which foreign interest blocs could constrain and shape China's institutional transition as well as relevant intellectual thinking.

Import was always coupled with export. This change in the mechanism of opening up started with the 1998 imported crisis caused by external financial crisis (the 1997 Southeast Asian financial crisis generated by international hot money flow) which forced China to urgently open its economy still at the stage of industrial capitalism.

On that basis, we propose a hypothesis that: it was because China and the West were situated in two different phases of capitalist civilization—respectively industrial capitalism and financial capitalism—that China would have an induced change in the content of its export structure.

Before 1998, China was still in the industrial capital expansion stage propelled by structural adjustments, which was completely different from the USA. In the latter case, the virtual expansion of financial capital took place simultaneously with outward transfer of industry. The USA recorded long term trade deficits while capital account surplus was growing. Back then China's economy was yet to be highly dependent on foreign markets. Domestic and foreign markets mainly served China's industrial capital expansion. They were mutually replaceable. Large increases in import were usually offset by large decreases in export. As seen in graph 4–6, the import growth rate and export growth rate curves went in opposite directions most of the time during 1980–1990. The turning point was the 1997 Southeast Asian crisis when public debt driven investments became the key impetus of growth.

Figure 8 shows a high correlation between import growth rates and China's economic situation. For example, the two economic surges in 1982–1985 and 1992–1993, caused by domestic industrial capital expansions led to drastic increases of import while export over the same periods decreased. Furthermore changes in export were more sensitive to stimulating policies. For example, there were high export growth rates in 1987 and 1994 responding to policy adjustments on trade. Yet after

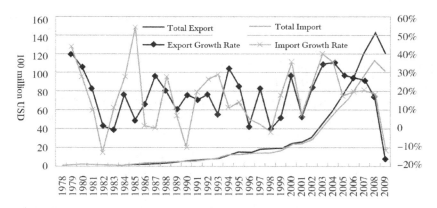

Fig. 8 Changes in China's trade structure since 1978 (Data source: China Statistical Yearbooks)

1998, import and export trends went almost hand in hand in the same direction.

While the world economy was emerging out of the slump from 2002 until 2008 before the Wall Street financial crisis, China shifted towards the trade model of manufacture processing wherein both ends of trade (raw material supplies and product markets) were on the outside. Hence import and export were rising simultaneously.

As China's participation in international trade was largely in the form of manufacture processing after 2002, the volume of general trade (import and export) accounted for around 40–50% out of the total trade volume.

When foreign investments entered into China in the 1980s, they were interested in the potential of China's enormous consumption market. At that time the principal force in creating export and foreign exchange reserve were domestic enterprises. By the 1990s when China sought to release excess capacity into international market, even though the proportion of export by foreign-owned enterprises had grown substantially it was still lower than domestic enterprises. However, since 2000 foreign owned enterprises accounted for more than 50% of China's total import and export trade. The share of foreign-owned enterprises in export accounted for 52.2% in 2002, 58.2% in 2006 and over 60% in 2011. In the South Suzhou region where the structure of manufacturing had already been shaped to facilitate industrial capital in the Yangtze delta area, the characteristics of export-oriented economy were even more pronounced. The proportion of import and export by foreign enterprises exceeded 70% (Figs. 9 and 10).

China's total import and export in 2001, the year of its accession to the WTO, valued at US$ 509.8 billion. Seven years later in 2008 when the Wall Street financial crisis broke out, the total value already grew up by five times to US$ 2.56 trillion. The average annual growth rate over these 7 years was as high as 26.1%. Meanwhile, China's share in total world trade rose from 4.06 to 7.88%.

China's dependency on international trade maintained at around 70% for a relatively long period. It relied on overseas demand to drive its annual GDP growth up to double digit and was increasingly blended into the global capital regime led by the U.S.A. at accelerating pace of

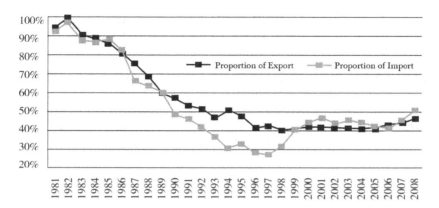

Fig. 9 Proportions of general trading in China's total import/export (Data source: China Statistical Yearbooks)

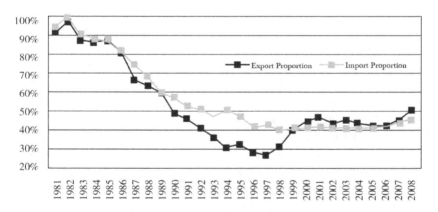

Fig. 10 Shares of foreign enterprises import/export in China and Jiangsu Province (Data source: China Statistical Yearbooks)

financial deepening. Then the Wall Street financial crisis, much more violent and with a more profound impact than the Asian crisis ten years ago, broke out.

4   The Ninth Crisis: Policies Responding to the 2008 Financial Crisis and Impact

Since the 1980s the capitalist economy in the West was "upgraded" to financial capitalism led by the USA. In a short span of 20 years the U.S. capital market already created more than 2,000 types of derivatives, thereby promoting the low cost global expansion of the financial economy. Simultaneous to that, the enormous institutional cost corresponding to this development was inevitably accumulating while astronomical amount of financial capital marched into the brave new world of the virtual economy. That accumulated cost manifested itself continuously as a series of financial crises that moved gradually from the periphery (Latin America, East Asia etc.) towards the core (the USA where financial speculation was most intensive) in the world financial system.

In the summer of 2008, with the deterioration of the Subprime Crisis in the previous year, Lehmann Brothers, the fourth largest invest-ment bank in Wall Street filed for Chapter 11 bankruptcy. The two largest mortgage loan companies Fannie Mae and Freddie Mac as well as the largest insurance group AIG were temporarily "nationalized". The curtain was drawn open for the global economic crisis caused by the Wall Street financial tsunami.

The rest was history most people are familiar with. However what many around the world do not know is that during this advanced phase of capitalism, financial capital with its dominating position in global economy and by the command of the country holding the unipolar hege-mony, was capable of transferring the institutional cost outwards and downwards. In addition, it also held the institutional power (a soft power constructed to protect this international politico-economic order) and discursive power—a smart power working hand in hand with the former. They were mutually dependent, spreading worldwide in the company of globalization and becoming the root of the general aphasia among intel-lectuals in developing countries who lost sight of their responsibility of localized knowledge production. While the crises were moving from the periphery toward the core, these intellectuals were busy at parrot talking and lost the ability to understand what was happening in their own countries.

The positive experiences that China had gained in dealing with crises also fell into oblivion amidst that aphasia.

China's Domestic Situation Before the Crisis

As a response to the crisis in 1997–1998, the large scale public debt-driven investments aiming at spurring domestic demands had been mostly put into infrastructure construction and improvement, thus facilitating China with the hardware to further integrate with the global economy. Since the second half of 2002, with the revival of global economy and the re-setting of international industrial layout directed by the advanced countries, China became the most attractive country for foreign direct investments, given that its infrastructure was in a much better shape than developing countries in general. The impetus led to a new wave of high speed economic growth in China.

As compared to the past, before the eruption of the 2008 crisis China's economy manifested some new features in terms of the development mode and structure.

China's Economy was Further Integrated into the Great Global Economic Circulation Dominated by the USA

Around the turn of the twenty-first century, global financial capital developed further into excess and over expansion, driving advanced countries to undertake structural adjustments and upgrade traditional industries to information industry. Following that, the international industrial configuration also saw profound changes.

Box 7: International Industrial Transfer in the Twentieth Century

International industrial transfer in the twentieth century can generally be summarized into three waves.

The first wave took place in the mid-twentieth century, as a consequence of the seismic shift in the centuries-long western imperialist geo-political configuration, a shift brought about by the Second World War caused by the power collision during industrial capitalist expansion. The two emerging super powers, the U.S.A. and U.S.S.R., in order to consolidate their geo-political controls, both deployed industrial exports in a "flying-goose formation"—the U.S. towards Western Europe and Japan, and the U.S.S.R. towards Eastern Europe and China. The difference between the two was that, the U.S., having completed the outward industrial transfer to facilitate its geo-political strategy, took the lead into financial capitalist expansion, while the USSR's outward industrial transfer was halted midway due to its controversies over sovereignty with China, foreshadowing its subsequent disintegration.

The second wave of industrial transfer took place in the 1960s. In general it could be regarded as the process in which the spillover effect of manufacturing capital resulted in rising cost of production factors, thereby driving developed countries to transfer manufacturing outwards. With the development of science and technology, labor cost in developed countries continued to inflate. Furthermore, given the increasingly intensified labor and capital conflict that was inevitable in industrial capitalism, the world then saw a new wave of global industrial structure adjustments, with developed countries in the lead. Labor-intensive industries were transferred from developed to developing countries, leaving the former to focus on development of technology and capital intensive industries, realizing upgrades in economic structure.

In the 1960s and 1970s when the Cold War still at its height, those countries and in the Western camp and along the frontier had been the first to receive this round of industrial transfer. As their societies and cultures were somehow similar, the process was smooth with little institutional friction. Likewise, Korea, Taiwan, Singapore and Hong Kong—countries and regions that shared Confucian civilization—received industrial transferal from Japan to launch 'export-oriented' strategy, putting priority on labor-intensive processing manufacturing.

In a short span of time they were able to realize economic upsurge and referred to as 'Asia's four little dragons'.

Since the four little dragons were small geographically, the spillover effect of receiving capital from international industrial transfer rapidly led to resources re-pricing within their realm. To secure profit margins, capitals seeking optimal return then flowed into countries and regions around the four little dragons, where the prices of essential factors such as land, resources and labor force were still relatively low. The Asia's 'four little tigers' thereupon developed rapidly.

China resumed diplomatic ties with the West in 1972. Simultaneously, the second round of opening up had started. Western equipments were brought in on a large scale to adjust its industrial structure. It was against this backdrop the 'processing manufacturing and repayment trading' model in Pearl River delta region emerged while the cities along the Yangtze River specified in heavy and chemical industries started to make structural adjustment.

In early 1970s, after Mao Zedong accepted the military assessment that a new world war would not break out within 20 years, China resumed diplomatic relations with Europe, the USA and Japan. Western capital was thereupon introduced into industrial cities in coastal regions where industries were more concentrated. In mid to late 1970s, the international situation had progressed in a direction favorable to third world countries with regard to receiving industrial transfer. At the same time, the tension in China's eastern and southern coastal region (due to the antagonism with Taiwan) had also eased up. Guangdong province which previously had a relatively weak industrial base was able to rapidly accumulate domestic and foreign resources with the help of policies favoritism from the central government and the advantage of proximity to Hong Kong and Macau, from which labor-intensive industry was transferred into the province. An exogenous industrial structure corresponding to the process gradually took shape. Guangdong rapidly developed into an economically prominent region, drawing the curtain of China's third opening up with local governments in the lead. (The first opening up referred to the 1950s aiming at primitive capital accumulation, the second in early 1970s attempting to adjust industrial structure. Both had been executed in the name of the state. The only difference was that in the first round the foreign capital came from the USSR while in the second round Western countries and Japan.)*

In Asia, the flying goose formation industrial structure with Japan at the tip stabilized gradually. Japan located at the apex of East Asia's economic hierarchy exported top-end technological products to East Asian countries and bought relatively low-end products from the latter which received Japan's obsolete industries. The reliance of those late-developing countries on Japan's high-end products and on Japan's market for selling their low-end products constituted Japan's structural support on East Asian economic development.**

The international industrial transfer taking place around the turn of the twenty-first century can be regarded as the third wave, largely the outcome of the rise of IT industry. Since the 1980s when the international political situation eased up, a large number of military technologies achieved in advanced countries during the Cold War were converted to civilian use, giving impetus to an industrial upgrade with the knowledge economy as its base. It continued to be the driving force for developed countries' outward industrial transfer (see next column).

*Wen Tiejun, '新中国三次对外开放的成本与收益'(New China's Three Rounds of Opening Up: Costs and Benefits), in 我们到底要什么(What In Fact Do We Want). Huaxia Publishing House, 2004; Wen Tiejun et el, 广东省产业结构和发展战略调整研究课题报告 (Report on Guangdong Province's Industrial Structure and Development Strategy Adjustments), 2008.

**Ju Hailong(鞠海龙), '破日本雁阵 中国—东盟布新局' (Breaking Japan's Flying Goose Formation: the New China-ASEAN Layout), 时代周报(Time Weekly), 23-4-2009.

The USSR disintegrated in the 1990s and the post-cold war world turned into an arena of globalized competition dominated by financial capital. The approach to make profits by the financial empire, given its unipolar hegemony, underwent a fundamental change. It increasingly relied on inflow of capital to drive up the capital markets. Financial capital seeking liquidity for profit making in the virtual economy was increasingly alienated from industrial capital. Transnational corporations transferred processing manufacturing segments to developing countries.

This round of transfer had different features. Labor-intensive industries that no longer had comparative advantage in competition in developed societies continued to transfer outward to developing countries. At the same time technology and capital intensive industries began to be transferred. Apart from the raw materials industry, processing and general manufacturing, now service industry and high-tech industries became the focus, such as finance and insurance, trading services as well as capital intensive heavy industries including steel, automobile, petroleum and chemical industries, etc.

This round of industrial transfer was generally referred to as a revamping of global industrial capital configuration. Yet it was still a two-way selective exchange process. Advanced countries made the strategic adjustments of keeping the research and development sector and moving the production sector closer to the markets, while late-developed countries opened their markets for capital and technology in order to accelerate domestic industrial development.

The motive for this new round of industrial transfer was consistent with the global geo-political strategies of developed countries since colonialist expansion began 500 years ago. Take heavy and chemical industries as example. Developed countries markets had reached full capacity and the profitability was declining whereas in East Asia, emerging industrialized countries got stronger in manufacturing. The profit rates of heavy and chemical industries were consistently rising. Some even towered over other sectors. Therefore transnational collaboration with Chinese enterprises in heavy and chemical industries was imperative for competing in this emerging market. Japanese and Korean heavy and chemical industries had developed under trade protectionism. Their target markets were the downstream export-oriented industries. Given their proximity to China, over the past two decades their upstream industries had already enjoyed the fruits of China's development in light industry. Yet as a whole, they were only second class in the world (excepting Japanese automobiles). The first class players were still European and US heavy and chemical enterprises. Now, those Fortune 500 giants made high profile presence in China to join forces with local enterprises. It could possibly crowd out similar Japanese and Korean products that had relatively higher production factor prices. That was the outcome of global industrial chain revamping since 2002 as global economy was booming. The capital bubble was growing while the cost of production factors kept rising. The reshaping of global industrial configuration was an interaction of colliding forces.

US Dot-Com Bubble and FDI Flooding into China

China became one of the largest FDI recipients in the world may be contextualized in the rise of IT industry in the US.

Box 8: US IT Industry's Roller-Coaster Ride: 1995–2001

The predecessor of contemporary information technology was intelligence technology, originated at the end of the nineteenth century and widely applied during the Cold War (1).

In 1994, the Mosaic browser and the World Wide Web had attracted the public's attention. At first people simply took notice of internet's free publication and real time information from around the world. Gradually people began to adapt to two-way online communication, and further started using internet as the medium for electronic commerce and worldwide instant communication.

This new media technology that could contact millions of people around the world quickly at low cost and could connect buyers and sellers as well as advertisers and consumers immediately, brought changes to traditional commercial creeds such as advertising, mail order and customer relationship management. The internet brought about all kinds of new business models that were impossible just a few years back, thus attracting venture fund investments.

Netscape was listed on the stock market on 9 August, 1995, officially announcing the arrival of internet era and later leading to internet stock bubble as well as over-investments in optical fiber cable. As Netscape's former CEO Barksdale had said, 'We have initiated the internet bubble.'

A typical "dot.com" business model relied on a sustaining net effect, and for that it had to pay the price of running at a net loss to acquire market share. The company hoped to build sufficient brand recognition in order to gain return on subsequent service provision. The slogan of 'grow big fast' explained this strategy. During the period of running at a loss, the company would have to rely on venture funds and fund-raising at initial public offering (IPO). The novelty of these stocks as well as the inestimable value of the company pushed the price of many stocks to dumb-founded highs, and brought huge wealth on paper to the primary shareholders.

A small number of founders had acquired enormous wealth upon IPO of their companies during the early stage of the Dot Com bubble. These early successes made the speculation even more active. During the bloom it had attracted unprecedented number of individual investors. The media reported cases where people would resign from their jobs to focus on stock speculation.

As Su Guangping said, "The stock market's sensitiveness, amplification and feedback towards the economy have provided sufficient room for speculation. In stock market, as long as there are good stories there would be people speculating and believing. The concepts of advanced information technology, particularly the internet, were novel and non-comparable, making them ideal stories for speculators. Hence there were people suggesting that '3 years of internet economy is equivalent to 70 years of industrial economy' and some even claimed that 'the internet has subverted all economic rules'. Spurred on by the lead of venture funds, capital from domestic and foreign sources in a short span of time swarmed the internet realm in which the profit model was obscure. At the same time it also drove up the stock price of other IT enterprises. More and more people were being attracted to enter the market with anticipation of future rise, thereby pushing up the price further in a spiral. An exuberant bull market therefore took shape."

In various stock markets in Europe, America and Asia, the price of technology and internet related company stocks rapidly rose. On 10 March 2000 the NASDAQ index had reached the peak with the day high of 5048.62.

Yet an over-inflated stock market bubble could not possibly be sustained. Once the fact of continued losses of internet businesses set up the general anticipation of going short, the unrealistic stock price turned south and fall, resulting in a market crash.

> The crash amplified the recession in real economy. The internet bubble bust wiped away around US$ 5 trillion of market value from technology companies between March 2000 and October 2002.
>
> Some suggested that the internet bubble's burst stimulated the emergence of housing bubble in the USA. Yale University's economist Robert Schiller said in 2005, "Once stocks fell, real estate became the primary outlet for the speculative frenzy that the stock market had unleashed. Where else could plungers apply their newly acquired trading talents? The materialistic display of the big house also has become a slave to the bruised egos of disappointed stock investors. These days, the only thing that comes close to real estate as a national obsession is poker" (2).
>
> References:
> (1) http://baike.baidu.com/view/4402048.htm.
> (2) Quoted by Jonathan Laing, 'The Bubble's New Home,' *Wall Street Journal*, 20-6-2005.
>
> *Source*: http://baike.baidu.com/view/780.htm?fr=aladdin, Su Guang-ping(苏广平), '关于IT经济泡沫的反思(Reflections on the IT Bubble),' 2004-7-21, http://www.eepw.com.cn/article/27.htm.

The U.S. internet bubble went bust in 2001. Even though it was no more than one of the manifestations of economic cycle in the phase of capitalism civilization, "from a historical perspective, the prosperity of internet economy could be regarded as similar to other technological prosperities, including the railroad in the 1840s, the automobile and radio in the 1920s, the transistor in the 1950s, timesharing computer systems in the 1960s as well as personal computers and biotechnology in early 1980s".[20] It did in fact give Asian countries an opportunity to go against the trend and take a ride on the IT express.[21]

The reason was before the dot-com bubble bust, overinvestment into the real economy had been frenzied. One typical case was information network construction. During the time when the internet bubble expanded, the growth of internet communication capacity was forecasted

---

[20]http://baike.baidu.com/view/780.htm?fr=aladdin.
[21]Thomas Friedman, *The World is Flat: A Brief History of the Twenty-first Century*. London: Penguin Books, 2006.

to double every 100 days. The funds invested into networks in 1999 had reached US$ 100 billion, exceeding the total in the previous 15 years. Between 1998 and 2001, the number of underground fiber-optic cables laid increased by 5 times. By the time the internet bubble collapsed, the length of underground optical fibers in the U.S. was around 39 million miles.[22]

Prosperity in the stock market meant that the invested funds were cost-free. In 5 to 6 years, communication companies had invested a total of around US$ 1 trillion to lay all kinds of optical cables, and no one had ever questioned the future demand (Friedman 2006).

Adding to that, technological advancement raised the communication capacity of optical cable. The overall communication capability of U.S. fiber-optic network had increased by tens of times in the short span of a few years. Yet the growth in demand was lagging behind. Even during the early period of high speed development, the growth in internet communication capacity was only doubling every year. The rate of growth in the later period was even lower. In 2002 the growth in internet capacity worldwide was less than 40% (Su 2004).

Another typical case was the semi-conductor industry. At the end of the last century, given that the semi-conductor market had grown substantially due to the rapid expansion of electronic equipment market, various semi-conductor manufacturers competed to invest enormous amounts into building production lines for new generation chips. First they competed in the 8 inch production line that cost at US$ 1 billion each, then 12 inch production line at US$ 2 to 3 billion (ibid.).

Such overinvestment was of course highly risky from economic perspective. Yet from technological perspective, "they also often do drive innovation faster and faster, and the sheer overcapacity that they spur—whether it is in railroad lines or automobiles—can create its own positive consequences...Unlike other forms of Internet overinvestment, it was permanent: Once the fiber cables were laid, no one was going to dig them up and thereby eliminate the overcapacity. So when the telecom companies went bankrupt, the banks took them over and then sold their fiber

---

[22]Su Guangping, 'Reflections on the IT Bubble,' 2004-7-21, http://www.eepw.com.cn/article/27.htm.

cables for ten cents on the dollar to new companies, which continued to operate them, which they could do profitably, having bought them in a fire sale....[T]he capacity of all the already installed fiber cables just keeps growing, making it cheaper and easier to transmit voices and data every year to any part of the world" (Friedman 2006:71–75).

It was precisely these internet infrastructure built during the internet bubble period with enormous amounts of investments that created a big market for all kinds of virtual space based on that infrastructure. It narrowed the digital gap between developed and developing countries as well as the industrial gap between them. It could be said that the speculative funds invested during the peak of the internet bubble spilt over to other industries and eventually integrated with the real estate sector, to a very large extent raising the operating costs of real industries in those countries at the internet bubble core, forcing industrial capital in these countries to transfer outward to developing countries. And the narrowed digital gap strengthened the feasibility of this move economically and technologically.

"Off-shoring" appeared in accordance with this. That and "service outsourcing" together would explain the changes in global FDI flows since 2001. Similar to the process in the 1960s when manufacturing companies in developed countries out-sourced part of their operations off-shore, the rapid development of offshore service outsourcing in the past decade has become another characteristic of service outsourcing. According to estimations, in 2001 the total market for off-shore service export had amounted to roughly US$ 32 billion. The principal service providers were Ireland, India, Canada and Israel. Based on statistics from International Data Corporation, global expenditures on service outsourcing increased from US$ 99 billion in 1998 to US$ 150 billion in 2001, then to US$ 300 billion in 2004, with a compound annual growth rate of 12.2%. The rate for Asian regions was 15.1%. Among this, the market for software foreign out-sourcing grew by 29.2%. Offshore services related to IT had the fastest growth rate. Based on estimation of UNCTAD, the offshore out-sourcing driven by IT sector was around US$ 1.3 billion in 2002, accounting for 1% of total global outsourcing.[23]

From 2001 to 2003, global FDI declined from the previous year by 41.1%, 17% and 17.6% respectively. Examining global FDI flows by region would give even more meaningful findings.

FDI into developed countries had declined in 2003 from previous year by 25% overall, amounting to US$ 367 billion. Of this, FDI into the USA decreased by 53%, from US$ 63 billion to US$ 30 billion, the lowest level in 12 years. The total flow into the EU dropped by 21% to US$ 295 billion.

In that same year, the FDI outflow from developed countries went up by 4%, amounting to US$ 570 billion. Of this, the outflow from the USA grew by almost 1/3, reaching US$ 152 billion. Next were Luxemburg (mainly investments in transit), France and U.K. The FDI outflow from the United States increased while inflow decreased. The net was an unprecedented outflow of US$ 122 billion.

The reduction in FDI to developed countries did not flow evenly to developing countries.

FDI inflows to Central Europe and Eastern Europe were weak in 2003, decreasing from US$ 31 billion to US$ 21 billion while recovery appeared in developing countries as a whole, with FDI inflow growing by 9% to US$ 172 billion. Of this, Africa, Asia and Pacific region showed increases whereas Latin America experienced sustained decline (Table 4).

FDI inflows to Asian regions increased in 2003 from previous year by 14%, reaching US$ 107 billion. Of this, inflows increases were seen in 34 economies and decreases in 21 economies. The inflow was concentrated in Northeast Asia and in service industries. China became the second largest FDI recipient, next only to Luxemburg (which had mainly investments in transit, therefore not comparable). The amount was US$ 53.51 billion. The flow into Southeast Asia was increased by 27%, amounting to US$ 19 billion. South Asia had US$ 6 billion, with a growth of 34% while central Asia had US$ 6.1 billion, a growth of 35% and West Asia

---

[23]Zou Quansheng (邹全胜) & 王莹 (Wang Ying), '服务外包: 理论与经验分析 (Service Outsourcing: Theoretical and Empirical Analysis),' 国际贸易问题 (Journal of International Trade), 2006(05), pp 54–61.

Table 4 FDI In-flows to regions around the World 1992–2003 (Unit: US$ billion)

Region/Country	1992–1997 (annual average)	1998	1999	2000	2001	2002	2003
Developed countries	180.8	472.5	828.4	1108	571.5	489.9	366.6
Western Europe	100.8	263	500	697.4	368.8	380.2	310.2
Japan	1.2	3.2	12.7	8.3	6.2	9.2	6.3
U.K.	60.3	174.4	283.4	314	159.5	62.9	29.8
Developing economies	118.6	194.1	231.9	252.5	219.7	157.6	172
Africa	5.9	9.1	11.6	8.7	19.6	11.8	15
Latin America & Caribbean	38.2	82.5	107.4	97.5	88.1	51.4	49.7
Asia	74.1	102.2	112.6	146.1	111.9	94.4	107.1
Pacific Region	0.4	0.2	0.3	0.1	0.1	0.1	0.2
Central and Eastern Europe	11.5	24.3	26.5	27.5	26.4	31.2	21
Global	310.9	690.9	1086.8	1388	817.6	678.8	559.6

Source: Xin Jie (辛洁), 全球FDI向服务部门转移的趋势分析和对中国的政策建议 (Trend Analysis of Global FDI Shifts towards Service Sector and Policy Suggestions for China), Nankai University Master thesis, 2005

US$ 4.1 Billion (14%). The various Pacific Islands had US$ 0.2 billion (details shown in the Table 5).

The cross-sectional statistics for 2003 provided a wealth of information. If the vertical data were added, it would be seen that China's FDI inflow changes showed a saddle-shaped trend: from 1998 it showed a sharp drop due to the East Asian crisis and 2001 marked the start of a rising trend coincidental with the year of U.S. dot-com bubble bust (Fig. 11).

Inflows of FDI to developed countries were mostly founded on investor's anticipation of high yield from the capital market whereas investments to China from developed countries mostly focused on the manufacturing sector, amounting to around 2/3. FDI investment into China's secondary industries as a proportion of total FDI was consistently rising from 1999 to 2002, reaching 74.8%. It remained stable at around 74% from then on to 2005. Among secondary industries, FDI

Table 5 China's actual use of foreign capital 1983–2012 (Unit: US$ billion)

Year	Foreign loans	Foreign direct investments	Other foreign investments	FDI's weight in GDP (%)	Total foreign investment actually used
1983	1.07	0.92	0.28	0.3	2.27
1984	1.29	1.42	0.16	0.5	2.87
1985	2.51	1.96	0.30	0.6	4.77
1986	5.01	2.24	0.37	0.8	7.62
1987	5.81	2.31	0.33	0.7	8.45
1988	6.49	3.19	0.55	0.8	10.23
1989	6.29	3.39	0.38	0.8	10.06
1990	6.53	3.49	0.27	0.9	10.29
1991	6.89	4.37	0.30	1.1	11.56
1992	7.91	11.01	0.28	2.3	19.20
1993	11.19	27.51	0.26	4.5	38.96
1994	9.26	33.77	0.18	6.0	43.21
1995	10.33	37.52	0.29	5.2	48.14
1996	12.67	41.73	0.41	4.9	54.81
1997	12.02	45.26	7.13	4.8	64.41
1998	11.00	45.46	2.09	4.5	58.55
1999	10.21	40.32	2.13	3.7	52.66
2000	10.00	40.72	8.64	3.4	59.36
2001	–	46.88	2.79	3.5	49.67
2002	–	52.74	2.27	3.6	55.01
2003	–	53.51	2.64	3.3	56.15
2004	–	60.63	3.44	3.1	64.07
2005	–	603.3	3.48	2.7	63.81
2006	–	63.02	4.06	2.4	67.08
2007	–	74.77	3.57	2.3	78.34
2008	–	92.40	2.86	2.1	95.26
2009	–	90.03	1.77	1.8	91.80
2010	–	105.73	3.09	1.8	108.82
2011	–	116.01	1.69	1.6	117.70
2012	–	111.72	1.58	1.4	113.30

Data Source: edited from *China Statistical Abstract 2013*

was mostly concentrated on manufacturing. That had to do with China's abundant supply of low-cost labor and raw material. Manufacturing could provide long-term stable returns on investment. Furthermore,

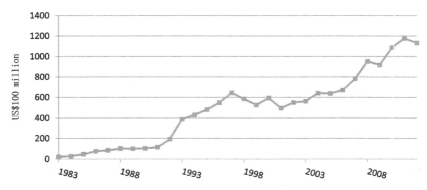

Fig. 11 1983–2012 China's actual use of foreign capital (Data source: Same as above)

China's tax favoritism policy helped foreign investors lower business costs, thereby increasing their competitiveness to access a wider market.[24]

This round of investments since 2001 were primarily concentrated on IT related manufacturing. Driven by internet development, IT industry production was gradually modeled by standardization and modularization. Developed countries and economies would therefore often transfer equipment manufacturing to China.

A noteworthy change was that FDI to China's tertiary sector as a proportion of total FDI went from 24.74 to 41.72% during 2005–2008, increased by 16.98 percentage points in a short span of 3 years. At the same time, the proportion of secondary industry FDI declined from 74.07% to 56.66%, a drop of 17.41 percentage points. By the end of 2008, China's actual use of FDI in the primary, secondary and tertiary industries as proportion of total foreign investment were 1.29%: 56.66%: 41.72% (Peng and Liang 2010).

Under the wave of global industrial transfer and reconfiguration of industrial value chain, China's opening up underwent a change in its mechanism, with devaluation of domestic currency and endeavors of

---

[24]Peng Tong (彭疃) & Liang Shuang (梁爽), '外商直接投资在三次产业中的分布及评价 (Distribution and Evaluation of Foreign Direct Investments Among Tertiary Industries),' *China Venture Capital*, 2010(4): 47–50; Li Wenjing (李文晶), '中国FDI与经济增长的产业分析 (Industrial Analysis of China's FDI and Economic Growth),' http://ems.nwu.edu.cn/economic/26/lianjie/papers/3.htm.

local governments to attract foreign capital. At real economy level, the impetus for China to join international trade changed from domestic overcapacity to external demand. With regard to the financial system, China actively took part into the new international economic circulation dominated by financial capital of the core countries with U.S.A. in the lead, which meant the emergence of China's "financial dependence" on overseas market, as stated by Wang Jian in earlier section.

Structural Contradiction in China's Economy—Three Overcapacities and Worsening Imbalance of the Troika

The surge of China's economy since 2003 was in synch with the blooming cycle of international economy. From 2003 to 2007, China's GDP sustained high growth rates at double digit for 5 consecutive years. By 2007 it reached the peak of 13%.

Justin Lin Yifu pointed out in 1999 that a vicious cycle under the condition of "double overcapacity" had emerged in China's macroeconomic operation. What he was referring to at the time was excess labor force and excess general manufacturing capacity. Adding the excess in financial capital that emerged after the financial reform was completed at the turn of the century, there would be three major overcapacities. Following China's deepening participation in global economic regime, the structural contradiction of these three overcapacities was further reinforced during the economic surge.

Excess labor force had been a problem China was faced with since the modern era, even though in the course of industrialization over a century, a large number of excess rural population had already been relocated to cities and China's urbanization rate had reached 46% in 2008 (this data was based on the newly revised definition of urban population in statistical sense). The academic community was generally skeptical about the extent of urbanization. There were still around 130 to 200 million excess labor force in rural regions (Nie Minghua & Yang Feihu 2010). With regard to excess capital, structural imbalance appeared in the consumption market in early and mid-1990s with insufficient consumption power among low-income groups and under-development of high-end consumption markets. Moreover, domestic saving rate also went up significantly. Since 1994 the banking system began to record positive deposit differential. By the third quarter of 2007 the deposit differential in financial institutions had reached 1251.97 billion yuan. The loan to deposit ratio was 69.5%. That was an indication of worsening problem of excess financial capital. Regarding general manufacturing capacity, spurred on by proactive fiscal policies, a sudden increase of supply worsened the problem of overcapacity that had already emerged by the end of 1990s. This sudden expansion was due to the completion of a large number of heavy industry projects and being put into production from the second half of 2002 to first half of 2007.

In company with the worsening situation of three major overcapacities, the imbalance of the Troika, the "three-horse carriage" (investment, consumption and export) also deteriorated.

Domestic consumption should have been the main impetus of economic growth. However it had long been depressed in China since mid-1990s. In general, it was regarded as a problem of weak consumption power. With almost unlimited supply of labor in absolute excess, general labor wage was suppressed over a long run. In particular, an enormous number of peasant households relying on cash income had very low purchasing power, resulting at general under consumption. Furthermore, the widening income gap between the rich and the poor made under consumption even worse. Oversupply of manufactured goods had to be digested by export, in turn boosting the trade surplus.[25]

Since mid-1990s, China was consciously or semi-unconsciously oriented towards globalization and continued to be integrated into the mainstream global economic trend. Alongside insufficient domestic demand, investments and external demands were growing robustly. Since early twenty-first century, monopolistic financial capital in excess began to alienating itself from industrial capital, integrating mainly with real estate sector and stock market, which in turn spurred on the rapid development of real estate, funds, stocks and futures trades. That was also

---

[25]Wang Jian, '防过热更需防过剩 (Caution on Overheat and More Importantly Overcapacity)', 中国经贸导刊 (China Economic & Trade Herald), 2007(17).

the regular trend with which western core countries or core sectors had maintained economic growth. As for local governments, given that fiscal and financial means were monopolized by the central government, they could only rely on more debt-driven investment through land financing, following the path dependence of "high investment + high indebtedness = high growth" model.

External demand contributed a higher and higher proportion to China's economic growth. China's general domestic overcapacity and under-consumption was complementary with the expanding overseas demand as international industrial capital shifting to the emerging industrial state. As a result, China's national economy became over dependent on the export sector. China's trade dependence ratio (import + export)/GDP) had reached 66% in 2006. In comparison, the ratios of the U.S.A., Japan, India and Germany remained stable at 14–20% level from the 1980s to 2001 (Shen Jiru 2004). Even taking into consideration differences in calculation specifications, China's dependence on trade was still much higher than the developed countries and large developing countries in comparison. The overcapacity in basic industries could only be dealt with by means of "overdrawing tomorrow's overcapacity to digest today's capacity".[26]

Under such a structural imbalance, China's economy actually proceeded at a fast but extremely uncoordinated pace, with two "wild horses" (investment and export) pulling a "lean donkey" (domestic consumption).

Corporatized Local Governments "Cashing in Land": The "High Investment + High Indebtedness = High Growth" Model Led by Urbanization

China's endeavor to attract business as well as capital, and the supply of capital that arose in excess international industrial capital's pursuits of factor price valley, were in fact the two facets of the same process.

---

[26]Lang Xianping (郎咸平), '美国正把中国复制成第二个日本 (The USA Is Turning China into a Replica of Japan)', 中国物流与采购 (China Logistics and Purchasing), 2010(12).

The formation of the investment-driven model to growth was related to the centralization of fiscal power by the central government amidst the fiscal crisis in 1993–1994 and financial power amidst the crisis in 1997–1998.

In the 1980s, the capitalization of factors such as finance, land and labor had been conducted at the local level. The first two were by nature local whereas the third (labor) was not free to migrate back then. With the bloom of rural enterprises, localized industrial development had taken shape and the gains from capitalizing the three essential resources were by and large kept within the *sannong* sector.

Yet from 1994 onward with the new Tax Division System, and in 1998 with comprehensive reform of the financial system, local governments' fiscal and financial powers were significantly weakened. Furthermore, as labor force was free to migrate (even if not migrating local governments no longer had the subjective and objective conditions to make use of a scale effect of labor to substitute capital in upgrading industrialization), the only remaining resource that local governments could mobilize in the name of the state was land. When the macroeconomic environment became favorable again, local governments took to capitalize land to promote high speed export-oriented development, attracting capital to their respective jurisdictions. And even if not trying to introduce foreign capital, many top local officers would appropriate land haphazardly for conspicuous constructions such as government buildings to create a track record of good political achievement by having brought in capital from banks.

However, such non-productive investments ended up as large-scale indebtedness for which local governments did not have to take the responsibility. And since the central government found it hard to bear that increasingly heavy debt obligation either, continuous expansion of money supply became the only available means.

We may take a look at how it worked.

Due to regulation constraint as well as high transaction costs in dealing with scattered peasants, prospective land users and even developers would not directly deal with the peasants who worked on the land. On one side, local governments would appropriate the land at a very low cost, made possible by their monopolistic authority. Then through various financing agents such as land reserve centers, urban investment companies, development zone management committees, etc., they would mortgage the land to banks to obtain loans for infrastructure constructions. By 2006, around 60% of investments worth tens of billions into infrastructure in counties and towns along the southeastern coast had been financed through land. In the western regions, funding through bank loans had even accounted for as much as 70–80% of urban infrastructure investments (Jiang Sheng San & Liu Shouyin et el 2007)

On the other side, local governments accelerated urban expansion in order to increase the scale of various types of local taxations as well as revenues from land concession. By 2002 local business tax had rapidly risen to become the largest source of tax revenue for local governments. By 2006, the proportion of business tax out of total local taxation reached 43.3% (the next in line was profit tax at 18.1%). The business tax was mainly levied on construction and tertiary industries. That motivation made it a pressing matter to expand urban regions, in turn the construction industry for increasing business tax revenue. A research by the World Bank pointed out that, driven by the motivation of increasing fiscal revenues, local governments enthusiasm towards land development, infrastructure investments and expanding the scale of local construction had been unprecedented since 2002 (World Bank Urbanization and Land System Reform Project Team 2005).

In a research report published during that same period, we referred to this process between local governments and banks as "cashing without land". We believe it suited financial capital's urge to integrate with the real estate sector after its alienation from general industries, as a result driving urban expansion. The first thing it pushed up was the windfall real estate profits, making it "the channel for local governments to repay the enormous loans for urban infrastructure investments as well as to realize revenues from land concession." Real estate became the realm into which excess capital jostled for entrance. Spurred on by infrastructure construction and real estate, related industries were blooming. Since 2002, the proportion of fixed investments stayed at 60% of total new demand (Wang Jian 2006).

In this way, with the third round of land enclosure as the starting point whereby local government "cashing out land", the development model of "high investment + high indebtedness = high growth" founded on "high land closure" gradually took shape at the beginning of the new century. And since 2002 local government fiscal deficits were increasing rapidly. Furthermore, the excess financial capital at central level also added fuel to the speculative markets, which ushered China's rapid economic surge in the new millennium.

How the "New Pro-People's Livelihood Policies", Represented by the *Sannong* Strategy, Facilitated the "Soft Landing" of 2008 Crisis

"*Sannong* New Deal": Background and Contents

In late 1990s, because of the volatility in macro-economy the third crisis in rural governance had occurred.[27] We believed that rural governance crisis was mainly the outcome of costs transfer towards underprivileged groups or sector by powerful agents maximizing their institutional gains during institutional transition. That would be pertinent to understanding the background for the introduction of the "*Sannong* New Deal".

It is well known that in modern society agriculture has to face the double risk factors of market and nature. Consequently agriculture as compared to other modern industries would be more vulnerable. During the transition from traditional to so-called modern society, the *sannong* also has to face the third risk: the cost of institutional transition, an institutional risk in political-economic sense that arises due to the domination of powerful interest blocs over policy decisions.

Therefore, whether during economic crisis or rapid economic development in urban sector, fundamental factors in the *sannong*, scarce resources such as funds and land, saw outflows at an accelerated rate. And even rural funds would find it increasingly difficult to integrate with the factor of labor given the latter's seasonal migrations. Not only had it resulted in deterioration of rural economy, society and culture, it even

---

[27]See: Dong Xiaodan & Wen Tiejun, '宏观经济波动与农村"治理危机" (Rural Governance Crisis and Macro-Economic Volatility)', 管理世界 (Management World), 2008(9).

exacerbated the third crisis of rural governance since 1997. The crisis was not alleviated even with the revival of the macro-economy although there had been a structural change since 2004 following the abolition of agricultural tax.

After China entered a period of high economic growth in 2003, rural labor once again flocked into cities in large numbers. Agricultural employment decreased from 365.46 million in 2003 to 306.54 million in 2008, which implied a decrement of hidden unemployment by 58.9 million people, as high as 16.12%. However, employment opportunity did not necessarily lead to income growth. Following the emergence of export-oriented economy consisting mainly of processing manufacturing, Chinese factories and workers only shared the smallest portion of the total added value in the entire industrial chain. The wages for migrant workers were generally suppressed. In a research conducted by the Department of Labor Security that compared labor costs in manufacturing between China and 20 countries, it was found that average labor costs in developed countries generally accounted for around 35–50% of the added value, other country categories generally 20–35%, while China's was only 9.3%. Furthermore, according to related studies, minimum wages in many countries were generally at 40–60% of the average wages in the society. In China that percentage was notably low overall. In the Pearl River delta region the number was generally as low as 30%.[28] And after these good quality workers were thus exploited in urban sector, their retirement and social security had to be borne by the home village. That meant not only did the rural regions not have enough labor force to support rural development, they had to bear a social burden.[29]

In the cyclical crises that took place before 1998 largely due to endogenous factors, rural regions had been the primary recipient of cost transfer from urban sector. By the two crises during 1998–2009 that arose mainly

---

[28] 中国农民工调研报告 (Survey Report on Chinese Migrant Workers), China Yan Shi Press, 2006, p 31.

[29] For the concept of "multiple exploitation" see: Pan Zequan (潘泽泉), '全球化、世界工厂与中国农民工发展的经验教训 (Lessons from Globalization, World Factory and China's Migrant Worker Development)', *Guangzhou Social Science*, 2008(1).

due to exogenous factors, China had already entered the phase of industrial overcapacity. Upon "farewell to shortage," the government's policies in response were obviously different from earlier occasions. The key manifestations were stronger macro coordination and rebalance on three major gaps: rural and urban, the east and the west, as well as the rich and the poor. Nevertheless, on one side the institutional costs of 'government retreat' from the urban economy in the 1990s could not possibly be offset in a short span. On the other side, given the diversity of local regions they were indeed hard put to accept the central coordination. The only realm that could most embody the central government's "People-oriented Scientific Development" concept and "People's Livelihood New Deal" was the *sannong*, to which the local interest groups had already become indifferent.

A year before putting forward the notion of "people-orientation" as the premise for development in 1999, the CPC had taken the opportunity of the 20th anniversary of Household Responsibility Contract System to pass the Central Bureau's decision on 'Certain Important Issues Regarding Agriculture and Rural Regions' in the third plenary of the 15th Congress. The direction was to "steadfastly execute the extension of the land contracting period for another 30 years, and at the same time take initiation in setting laws and regulations to ensure long term stability of the land contracting system, granting to peasants the land usage right with protection on an on-going basis." It would go down in history as the second round of household land contracting with an even land re-allotment in accordance with the population in village, established as the basic economic institution in Rural China.

Under this context, when the 16th Congress of the CPC put forward the major target of "building a moderately prosperous society in all aspects", President Hu Jintao pointed out clearly in the report that to achieve the goal the focus and the difficulty would both be in the rural regions. He later stated again that future *sannong* policies should place priority on giving peasants tangible benefits. Later, in the rural working meeting convened by the party central committee in January 2003, President Hu emphasized again that "the *sannong* issue is the most important of all important party work", to counter against the situation in which relevant departments lagged in following the central strategic adjustments. Over the next 5 years, the central government reiterated twice every year that theme of "the *sannong* being the most important of all important issues", first in the CPC plenary meeting as well as the People's Congress and then in the Political Consultative Conference. During those years, President Hu also made the important assessment of "two stages and two nurturing". [In the past agriculture supported industry. Now industry should nurture agriculture]. In the fourth plenary meeting of the CPC 16th Congress in 2004, he gave the directive for resolving *sannong* issues, setting the keynote to shape the mechanism of industries nurturing agriculture as well as cities supporting the rural under new circumstance. To mobilize peasants' pro-activeness in producing grain crops, China began to allocate a portion of the subsidies previously dedicated to the circulation regime to directly subsidy the peasants cultivating grain crops.

In the CPC 17th Congress in October 2007, the theme "*sannong* being the most important of all important issues" was adopted as a guiding principle of the CPC, and reiterated with emphasis in the political report for the Congress in an unprecedented manner.

While that proposition had been stressed on continuously, in September 2005 the Central Political Bureau put forward the opinion that China's 11th 5-year plan must comprehensively follow through with the 'scientific development view' and the strategy of "building socialist new countryside". Afterwards, the fifth plenary session of the 16th Congress convened by the CPC Central Committee in October officially established "building the socialist new countryside" as the topmost strategy in a list of eight.

The 19th meeting of the 10th Standing Committee of the People's National Congress passed the resolution on the 29th December 2005 to repeal the "Agricultural Tax Law" on January 1, 2006. That meant the agricultural tax that had existed in China continuously for over 2000 years officially became a bygone in history.

The 2006 CPC Central Committee Document No. 1 gave concrete policy requirements in building the socialist new countryside, supplemented by concrete measures on financial transfers and payments as well as 'industries nurturing agriculture' (Table 6 and Image 1).

Table 6 Pro-peasants policies introduced since 2003

Year	New pro-peasants policies contents
2003	Supported the *sannong*. Rural taxation reform. Plan to establish new rural cooperative medical system
2004	Suggested abolish agricultural tax in 5 years. Introduced three types of subsidies to rural regions
2005	Certain provinces and urban regions abolished agricultural tax on 'self-funded' basis
2006	Total abolition of agricultural tax. Launched integrated agricultural subsidy. Exempted rural regions in west China from tuition and fees for education. Permitted three types of rural financing pilot scheme: peasants mutual financing, micro finance and village township banks
2007	Free education in rural regions. Promoted New Rural Cooperative Medical Insurance & Rural Minimum Living Security. Promulgated the Specialized Peasants Cooperatives Law
2008	Increased integrated agricultural subsidy. Raised participation rate in the New Rural Cooperative Medical Insurance. Comprehensive exemption of all school fees and expenses. Revised new law on obligatory education. 562.5 billion yuan of *sannong* budget, an increase of 130.7 billion from previous year. Adopted ten important measures to support agriculture and grain crop production
2009	Implemented new rural pension insurance. Developed middle level vocational education in rural regions and phasing in fee exemption. Increased *sannong* budget. Eliminated obligatory financing to upper tiers' investments of large agricultural counties. Expanded agricultural financing and insurance pilot sites. Subsidies to peasants in purchase of home appliances
2010	'Home appliances going to countryside': diverted to Chinese peasants the 13% export tax rebate which previously equaled to subsidies to foreign consumers; Unsalable home appliances in export sector sold to rural regions in large quantities, helping China to convert to domestic demand driven growth in a short time

Source: Based on the CPC Central Committee policies in recent years, Yang Shuai revised the table in a paper by Professor Wang Shaoguang of the Chinese University of Hong Kong at a conference in Sungkyunkwan University of Korea on 18 March 2007

Repairing the Regulatory Function of Rural "Capital Pool" and "Labor Pool"

At the same time as the central government began implementing new *sannong* policies, a whole series of pro-agriculture and peasants measures were introduced over a short span of time. On one side it gave rural sector the opportunity to recuperate, so that its regulatory function

Image 1 On the 9th February 2005, the Hebei provincial government announced the total abolition of agricultural tax in Chinese Lunar New Year. On the New Year day, a peasant from Hebei province by the name of Li Zhongjie brought his lion dance team to the government building in his county and displayed a couplet on scrolls to express the peasants' heartfelt joy on the abolition

as a 'labor pool' could be repaired. On the other side, it strengthened the county economy's regulatory function as a second 'fund pool' beside urban sector. Undoubtedly it had a positive effect on rectifying the structural contradiction of 'three overcapacities' and the unbalanced 'three-horse carriage' in China's economic growth, thereby raising the on-going sustainability of China's economy and development.

The concrete transmission mechanism consisted of the following:

One: unprecedented amounts of investment enabled the *sannong* to absorb the excessive portion of capital and production capacity in the national economy. The investments in support of the *sannong* during 2003–2008 totaled more than 1.4731 trillion yuan at current year prices.[30] Furthermore, based on estimation, the cumulated state *sannong* budget during 2003–2009 came to 3.097 trillion yuan, an average of 15,000 yuan per peasant household, and an annual average of 2500 yuan per capita. Not only did it increase the capital stock in the rural capital pool by a substantial volume, the infrastructure construction also provided large number of local non-agriculture employments, making it possible for the severely impaired regulatory function of rural labor pool to be partly mended.

Two: large amount of pro-*sannong* investments to a certain extent stimulated consumption demand in rural regions. Most of the policymakers in general agreed with the effect of new countryside construction in expanding domestic demand, with the view that rural sector was an enormous force driving domestic demand and promoted economic growth. According to a research by Ma Xiaohe et el, the marginal propensity on consumption for peasants was 75.3% during 2000–2004, compared with 69.5% for urban residents. During 2000–2003, the total annual increase in retail volume in consumption goods at county level and below was around 100 billion yuan. It more than doubled to 231.2 billion in 2004. Then it increased by another 148 billion in the first seven months in 2005. Some researchers estimated that the initiative of new countryside construction would give rise to a retail volume growth on consumer goods of more than 400 billion per year during the 11th 5-year plan period. The incremental contribution to GDP volume would be more than 2 percentage points.[31]

Third: With reversed flow of resources back to rural regions, wide spread confrontations between peasants and local grassroots governments, arising before out of economic tension, was alleviated and

---

[30]Based on data in China Statistical Yearbooks, investments from the central government covered agricultural support expenditure (including farming, forestry, irrigation, meteorology as well as integrated agricultural development), agricultural infrastructure expenditure, agricultural technology expenditure, rural relief funds, and so on. Due to data limitation, the figures for 2003–2006 included only agricultural support expenditures while figures for 2007 and 2008 included only farming, forestry and irrigation. Therefore actual total investments on agriculture and peasants should be more than 1.79 trillion yuan.

[31]Huang Wei (黄蕙), '社会主义新农村——农村是拉动内需被忽视的动力 (Building the New Socialist Countryside—The Countryside Was the Neglected Impetus in Domestic Demand Stimulation)', 瞭望 (Outlook), 2005-11-23. http://www.agri.gov.cn/jjps/t20051123_500588.htm.

transformed into general disputes over money interest within rural communities. Stability in rural regions improved overall. That was the social foundation upon which the *sannong* could once again be relied on to bear the cost transfer of crisis.

All these were the fundamental conditions that afforded China's economy with the leeway to respond to the Wall Street financial crisis without sustaining damages.

2008–2009: China's Response After the Second Imported Crisis

In face of the second imported crisis took place since merging into globalization, Chinese economy's sensitivity and vulnerability to external demand volatility were obvious. Fortunately, central government's enormous investments into the *sannong* before and during this period had laid down a rather smooth road for China's imbalanced, fast moving economic 'carriage'. It was on the solid base of the continuous investments into the *sannong* over consecutive years that China was conferred with the conditions of making a 'soft landing' in the crisis.

The Global Financial Crisis and Its Impact on China

On 15 September 2008, the news that Lehmann Brothers, the fourth largest investment bank in the United States, officially declared bankruptcy while Merill Lynch was bought out by the Bank of America sent the global stock markets into violent crashes. Wall Street experienced the worst day since 911 with the Dow Jones Industrial Index falling by more than 500 points or 4.42%. Some major European indices fell by more than 5% at one time. Financial stocks in Asian regions generally fell while the Taiwan Stock Exchange Weighted Index dropped by 4.1% to its lowest level in 3 years. In Russia, due to heavy losses in the stock market the government ordered a halt in trading in all exchanges on 17 September. Consequentially, US$ 5.79 trillion of market value was evaporated in the month of October. After the crisis, within a short span of time there were 14 bank bankruptcies in the USA alone. Most major financial and securities markets around the world suffered heavy blows.

This crisis that erupted in the core zone of capitalist core sector unfolded in less than a month into a total economic crisis and spread to other developed economic bodies. On 23 October 2008, White House spokesperson Perino indicated that although the federal government had adopted bold measures to rescue financial institutions, economic growth in the U.S. would still be facing difficulty. The October economic report published by the Japanese government believed that Japan's economy was receding. The data announced by the U.K. government on 24 October indicated that the country experienced a GDP decline of 0.5% compared to previous month for the first time since 1992. The basic economic situation of the Euro zone also deteriorated at an accelerated rate. The extent to which manufacturing shriveled in Germany, France, Italy and Spain exceeded expectations.

The deterioration in the financial, economic and trading environments around the world gave rise to the challenges of shrinking trade and capital outflows in emerging countries, given their reliance on export expansion strategies for fast growth. China as the world's top exporting country also encountered drastic decline in exports, and in relation to that a serious domestic economic crisis emerged. China's seriously misbalanced economic structure was immediately under impact. On one side, it severely damaged the export economy relying on overseas demand. The export sector's contribution to GDP fell from 2.6% in 2007 to 0.8% in 2008. Large scale layoff of migrant workers was remarkable in coastal regions specialized in export sector (see column below). On the other side, as international hot money swarmed into commodities markets after the Fed's Quantitative Easing, the price of primary products surged and serious exogenous (or "imported") inflation emerged.[32] The PPI rose from 5.4% in 2007 to 8.1% in April 2008, and the domestic CPI in 2008 saw a monthly high of 8.7%. China's economy, with insufficient domestic demand and hence over-reliance on export and investment, was immediately impacted. In addition, the

---

[32]Wang Jian, '关注增长与通胀格局的转变点 (Pay Attention to the Turning Point of Growth and the Inflation)', 宏观经济管理 (Macro Economic Management), 2008 (8).

macro regulation policies being implemented began to take effect. The GDP growth rate for 2008 declined to 9%. Even though still at a relatively high level, it showed a depressing trend compared to previous years (Fig. 12).

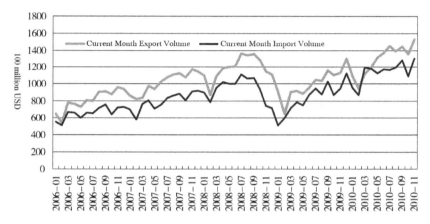

Fig. 12   Impact of 2008 financial crisis on China's export

Box 9: Global Economic Crisis Causing Business Close-downs and Unemployment

Based on information provided by relevant governmental departments, there were 25 million migrant workers being laid off in 2009, mostly due to wide spread business closing-down along the coastal regions with the onslaught of the global economic crisis. According to surveys, the number of small and medium size enterprises that had closed down in Guangdong during January to September 2008 came to 15,000, mainly in labor-intensive processing manufacturing including textile, clothing, electronic components, plastic, etc. Among the migrant workers who returned to home villages after layoff, 71.3% of them had worked in manufacturing and construction.

Jobs	Migrant workers distribution %	% Returning home due to impact of crisis
Manufacturing	38.9	44.1
Construction	19.1	27.2
Domestic and other Services	11.3	6.4
Accommodation & Catering	7.3	3.4
Wholesale & Retail	6.7	1.9
Transportation, Warehouse and Postal	5.4	3
Others	11.3	14

Surveys by the Population Services Management Division of the National Population and Family Planning Commission also showed that majority of the migrant workers who returned home after layoff were previously concentrated in a few sectors—mainly in manufacturing and construction along the southeastern coastal regions, with geographically 49.2% in Guangdong, 15.3% in Zhejiang, 8.6% in Shanghai and 5.8% in Jiangsu. In terms of their urban employment structure, 55.7% were in manufacturing, 20.8% in construction, while the proportions in wholesale and retail, accommodation and catering were relatively small.

Source: Sheng Laiyun (2009); quoted from Cai Fang (2010).

FDI and China's Financialization

Foreign investments which had made significant contributions to China's pre-crisis wave of economic growth still showed a relatively large increase in 2008.[33] Nevertheless that inflow was obviously blocked in 2009 due

---

[33]Before 2008, the regions around China were in competition with regard to attracting foreign direct investments. FDIs to China during 2006–2008 continued to grow. However, its weight in the world as a whole had ups and downs. The proportion had been falling from 2005 until 2008 when there was again a substantial rise. One major factor was that emerging countries such as Vietnam, Thailand and India begun competing for FDI, taking advantage of low labor costs and favorable policies. China by contrast had new factors such as the rapid rise in wages, improvements in labor protections, rise in land price and appreciation of the renminbi, which made China less attractive to foreign investments. During the financial crisis in 2008, the investment environment in China became relatively better in comparison. FDI that had flowed

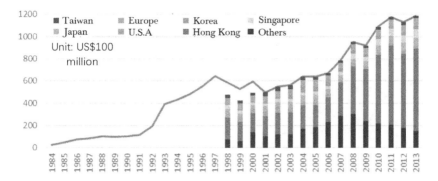

Fig. 13 1984–2013 total foreign investment actually used by China and sources (Source of capital—bars bottom to top: Others, Hong Kong, U.S.A., Japan, Singapore, Korea, Europe, Taiwan)

to repatriation of capital back to developed countries and showed notable fluctuations (Figs. 13 and 14).

It can be seen from the above graph that declining foreign capital and overseas demand resulted in a major decline of their impact on China's M2 supply, from the high of 60% in 2008 to less than 20% in 2009. Simply looking at it from this perspective, the sudden drastic drop can unquestionably be defined as a round of "quantitative tightening" that had tangible effects.

The trend shown in the above graph not only represented China's accelerating financialization catalyzed by globalization since the 1990s (indicated by the effect of increased money supply due to foreign investment inflows), it also showed that under globalization China's economic volatility showed cyclical patterns.

The Price of Joining WTO.

---

to other countries moved back to China. Year over year FDI movement in 2008 recorded a decline of 14.2% worldwide (29.2% in developed countries) and growth of 17.3% in developing countries, 29.7% for China, and 25.9% for economies in transition. Pu Changmo (朴昌模), '韩中外资政策的演变及其效应的比较研究 (Comparative Studies of Changes and Effects of Foreign Capital Policies between Korea and China)', Master Thesis, University of International Business and Economics, 2010; United Nations Conference on Trade and Development, *World Investment Reports 2009 & 2012.*

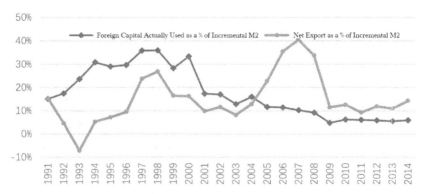

Fig. 14 1991–2014: Foreign capital inflow and attributable fraction on China's Monetary Issuance

In fact, even if there was not the Wall Street financial crisis, China's model of relying heavily on international market to achieve high speed growth would become increasingly difficult.

Based on the 2011 special report in *Business Weekly* 'Ten Years after Joining WTO,' China's export-oriented economy was facing several important constraining factors, such as anti-dumping investigations, intellectual property protection, vulnerable domestic industries being forced to face competition (see Box 10). Ten years after its accession to the WTO, China's export-oriented economy arrived at cross-roads.

Box 10: China into WTO Ten Years Later: Brilliant Achievements, High Costs

(1) Investigations on Anti-Dumping in Trade

Statistics from WTO's secretariat showed that in 2008 there were 208 anti-dumping investigations and 14 countervailing probes, with China being the target in 73 and 10 cases respectively, accounting for 35% and 71% of the total. China was the main focus of global anti-dumping investigations in 15 consecutive years, losing over US$ 30 billion annually in relation to the investigations. In the year 2009 when the global economy was the most dismal with the onslaught of the financial crisis, China's export accounted for 9.6% of the global total, while

---

anti-dumping disputes reached 40% of the total and countervailing cases reached 75%. The number of trade investigations that China was subject to accounted for 43% of the worldwide total for the same period.

In a report published by the World Bank in March 2009, 17 out of the 20 countries having made the commitment of "guarding against trade protectionism" in the G20 financial summit in November 2008, introduced 47 protectionist measures less than 3 months after. Of these, many were targeted against China. For example, India prohibited the import of Chinese toys, while Argentina implemented non-automatic import licenses on textile, television, toys, leather goods, and so on. That report also pointed out that in the last few months of 2008, the number of anti-dumping and countervailing cases had a clear increase. For example, countries around the world in general gave subsidy to the automobile industry, with the total as high as around US$ 4.8 billion, usually in high-income countries (accounted for US$ 4.27 billion).

In February 2009, the new Obama administration passed the 'American Recovery and Reinvestment Act' totaling US$ 787 billion, four months after the Bush administration announced rescue plans. The plan included terms of "buying American goods", requesting public construction and public projects supported by the stimulation funds to use American made steel, iron and manufactured products (with exemptions based on public interest considerations or when not available or costs not feasible). Besides, the Home Security Department should purchase only textiles and clothes made in America.

Under pressure from Europe, terms relating to 'buying only American products' were eventually revised. However the determination of U.S.A. to rebuild manufacturing did not change since that was considered by the Obama administration as an essential tactic for America's "economic rebalancing".

(2) Disputes over Intellectual Property Rights cutting into China's Export Gains

Entering the new century, China became the biggest producing and exporting country of DVD players. However the core technologies were entirely controlled by foreign enterprises. Chinese factories only conducted simple assembling. When the DVD players market and strength of China's companies rapidly grew, foreign patent holders in the realm organized alliances, including the 6C (constituted of Toshiba, Mitsubishi, Hitachi, JVC, Panasonic and Time Warner; later IBM also joined but it was still referred to as 6C), 3C (Philips, Sony and Pioneer; then LG joined to became 4C), 1C (Thompson) and several patent fee collection organizations like MPEG-LA (formed by 16 patent holders). They began to exercise their intellectual property rights. On 19 April 2002, China Audio Industry Association, after multiple negotiations over more than two years, finally reached an agreement with 6C stipulating that Chinese manufacturers would pay patent fee of US$ 4 for each DVD player exported. Following that, similar agreements were signed with 3C at US$ 5 for each DVD player, with 1C at 2% of selling price (minimum US$ 2) and US$ 1 for each Dolby equipment, with MPEG-LA at US$ 4 (adjusted to US$ 2.5 in 2002) (Reference: 'Dispute over DVD Player Patent Fee,' *Business Weekly*, 5 November, 2005). However, the price of DVD players in the international market was consistently falling. By 2005 the retail price of DVD players on the U.S. market was only US$30–40. Yet Chinese enterprises had to pay patent fees of totally US$ 12 on each, leaving almost no profit. Quite a few companies had stopped producing or bankrupted.

Having been inspired by the DVD players case, foreign manufacturers also raised requests for patent fees on television, USB flash drives, CD, CD recording machines, digital cameras, motor cycles, and so on. In a 2004 research report by China's Science and Technology Development Research Center, the patent compensation payments on China's television export amounted to almost Renminbi 20 billion in 2002, accounting for 1.5% of total electronic equipment export or 30% of the profit on electronic equipment export. Since joining the WTO, the amount of compensation relating to intellectual property disputes had amounted to more than US$ 1 billion.

(3) Entering International Market at the Cost of "Beheading" Domestic Industries

With the end of the WTO transition period in 2005, developed countries took a step further to request China open up the market.

In the post transition period, China introduced various market opening policies including limitations on agricultural subsidies, cancelling tariff quota on some import products, reducing import tariff year over year by a substantial extent or completely abolishing tariff. Furthermore, China promulgated in 2002 the "Interim Provisions on Restructuring State-owned Enterprises by Utilizing Foreign Capital", such that the introduction of foreign capital would have impact on "optimizing industrial structure and pushing state-owned enterprises ownership reform," in addition to the function of bringing in funds and technology, promoting economic development. Soon after, "beheading by foreign enterprise" (transnational companies acquiring and merging with leading Chinese enterprises) became a trend.

A report published by the State Council Research and Development Center in July 2006 mentioned that in China, out of the already opened industries, the top 5 companies in almost every industry were controlled by foreign capital. Out of 28 Chinese key industries, foreign capital had majority asset controlling right on 21. Out of 18 state-level key home appliances enterprises, 11 were joint ventures with foreign capital. The cosmetic industry was controlled by 150 foreign enterprises and 20% of pharmaceutical enterprises were in the hands of foreign capital.

On 8 September 2006, to subdue the wave of 'beheading', China introduced the "Provisions on Merger and Acquisitions of Domestic Enterprises by Foreign Investors", tightening the loose approval process in the past.

In January 2011 Gary Locke, then U.S. Secretary of Commerce, expressed unconventionally ahead of President Hu Jintao's visit to the United States, that the trade policies and approaches that China executed over the past few decades would no longer be adequate in handling the bi-lateral trade relationship between the two countries in future. He said that the era of indebted consumption in developed countries was over and China should no longer rely on export.

Source: 商务周刊 (Business Weekly) Special Report 'Ten Years after Joining WTO'. http://finance.ifeng.com/news/20110321/371 1209.shtml.

The situations described above would indicate that if the Chinese did not have institutional and discursive rights in globalization then they could only be tamed sheep under the lead of the shepherds, no more than an "economic herd" in the globalized game.

In its integration into the project of globalization on all fronts since the 1990s, China was continuously learning the lessons and gradually building up the ability to respond to challenges. Among them, the most effective measure was to replace external market demands with domestic demands. This experience has been one of the grounds upon which we emphasize on the theory of "resolving the risk of externalities by internalization". It was also the major competitive advantage that a large country with vast geographical width and depth had in particular to face the global competition.

How Did Chinese Government Deal with the Crisis

Generally speaking, the Chinese leaders executed with full confidence in dealing with the negative impact on economy by this global crisis and maneuvered the situation on a solid footing. Perhaps it was because China had already taken precautions through macro regulations and New Countryside Construction.

The central government's responses were still to focus on both aspects of domestic and external demands.

The similarity to the previous "imported" crisis was the proactive deployment of investments to drive domestic demands. The central government put forward in 2008 the decision to increase investments by 4 trillion yuan before the end of 2010 (of this, the central would provide for 1.18 trillion). In the 4th quarter of 2008 alone, new funds invested by the central government as well as the investments it stimulated from local and social sources came to totally 400 billion yuan.

The difference from the proactive fiscal policy in 1998 was the realm of investment deployment. In 1998 it was mainly on infrastructure construction. This time in 2008, out of the central government's new investments of 120 billion yuan, 10 billion was invested on security housing, 34 billion on rural livelihood projects and rural infrastructure constructions. Major infrastructure constructions such as railway, highways and airports accounted for 25 billion, development of social initiatives such as medical and health care, education, culture and so on

13 billion, energy-saving and carbon emission cutting as well as ecological and environmental projects 12 billion, and support to innovation as well as industrial structure adjustments 6 billion. Furthermore, a 20 billion budget of 2009 for rehabilitation projects relating to the 2008 earthquake were paid in advance in the same year. It can be seen that this round of fiscal investments for countering the crisis not only mostly applied to livelihood projects, but also more than 1/3 was devoted to the rural sector. Only 25 billion was used in infrastructure construction.

On external demand, the idea was generally similar to that in the previous crisis. However the policy support was even stronger. The key measure was to raise the export tax rebate rate to stimulate export under the condition of a stable exchange rate. From August 2008 to December 2009, the central government published 7 consecutive documents to raise export tax rebates on relevant goods, in an attempt to alleviate the blow on China's export oriented economy while demands in the international market shriveled.

Function of the Rural Labor Reservoir in Stabilizing Society

One notable difference of China's response to the crisis this time was its fore-sightedness: Premier Wen Jiabao had reminded in the summer of 2004 various officers around the country to guard against economic over-heating and over-appropriation of arable land. At that time he already clearly put forward the idea of macro-regulation. In order to narrow the "3 major gaps", the central government began in 2005 to increase investments on strategic adjustments including projects like "Central China Rising" and "Building the New Countryside". That meant by the time overseas demand fell in 2008 due to the global financial crisis, Chinese leaders had already started three years before to increase substantially public debt-driven investments on domestic projects.

The central government's policy to increase investments in the central regions and rural sectors was originally a directive of the 11th 5-year plan, not intended as market rescue measures to alleviate economic downturns in face of crises, not to mention global financial crises. Nevertheless, it had in practice the effect of building the county-level economy as a 'second assets pool', effective in raising domestic demands, attracting excess domestic financial capital into investments, and absorbing larger number of inland rural labor to promote rural "townization".[34]

Although these measures had faced criticisms from many scholars who advocated radical capitalist reform, the consecutive years of large scale investments did indeed single-handedly bring about infrastructure improvement in central and western regions, as well as increase non-agricultural employment by tens of millions. The practical effect was that when the global economic crisis broke out, causing bankruptcies of many export oriented businesses in coastal regions and unemployment of more than 20 million of migrant workers. The landlocked regions were thereby able to absorb in time the labor force returning to home towns, alleviating the pressure on urban unemployment and social stability. For the new generation of migrant workers that did not have a plot of land to work on farming, the employment opportunity thus generated was particularly important.

According to Sheng et el (2009), it was estimated 64% of those migrant workers who no longer returned to cities by the end of the first quarter of 2009 stayed locally to engage in agriculture. And after the 2009 Lunar New Year, the number rose to 67.6%.[35]

Therefore, we may conclude that China was able to achieve 'soft landing' with the *sannong* as the vehicle after the 2008 crisis only because of large-scale investments into the *sannong* beforehand and the pro-peasants policies continuously introduced. That was entirely different from the previous approach of simply dumping the costs of urban industrial capital crisis onto the *sannong* as it had happened repeatedly in the past half century.

Similar to the past, China had to pay a price to achieve the soft landing of this crisis. The most important negative impact was still that those inland and rural infrastructure constructions had to appropriate

---

[34]A mode of urbanization at appropriate scale at county level, integrated organically with the villages.
[35]Sheng Laiyun (盛来运), Wang Ran (王冉), Yan Fang (阎芳), '国际金融危机对农民工流动就业的影响 (Impact of International Financial Crisis on Flow and Employment of Migrant Workers),' *Chinese Rural Economy*, 2009(9).

large areas of land. The conflicts that ensued and the related institutional transition were still essentially a transfer of the institutional cost of industrialization and urbanization. The long term impact and how it may differ from before would have to be observed with time.

Brief Comparison Between the Two Imported Crises Regarding Responses and Conditions

Reflecting on the economic crises that took place in the past 3 decades since the start of reform in 1978, in particular comparing the crisis and the measures in the 1990s to this one, it could be seen that the situation in 2008–2009 was entirely different from that 30 years ago in 1979–1980 and 20 years ago in 1988–1989 while China was still in a stage of capital scarcity. Yet it had been highly similar to ten years ago in 1997–1998 when China had just entered the stage of excessive industrial capital. From the perspective of economic cycle, both imported crises coincided with the central government's macro-regulation to cool overheated economy.

The process down to the eve of 1997–1998 imported crisis could be summarized in general as follows. The economy had picked up speed after the stimulation by Deng Xiaoping's Southern inspection in 1992. It became over-heated in 1993–1994, with CPI as high as 24.1% in 1994, the highest in 30 years since the Reform. During the period there were three radical reforms—the merging of official and market foreign exchange rates, the tax division system reform and the state-owned enterprises reform that focused on headcount reduction to raise efficiency. These combined with a whole series of structural adjustment measure such as expanding fiscal deficit, expanding money supply, and liberating the securities as well as real estate markets. With these adjustments and measures to facilitate the reforms, the target of realizing "soft landing in 3 years" was eventually achieved in 1997. It was right at that point that China encountered the Southeast Asian financial crisis which led to substantial decline in overseas demands.

The process down to the 2008–2009 imported crisis could be summarized in general as follows. In December 2001 China joined the WTO, bringing in a large number of foreign companies. China completed financial market reforms in 2002. A new administration of central government took office in 2003. The third round of land enclosure by local governments then took place around the country. Over investment and over dependency on overseas markets emerged. These factors pushed in synchronization Chinese economic growth up to more than 11% annually. When over investment was worsening domestic industrial overcapacity, the 2007 Sub-prime crisis and 2008 Wall Street financial crisis hit hard the overseas demand on which China had become over dependent. Large numbers of businesses along the coastal regions went bankrupt giving rise to tens of millions of layoffs.

From the perspective of measures responding to the economic cycle, the fundamental condition for dealing with both imported crises was the institution of "whole-nation system": gathering force under central coordination to work on major tasks. In the summer of 1998 when there had been difficulties in adopting expansionary monetary policies, the central government made a timely switch to proactive fiscal policies through utilizing large-scale issuance of public debts to stimulate investments in infrastructures. Economic growth could thereby be sustained at the target level. When the crisis occurred in 2008, the early response had also been to take a loose financing policy. However it faced the same situation as the increased fund supply could not be effectively channeled to the real economy through lending. Then the measures were switched to public debt-driven investments.

From the perspective of effect, while the expansionary fiscal policy in 1998 had led to a substantial increase in the debt ratio (fiscal deficit/GDP) of the Chinese government, yet it did indeed improve to a large extent domestic infrastructure and build the "first asset pool" in major cities along the southeastern coast, thus providing the necessary condition for foreign direct investments marching in after being admitted into the WTO. It could be said that previous round of macro-regulation of using public debt-driven investments to counter economic decline was proven effective by subsequent economic stability as well as the next round of high speed growth. And the measures adopted after the 2008 crisis were not short of mega infrastructure projects either. The important difference lay with the precautions taken three years prior to the crisis. The development of the county economy had built the second capital pool and the rural labor pool.

In terms of macro-economic context, China's economic development was situated in a different condition during the 2008–2009 crisis compared with ten years ago. In that earlier case the context was a generally rising market demand. The marketization reform, while being too radical and thus giving rise to enormous social costs, had been able to generate comprehensive institutional gains overall by focusing the whole nation's power to deal with the imported crisis. In comparison, the context in 2008 was declining demand. If the policy-makers still insisted on having recourse to market as the means to allocate economic factors, as ideologized by radical reformers as "new market economy", the government would often have to pay even higher institutional costs implementing strict macro regulation after market failure.

Moreover, few could have forecasted the emergence of an imported crisis. People's understanding of the 'cyclical economic crisis' could only develop on a gradual basis.

Put it concretely, the greatest difference between the two crises was that although the situation in 1998 was difficult and the following years 1999–2000 were a period of depression in accordance with economic law, the central government's strong push to a comprehensive "monetization of the economy" did indeed catalyze new demands, such as commercialization of housing and banking in 1998, as well as the industrialization of medical and education systems. These new demands all had the practical effect of absorbing large quantity of money, creating the fundamental condition for the government to increase money supply, rapidly driving the monetization of the economy. GDP growth was thereby pushed up. The total monetary volume was enlarged. The expanding government debts were therefore diluted and neutralized.

What came after were the general new demands generated by market structural changes, such as the booming demand for vehicles, housing, and related consumption. Following that, this type of structural upgrade in consumption gradually became an important impetus to China's economic growth since 1999.

The 1990s was a special era in which Chinese government adopted radical reform to abdicate its obligation of public goods provisions. That had generated a surge of booming demands which neutralized the greatly expanded money supply as a way for the government to deal with fiscal problem. Into the twenty-first century, that condition became a historical bygone.

In the new century China had completed the total monetization of the economy. Furthermore, domestic financial capital was already in a state of relative excess. The impetus of investments and overseas demands both became spent forces. Furthermore, the institutional gains from the central government's effective, rapid monetization and capitalization during the 1997–1998 crisis were already mostly eaten up by interest groups, while the institutional costs continued to accumulate without being resolved, hence often manifested as social conflicts.

Besides, the comprehensive marketization in mid and late 1990s could still be endorsed to some extent by the central government's authority. Fiscal and financial sectors were still functioning complementarily like the two pockets of the government executing macro-regulation. By that time, state owned financial sector had not yet become an independent capital force, alienated from industrial capital, in pursuit of higher liquidity for profit. Entering the new century, China's banking sector had completed commercialization mostly after the U.S. model. The allocation of funds needed for macro-regulation must be executed by a centralized regime. That inevitably resulted at a head-on collision with the commercialized financial sector which was largely motivated by profit-seeking. Now the real economy was plagued by industrial overcapacity generated through a decade of high investment and high indebtedness. Unfortunately, the debt repayment cycle coincided with global recession. From the financial point of view, supporting the manufacturing sector by providing lending would end up with the accumulation of non-performing debts and even an endogenous financial crisis. The interest of an independent, profit-seeking financial sector clashed naturally with the state's obligation to regulate the economy for the optimal benefits of the society as a whole.

In summary, the complicated situation China faced was a result of the procrastination to resolve the enormous indebtedness accumulated through decades of "high investment, high indebtedness, high growth" model.

Finally, we must not neglect the international factors. China was long troubled by exogenous inflation since the 2008 crisis. It was because China, being the largest industrial country in the world, relied heavily on importing raw materials. However, the international primary commodities markets were flooded by hot money generated by the US Fed's Quantitative Easing as a way to save US financial system from crumbling. In a word, the USA transferred the cost of its crisis to other countries around the world, especially those developing countries relying on primary commodities from international markets. We were in a strange world where the USA practically recorded deflation after monstrous expansion of money supply and its M1 was even lower than its M0 after 2008. It was because the inflation was being transferred to the other parts of the world along with the flooding of hot money.

That was the root of the stagflation plaguing China, characterized by inflation and overcapacity. As what China faced was an "imported" or exogenous crisis, it would be hard to resolve by domestic policies alone. If China failed to partake in setting the rules of international institutions, these domestic policies would be very costly to be truly effective.

6

Unfolding Crisis and Great Transformation (2013–2020): From Globalization to Ecological Civilization as Localization

1 The Crisis of Globalization and the New Cold War

Entering 2020, China's tenth economic crisis since 1949 broke out in a dramatic conjuncture. Unlike the previous nine crises, this crisis was no longer a cyclical economic crisis in the classical sense.[1] The cycle of industrial capitalist crises was subverted by the 2008 Wall Street financial crisis. In the ten or twelve years after the crisis, the global economy was still characterized by the classical cyclical crisis of the twentieth century. For example, after the end of QE policy during 2013–2014, China experienced monetary contraction along with overproduction. Out of a status of dependency and structural complementarity, China strove to make use of its overproduction at the expense of environmental and social welfare to complement the US economy, attempting to sustain this unequal relationship. Under such unfavourable conditions, China

---

[1] In classical sense, crisis is caused by overproduction and declining profitability. An economic cycle is expressed as the fluctuation of prices and enterprises life cycle. In financial capitalism, a large part of capital does not flow into real economy. Hyman Minsky supplemented it with the financial cycle through credit creation.

© The Author(s) 2021
Wen Tiejun, *Ten Crises*, Global University for Sustainability Book Series,
https://doi.org/10.1007/978-981-16-0455-3_6

still desperately endeavoured to pursue the path of modernization which has unfolded as globalization in the last 30 years. However, the golden age of globalization might have come to an end.

Early 2020 marked the end of an era both for China and the world.[2] If the 2008 crisis had been the crisis of financial globalization, then the 2020 crisis was the crisis of globalization itself. In 2020 people was witnessing the historical seismic shift of the global system itself. After a hundred year of reckless pursuit of industrialization and urbanization, China was confronted by the crisis of globalization, in fact the crisis of modernization itself. Nevertheless, many who strongly believed in this path were still dreaming of "back to business as usual". They were conceiving of all sorts of measures attempting to resume normal economic operations. However, blind to the essential shift in global political conditions, one would be almost irrational if still clinging to economic rationality. Borrowing a famous slogan at the beginning of globalization, it may be expressed as "It is politics, stupid!"

Debt Regime and the Heavily Indebted Hegemony

Another characteristic of the time is debt becoming a new institutional arrangement. It can be seen, entering the twenty-first century, the global debt regime has been turned upside down. Now the most powerful country has become the most heavily indebted nation. It is the debtor country which holds the institutional power and repudiates debts. The powerful debtor has become a shameless repudiator. It may be less surprising if the readers are reminded that modernization is always intrinsically costly. The more modernized an institution, the more costly it is. In the age of financial capitalism, the high costs of ultra-modernized institutions (such as modern government, welfare and democracy) are sustained by mounting debts. The difference between the USA and China rests with the former being indebted to other countries while the latter is indebted internally.

---

[2]Some may believe that the twentieth century ended at 1991 when the USSR collapsed. Some ideologues even claimed it the end of the history. However, viewed from the reckless pursuit of modernization, the long twentieth century may have ended at 2020.

Now debt has become a new regime with new institutional arrangement. In the past, the heavily indebted countries were requested to transform their institutions, making their people suffer, usually according to neo-liberal tenets. Nowadays, the powerful debtor country in turn requests creditor country to transform its institution to benefit the former. Ironic and ridiculous it may seem, eventually the country which holds the international institutional power and discursive power can twist the principles it once sanctified[3] in order to maintain its privilege. The developing countries which fell into the debt trap since the 1980s might find it revealing that even if they followed the instructions to transform their institutions, the global debt problem would be not solved. The outrage lies with the powerful debtor country transfering their institutional outward cost through indebtedness while requesting its creditor to change their institutions. Even more ridiculous, the ultra-modern institution, which is shored up by increasing indebtedness and barely sustainable, is in turn taken as the example to be emulated by the creditor country. Such is the farce of the times.

The countries which hold the institutional power cling to the old path whereas those countries without institutional power have little reflection and institutional innovation. The whole global regime therefore becomes increasingly degenerate, probably until it implodes.

Recourse to Cold War Strategy

With the lack of the capacity of innovation in thinking and social institution, the old hegemony which is now heavily indebted is clinging firmly to its obsolete institutional and discursive power. Hence, unsurprisingly it has recourse to the old experience of Cold War victory out of path dependence. As a reactionary response to the challenge of the crisis of globalization, a New War has become increasingly irrational and even strips bare the old mantle of political correctness. It is the hegemony's desperate effort to sustain its privilege to transfer the cost of debt crisis to the world.

---

[3]The Washington Consensus can be boiled down into two core tenets: free capital flow and absolute creditor right.

From Delinking to Re-Linking to US-China Decoupling

During the first two decades of China's participation into globalization, the two continental nations were actually in a state of symbiotic complementarity in term of economic structure, despite constant political disputation. China's rapid industrialization was concomitant and complementary with the USA's deindustrialization and deeper financialization. The key mechanism coupling China with the USA was the great dollar circuit between them. US dollars circulated into China through trade deficits and recycled back to the USA through China stocking up treasury bonds. This great dollar circuit was a particular international institutional arrangement. The post-WWII international trade regime had been shaped and dominated by the USA. China's initial integration into globalization was possible only because the USA granted it the institutional right to take part into the global trade regime after the diplomatic rapprochement in 1979. China was allowed to take a ride on the accelerating train of global trade led by the USA. But it was not a free ride. Indeed the costs have been substantial, considering the ecological cost and labour force China has contributed during these decades, not to mention the astronomical profits US transnational corporations have earned from it and the improvement of the natural environment in the US due to deindustrialization. Viewed in this way, the dollar circuit as an international institutional arrangement was a form of seigniorage. The USA is the only nation on the planet that is able to keep trading what it desires from other countries simply by creating numbers out of nothing on a balance sheet.

As a consequence, China became increasingly dependent on the USA economically and institutionally.

Compared with the last nine major crises since 1949 we have elaborated in previous chapters, the unfolding tenth crisis shared many of the main characteristics but also had its particularity in this specific historical moment.

Similar to the second to fourth crises in the late 1950s to 1960s, China was punished because of its insistence on maintaining its relative independence and sovereignty and not totally submitting to the dominant hegemony. During the 1960s, China was forced to take the path of self-reliance after the interruption of Soviet assistance and sanctions by the West. It thereby achieved "delinking." However, since the early 1970s, China once again brought in foreign capital. And by the late 1990s, China had been integrated into globalization. As a result, China's industry and economy again became dependent on the West.

Nearly fifty years after China began accepting the inflows of western capital and twenty years after its reintegration into the global economy, the USA, while still dominating international institutional power and holding currency hegemony, threatened to punish China through a "trade war". Superficially, the reasons were to do with the huge trade deficit as well as allegations like forced technology transfers and theft of intellectual property as well as trade secrets. In fact, imposing heavy tariff on Chinese products would not improve the trade deficits. It might help little to motivate the reshoring of manufacturing back to the USA. The imbalance of the US economy originated from its structural problems at the advanced stage of financial capitalism. In fact, American enterprises and consumers would not benefit from the trade war. This was demonstrated by its rising trade deficits as well as by various studies.[4]

The Obama and Trump administrations were actually quite consistent in the strategic aims they claimed to be attempting to achieve, namely re-developing the real economy (manufacturing) in the backdrop of the hyper development of financial capitalism. However, it was doubtful that Trump would succeed where Obama had failed. The practical consequence of the trade war was in fact an effort to reshape the global economic structure and to prevent China's attainment of economic optimization and relatively greater independence through its development of technology and its fine-tuning of the international trading structure. Its strategic goal was not different from the Transpacific Partnership (TPP) advocated by Obama administration, which aimed at remaking global trade rules. In either case, China was in fact given two options: greater submission or be excluded from the new global trade regime with the US still at its core. The so-called structural reform the USA requested in

---

[4]See, P. D. Fajgelbaum, P. K. Goldberg, P. J. Kennedy, A. K. Khandelwal, 'The Return to Protectionism'; Trade Partnership Worldwide. LLC, 'Estimated Impact of Tariffs on the US Economy and Worker 2019'; M. Amiti, S.J. Redding, D. Weinstein, 'The Impact of the 2018 Trade War on U.S. Prices and Welfare'.

fact constituted for China greater submission or structural dependency. Meanwhile, no country on this planet is able to impose structural reform on the USA, its structural imbalance of which has become a major source of instability in the global economy. Herein is US exceptionalism. The USA is not just an equal member of the global community. She is the rule maker. The post WWII global trade regime was created by the USA to serve its interests. It is the only country in the world being able to stay prosperous in spite of decades of growing trade deficits.

In reality, those who have benefited most from China's incorporation into the global economy were transnational capital (especially US capital) and Chinese capitalist elites. All this occurred at the great expense of ecological degeneration and the extraction of surplus value from labour. Nonetheless, China did demonstrate substantial development. However, its industry was still highly dependent on the advanced countries. Transnational corporations took the largest share of the added value created in China. In the financial sector China still insisted on its sovereignty, which induced discontent from foreign financial capital hoping to seek higher profitability in China.

The dependent status of China in the two decades of integration into globalization could be partly reflected by its incomplete currency sovereignty. As stated above, for a long period China's money base mechanism was exogenous and dependent on its foreign exchange stock as it is accumulating a huge amount of foreign exchange reserve mainly consisted by US dollar. Therefore, China's monetary policy was susceptible to the Federal Reserve's policy and US monetary strategy and ineffective in regulating the domestic economy.

From Structural Complementarity to Institutional Delinking

China's inferior status in the global trade regime could also be reflected in its lack of rights in the pricing of major commodities. Despite being the largest importer, China lacked the right to negotiate the price-setting of major commodities as the major settlement currency is the US dollar and the international commodity markets are highly speculative. In recent years, China has been establishing its own commodity markets to gain bigger pricing power. One effort was the emergence of the Petro RMB, which was naturally regarded by the USA as a threat to the petro dollar, the cornerstone of US national interests since the 1970s. In other words, China was endeavouring to set up a preferable international trade regime, if the existing regime could not be fine-adjusted to more favourable conditions.

Of course, inside China there were two strategic stances concerned with how China should relate with the USA. One line claimed that it was actually more beneficial to China continuing and even deepening its submission to the USA. However, the problem was how the USA could avoid the mentality of the Thucydides Trap as it had successfully put a curb on Japan and later Europe, not to mention its much praised victory over the USSR.

Another line of thought believed that lesser dependency on the USA was vital to the further development of China. Made in China 2025 strategy represented the country's effort to develop core advanced technologies as a way to shake off the status of industrial dependency. It was not a coincidence that US elites decided to launch a trade war against China at this particular historical moment.

Economic Iron Curtain: From TPP to Economic Prosperity Network or Other Future Initiatives

The 2008 global financial crisis marked the end of the golden age of globalization. Since then both the USA and China were pushing strategic transformation in economic structure as a response to crisis. The consequence was a seismic shift of the strategic relationship between the two great powers. As early as in 2015, while terms like "Chimerica" and "G2" were still sort of fads in academia and media, we had proposed the imminent US-China Decoupling.

The strong rhetoric and idiosyncrasies of the Donald Trump Administration might make people forget that the US trade war against China actually had its origin in the Trans-pacific Partnership pushed by Obama administration. After the 2008 financial crisis, US government had consolidated its strategy of transferring its cost of financial crisis to other countries, including emerging countries such as China. At the same time the Obama administration also launched the high-key Rebalance Strategy and pushed the exclusive TPP initiative. Despite disparity in strategic style, American leaders were in fact highly consistent in the attempt to exclude China from the global regime in which the USA still played a dominant role. Whether it was the aborted TPP or the trade war against China in 2018 launched by the Trump administration and the latterly proposed Economic Prosperity Network, the strategic aims were in fact quite consistent, namely firstly attempting to put a curb on China's effort to shake off dependence and secondly punishing by exclusion if China refused to yield to the yoke in greater submission; nevertheless, it was dressed up by the New Cold War ideology as China taking a free ride of globalization but without embracing western democracy.

The Chinese leadership proposed in 2012 a "New mode of Major Power Relationship" as an attempt to define the US-China relationship based on common interests and despite divergence. However, it turned out to be wishful as the Obama-Hillary Clinton Adminstration instead pushed forth the Rebalance strategy to contain China in the region. In December 2017 the National Security Strategy of the United States redefined China from a "stakeholder" as one of the revisionist powers, which challenged the US-led world order. In other words, in spite of China's wishful vision of strategic partnership, the USA now regards its counterpart as a major strategic competitor and even potential threat of hot war not unlike countries like Iraq and Iran. On March 22 2018, the US Presidential Memorandum blew the bugle calls of the Trade War.

A systematic strategic containment of China became the consensus of US top political elites. It was not a result out of the spontaneity of an idiosyncratic leader, nor the preference of a single party.

Reverse-Globalization or the Exclusion of China from the Global Trade Regime

The 2008 crisis had been a crisis of the financial globalization. The globalization regime kept working for ten more years but failed to fully recover until this full-scale crisis of globalization as a whole. After globalization had exhausted its first phase resulting in widening wealth disparity around the world, some populist demagogues adopted a sort of anti-globalization discourse as a way to please their constituencies. However, upon a closer look at their policies, we found little evidence of practices of deglobalization[5] although there would be a trend of reshoring in certain key strategic sectors.[6] The present trend was more a reconfiguration than the disintegration of globalization. The result might be just an altered form of globalization at a lesser scale but no less intrinsically pro-capital and pro-elite. What was unfolding may be regarded as reverse-globalization. Or it might be called global regionalization.

In retrospect, China was admitted into the global trade regime in 1972 led by the USA because of the latter's half a century long rivalry with a chief opponent, the USSR. The first phase of the globalization started at the end of the Cold War. The so-called victory in a political and ideological war over a major enemy had granted the USA with the confidence to open its global trade regime to any country willing to play the game. At this phase, the globalization regime was a gigantic profit machine based on highly complicated global supply chains and extraction of cheap production factors, such as labour, land and resources.

---

[5]It depends on how one defines globalization. We think that during its prime time in the last three decades, the unit of globalization has always been nation-state. Certainly, globalization is characterized by the permeability of state by capital. But the erosion of state power is only relevant to countries in a less privileged position in the global regime. For the powerful core countries, it is not the case. Therefore, a revival of nationalism in political discourse does not necessarily imply genuine de-globalization in practice. For us, a genuine de-globalization should be pro-people's wellbeing and empowerment, not to mention pro-ecological regeneration. However, many of the populist demagogues are in reality highly elitist and pro-capital.

[6]Reshoring was not a strategy limited to the USA. Japanese government also planned to offer subsidies up to $2.25 billion to Japanese companies bringing supply chain back home.

Nevertheless, the second phase of globalization (or post globalization era if one likes it) would be more about alliance of ideological and geopolitical compatibility than merely profit-making. In a sense, it was an endeavour to retrograde to 2001 before China joined WTO, or even to 1972 before China had rapprochement with the USA.

Global Regionalization

So far, what we have witnessed at the beginning of the post-globalization era is the formation of global regionalization, which may be an alter form of globalization. The NAFTA has been reshaped into the United States-Mexico-Canada Agreement (USMCA). Launching a New Cold World, the USA is mobilizing like-minded countries to form an anti-China geopolitical and trade alliance. In fact, apart from the trading regime, the US under Trump Administration is attempting to decompose and reconfigure almost all international institutions with only one principle: to form an anti-China alliance. The Anglophone Five Eyes Alliance members have often also been the *ex officio* core members of most of US geopolitical initiatives. India, regarding itself as the regional competitor of China, would be also keen at joining any US initiative aiming at containing China and see themselves as possibly benefiting from the ripping of Chinese supply chain.

The European Union, after continuous shocks of PIIGS Sovereignty Debt crisis, Brixit and COVID-19, is struggling to regain its footing to rebuild the solidarity of Europe. To help fiscally less favourable members to recover from the blow of COVID-19, Germany and France proposed a €500 billion Recovery Fund providing grants to European countries in need. The European Commission would raise money by borrowing on the markets, which would be repaid from the EU budget. Most importantly Germany has changed her firm position of rejecting debts-sharing. It might mark an important step toward the fiscal unification of the EU. It is well known that the design of Euro was defective in the deficiency of fiscal unity among EU members. Fiscal unification might strengthen Euro's presence in the global financial system. EU bonds would be an alternative to the US Treasury Bonds. Then Europe might become an equivalent strategic competitor to the USA.

Undoubtedly, the EU would continue to play an important role in the world. However, caught in the confrontations between the USA and China, as well as the USA and Russia, it would have to seek a balance between these powers. Lack of a united administration and without its own independent arm force, the EU would find it not competent enough to deal with the overspill of conflicts in some of the turbulent regions proximal to Europe.

In Asia, the regional integration of China, Japan, Korea and ASEAN appears to be the most beneficial direction for all countries in the region. However, Japan and Korea, lacking complete military autonomy, would have to struggle in the dilemma of whether to befriend a non-negligible neighbour with which it has close economic ties or yield to their *de facto* military suzerain. ASEAN countries, likewise, have close economic connection with China. However, the region has been plagued by complications arising from the South China Sea dispute, which has been proactively inflamed by the interventions of external powers.

Entering the twenty-first century, China appeared to have the greatest international presence since the late nineteenth century. However, after forty years of relatively peaceful times and having waived its competitiveness in institutional and discursive power, China suddenly finds itself in an increasingly hostile geo-political surrounding. At the international level, decades of China-bashing in international media precipitated into blatant demonization after the COVID-19 outbreak in 2020. The third decade of the twenty-first century would not be an easy era for Chinese diplomacy.

Fast Track to a New Cold War

An epidemic by an unknown coronavirus later dubbed as COVID-19 broke out in China. After having confirmed its contagiousness and fatality, Chinese government responded swiftly in the January of 2020 with decisive measures including locking down Hubei provinces, the epicentre of the epidemic and halting all non-essential economic activities nation-wide. The central government mobilized the whole nation's power to take on an unforeseen challenge. These measures and efforts proved to be effective in containing COVID-19.[7] The outbreak and its containment in China also showed that a functional and well-coordinated administration is invaluable to any nation. China's administrative effectiveness has been an institutional legacy since the revolution era, despite much demonization and criticism by the West.[8] In some western countries, the official and mainstream epidemic discourse implied an innuendo of social Darwinism whereas personal freedom was hailed as prior to collective interests and the poor, the aged, the coloured and the underprivileged were the most seriously impacted social group, economically and pathologically. While many countries were still paralyzed by this century epidemic, China was among the first to resume normal daily life and economic activities. However, the US government failed to contain the epidemic while the leadership took a scapegoating approach and blamed China for spreading the coronavirus, despite international medical professionals generally speaking highly of China's efforts in containing the epidemic.

After the trade war and COVID-19 outbreak in 2020, the Sino-American relationship fell to its worst moment since 1989 and showed no sign of relief. The 1990s was the time when globalization was rising and international capital was seeking after cheap production factors. Therefore the 1989 sanction lasted only for a few years. Soon after that China was re-admitted and fully integrated into globalization. Nevertheless, after three decades the situation has become different. Now globalization has come to the bottle neck. And most importantly, three decades after the Cold War, China emerged from being the second to the major opponent of the USA. In a sense, the US-China relationship has retrogressed to the situation prevailing before 1972. Just that China

---

[7]"The outbreak containment strategies in China based on non-pharmaceutical interventions (NPIs) appear to be effective...Without NPIs, the COVID-19 cases would likely have shown a 67-fold increase (interquartile range 44–94) by February 29, 2020..." in S. Lai, N.W. Ruktanonchai et al. "Effect of non-pharmaceutical interventions to contain COVID-19 in China," Nature, 4 May 2020. https://www.nature.com/articles/s41586-020-2293-x. Also: "An investigation of transmission control measures during the first 50 days of the COVID-19 epidemic in China," Science, 8 May 2020.

[8]About the US administration's poor performance in handling the outbreak, read Joseph E. Stiglitz, "Plague by Trumpism" March 9, 2020, Project Syndicate. https://www.project-syndicate.org/commentary/trump-coronavirus-failure-of-small-government-by-joseph-e-stiglitz-2020-03.

now took the place of the USSR as the prime enemy of the USA. As a Newsweek essay put it, "Thus, a growing number of policymakers, current and former, and China hands old and new, acknowledge the obvious: Cold War 2.0 is here."[9] And Joseph Bosco, a former Pentagon strategic planner and vociferous Anti-China hawk, expressed it in an unmistakably Cold War language: "Another long twilight struggle may be upon us and it may make the last one look easy" (ibid.).

In US strategic conception, its competition with China was full scale and in all major fields: Economy (extending to finance and currency), Military Superiority (extending to the space), Geopolitics, Technology, National Security, International Institutions and Ideology.[10]

As for the economy, what was taking shape would constitute a seismic shift splitting the global trade regime that would shake the world order. Be it passively or proactively, to save its survival in the global industrial chain, China had to establish an alter-international trade system, splitting from the old regime currently which was reshaping itself, with the USA still as the core. The problem was that the USA increasingly took to adopting a New Cold War approach. In its official discourse[11] and high ranking officers' speeches, the USA's engagement with China was raised to the level of an antagonistic rivalry between two opposite ideologies and even civilizations. Worse still, the USA was obsessed with forcing other countries, enterprises and international institutions to take sides

---

[9] Bill Powell, "America Is in a New Cold War and This Time the Communists Might Win" 18-05-2020, https://www.newsweek.com/2020/06/05/america-new-cold-war-this-time-communists-might-win-1504447.html.

[10] US Congressman Michael McCaul, Republican Leader on the House Foreign Affairs Committee, announced on 19 May 2020 the pillars of the China Task Force: National Security, Technology, Economics and Energy, Competitiveness, and Ideological Competition. He said, "*Each of these pillars represents a key focus area where U.S. leadership and democratic values counteract Chinese Communist Party (CCP) malfeasance globally. The five pillars reflect the key aspects of our strategic competition with China, as identified by our members: military superiority and homeland security; advanced technology; economic strength; increasing our competitiveness; and the battle between democracy and authoritarianism. We must take decisive action across each of these vital domains to better secure our future.*" https://gop-foreignaffairs.house.gov/press-release/mccaul-announces-china-task-force-pillars-and-co-chairs/.

[11] See: *U.S. Strategic Approach to the People's Republic of China.* This report by the White House articulated its whole-of-government approach to China under the 2017 National Security Strategy. https://www.whitehouse.gov/wp-content/uploads/2020/05/U.S.-Strategic-Approach-to-The-Peoples-Republic-of-China-Report-5.20.20.pdf.

by measures such as poison pill provisions, supply chain blockades and sanctions.

It might be too early to call whether the new cold war would lead to full scale military confrontation. If it is a soft delinking, what we would witness might be the emergence of two economic cores with overlapping supply chains and markets to some extent. For a certain period, the two cores would still be interwoven in a complicated manner. However, if the confrontation escalates and eventually leads to a hard decoupling, then the probability of regional military tension and even proxy war cannot be not excluded. Bill Powell put the US new mission concisely: "Wage the 21st century's Cold War, while ensuring it never turns hot" (ibid.). However, the historical lessons of the World Wars I & II show us clearly that any attempt of playing a rival game to gain greater supremacy while believing one could avoid full scale military confrontation is an illusion.

During this great splitting of the most important relationship in the world, what is truly worrying is less about the so-called Thucydides Trap. The mentality of the an alpha nation not tolerating the rise of a potential competitor might not necessarily result in a disastrous clash. It is the unsustainability of the present debt regime that should bother us. The old financial regime with the Federal Reserve mechanism as the core has increasingly become similar to a Ponzi scheme. Many major central banks in the world had reverted to quasi-quantitative easing of various sorts because there was not enough private demand to keep the game going. If China refuses to continue playing the role of paying tribute to the suzerain as it has in the last 20 or 30 years after the decoupling, would the world find a contributor big enough to sustain the game? If the big game of debt is no longer sustainable like the situation before the WWII, does it imply a new world war looming on the horizon?

The two nations are heading towards strategic collision in this post globalization era. This great shift may bring forth an even more complicated scenario in a world plagued by debt, recession, unemployment, widening wealth disparity, social turmoil, political conflicts and ecological catastrophe.

2   Post-epidemic Impact: Towards a Hard Delinking

After months of intense dispute, China and the USA reached an agreement in January 2020 aiming at easing the trade war stage by stage. According to the deal, China had to commit to increasing imports from the USA by at least US$200 billion above 2017 levels and strengthening intellectual property protection. Other terms included opening up market access for financial service and easing legal action over so-called "trade secret theft". The scale of the purchase promise was so large that people generally regarded China had made major concession to the USA allowing both sides a way out of the scenario of full-scale confrontation.

However, no matter how much Chinese government was willing to concede with promises to balance trade and open up financial and capital markets, the US ruling elites did not appear to be not easily appeased. A tentative trade agreement with China did not stop the US government from further ripping global supply chains from China, including banning leading Chinese IT enterprises from getting advanced technologies related with US companies. This amounted to a technology blockade.

Box 1: US Technology Blockade

On May 15 2020, US Bureau of Industry and Security announced plans to restrict the leading Chinese IT enterprise Huawei from making use of U.S. technology and software to design and manufacture its semiconductors on the ground that it was "engaged in activities that are contrary to U.S. national security or foreign policy interests".

However, beneath the pretext of national security, the genuine reason of the technology blockade against China was expressed unabashedly by William Barr, US Attorney General, in a public speech:

> It is the pivotal nature of 5G technology and the threat arising from the Chinese drive to dominate this field. 5G technology lies at the center of the technological and industrial world that is taking shape. In essence, communications networks are not just for communications anymore. They are evolving into the central nervous system of the next generation of internet, called the "Industrial

Internet," and the next generation of industrial systems that will depend on that infrastructure. China has built up a lead in 5G, capturing 40 percent of the global 5G infrastructure market. **For the first time in history, the United States is not leading the next technology era** [bold added].[1]

It was out of this anxiety of being surpassed in technological competition for the first time in more than a hundred years that the US was determined to contain China's technological advancement by all means.[2]

In fact, it was not the first time the USA applied non-market means in an attempt to defeat potential competitors, even US allies. In the 1980s, the rise of Japanese enterprises in the semi-conductors market had threatened the USA's bellwether status. In 1985, Japan surpassed the US to become the largest semi-conductors producer in the world. In 1989, Japan held 53% of the world market whereas the US merely 37%. On the pretext of national security threat, the US government started to make use of various means to suppress Japan's lead in the field. By a series of US-Japan Semiconductors Agreements since 1986, along with the Plaza Accord in 1985, the US succeeded in gradually strangling Japanese semi-conductor industry. By the 2010s, Japan had basically lost its share in the global chip market.

Of course, the US selective technology blockade against China was a gamble. In 2018, China imported US$312.1 billion of integrated circuit products, comprising two third of the global trade volume of semi-conductors, with a trade deficits of more than US$200 bn. The blockade might in turn hurt US enterprises and eventually undermine its lead in the industry. A report by Boston Consulting Group, *How Restrictions to Trade with China Could End US Leadership in Semiconductors*,[3] expressed this concern. If the Chinese semiconductor industry could survive, China might achieve delinking from its technological dependence on the USA. However, out of strategic path dependency, the US considers it imperative to knock out any potential competitor, especially when it is not considered an ally but instead a strategic competitor.

References:

1. https://www.justice.gov/opa/speech/attorney-general-william-p-barr-delivers-keynote-address-department-justices-china.
2. The *Wassenaar Arrangement on Export Controls for Conventional Arms and Dual-use Goods and Technology* also affords the US with the

power to put pressure on the signatories in exporting goods and technology which the US considered may be used for military application and contrary to US interests.

3. https://media-publications.bcg.com/flash/2020-03-07-How-Restricti ons-to-Trade-with-China-Could-End-US-Semiconductor-Leadership. pdf.

Furthermore, the US government planned to attach a "poison pill" provision in all trade agreements with trade partners, which endowed the USA with the veto over its partners making trade agreement with so-called "non-market country" it defined. The provision was widely regarded as specifically anti-China.

From the standpoints of transnational corporations which had benefitted most from globalization, the reconfiguration of global trade regime or reshoring to the USA in fact harmed their short-term profits.[12] However, what the US political elites were concerned with was the long-term national strategies. For this major strategic adjustment, the US enterprises were requested to endure the shock of global reconfiguration of the trade regime.

The COVID-19 global outbreak staged another episode of the ongoing saga with further dramatic conflicts. The epidemic terminated the 128 month boom, the longest record in US history since 1854.[13]

---

[12]Thomas J. Donohue', CEO of the U.S. Chamber of Commerce, warned on April 2020 that ripping US supply chain out of China by over reshoring could harm the US economy. https://www.reuters.com/article/us-health-coronavirus-supply-chains/bus iness-group-cautions-u-s-on-reshoring-too-much-china-supply-idUSKBN22V2VO. Bill Powell reported, "In the U.S., a lot of companies simply do not want to reduce their exposure to China. They spent years—and billions—building up supply lines and are loath to give them up. Consider the semiconductor industry, a critical area in which the U.S. is still technologically more advanced than China. A complete cessation of semiconductor sales to China would mean U.S. firms lose about 18 percent of their global market share—and an estimated 37 percent of overall revenues. That in turn would likely force reductions in research and development. The U.S. spent $312 billion on R&D over the last decade, more than double the amount spent by its foreign competitors—and it's that R&D which allows them to stay ahead of competitors" (Newsweek, 18-5-2020). https://www.newsweek.com/2020/06/05/america-new-cold-war-this-time-communists-might-win-1504447.html.

[13]National Bureau of Economic Research Business Cycle Dating Committee. https://www.nber. org/cycles/june2020.html.

And the US economy plunged into recession. Under much criticism in mishandling the crisis with a death toll of over 120,000 (as of June) and the worst economic conditions since the Great Depression,[14] the US leaders sought recourse to a strategy of scapegoating China, as it was the first country known to discover the outbreak. Xenophobia, racism and conspiracy theory was orchestrated with a distorted form of epidemiology despite disapproval by scientists.[15] Amidst the outbreak and the US leaders demonizing China, a survey by the Pew Research Center showed that 66% of the Americans had an unfavourable view of China, the most negative rating since the Center began similar survey in 2005.[16]

We should not forget that the rise of conservative populism was an aftermath of unfettered globalization. Globalization was a process of captialization of resources (or the commons) followed by the virtualization of capital. Financial globalization made it worse as financial capital was in essence exclusive. Therefore, financial capitalism is not about free markets in general sense. It is an exclusive development in which a small group of people takes control of increasingly large amounts of capital. The consequence of financial capitalism is inevitably the widening gap between the rich and the poor, the have-all and the have-nots. It was not an accident that the development of hyper financial capitalism in the 1920s resulted in the rise of fascism while in the 2000s, it led right wing populism. Populism is in fact an irrational reaction to this widening gap by the lower and middle class.

---

[14]The US unemployment rate was 14.7% in April. As of 9 May, the number of unemployment was 36.5 million. The Federal Reserve Bank of Chicago indicated that the real unemployment rate might be as high as 30.7%. Low income households were hit hard. A Federal Reserve survey showed that 39% of low income Americans (with annual income below $40,000) lost their jobs over the period (compared with 13% of households with income over $10,000). Over 100,000 enterprises were closed permanently due to the epidemic. 42% of work opportunity might be lost permanently. US industrial production in April decreased by 11.2%, the worst in 101 years. The Federal Reserve Bank of Atlanta predicted the Q2 GDP might be contracted by 42.8%. The homeless population might increase by 45% at the end of 2020.

[15]See "Stop the coronavirus stigma now," *Nature*, 7 April 2020. Also Richard Horton, the editor-in-chief of *The Lancet* pointed out it was unfair to blame China for the COVID-19 pandemic in an interview with Chinese state media. See South China Morning Post, 2 May, 2020.

[16]K. Devlin, L. Silver & C. Huang "U.S. Views of China Increasingly Negative Amid Coronavirus Outbreak". https://www.pewresearch.org/global/2020/04/21/u-s-views-of-china-increasingly-negative-amid-coronavirus-outbreak/.

Faced with uncertainty, many US companies planned to adjust their supply chains and lessen their dependency on China. As an economist in the Federal Reserve Bank of New York's Research and Statistics Group stated that, "[g]oing forward, COVID-19 is likely to give further impetus to trends that already began in previous years [due to the trade war]. It is likely to lead firms to consider bringing some critical activities back to the United States or to set up backup suppliers to reduce the firms' exposure to any single supplier or country. While introducing such additional safeguards is going to reduce the efficiency of supply chains in normal times, it may well improve performance in the longer run by mitigating the high costs of supply chain disruptions."[17]

The technology blockade and the not totally unlikely possibility of a financial war has alarmed China of its over dependency on foreign core technologies. The government has set its goal of increasing chip self-sufficiency from the current 25 to 75% in five years. In the Fourteenth Five-year Plan, the state has proposed the principle of independent scientific research capacity and technological self-sufficiency as the foundation of the nation. The aim is to build a Digital China with its own independent IC-chip, 5G, new energies technologies and new material science. The central government has called for an overhaul in education(talent), scientific regime(know-how), economic system (with a coordination of capital, industry and market) and administration. Whether this great expectation may be successful or not would be one of the global focuses determining the course of history in the next 15 years.

People generally believed the China-US relationship would never be the same after the COVID-19 epidemic. It appeared that the bifurcation in scenario would lie at whether the delinking would take place in a smooth and orderly manner or abruptly by some black swan or grey rhinoceros event.

---

[17]Sebastian Heise, "How Did China's COVID-19 Shutdown Affect U.S. Supply Chains?," Federal Reserve Bank of New York, 12 May 2020. https://libertystreeteconomics.newyorkfed.org/2020/05/how-did-chinas-covid-19-shutdown-affect-us-supply-chains.html.

The Formation of an Exclusive Global Financial Regime

As finance lies at the heart of globalization, the strategic exclusion of China naturally extended to the US-led international financial regime. Global dollar liquidity regulation has been one of the fundamental mechanisms of this regime. Every time when there was a financial crisis, global dollar liquidity would be in a state of contraction. However, because of the lack of alternative source of international credit, the global contraction of dollar liquidity would in turn strengthen the status of dollar as the global currency. The expansion of the currency swap agreement between the US Federal Reserve with foreign central banks beyond the core became an important strategy toward the exclusion of China from the global financial regime.

Box 2: Currency Swap Agreement

On 31 October 2013, the U.S. Federal Reserve, the European Central Bank, the central banks of United Kingdom, Japan Canada and Switzerland had come to a long-term currency swap agreement to replace temporary mutual liquidity swap agreements. Given the situation of contracting U.S. dollar liquidity, the monopoly system of the six central banks will dominate the polarization of the global monetary, financial and economic system. Monetary and financial markets that entered that system would have liquidity support as well as a 'crisis bottom line premium' assessed by international capital. Economic systems worldwide that did not have the good fortune of sharing that network would be vulnerable to attacks in currency exchange rates and in the financial markets.[1]

Due to the outbreak of COVID-19, the U.S. stock market crash prompted the Federal Reserve take on a new round of Quantitative Easing (QE), which started with USD 700 billion on 15 March 2020, then announced "an open-ended commitment to keep buying assets under its quantitative easing measures."[2] On March 19, 2020, the Federal Reserve announced the establishment of temporary U.S. dollar liquidity arrangements (swap lines) with nine more central banks. "These

---

new facilities will support the provision of U.S. dollar liquidity in amounts up to $60 billion each for the Reserve Bank of Australia, the Banco Central do Brazil, the Bank of Korea, the Banco de Mexico, the Monetary Authority of Singapore, and the Sveriges Riksbank (Sweden) and $30 billion each for the Danmarks National Bank (Denmark), the Norges Bank (Norway), and the Reserve Bank of New Zealand. These U.S. dollar liquidity arrangements will be in place for at least six months."[3]

In this way, the monetary system of the West in the financial globalization era is forming a layout similar to that revealed in Immanuel Wallerstein's world system theory, "core – semi-periphery – periphery": the U.S. dollar remains in the central position, and together with the currencies that orbit around it, the Euro, British Pound, the Yen, the Canadian dollar and Swiss Franc, formed the core monetary system. Other economic systems that are of compatible ideologies can make relatively large-scale currency swaps with the six central banks and as such have the nature of a secondary center. The nine newly joined central banks become semi-peripheral. Those economic systems that are excluded from making swaps with the core central banks have the peripheral position.

Sit Tsui

References

1. Xu Yisheng, "From 'Jamaican System' entering into 'New Atlantic System'", *China Business News*, 3 December 2013.
2. https://www.cnbc.com/2020/03/15/federal-reserve-cuts-rates-to-zero-and-launches-massive-700-billion-quantitative-easing-program.html; https://www.cnbc.com/2020/03/23/fed-announces-a-slew-of-new-programs-to-help-markets-including-open-ended-asset-purchases.html.
3. https://www.federalreserve.gov/newsevents/pressreleases/monetary2 0200319b.htm.

The liquidity swap agreement should have been an important international arrangement to stabilize the global financial system. However, the exclusion of the second largest economy in the world made the motivation of the agreement dubious. The arrangement would function to stabilize the core nations of the global financial regime. Countries at the semi-periphery might also benefit from this at the price of their economies being further dollarized and dependent on the dollar regime. Other economies not included into this arrangement had to face greater risk of financial instability as the global economy became increasingly unstable.

3   A Brief Recapitulation of Major Domestic Economic Aspects During 2013–2020

This round of crisis actually had its root as early as in 2013 when the US Federal Reserve ended the Quantitative Easing III. Most of the emerging countries were seriously impacted. Even though still ranking among the top in the world, the speed of China's economic growth was slowing down consecutively since 2013, a drop by nearly half from the peak, a situation unprecedented in 20 years. In the official discourse, it was described as the "New Norm". In other words, the old model of globalization into which China had integrated itself exhausted its momentum and the negative externalities accumulated in three decades were biting deep into the society, economy and ecology.

This prolonged economic downturn was an extension of the previous 2008 crisis in the USA. The weak global demand since 2012 had thrown China into deflation. The termination of the US Federal Reserve's QE policy in 2013 had great impact on emerging economies around the world. China was not an exception, though the impact of the Fed's QE policy on it is less serious thanks to its capital controls and more solid economic base. In response to the crisis, the government engaged in "supply side reform" and took measures which were basically "procyclical": going along with rather than against the trend. That meant while the economy was going down, the government took contractionary instead of expansionary measures, unlike the counter-cyclical (expansionary) measures in the cases of 1997 and 2008 to save the economy from further crumbling. For example, during the worrying trend of 'deindustrialization,' the government took to forcibly cutting excessive industrial production capacity. However, while the industry was contracting, the financial sector was expanding fast. Driven by the enthusiasm for radical financial reform as advocated by the rising financial interest bloc against the backdrop of declining manufacturing industrial profitability, the frenzy of rapid financialization led to the stock market crash of 2015,[18] followed by the foreign exchange reform which resulted in pressure placed on RMB's exchange rate. The government had to put as much as a trillion US dollar of its foreign exchange reserve in the market to stabilize the exchange rate of RMB.

We may give a quick sketch of Chinese economy in six major aspects which would continue to be of importance in the coming future.

Rapid Financialization Crowding Out Industrial Development

The most prominent feature of the situation during 2013–2018 was the trend of financialization of the economy crowding out industrial development. China's money supply mechanism in the last 20 years relied heavily on the inflow of foreign exchange reserves. By regulation, all foreign exchange flowing into China was obliged to be sold to the central bank, accordingly expanding the money base. Therefore, enormous trade surplus was rendered into rapid expansion of the money base (M0) from RMB 3 trillion in 2008 to more than 8 trillion at 2018 while M2 from 40 trillion in 2007 to 182 trillion at December 2018. As a consequence, liquidity increased without a corresponding growth in the real economy. During this period, the expansion rate of M2 was almost twice the GDP growth rate. Furthermore the defects in monetary conductive mechanism in banking sector made it difficult for small and medium enterprises in the real economy to obtain credit from banks. Faced with declining profitability in manufacturing and the real economy, capital was driven into the speculative sectors such as the stock and real estate markets. As a consequence, China experienced great fluctuations in the stock markets

---

[18]It was estimated that the government had totally spent RMB 2-3 trillion to save the markets from further crumbling.

during 2013–2018.[19] After the stock market crumbled in 2015, hot money flowed into real estate sector to create a big asset bubble. This financial crisis was essentially the institutional cost of China being incorporated into global financialization under the pressure of excess financial capital.

The drive towards financialization in China was both endogenous and exogenous. One the one hand, the profitability of general manufacturing was declining due to overcapacity and weak global demand. After the Wall Street financial crisis in 2008 and the subsequent crises in the West, global demand crumbled and diminished the profitability of manufacturing. Although China became the largest manufacturing country in the world, most of its products still generated relatively low added value. Now with its industries being yet to upgrade itself technologically with higher added value, China was threatened by deindustrialization.

On the other hand, China was increasingly participating in financial globalization. After the crisis of 1993, the Chinese banking sector became commercialized along the lines of the Anglo-Saxon model. As a policy to emerge from the 1927 crisis, the Glass Steagall Act (1933) ensured that the functions of commercial banks were strictly separated from investment banking in the USA. This held sway until the Act was repealed in 1999 by the so-called Financial Services Modernization Act. In China, however, the new-born commercial banks in the 1990s dived head-on into the brave new world of high finance capitalism. After two decades of development, China's financial sector has become one of the biggest interest blocs,[20] increasingly intermingled with the global financial capitalism.

Consequently, the financial sector increasingly became alienated from the real economy. This had two obvious consequences. Whereas small and medium enterprises as well as manufacturing sector found it hard to get credit from banks whose preference was to give infrastructure

---

[19]At its peak at June 2015, the total value of Chinese stock markets amounted to US$ 10 trillion, second only to US stock markets.

[20]At its peak, the US financial sector was weighted about 7.6% of US GDP. However, China's counterpart recorded 8.4% of the GDP in 2016. The total assets value of Chinese financial institutions ranked as number one in the world.

building, state-owned enterprises, real estate or loan with land or property as collateral, a handful of China's financial giants sucked most of the national economic returns.[21] The real economy was in turn crowded out by the imperatives of finance. As the real economy hollowed out, the financial interest bloc was pushing for further radical financial reforms, drawing excess liquidity into speculative sectors and creating asset bubbles and expanding debts.

China's financial system at its present mode is not supportive of manufacturing and the real economy. Its stock markets failed to fulfill its supposed function, namely to effectively channel excessive liquidity into the real economy to promote industrial upgrading. After the 2015 crash, hot money seeking profitability left stock markets and rushed into other speculative sectors, the most prominent being real estate. And real estate prices in major cities have sky-rocketed beyond the affordability of most people. To compound the problem, local governments developed a dependence on land and real estate as sources of fiscal revenues.

The stock market crash of 2015 did not halt the financial frenzy. Financial products and derivatives have continued to grow exponentially. As estimated, the value of total assets managed by various financial institutions in 2018 amounts to more than RMB 100 trillion. With a weak economy and declining profitability in the real economy, it is reasonable to be worried with the exponential growth of financial investment and the scenario of Ponzi scheme. The rapid financialization of the last decade has reshaped Chinese economy increasingly to share the traits of a casino economy.

Nonfinancial Enterprises Financialized and E-Finance Bubble

Moreover, financial investment and real estate speculation become important sources of revenues for many nonfinancial enterprises. Some

---

[21] Eight of the top ten listed companies were banks. And the top four were all state-owned banks. In 2017, the banking sector swallowed half of the total returns of listed companies in Chinese stock markets. The total profits of banks, real estate, securities and insurance companies (the FIRE sectors as dubbed by Michael Hudson, about 300 in number) amounted to 70.3% of the stock markets while the other 3200 listed companies have to share the remaining 30%.

researchers estimate that in the last ten years, 40% of the fund raised in stock market has gone to the purchase of financial assets, real estate speculation and all sorts of financial investments.

Hot money also found its way into e-finance along with the rapid development of internet. Since its birth in 2011, the total transaction volume of e-finance has grown over RMB 17.8 trillion. In July 2018, many Peer to Peer financial platforms closed down. The total loss is estimated to be up to a trillion RMB. The internet has become an indispensable part of economy. However, when the internet goes hand in hand with financial disorder, the systematic risk is worrying.

At the end of 2017, the total value of the assets of China's financial sector has amounted to RMB 250 trillion, topping the rest of the world.

Faced with the grey rhino of a looming global financial crisis, greater financial liberalization to deepen and accelerate financialization remained a major target of policy-making. Financial interest blocs have apparently taken a firm grip on China's policy decision making.

Worried by the trend, the top leadership warned on different occasions against the risk of disordered financial expansion. On June 2020, the State Council issued "Suggestions on Accelerating the Perfection of Socialist Market Economic System in the New Time," emphasizing the aim of finance being at service of the quality development of economy and society and the urgency of rectifying market disorder. At a summit on 24 October 2020, Wang Qishan, China's Vice-Chairman, reiterated the importance of finance to the service of the real economy and warned that the financial sector should not go astray with speculation and gambling, or even become a Ponzi scheme. Financial safety should be always prioritized over liquidity and profitability.

The Fourteenth Five-Years Plan as put forth in 2020 has set the goal of China becoming a "Strong Manufacturing Nation" and developing digital economy. How to reverse the crowding out of manufacturing by financialization in the last decade and ensure that finance would function as a humble servant of real economy would pose a great challenge.

The Lesson China Should Learn from the Crisis in the West

The deepening of financialization and further opening up of domestic financial market had been a well-defined policy in China, which might have its reason considering the excess of financial capital. Amid the COVID-19 epidemic, China further opened its financial market on April 1 2020 as planned. At the time that this chapter was being written, it was not clear what its impact would be on Chinese economy. However, the global financial instability due to the epidemic outbreak should be considered as an alarm to this obsession with financialization. The western financial system should not be worshipped as an assumedly better institution. China should not simply copy the western capital market system which has been proven to be prone to instability, conducive for social inequality and bound for crisis. It would be irrational to simply duplicate a system that has such an increasingly poor track record.

Instead, China should look for new policy orientation and alternative path.

Monetary Sovereignty

As described in previous chapters, foreign exchange used to be a valuable resource for China as a developing country to repay foreign debts and stabilize its domestic currency. The state thus stipulated that all foreign exchange flowing into China had to be sold to the central bank. As China's foreign exchange reserve was expanding, so did its money base. As a consequence, the central bank money supply became exogenous. It led to the ineffectiveness of monetary policy as a tool of economic regulation. Hence, the restoration of an endogenous monetary mechanism became essential.

On 16 January 2019, an officer from the Treasury Department in the Ministry of Finance released the message of planning to link national bond issuance with the central bank's monetary policy operation. In other words, the state's credit would become the basis of monetary issuance, which is a common practice for many major economies in the world. For example, the total assets of the US Federal Reserve balance sheet in 2020 amounted to over $7.1 trillion, mostly comprised of US treasury bonds, mortgage backed securities and institutional bonds. However, in comparison, China's central bank, as of July 2020, held foreign assets worth of RMB 21.8375 trillion in its balance sheet while merely RMB 1.5250 trillion of claims on Chinese central government. This striking structural imbalance could be viewed as a sign of incomplete monetary sovereignty upon which an economy could create money based on national credit to support its development.

If the RMB would no longer be pegged to the dollar and China's monetary mechanism would no longer rely on holding foreign assets, then the search for a new foundation of monetary value becomes imperative.

Moreover, confronted with the scenario of financial war imposed by the USA in which China might be forcibly delinked from the international US dollar system, seeking an alternative to the dollar in international settlement also becomes a pressing problem.

A Race of Post Dollar Hegemony: Digital Currency and New Global Financial Order

US global interest was sustained by dollar hegemony, a legacy of the Bretton Woods system and post Bretton Woods regime. The dollar was yet to be challenged as the global reserve currency and the default currency of international trade and settlement. As the value of money was backed almost solely by the creditability of the state behind it, the value of the dollar was secured by unchallenged US military dominance and the political and social stability of the USA. It remained the most preferred foreign exchange reserve many countries stock to stabilize their currencies. Because of it, the USA became the only nation on the planet able to prosper by perpetuating trade deficits and debt rollover.

The current international financial system was functioning only because of the dollar system. Without SWIFT and CHIPS (Clearing House Interbank Payments System), the global financial system would come to a halt. However, it virtually also afforded the USA the monopolized power of financial sanctions. Apart from direct military intervention, financial sanction through international clearing system became one of the most important and effective means to extend US global hegemony. Russia, Europe and quite a few countries were conceiving new alternative international clearing systems capable of bypassing the control of the USA.

With the rise of block-chain technology and cryptocurrency, it seemed that an alternative global currency and international settlement system eventually became conceivable and viable after more than 70 years of U.S. dollar hegemony. Nevertheless, decentralized cryptocurrencies like Bitcoin seem to be speculative fads boosted by the ideological fantasies of the Austrian School rather than practical tools to improve the economic well-being of people. Blockchain technology has yet to solve the trilemma of decentralization, creditability and cost. However, we should not underestimate the significance and impact of cryptocurrencies issued by big financial institutions or IT giants, which may pose a threat to sovereign currencies, especially of small economies. Furthermore, if the USA came up with a form of cryptodollar, then dollar hegemony might rise to a new level. It might mark the death of monetary and financial sovereignty of most of the countries in the world other than the USA.

It was against this backdrop that China prominently embraced the potentials of blockchain and cryptocurrency technology. As a leader in electronic payment, China, after six years of research for, launched in May 2020 a pilot scheme of DCEP(Digital Currency Electronic Payment) in four cities. It was a digital currency exclusively issued by the Chinese central bank. DCEP was supposed to be the replacement of M0 and pegged to RMB as legal tender generated and regulated by a centralized and exclusive model (being the only legal digital currency in China). However, it was more than a simple digitization of cash. In combination with big data, DCEP may improve the effectiveness of the central bank's monetary policies. As Huang Qifan, chairman of the China International Economic Exchange Center, put it in a speech at the China Finance 40 Forum,

DCEP can achieve real-time collection of data related to money creation, bookkeeping, etc., providing useful reference for the provision of money and the implementation of monetary policies.[22]

Apart from improving the efficiency of monetary policy and general transaction, its traceability may also help to monitor criminality.

Last but not least, whether being a pioneer in electronic payment and digital currency might facilitate to promote the RMB as a regional currency was still uncertain, especially against the backdrop of a growing hostile international geopolitical environment.

No doubt, the race for post-dollar hegemony was set on. How the global economic and financial regime was going to be reshaped was still unclear as of this chapter was written. However, a seismic change would be taking place.[23]

And at the domestic level, would the emergence of a digital currency improve the efficiency, transparency and creditability of industrial and financial chains and make finance really serve the real economy? Or would it open up a new round of speculative frenzy?

From the perspective of rural regeneration, we are more concerned with how to apply blockchain technology to the local community in building a local credit system. It may serve the development of rural endogenous cooperative finance. Unlike the "nobody trusts anybody" ideology, we are interested in how to localize blockchain technology and, hence, facilitate the cooperation and trust among rural communities and citizen-supported agriculture.

The Astronomical Expansion of Debt

The expansion of debt is always concomitant with financialization, as debt and finance are the two faces of the same coin.

At the end of 2000, the total balance of credit in China's financial system was RMB 9.9 trillion. By July 2014, it had grown to 78.02,

---

[22]https://boxmining.com/dcep/.
[23]See: Gustavo Moura, Paulo Natakani & Erebus Wong, "Dollar Hegemony under Challenge and the Rise of Central Bank Digital Currencies (CBDC): a new form of world money?," in *Wealth and Poverty in Contemporary Brazilian Capitalism*. Palgrave Macmillan, 2021.

an increase of 688% meanwhile the nominal GDP growth was merely 473%. The expansion of credit was obviously greater than the growth in real economy.

According to the Institute of International Finance, China's total domestic debt as of the first season of 2020 amounted to 317% of GDP, the highest historical record (Fig. 1).

Top to Bottom: Financial sector debt, government debt, household debt, non financial corporations' debt.

In recent years, China has put much effort in deleveraging its economy. Nevertheless, while the growth of debts in other sectors has stabilized or declined, the growth of household debt has been striking. As of 2019, household debt has amounted to 54.3% of GDP. Personal consumption based on debt is expanding. China is gradually shifting from traditional society with a high savings rate to a consumerist society based on debt.

Corporation debts have comprised the largest portion in the domestic debt stock. Since 2014 with the economic downturn, corporations have

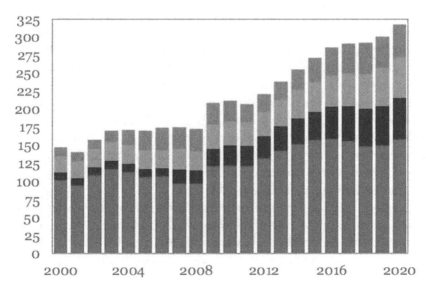

Fig. 1 Debt to GDP (%) in China (as of March 2020) Original graph: MarginalLab

found it increasingly difficult to fulfil their debt services. The numbers of bad default cases became obvious in 2019 ($17 billion in the first eleven months).[24] It was expected that the covid-19 epidemic in 2020 would worsen the situation.

Local government debt is another issue of concern. Due to regional imbalance in economic development, only very few local governments have recorded fiscal surpluses. As of the end of 2019, the total local governmental debts were up to RMB 21.3 trillion, almost two times of general local budgets, not to mention many off-the-books and hidden debts. Many local governments maintain their functions and pay debt services by rolling over loans. China may need new monetary and fiscal mechanisms to tackle the problem of local government debts.

As of the end of 2019, China's foreign debts have amounted to $2.05 trillion while it held $5.5 trillion of foreign outstanding claims, of which over $1 billion was US treasury bonds, which might never be repaid. The rest were mostly owed by developing countries, which became increasingly dubious in repayment as uncertainties in the global economy were mounting.

Of course, debt expansion is not exclusive to China. It is a global phenomenon under the financial capitalism regime. According to a report by the Institute of International Finance, as of March 2018, the total debt in the world (including governments, corporations, households and financial institutions) amounted to US$ 247 trillion, a growth of 43% since 2008 while the GDP growth during the ten years after the crisis was only 37%. Global debt/GDP expanded from 2.9 to 3.2. The new increase in private corporate debt was US$ 28 trillion, two thirds of which was held by Chinese companies. China has functioned as the growth engine of the world. As the economy is slowing down, the burden of debt servicing may become troublesome.

Admittedly, a large part of debts in China is related with infrastructural construction. As long as the national economy keeps growing, they are productive debts. The truly worrying parts are non-productive debts such as mortgage and financial debt seeking virtual profits in speculation.

---

[24]It was still relatively mild considering the total $4.4 trillion on-shore corporation bonds market.

And we should not forget the mother of all debts, the US Federal Reserve Notes known as the dollar. Technically, the USA has been insolvent, especially after the new round of unlimited QE in 2020. The financial orgy goes on with perpetual debt rollover because the USA is still the greatest unchallenged political and military power in the world. The global economy has increasingly become a Ponzi scheme.

The expansion of debt is hanging over the world as well as China like the sword of Damocles. The USA's heavy indebtedness with endless roll-over and even repudiation can only be sustained by its unchallenged hegemony. In comparison, China can only rely on domestic debt expansion. Its mounting internal debt can only be sustained and guaranteed by a centralized system. Here lies the greatest mental confusion. Financial capital and its appendages have long claimed that Chinese institutions should be transited to the western model without acknowledging that western institutions are now built on the increasingly shaky ground of mounting indebtedness, which are not to be emulated by other countries.

Land Issues: Land Finance and the Expansion of Real Estate Sector

For China, land is not a generic issue. As elaborated in previous chapters, land had functioned as the key to resolve crises in different occasions. We may put it in this way: land is the foundation of the political regime in China.

However, since the tax revenues division reform in 1994 (see Chapter 3), many local governments have increasingly relied on land-related revenues as the main source of general fiscal revenues. As seen in the following chart, of 30 major cities in China, over 26 were dependent on land finance (over 50% of fiscal revenues). 12 cities were heavily dependent (over 100%).

Over-dependency on land finance led to problems such as enclosure of arable land, violation of peasants and citizens' right, inefficiency of land use and unreasonable expansion of urban areas etc. Furthermore, it also played a part in the creation of a real estate bubble (Fig. 2).

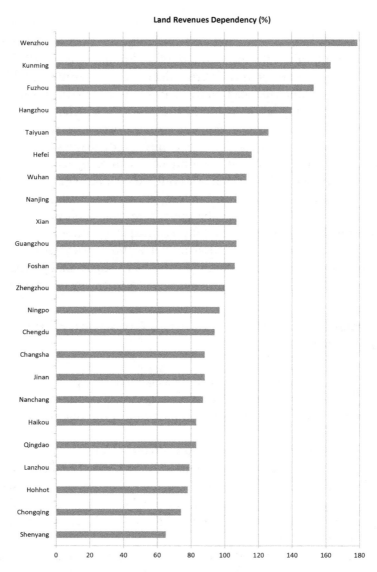

Fig. 2 Local governments land revenues dependency: land revenues/general fiscal revenues X 100%. Original chart: https://finance.sina.com.cn/china/gncj/2020-04-28/doc-iirczymi8742353.shtml. Chart: Land revenues dependency in 30 major Chinese cities, 2019

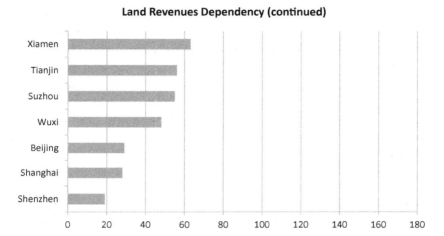

Fig. 2 (continued)

Local Fiscal Budget Deficits

Over dependence on land revenues is a consequence of long-term fiscal difficulties faced by local governments. Fiscal constraint had been a long-term problem for many local governments except some developed provinces and municipalities.[25] The economic lockdown in the early 2020 further worsened the problem. The national fiscal revenues dropped by 21.4% and 26.1% in February and March 2020 year on year, the worst numbers since 2008. The first season recorded a minus 14.3% in fiscal revenues growth, compared with 6% last year. 2020 was the most difficult year for local fiscal budget since the tax division reform in 1994, not to mention the enormous expenditures on epidemic control (RMB 145.2 billion as of 19 April) and general relief (156 billion). The local budget deficits might reach 56% in the first season of 2020.

The authorities responded by an expansion of local infrastructure projects bond, RMB 1160.7 billion as of 15 April with another 1000 billion before the end of May.

---

[25]Only 8 out of 31 provinces and municipalities recorded a revenues/expenditures ratio over 50% in 2019. See: 羅志恒 范城愷 "當前財政形勢分析" (An Analysis of Current Fiscal Situation).

To release local governments from over-relying on land revenues, it is pivotal to reform the taxation system which after all functions as the wealth-redistribution mechanism of a society. Land revenues are usually generated at the expense of transferring rural land resources to the urban sector. Inflationary land prices imply an implicit land tax on lower and middle classes as their costs of living and commerce are also being inflated. China's current taxation system mainly taxes individual income, goods trading (value-added tax) and services. Such a system in fact discourages involvement in the real economy and motivates people to speculate. It results in an unfair burden among classes. According to estimate, the richest class who own over 50% of the total wealth in China have contributed less than 10% of personal income tax while 60% are paid by wage earners. The current practice apparently fails to redistribute wealth among different classes in an equitable manner. A sensible taxation system should keep low tax rates on earned incomes from the real economy, including salary and profits of manufacturing and commerce. It should instead tax non-productive unearned income (rent-seeking) of the *rentier* class and capital gains, such as by property tax or assets-holding tax. Only through conversion of the current pro-speculation tax structure can China prevent its economy from hollowing and orient its society towards wealth redistribution in favour of the lower and middle classes.

Real Estate: The Sisyphus Boulder of the National Economy

Inflationary real estate price has caused a distortion in the Chinese economy.

According to a report by the National Bureau of Statistics, the total value of real estate in 70 major cities China amounted to US$ 65 trillion in 2018, more than the sum of the value in the USA, EU and Japan as a whole. Meanwhile, the value of the Chinese stock markets was merely one tenth of the value of the above big three (Fig. 3).

There was an apparent distortion in Chinese citizens' wealth port-folio structure. According to a survey, the net value of housing property constituted 66.35% of Chinese household wealth in 2017. It was

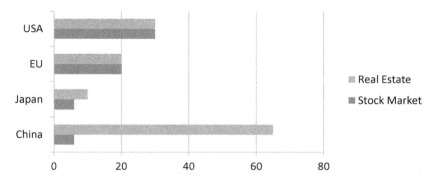

Fig. 3 Stock market and real estate total values 2018 (Unit: US$ trillion)

a worrying trend. Mortgage expenses have sucked household dry of consumption power. The growth of citizen's disposable income lagged behind economic growth. Household savings even started to decline. It is contradictory to China's strategy to stimulate domestic demand as the main growth engine as the export-oriented and infrastructure structure investment-propelled models have exhausted their momentum. Real estate became an unbearable burden on Chinese society and economy. Chinese government got caught in a dilemma. On the one hand, the real estate bubble had to be restrained from growing further; on the other, crash in real estate prices would equally be a serious problem.

The authority expressed its concern. President Xi Jinping has emphasized in 2016 Central Economic Working Meeing the necessity of suppressing real estate bubble, emphasizing that "houses are meant for people's habitation, not for speculation". On the 19th National Congress of the CCP in 2017, he reiterated the principle again.

Last but not least, it is essential and also a challenge to maintain rural land collective ownership intact. As elaborated in previous chapters, collective land ownership can serve as a solid foundation for rural cooperative economy and self governance, which in turn are vital for rural social stability and eventually the stability of Chinese society as a whole. However, in the name of granting peasants full ownership, some policy researchers constantly suggest the privatization of rural land, which might destabilize the economy and eventually shake the foundation of the regime.

Structural Imbalance and Rebalance in Three Aspects

Chinese economy and society has long been characterized by structural imbalance in three aspects: rural-urban divide, income/wealth gap and regional disparity in development. Balancing these three disparities has been the targets of the essential structural adjustment in the last phase of development.

Since the 1998 the central government has consistently been investing into rural development. The rural-urban divide is to a certain extant being narrowed while the rural income in general is rising. However, the gap is still obvious. Of the total population, 330 million enjoy GDP per capita of more than US$25,000, while the other 1.05 billion have less than $4500. The great divide is mostly drawn along the rural-urban disparity.

The income level of the nation as a whole has impressively multiplied in the last four decades. However, the wealth gap is also widening. In 2019, the average disposable annual income is about RMB 30,000. Meanwhile, 610 million people (including non-working persons) on average have a disposable monthly income of merely RMB 1000. Admittedly, a widening wealth disparity is a common phenomenon plaguing the whole world. The global capitalist regime is a highly effective wealth-generating machine. However, it fails disgracefully manner when it comes to ensuring an equitable distribution of wealth, concentrating wealth into an exclusive elite bloc. Undoubtedly, China has successfully eradicated absolute poverty, one of greatest achievements in human history. Nevertheless, the sign of a widening wealth gap is indeed worrying whereas the aim of becoming a moderately well-off society has yet to be achieved in China.

New Infrastructure Building and the Worry of Economic Polarization

Amid the impact of the pandemic, Chinese government launched the New Infrastructure campaign, aspiring to regain economic momentum.

The New Infrastructure was not a response to the crisis. Chinese government first proposed the New Infrastructure Building in December 2018, which was closely related to the "Made in China 2025" initiative. The crisis along with external pressure no doubt drove the country to add a larger stake on the game. "New Infrastructure" projects were focused in cutting-edge areas considered to be decisive in the coming industrial era: 5G networks, industrial internet, data centers, artificial intelligence, ultra-high voltage, and new energy vehicle charging stations. The investment was estimated to be worth about 100 billion yuan. These represented the nation's efforts to upgrade its economic structure when the old export-oriented model had come to an end.

Like the previous two crises, one of the aims of the New Infrastructure building was to create effective domestic demand to keep the economy growing. However, the New Infrastructure was different from the old infrastructure-driven model in an essential way. The new economy related with the new infrastructure was highly capital-intensive and generally labour-exclusive, especially the automation of production and service. Even if it could facilitate the creation of new economic model with new job creation, it does not appear that enough work opportunities might be created for those labours with lesser know-how and education. The new economy model, if not properly and carefully conducted, might further worsen the polarization of China's economic structure and national income and widen the above disparities which had long been troubling China.

The Regional Mega Integration and the Dilemma of Regional Rebalance

As for the third structural imbalance, regional rebalance has long been an important national strategy, as elaborated in previous chapters, with substantial investments into the western and northeast regions since the turn of century. The Belt & Road Initiative has facilitated the relocation of industrial hubs toward the western part from coastal regions. However, as the international geo-political environment becomes increasingly hostile, uncertainty may be cast on the sustainable development of the western regions.

We also saw a spatial shift in China's regional disparity. During the last ten years, north-south disparity has replaced east-west (coastal-hinterland) gap as the main feature of regional disparity. In 2009, the greater northern regions accounted for 43% of the total GDP. However it has dropped to 35% in 2019.[26] In 2009, the northern regional GDP was 176% of the southwest which were traditionally the poorest regions in China. However, the situation was reversed in 2019 when the former's GDP accounted for merely 84% of the latter's.

Furthermore, this disparity is likely to be consolidated as the state pushes forth in recent years regional integration in Yangtze River Delta Zone, Guangdong-Hong Kong-Macao Greater Bay Area and Beijing-Tianjin-Hebei region as the most essential national strategy meanwhile we see so far no major strategic development plan for the northeast. The strategy should be understood against the changing international background in which the trend of reverse globalization, the rise of unilateralism and protectionism and the uncertainty in an increasingly hostile geopolitical environment have posed serious challenges for China. Four decades of China's participation into globalization has come to a turning point. It may be reasonable to focus resources on advanced regions which already hold the advantage. Nevertheless, the decades-long aim of structural rebalance would be confronted with even greater challenge.

Dual Circulation Strategy

The Chinese leadership has proposed in 2020 the new strategy of Dual Circulation, facing enduring weak demand in global market after the ending of QEIII in 2013, rising protectionism and uncertainty in geopolitical surrounding, mainly arising from increasing antagonism by the USA and its allies. Domestic demand is once again staged as the mainstay after 30 years of relying on international trade as the main growth engine. In fact, the weight of export in GDP has declined from 35.4% in 2006 to

---

[26]https://www.huxiu.com/article/341548.html.

17.4% in 2019. In other words, domestic demand has already accounted for 82.6% of the GDP. The strategic adjustment reflects a natural transition in the trend of the tapering of the export-oriented sector. In fact, the authority has given up setting a rigid GDP growth target and instead aims at quality rather than quantitative growth.

However, the Chinese authorities have stressed that it does not imply a closed and isolated domestic market. International cycle (trade) will continue to function as an indispensable supplement to the domestic cycle. Given the massive volume of its economy, China's domestic market would continue to be a major epicentre of global supply chains. The Chinese authorities therefore emphasizes that it will keep its market open to foreign investment. In fact, a significant change in recent years has not only been in the export of manufactured goods but also in industrial standards, such as high speed railway system and 5 G technology. If the current trend of US-China decoupling goes on and even escalates, the global economy may diverge into two or several major supply chains networks, each with its own industrial standards.

Needless to say, the key to the feasibility of the Dual Circulation Strategy is how to develop a healthy and balanced domestic market. It is highly correlated with many of the major problems we have discussed as above. How to boost domestic demand by raising national income level in general? On the one hand, how to raise the 1 billion rural and urban lower class with less than $4500 GDP per capita to a level closer to their 330 million fellow countrymen and women? How to achieve rebalancing in the three aspects, namely the rural-urban divide, wealth gap and regional disparity? How to avoid the widening of regional disparity while concentrating resources in the three leading regional mega zones? On the other hand, how to avoid the consumption power of urban middle-class being increasingly depleted by expenditures in housing and mortgage? How to reform the taxation system to release consumption power? These challenge would require a thorough modification of the economic system.

Of course, the prerequisite of the viability of the Dual Circulation strategy is that the two basically antagonistic international supply chains systems find a way to co-exist in a competitive but relatively peaceful manner without eventually ending up with fatal confrontation.

4   Ecological Civilization: Localization as Alternative to Globalization

Policy Adjustment: Rural Revitalization

China is facing a multi-dimensional crisis with exogenous and endogenous factors. How to deal with the problem of deindustrialization as capital moves into the speculative sector seeking higher profitability? How to prevent deindustrialization from leading to large scale unemployment? How to avoid systematic financial crisis? How to secure the survival of small and medium enterprises and improve their competitiveness? How to convert the over dependency on international trading by promoting domestic demand? How to prevent consumption from being squeezed by real estate and finance at the national level? How to prevent the intensification of class struggle (labour-capital conflict) under such a crisis? The key is to let the majority of the citizens share the fruit of growth in a more equitable way. It requires containing various interest blocs within the polity. Decades of developmentalism has brought about severe ecological degeneration, income disparity, class tensions and moral hazard behaviour. China has to deal with a highly complicated relationship: domestically and internationally, between central and local governments, between finance and the real economy, between the state and society etc.

Since 2017 the government has adjusted its policy by returning to counter-cyclical measures through creating effective demand. Another important policy is to foster an eco-friendly economy as an alternative development strategy. Hence the slogan, "green mountain is gold mountain; clean river is silver river". One of the major strategies of rural vitalization is the valuation of natural resources in villages as well as the "capital-deepening of eco-economy" as ways to resolve the crisis of excess money-supply caused by the trade surplus and the inflow of foreign capital.

In a word, the current moves on the economic front constitute China's proactive effort to steer away from decades of developmentalism in line with the western model of modernization. "Beautiful villages" are conceived to be the carrier of "beautiful China". The national development strategy is gradually adjusted toward inclusive sustainable development which is resource-efficient and eco-friendly. Ecological civilization, rural vitalization, and poverty eradication are among the essential strategies of transformation.

COVID-19 Epidemic as a Strategic Time Window

Although the epidemic was unexpected its impact was in fact not a surprise. This historical juncture of US hostility along with an epidemic outbreak urged people to have a timely and profound reflection on the old development model of over-relying on export-oriented economy, a rough extensive growth model which focused on quantity rather than quality, with risk accumulating. The guiding strategy should not be the "back to business as usual" mindset attempting to sustain the old model and put patches on the fractured global industrial chain. Nearly four decades of practices have proven that the export-oriented model was actually a prolonged overdraft on the eco-system and social reproduction. The price of overdraft would inevitably turn into social conflicts. China should take this chance to really steer the economy and society as a whole toward ecological civilization with the ecologization of industry. Then this crisis would become a chance.

Rural Society as the Condition of Crisis Soft Landing

The urban economy that is comprised of concentrated profit-seeking capital is characterized by risk. In comparison, rural society is based on household and community cooperation, which is an effective means to internalize negative externalities. Whereas the urban economy is driven by economic rationality which often leads to irrational behaviour, the rural community is maintained by what can be considered cooperative rationality. We have proposed that for decades Chinese rural society has served as the buffer to absorb negative externalities generated by the urban economy and as the vehicle for soft-landings to crises. However, in recent years, the foundation of rural society's capability to absorb negative externalities has been eroded. This is due to several reasons. For decades, production factors (labour, capital, land etc.) have been draining out of rural communities. Peasants have become disorganized, therefore rural governance has deteriorated. The rural household economy has become underdeveloped compared with the capital-intensive urban economy.

Developing the cooperative economy is the key to rebuilding a robust rural society, which may once again serve as an antidote to the risk-based and risk-accumulating urban economy. Based on principles and practices of a cooperative economy, peasants can organize themselves, which in turn can consolidate the foundation of rural governance. The localized capitalization of rural resources based on cooperatives may help to shape a strong and healthy domestic demand.

The Valuation of Rural Ecological Resource and Cultural Assets

After a few years of fruitless policy, the central government proposed the strategy of rural vitalization in 2017. The government has adjusted its agrarian policies, which amount to:

1. A diversion from the policy of accelerating urbanization in recent years. Instead it has begun to emphasize the priority of agriculture and the rural.
2. An assertion that rural vitalization is the most creative aspect of China's development in the twenty-first century.
3. An abandonment of the path dependence of quantitative growth and a turn towards eco-friendly (quality) growth and development.

Despite the limited nature of present discourses, the policy-makers have turned their perspective to rural China and once again emphasized the importance of the rural sector. Can it save China again as it did in previous crises? Facing the current crisis, we should remain cautiously optimistic.

New Infrastructure Building Should Steer Toward the *Sannong*

The post-pandemic investment into New Infrastructure should not be a simple expansion on the old infrastructure. Neither should it be over concentrated on the urban sector. The fiscal and financial policy should be favourable to the *sannong* as a way to revitalize the rural sector. The valuation of rural ecological resources and cultural assets based on village collective and cooperative economy could serve to enlarge the national real assets pool. Then China's money supply would no longer have to rely on foreign exchange reserves. Instead, the value of Chinese currency should be pegged against the monetarization of national resources. The reconstitution of monetary sovereignty could lay a solid foundation for financial risk management. So-doing would safeguard the national economy against the probable impact of increasingly serious global financial crisis in a world market flooded with unlimited quantitative policies by advanced countries.

China's current M2/GDP is up to 200%, among the highest level in the world. However, we should not simply conclude from this that Chinese economy is shaky due to money oversupply. Compared with other advanced economies, China is characterized by a feature: many assets in rural regions have not yet been valued and priced, or their value remains implicit. Capital in the urban sectors is currently in excess and seeking the opportunity for the capitalization of resources. For this reason, the trend of capital flowing into the rural sector seems to be irreversible. Viewed another way, it may be a chance to reverse the decades-long draining of production factors (labour, capital and land) from the rural sector. The problem becomes how to avoid malicious and destructive enclosure of rural resources by capital and finance. The formation of cooperatives becomes a key element in this process. Supported by the national strategy of ecological civilization and rural vitalization, rural community cooperatives can become effective agents in the valuation of ecological and cultural assets. Through appropriate institutional innovations, a part of the property rights can become exchangeable assets on a well-designed special market, while the fundamental ownership of vital resources like land remains with the community cooperative. This may attract capital flowing into the rural sector in a healthy and constructive way. Factors like labour, capital, technology and land may contribute to localized rural vitalization. The fiscal pressure of eco-infrastructure and rural construction can be partly relieved through this form of financing at the same time that excess liquidity in the urban sector can be channelled into the rural sector. This can promote peasant income growth while preventing the formation of financial bubbles in the national economy. Income increment can serve as a foundation for economic reproduction, the provision of public services for rural communities, the protection of ecology and the improvement of rural governance.

To achieve this, the state must stick to the principle of inclusive finance. The central government must make good use of its monopolized financial sector to establish financial mechanisms below county level to serve the new rural reconstruction. Finance must not only seek the maximization of profits. State-run finance especially has to fulfil its policy-oriented functions to stabilize rural society, create job opportunities in rural regions and promote community welfare.

As long as institutional arrangements and innovation are appropriate, the valuation of implicit cultural and ecological assets can easily absorb the money stock which, otherwise, will turn into excessive liquidity leading to financial bubbles.

From Globalization to Localization: Rural Vitalization

In the post-globalization world, China is facing both industrial over-capacity and capital oversupply. Chinese political and economic elites therefore feel compelled to expand their presence in the world. However, the world has changed. After decades of globalization and neoliberalism, worldwide social reactions (Polanyi's double movement) have raised vociferous and strong protest against their progress. Ecological degeneration and climate catastrophe have signalled the limit of the prevalent growth model. Even if these Chinese elites emphasize that China is merely seeking equal and bilateral cooperation for development opportunity, the unipolar power, which has remained unchallenged for nearly 30 years and indulging in the ingrained Thucydides trap, naturally regards it as a challenge to its hegemony. Every move by a big country like China will be taken as a transgression against the presence of the dominant geopolitical power. Advancing with an expansionist strategy in the post globalization age, China has to face vicious competition and even a new cold war. Admittedly, the alternative option is not isolationism or autarky. However, an indispensible and more intelligent strategy would be to re-emphasize domestic economic circulation by ameliorating the gap between the urban and the rural, the rich and the poor, different regions, and different sectors. The external circulation (international trade) would serve as a complement to the internal one.

If China persists with the strategy of rural vitalization, determined to pursue the path of ecological civilization, its heretofore capacity to deal with global crises might still remain intact.

Conclusion: Ecological Civilization as New Paradigm for Developing Countries

The once-shining so called 'emerging economies' (so dubbed ideologically) are still struggling to keep their footing after the post-2008 shock. Except for China which is still not recognized as full market economy, most of them are plagued to a certain extent by industrial degeneration. Some have even retrograded to pre-modern mode of resources export.

Most of the developing countries in the last 100 years have been pursuing modernization according to the western model and pushing developmentalism. However, at the end of the day, many of them found themselves ensnarled in the development trap. The reason may be attributed to the irreplicability of the western development path: colonization. (On the side of the West, it becomes a sort of path dependence.)

China is a late developing, populous 'continental economy'. Colonization was never an option. Hence it went through a path different from the West. By the extraction of surplus from the *sannong* as evaluated in previous chapters, China accomplished the primitive accumulation needed for industrialization and the subsequent expansion. However, China has to convert to an inclusive growth oriented towards ecological civilization if it wants to sustain development in the 'race to the bottom' global competition plagued by the cost transfer of financial capitalism.

The Institutional Experience of China's Late-Developing Introvert Industrialization

Unlike the West which developed by colonial plundering overseas during the fifteenth to early twentieth centuries and then transferred the cost of economic upgrading through global regime after the WWII, China achieved industrialization through introvert primitive accumulation in two ways: (1) extracting the surplus value of labours of the whole nation through highly collectivized social organization and the agricultural surplus through the price scissors between industrial and agricultural products; (2) investment of large-scale labour force into state infrastructure building. In the second, labour force resource was capitalized as a substitute for capital scarcity. This whole nation mobilization system afforded China with the capacity to accomplish the 'alarmingly dangerous saltation' of primitive accumulation for industrialization without compromising national sovereignty. However, the enormous institutional cost of this untypical development growth had to be carried by all citizens (and often unevenly).

The government corporatism with Chinese characteristics that took shape in the above process became 'path dependence' in later institutional transitions. Out of responses to crises known as reforms, a 'government-corporate market economy' emerged. This centralized system is much criticized for its monopoly by the state-run sector. Nevertheless, one should not neglect the fact that China manages to sustain a relatively complete and intact industrial structure because of this government corporatism.

From an institutional-cultural point of view, two effective mechanisms took shape in China's modern state-building. First, it made use of the historical legacy of collective and cooperative culture to dissolve the serious externalities of market economy through internalizing the cost into community cooperation. Second, rural households dealt with the

problem of capital scarcity by a non-monetized 'intensive labour investment portfolio' intrinsic to the millennial-year old peasant economy. We
believe these two mechanisms helped China to accomplish industrialization not achievable by many third world developing countries emulating
western institutions.

Ecological Civilization and Sustainable Inclusive Growth

Rural society as the carrier of soft-landing in various crises has experienced fundamental changes in the last two decades. Large scale migration
of young labour force out of villages renders the rural an aged society.
Most of the capital gains of rural labour force are taken by internal
and external capital as well as developed regions. Collective culture as
the foundation of rural society is disintegrating. As a result, the basic
condition of 'risk-internalizing mechanism' (sustaining gains through self
capitalization of household labour force and resources) based on peasant
household rationality[27] is also diminishing.

After 20 years of one-sided pro-capital mentality, the Chinese leadership switched to a pro-people well being policy orientation after 2003.
New Rural Reconstruction was put forward in 2005 as national strategy.
Then the idea of Ecological Civilization was introduced in 2007. A
year later, the goal of building a 'resource-conserving and environment-
friendly agriculture' was set up. Since 2005, over 8 trillion yuan (about
US$ 1.2 trillion) has been invested into rural development. Such a scale
of infrastructure investment into rural regions regardless of short-term
returns is unprecedented in the world including developed countries.
The effect is quite remarkable. Most of the villages in China now have
access to paved roads, piped water, electricity, communication and broad-
band internet. The business cost of rural small and medium enterprises
is significantly reduced. Diversified non-agricultural economy is spared

---

[27]Peasant household rationality as a sort of cooperative rationality is contrast to individualistic
rationality emphasized by modern economics. It is non-individualistic cooperation for the sake
of the benefit of the whole.

with the room to develop in villages, attracting labourers moving back to rural regions.

Nevertheless, local governments, by path dependence of government corporatism, cling to the developmentalist 'high investment—high debt—high GDP' model. Rural regions are still confronted with the problem of resource drainage and ecological unsustainability. The crux lies at whether it is possible to create an institutional condition to faithfully implement the strategic adjustments by the central government.

To build an ecological civilization, the first step is to abandon the GDP-supremacy mentality. Economy must be re-embedded into society and society into ecology. The idea of ecological civilization is a response to the social and cultural crisis of post industrial civilization. It calls forth a paradigm change in civilization. After all, the development of civilization is ultimately over-determined by ecology. The idea must question the development of capitalism in the last five centuries. It is high time we ponder upon our relationship with the nature, with society, with others, with ourselves, which are being shaped by capitalism (and worse still financial capitalism). If our existence is embedded into ecology, then we must hold nature in awe and constantly remind ourselves that nature is an end in itself rather than a means to other purposes, such as economic growth.

China is one of the very few civilizations that have evolved without break for a few thousand years. Its struggle to achieve modernization in the last 150 years is a tragic and heroic saga, a part of which this book attempts to illuminate. After all the pains and efforts, the revelation of the lesson is the idea of ecological civilization which questions morbid modernization we are still entrapped in. China's experiences in the last 70 years may be valuable not only to developing countries but also to the whole world.

7

Chronicle of Major Events 1949 to 2020

1949   **Land Revolution and 'Three Supplies-based Vehicles' to Alleviate Protracted Inflation**

The land revolution of "equal distribution" agrarian system embodied the fundamental demand of traditional peasants for the past several millennia. The war spurred the mobilization of the largest peasant population in the world to participate in the state-building. The hyperinflation that had started in 1937 during the Republic of China era was still a major problem. Yet with the revival of traditional peasant communities, not only were the peasants that accounted for 88% of the total population able to 'de-link' from the urban capital economy, it also enabled the state to establish an independent, autonomous financial system by anchoring the sovereign currency to those agricultural commodities that livelihoods depended on. That in essence rectified the error of the former regime, which gave up the monetary sovereignty and pegged the Gold Yuan against U.S. Dollar, thereby ushering in hyperinflation.

What it meant in practice was that, the new government, through measures such as "supplies-based savings", "supplies-based wages" and

Wen Tiejun, *Ten Crises*, Global University for Sustainability Book Series,
https://doi.org/10.1007/978-981-16-0455-3_7

"supplies-based public bonds", pegged the Renminbi to essential agricultural commodities like grain and cotton, and thus finally alleviated the two main predicaments that China had faced for over a century—hunger and inflation. However, the problem that the 'equal distribution' land reform had left behind was that the hundreds of millions of scattered and multi-occupational peasants became contradictory with the primitive accumulation of capital needed for urban industrialization.

In December 1949, Mao Zedong visited the U.S.S.R. by train to negotiate with Stalin over the return of Lushun harbor and the Changchun-Dalian Railway, as well as loans and aids from the U.S.S.R. In February the following year an agreement was signed.

1950   Korean War Broke Out; China Received Soviet Aids and Investments in Military Industries; The "*Sanfan*" and "*Wufan*" Movements

North Korea had completed land reform yet the South was against it, giving rise to domestic confrontations that turned into war on the Korean Peninsula. China participated in the war by sending "voluntary combatants", and therefore became included in the Soviet geo-political strategic regime. It also led China's urban industries out of the crisis and entered into wartime economy. The first wave of "state industrialization" was brought on, with the focus on the military sector, driven by foreign capital from the Soviet Union. The "*sanfan*" ("Three-Antis") and "*wufan*" ("Five-Antis") movements were launched nationwide to put a curb on the capitalism's primal drive of primitive accumulation. Back then the Chinese had not realized that foreign capital would inevitably transform into sovereign debts and lead to budget deficit crises. Because of that it was inevitable that as a rule emerging countries in general would fall into the development trap.

The most significant change that happened in the West after the WWII was that the previous situation of multi-polar powers contesting one another turned into a confrontational duopoly. MaCarthyism was prevalent in the USA. Since then, the world entered into the Cold War in which the U.S.A. and the Soviet Union competed for geo-political domination. It gave rise to the "wild goose formation" model of outward industrial capital transfer by the two superpowers—the USSR giving aids to industrial projects in China and Eastern Europe while the U.S. launching post-war aids and recovery plans to Western Europe and Japan. The manoeuvres of the superpowers were almost identical in form.

1951 The Chinese State Appealed to Twenty Million Peasants to Support Urban Industrialization; First PRC Five-Year Plan Drawn; Japan Started Nuclear Power Technology

The state industrialization model formed mainly on the basis of the imported facilities from the USSR had innately concentrated around military and heavy industries, capital-intensive while excluding labor. Although over ten of millions of young peasants had been mobilized by the state to go to cities in support of industrialization, what they were engaged in were labor intensive urban infrastructure projects—drainage, power lines, roads and land levelling that required "simple labor work". As a result, the demand for food grain in cities suddenly surged.

The first five-year plan was under preparation.

Due to strict geopolitical control by the U.S. over oil supply channels on the one hand, and the industrial revival because of the Korean War on the other, Japan was able to initiate the development of nuclear power and related technology. Yet it also foreshadowed the Fukushima nuclear crisis sixty years later.

1952 The State Planning Committee Officially Established; Land Reform Completed

The first five-year plan was launched under the guidance of Soviet experts. The small planning commission originally established in the Northeast Bureau to facilitate war-time investments from the Soviet military was brought to Beijing and became the "State Planning Committee".

The land reform was completed countrywide. A rudimentary form of cooperatives emerged in many rural areas with peasant households forming mutual-aid teams, sharing plowing equipment, cattle and even labor.

1953   The "General Line" Proposed; Korean War Truce; Stalin Passed Away

With the large-scale increase of Soviet foreign capital as well as the change in loan arrangements—from ten year loans to bartering trade, the 'Stalin model' remained prevalent in China and manifested as the 'path dependence' of state industrialization constrained by geo-politics—**the 'General Line of the Socialist Transition Period' completely replaced the 'New Democracy'. In essence, it was the transformation of private capital to state capital which held total control over important resources in the entire society.**

1954   The Cooperativization Movement and De-monetization

The state had difficulty in implementing the policy of 'unified purchase and distribution' of agricultural produce due to the geographically and economically scattered conditions of the four hundred million peasants. Mao Zedong's solution was to launch cooperativization. The four hundred million peasants were organized into four million elementary cooperatives in support of unified purchase and distribution by the State commercial capital. However, during this period the premise for increased deployment of industrial goods to the countryside had been a shrinkage of the industrial and agricultural 'price scissors'.

In East Asian region, in which the equal distribution of arable land was likewise completed and the peasant economy revived, rural co-op movements including unified purchase and distribution were promoted under different labels in different political institutions. Following that, the Japanese Liberal Democratic Party (LDP) came on stage. The Japan Agricultural Co-operatives (JA), similar in form to the Advanced Cooperatives in China yet completely opposite in terms of right entitlements, became the long-term strong supporter for the LDP.

1955   Two Important Meetings and Two Important Events

Two historic meetings took place this year:

First was the 20th Congress of the Soviet Communist Party during which Khrushchev denounced Stalin in a secret report. It meant that the Soviet Union entered into the phase of industrial capital expansion and exchange with the outside, having to articulate its economy with the markets in the west.

Second was the Bandung Conference in Indonesia during which China strategically joined the 'non-aligned movement' as its first endeavor to break the stranglehold of post-WWII geo-political control by the two world's superpowers, the U.S.A. and the USSR.

Two major events happened this year relevant to China's transformation: first, on 25 May the Soviet Union, on the basis of strategic interest, withdrew the troops stationed in Lushun Harbor. China thenceforth realized the hundred-year long dream of resuming an intact sovereignty; second, on 21 June, the U.S. State Department published the full content of Khrushchev's secret report, including Khrushchev's censure against the Chinese Communist Party. It foreshadowed the divergence between the two communist parties as well as the USSR's subsequent withdrawal of investments from China.

In December, Mao Zedong convened and presided over a meeting with the 34 heads of all ministries and commissions to discuss China's inclination towards 'across-the-board Sovietization'.

1956 'Agriculture Modernization' and Private Capital Reform in Service of the State Capital

The central government, in answer to the pressing request from the urban industrial sectors of selling heavy industrial products to rural regions, put forward the policy of 'agriculture modernization'. Its essence was to move forward the 'collectivization and mechanization' simultaneously. The advanced cooperatives with county as the unit were established to realize unified land operation scale of over a thousand hectares. Tractor stations and factories for repairing farming equipment were built to facilitate agricultural mechanization. In doing so, it realized the exchange between two major sectors, the industry and the agriculture, with price scissors embedded.

During the same period, the state capital completed the transformation of private capital. The high growth in state industrialization demonstrated the achievement of primitive accumulation of capital over a short period. Yet the concentration of industrial capital in urban sector also meant an intensification of risks. The potential for crisis was also being incubated as a rule during the process.

1957 "Second Five-Year Plan" Ended Half Way; "Anti-Right Movement"

By having the sovereign state take on an 'unlimited liability' of foreign debts, China was able to amass large scale foreign investment to drive a high-speed growth of state industrialization. Yet because of that an 'institution inertia' was quickly formed in the super-structure (ideology) constructed by the completely Sovietized sectors of the party, the government and the army. It was also the root cause of the incessant political movements in China.

The contradiction between China and the USSR with respect to sovereignty and ideology led to the cessation of the Soviet investments. The entire investment in the form of external aids that was previously anticipated in the second five-year plan abruptly ended. The central government's fiscal capacity dropped rapidly relative to that of the local governments. The situation was ominous of crises as opinions varied. Many people were denounced as "rightists". **However, many of their words and actions were in fact to oppose the exploitation of peasants and workers, the bureaucratism and dogmatism of the 'completely Sovietized' cadres.**

1958 The 'Great Leap Forward' to Muster Regional Initiative; Rural Communes were Set Up to Serve the State Industrialization

In the Zhengzhou meeting in January, the central government put forward the policy to muster "local initiative". On one side local investments were mobilized to continue with the state industrialization, filling the on-going demand of investment by industrial capital. A large number of industrial projects were completed and put into production. On the other side, multi-functional and integrated People's Communes were set up to utilize labor as a substitute for capital, transforming the development mode that had relied on foreign capital. The main reason for this had been the cessation of Soviet aids to the second five-year plan period, making it impossible for the central government's fiscal capacity to sustain the state industrialization. Yet in less than one year, in the third Zhengzhou meeting in November, the central government had to rectify the "local industrialization" process wherein various radical errors were committed due to inexperience, such as the "Great Leap Forward", the "Great Steelmaking ", as well as the "People's Communes Great Canteens". The essence of the problem was that the regional governments, suddenly gaining the opportunity of primitive accumulation of capital, forced the limited resources into crude and extensive 'capitalization' within a short span of time.

1959   High Economic Growth Turned into Deficit Crisis

The USSR reduced its financial aids and experts to China. The two major communist parties diverged. For a 'continental power' like the USSR, it meant losing one flank of the 'flying goose formation' strategy. The USSR failed to realize a successful geopolitical strategic control on two wings unlike the way the United States had made successful industrial and capital transfer to Western Europe and Japan, thereby securing its geo-strategic stronghold. It foreshadowed the USSR's defeat by the U.S. thirty years later. With regard to China, an economy in the process of primitive accumulation of industrial capital, it implied crisis—the first round of industrialization driven by foreign capital after 1949 was all of a sudden confronted with the situation of capital scarcity. The state's fiscal capacity dried up and it had to use up every last resource in the country to sustain the investments into the capital-intensive industrialization. The cost for this in the form of a deficit crisis began to emerge.

1960 The Cost of Urban Capital Crisis Transferred to the "*Sannong*"

The cost of primitive accumulation in the 1950s, first by the national capital and later the state capital, resulted in a major crisis—the various tiers of local and regional governments, in order to push ahead with the industrialization, had accumulated an enormous fiscal deficit which made it impossible for the state industrialization in large cities to continue. As a result, the central government launched the first "go up to mountains and go down to villages" movement to mobilize the urban unemployed youths, relying on the collectivized rural sector to take up more than 10 million of surplus urban laborers.

The government began to repay the debts to the USSR. Even though during the same period successive natural disasters resulted in a shortage of agricultural produce, the debt repayments were still being made, mostly with agricultural produces, safeguarding the fruits of China's industrial establishment.

1961 Policy Adjustments during the Economic Depression

The enormous costs of primitive accumulation of capital during the industrialization in the 1950s fully unfolded in this year. Although the key leaders did not yet transcend ideologies to have reflections on the crisis and depression, they already had policy adjustment in response to the crisis. An array of measures dealing with the difficulties brought on by natural disasters in the past 3 years, including household self-use plots, limited free market, self-finance and household contract, were debated at the "assembly of seven thousand" [*over seven thousand participants from central and regional governments at various levels, as well as the leaders of key enterprises*] convened by the Central Committee. In addition, the central government took back part of the fiscal power previously conceded to the regional governments, a move obliged by the urgent need of coordinating relief efforts around the country.

1962 Domestic Economy Recovered; Surrounding Geo-political Situations Worsened

The policy adjustments—the central government taking back part of the fiscal power and the revival of the peasant community system—took effect and the economy started to recover. Yet during this time China came under a complete blockade by both of the two superpowers through their geo-political control. The surrounding situations worsened in a "ring form". For example, the disagreements between China and the Soviet Union led to an across the board hostility between the two countries—military conflicts broke out along the borders between China and India; the West intervened into the regional wars in South East Asia; the Chiang Kai-Shek regime in Taiwan took actions on the 'counterattacks to the Mainland'; U.S. war planes and battleships intruded into China's territorial air space and territorial water for hundreds of times.

1963 The "Third Five-year Plan" Aborted; The "Four Modernizations" Proposed

Although the third five-year plan was ready, a plan that aimed at adjusting the weights between agriculture, light industry and heavy industry in accordance with the framework of a planned economy, it had to be aborted at the cradle due to the total blockade and the surrounding military threats. The focus was turned towards military construction instead. The State Planning Committee was therefore replaced by the 'small' planning committee that targeted on military infrastructure. At the same time, during the National People's Congress and the National Political Consultative Conference the central leadership announced the grand mission of "four modernizations" [the *modernization of industry, agriculture, defense and science-technology*].

1964 Three Lines Construction Launched; The State Industrialization Costs Abruptly Surged

Given the extreme tension in the geo-political situation, the national industries were forced to undertake a 'spatial translocation' from coastal regions and urban centers to inland mountainous regions, geographically scattered for more effective defense. However, not only was it unable to create added-value, the costs of state industrialization greatly increased. Adding to the debt repayments, both domestic and external, the military expenditure foreshadowed the second fiscal deficit crisis in China.

1966 The "Cultural Revolution" Broke Out; Decline of Urban Industries

Li Xiannian announced that China would no longer have foreign debts—in a matter of five years all the debts owed to the USSR were fully repaid, including the military expenses for the Korean War.

The Soviet superstructure by nature did not suit China's approach of mobilizing the masses to rebuild the economic foundations. That intrinsic contradiction which had been protracted—in ideological terminology of the party it was frequently referred to as the 'line struggles'—finally resulted in an eruption, in the form of the "Cultural Revolution" in cities. Because of that the urban industries controlled by the state monopoly capital came to a halt.

1967 Fiscal Deficit Mounting; Urban Industrial Crisis being Incubated

The 'three lines construction' as well as the military industry (including the research and development of nuclear weapons) had taken up a large amount of resources. The investments in urban industrialization declined and led to serious under-employment. When cities became engaged in the 'Cultural Revolution' the government turned its investments towards rural infrastructure such as irrigation, mobilizing the peasants to contribute their labor force at a large scale as a substitute to the capital in scarcity. That was the background of the campaign the 'Emulating Daizhai on Agriculture'. [Daizhai was a production brigade under Daizhai Commune in Shanxi Province.] After that, given the expansion of arable land, the grain production also increased.

For the first time China had industrial exports in the form of aids—the government signed agreements with Tanzania and Zambia to build a railway that would connect the two countries.

1968 Economic Crisis Broke out in China, Costs Again Transferred to the *Sannong*

Foreign debts repayment, three lines construction investments and military expenditure exhausted available finances. The remaining fiscal capacity was insufficient to develop the production of consumable goods in response to the needs of the people. The outcome was an accumulated deficit crisis. The second wave of 'go up to the mountains and down to the villages' movement was initiated to relieve the cities of millions of surplus labor. The urban crisis again ended with 'soft landing'.

1969 Zhou Enlai Announced the Pay-off of Domestic and External Debts; China Became a Model of 'De-linking' for the Third World

Military regimes appeared in the emerging countries supported by the U.S., in accordance with the latter's geo-political strategy. Struggles erupted one after another in the third world countries in defense of national sovereignty. Mao Zedong thought which transcended geo-political controls of the two superpowers became prevalent. Certain European countries which did not side with either of the two superpowers began to establish diplomatic relations with China. France was an example.

In light of the border conflicts between China and the USSR, the latter contemplated and proposed a limited nuclear attack on China but it was rejected by the U.S.A. Zhou Enlai arranged an analysis of the international situation by four veteran generals Chen Yi, Ye Jianying, Nie Rongzhen and Xu Xiangqian. Their conclusion was that China would not face a major war in the next twenty years. That conclusion differed from that of the military mainstream, and greatly impacted Mao Zedong's decision to relieve the tension in the relationship with U.S.A. and to readjust the domestic economic structure.

1971   A Year of Major Significance to China and the World: Disintegration of the Bretton Woods System and China's Ping Pong Diplomacy

The Bretton Woods System that was established in 1944, with U.S. Dollar pegged to gold and thereby facilitating the dominance of the Dollar as the major reserve currency in the world, was unilaterally repealed by the United States. Taking the advantage of acting as the *de facto* "Central Bank of the Western World", the USA was able to appropriate profits from its monetization and became the first to enter the financial capitalism phase. The new era of western geo-monetary strategy dominated by "political finance" began.

After many preparations and efforts, Mao Zedong met with Henry Kissinger. The United States lifted the blockade against China six months before Richard Nixon visited China.

1972   Zhou Enlai Proposed the "43" Plan to Bring in Foreign Investment; Mao Zedong Assented to it

The alleviation of the tension between China and the West led to enormous changes in the international situation. Mao Zedong assented to the "43 plan" [US$ 4.3 Billion] proposed by Zhou Enlai to import industrial facilities from the West. The plan was to make use of western capital to reconstruct the existing industrial structure that had been built with the Soviet investments and weighted toward the heavy industry and the military sector. That inevitably led to changes in the superstructure, including the management system. Subsequently, the leadership followed in that direction and turned 'from Sovietization to Westernization'. In the same year, the United States started to record constant trade deficits.

1973   The Fourth Middle East War Broke Out, Leading to Global Energy Crisis

With the fourth Middle East War, the oil price surged, cumulating in a global energy crisis. The U.S.A. led the signing of the "Jamaica Agreement". Oil exporting countries amassed a large amount of USD with the oil price surge. The value of the Dollar became in effect backed up by oil. No longer pegged to gold, the dollar entered the 'oil standard' era.

1974 Fiscal Deficit Crisis in China; The Costs Still Transferred to the *Sannong*

With the increasingly ambitious effort to import western equipments and invest in domestic ancillary facilities, China's fiscal deficit sharply rose and soon exceeded 10 billion yuan. The central government was obliged to rectify the process. The decision of launching another "go up to the mountains and down to the villages" campaign was made. That was the last attempt of this kind of campaign, with over 10 million of surplus urban labor being sent to the rural collectives.

The abnormal weather in two successive years resulted in worldwide grain production shortage. Along with the USSR's moves to buy up a large quantity of cereals, a global food crisis emerged. Furthermore, the oil crisis had caused a serious economic crisis among western countries given their reliance on energy consumption for their physical economy. Consequently, the western countries intensified thier industrial transfer outward.

The United States cut its loan aids to Latin America.

1975 Fiscal Deficit Crisis Continued; Budget Deficits Exceeded 10 Billion Yuan Consecutively

What happened during 1972–74 was similar to the case of introducing industrial facilites on a large scale from the USSR during 1950–1960, which gave rise to heavy debts, the budget deficit crisis, as well as consequently a series of 'political struggles' in the superstructure, whereas the economic contradictions were expressed in ideological terms. Now, foreign industrial facilities were again introduced on a large scale, but this time from the West. The results were once again high indebtedness and a deficit crisis. It also led to political movements—the 'denouncement of Lin Biao and Confucius' [Confucianism was regarded as reactionary and Lin Biao was accused of advocating it] and the denouncement of

Deng Xiaoping, as a response to the so-called "wave of rightist attempt to reverse the historical verdict".

1976   Earthquake in Tangshan; Zhou Enlai and Mao Zedong Passed Away

The arrest of Political Bureau members like Jiang Qing after the death of Mao Zedong became the focal point of politics. Since then, major leaders Deng Xiaoping, Hua Guofeng, Li Xiannian and others followed Mao Zedong's policy of "using foreign capital to reconstruct domestic industrial structure". A more ambitious plan (the "82" plan) was put forward to bring in US$ 8.2 billion of foreign capital. At one point, Deng had even proposed a scale of US$ 50 billion. The National Planning Committee members discussed the management system reform in Jiangsu province, which had earned the largest amount of foreign exchange among other regions. In view of the need for debt repayments, the state consented to piloting Jiangsu piloting the fiscal system reform, whereby a fixed proportion of fiscal revenue would be retained by the province, to be spent on the provincial needs on an autonomous and self-financing basis, similar to the concession in 1958. Following that, the local industrialization including the 'commune brigade' industries was re-vitalized.

1977   The '82' Plan and the 'Foreign Leap Forward' Facilitated High Growth; Fiscal Deficit Exceeded 10 Billion Yuan Again

The central collective leadership proposed the '82' plan to bring in USD 8.2 billion of western industrial facilities. The oil sector was requested to strive towards building a dozen or more oilfields like Daqing oilfield. These over-ambitious practices were later denounced as the 'foreign leap forward'. Large scale of investments through foreign loans as well as supplementary domestic investments drove a high growth. Yet the mounting deficits were also incubating another crisis.

1978 China on the Brink of Economic Collapse; "Educated Youths Returning to the Cities"

A large scale of foreign capital was brought in through loans towards the end of 1978. Contracts worth more than US\$ 2 billion were signed within the last 20 days of the year alone. Along with the expansion of imported western production facilities over a short span, the foreign exchange reserve recorded a severe deficit. Therefore, the export sector was prioritized in order to bring in more foreign exchange. At the end of the year, Hu Yaobang already foresaw in a conference that China was in face of a crisis. The Chinese economy was on the brink of collapse while the conduct issues of the party members reached a critical moment. However, the root of the problem was blamed on the Cultural Revolution instigated by the former leader.

1979 Another Fiscal Deficit Crisis Broke out; The Budget Deficit of the Year Equaled the Total of the 1950s

During the 1970s, China's industrial structure was in a process of adjustment. The "growth through debts" approach became a "path dependence". In addition with the military expenditures, the total budget deficit for this year amounted to almost 20 billion yuan. The crisis led to further changes in the export trading system. China committed itself to uplifting all the constraints over the inflow of foreign capital. Any projects that were beneficial to foreign debt repayments would be approved. Any practices commonly adopted around the world would be adopted by China. At the same time, the dual-price system reform was initiated—allowing both monopolistic pricing and market pricing on the same commodities.

1980 Rural Collectivization Approached Disintegration; Macroeconomic Adjustments to deal with the 'Hard Landing' of Urban Crisis Labelled as the "Reform"

Rural China had contributed too much surplus to the national industrialization over the past 30 years. In addition, the budget deficits forced the central government to cut financial support to the rural sector, implying the government's withdrawal from the agricultural sector which was the least profitable. The reform which in essence was the state offloading fiscal part of its fiscal burden started with agriculture.

Nevertheless, because of the disintegration of rural collectivization, the state lost the vehicles to readily transfer the institutional costs of this crisis—the most severe urban economic crisis in thirty years—to the rural sector. That was precisely the reason the peasants could finally have the breathing room to recuperate.

1981 "Youths Waiting for Employment" and "Two Crack-downs" amidst the Depression

The urban economic crisis had a hard landing in the cities. Many state-owned enterprises were closing down or merged. Some production lines stopped operation. The situation led to large scale unemployment—about 40 million surplus labor, referred to as the "youths waiting for employment", stayed idle in the cities. Crimes and delinquency became serious in the society. The government then launched strict 'crack-down' movements on criminal offences and economic crimes.

The China-U.S. relationship entered a honeymoon period. The UK and the United States worked hand in hand to foster financial deregulation and liberalization. The traditional geo-political strategy associated with the industrial capitalism in the West transformed towards a new phase of the 'geo-monetary-political' strategy of financial capitalism.

1982 Reform in China: "Offloading Fiscal Burden" and the Rural "Household Contracts"

Under the pressure of serious budget deficit, the central government put forward an array of reform policies that embodied the off-loading part of its fiscal obligation. On another front, the first State Council "Document Number One" was issued to permit the rural household contracts, an approach that allocated land to rural households by headcount, similar to the land reform of 1950. Since then, the "Documents Number One" issued in five consecutive years were packed with wordings of "approval" and "permission", expressing the state capital's concession to the peasant economy reverting to its traditional form. The essential agricultural production factors were effectively returned to the peasant households and the rural communities. A small number of production brigades and communes remained unchanged, not adopting the policy of household contract or giving up the practice after a brief attempt.

1983 The Government Alleviated the Urban Crisis by the "Workplace Unit" System

Obliged by the need to maintain stability, the government requested the state-owned enterprises to provide employment—"ten people sharing the pay of five"—and to establish other business units to employ more people, including the cadres' children. The outcome was the emergence of the early 'bureaucratic profiteering' companies making use of the dual-pricing mechanism to reap abnormal profits. However, it also disrupted from the inside the market order since the price reform.

1984 Three Major Fiscal System Reforms; Rural Regions Setting up New Superstructure; Local Re-industrialization Emerged as an Unexpected Force of Introvert Primitive Accumulation

After the collapse of the People's Commune system, there was no financial capability in rural regions to maintain the superstructure. Therefore, the government had to retreat further from the agricultural sector. Various rural official institutions were almost entirely closed down. The financial units such as the credit cooperatives, the supply/distribution cooperatives, the Grain Bureau and so on all recorded financial losses, which directly became bad loans in the agricultural finance sector. During the same period, the policy of dividing fiscal authority between the central and local governments was put in place. That led to the re-industrialization of rural regions as well as a surge of business enterprises in counties and towns, under the condition of a lack of relevant rural institutional regulations. That in turn resulted in the first wave of large scale land enclosure. The super land rent directly became the income of rural enterprises.

The State Council decided to open fourteen coastal cities. China had just emerged from the previous foreign debt crisis and almost immediately went into a new one due to the competition among local governments to bring in foreign investments. Hence the focus of the Opening Up shifted—now "the key was to promote exports in order to earn foreign exchange".

1985   Plaza Accord Driving Up Yen; China Affirmed the Strategy of Prioritizing the Prosperity and Development in Certain Regions

The western countries had joined forces in pushing Japan to accept the Plaza Accord—the exchange rate of Yen against the Dollar was doubled. As a result, Japan's low-end, labor-intensive manufacturing lost competitiveness and were transferred out at an accelerated pace. At the same time, a conference was convened in Lanzhou, referred to as the 'Western Conference' stressing the 'gradient theory', which was to allow the coastal regions and certain regions to have priority for development and prosperity. The coastal regions were to be the first to start the opening up process. The processing industry and trading brought in production lines by foreign capital. The domestic up-stream equipment manufacturing was therefore squeezed out of the market.

1986   China Accelerated the Reform and Opening Up to Promote Coastal Economic Growth; Rampant Profiteering, Hoarding and Corruption by Bureaucrat-related Businesses

High economic growth rate led to economic and social tension—inflation was met with ineffective regulation. The on-going high inflation gave rise to negative interest rates and the state-owned banks generally became engaged in rent-seeking. Furthermore, the hoarding by the profiteering corporations that were associated with government officials disrupted the market pricing system even more. Corruption was rampant and public resentment was seething. Nevertheless during that same time the rural enterprises were booming. The differential between rural and urban incomes was reduced to a historic low.

1987 Media Attributed High Growth to Reform which was Built upon High Foreign Debt

The "mega plan" regarding price and tax reforms was far more comprehensive and radical than the "500 Days Privatization Program" later adopted in Russia. However, it was not approved by the senior leaders in China. During this time, the priority of marketization versus securitization was also debated within the economists. The central government, partly in response to the demand by the state industrial capital for monopolistic interests to avoid competition, put forward the strategy of 'large volume import and export' promoting the import of raw materials as well as equipments and the export of finished product. In other words, China engaged only in processing manufacturing, further opening up the coastal regions.

1988 China's Institutional Change Crisis: Failure of Price Reform Resulting in Panic Shopping, Bank Run and High Inflation

The high inflation with an annual CPI over 18% was not so much an indication of the failure of the price reform. The causes for the crisis were as follows: first, the bureaucratic profiteering companies born out of the reform and reaping their first bucket of gold exacerbated the crisis with hoarding in large quantities, while off-loading the institutional costs of the primitive accumulation to the society as much as possible; second: with the Reform becoming an ideological object and even a fetish, the government did not have a plan B in preparation for possible failure, hence the delay in putting forth measures to deal with the crisis. Furthermore, to put a curb on the bank runs, the government simplistically and abruptly raised the deposit interest rate by a significant amount. The outcome was an enormous budget deficit of 50 billion yuan, arising from the losses taken by the state-owned banks.

1989 "Triangle Debt" and Production Stagnation

After raising the deposit interest rate to a high level for several months, the government was forced to also raise the loan interest rates due to heavy losses by the banks. The entire society was suddenly faced with an "official usury", giving rise to the so-called "triangle debts" [*due but unpaid receivables among enterprises*] countrywide. Hyper-inflation arose in company with production stagnation, a typical stagflation crisis. During the depression that followed, the crisis of stagflation led to waves of mass protests against bureaucratic profiteering and corruptions, which was known as the "political storm" [*the official term assigned to the June Fourth Tiananmen Square incident*]. It then resulted in a total economic sanction against China by the West.

1990 The Costs of Urban Capital Crisis Transferred, Impacting Rural Regions

Chinese economy was in a state of depression after the stagflation crisis and the sanctions by the West. The sales of agricultural produce and rural enterprise products were mostly sluggish. As a result the growth of peasants' income in the next three years declined at an accelerated rate. Yet the superstructures established locally after the central government 'off-loaded its fiscal burden' in 1984 had inelastic expenditures. The peasants had to pay more fees and charges in cash for public services. The urban-rural income disparity that had been once notably narrowed started to widen again.

1991 The Soviet Union and Eastern Europe Bloc Disintegrated; Their National Finance Systems Simultaneously Collapsed

The Soviet monopoly capital blocs had remained in the industrial capital phase in a protracted manner, refusing to monetize its economy. Subjected to western ideological propaganda, Russia and other East European countries prioritized the political reform. The outcome was a total collapse of their national financial systems, due to their complete reliance on national sovereignty to create monetary credit. Their industrial capital that was complete in structure was privatized and divided into separate entities. Added to that was the hyperinflation, and the outcome was an explosive surge in transaction costs within their industrial chains. The costs of institutional transition in the superstructure were directly transferred to the economic base. The reaction gave rise to the disintegration of their industries and general bankruptcy.

North Korea had realized a 70% urbanization rate much earlier than China. Yet the modernization of agriculture had to rely on tractors and oil. The disintegration of the USSR meant the disruption of these supplies to North Korea. Since then, under the sanctions by the West, the country found itself in constant crises of food and energy and turned towards the "Songun" [military first] policy.

1992 Deng Xiaoping's Southern Talk; The Year of the "Inauguration of Monetization"

China analyzed the disintegration of the USSR and East European bloc. In the 14th National Congress the CPC put forward the target of building a new socialist market economy. In the process, the government had to repeal almost all coupons, including those for food, due to fiscal deficit pressure. Chinese people began to have money in the true sense— the universal equivalence of commodities. It then led to the initiation of the "monetization of the economy", a change out of the Soviet model of goods bartering. Because of the repealing of consumption coupons, peasants were no longer constrained in their mobility. The wave of migrant workers moving about the country in large numbers seeking employment appeared.

Going along the monetization, three investment markets with speculative nature were kick-started—securities, futures and real estate. The economy then went into a frenzy. Yet paradoxically China did not yet have commercial banks in a real sense. The increase in fiscal deficits would still be covered by the overdrafts from the state-owned banks. After exhausting the banks' capital fund it started to eat into the deposits.

1993 The Sixth Occasion of Budget Deficit Crisis: Deficits in Three Sectors at the Same Time

Even though the central government emphasized macro-regulation, it failed to put a curb on the economic frenzy driven by the monetization as well as the three speculative markets. What followed were serious deficits in government's fiscal budget, balance of payments and financial sector. The total public debts exceeded 200% of the GDP. The inflation pushed up grain price. The central government requested the provinces and municipalities to subsidize grain and other produce. People protested against over-levying. The Premier Zhu Rongji, put forth an array of strict measures to put a curb on the overheating economy.

The U.S. lifted some of the sanctions against China after Japan and Europe had done so earlier. China accelerated its integration into globalization.

1994   A Very Important Year for the World; China initiated Three Major Reforms

The World Trade Organization (WTO), having included the liberalization of strategic sectors such as agriculture and finance, took the place of General Agreement on Tariffs and Trade (GAAT), signifying the age of globalization. Yet the North America Free Trade Agreement (NAFTA) and the European Union (EU) that had come into being on 1 January was an indication that the world also actually entered into regionalization dominated by hegemonic countries! On that very day, the indigenous Zapatista guerrilla in Mexico waged an armed struggle against NAFTA and globalization.

In Beijing, Mayor Chen Xitong was detained and interrogated. The state's macro-regulation was then effectively implemented. Yet a serious crisis had already emerged—the CPI up to 24%. The hyper-inflation was even worse than the case in 1988 due to the price reform. Under the pressure of debts, the volume of which was more than the GDP, the urban capital crisis had a hard landing, leading to three major reforms:

> First: a onetime devaluation of the RMB by 57%, merging the nominal official exchange rate and the adjusted exchange rate for foreign investors. At the same time, public debts and money supply as the ways of the government's credit creation were expanded.
>
> Second: the previous separation of fiscal obligation between the central and local governments was further institutionalized as the 'tax-division system'. It drove the local governments to a second wave of land enclosure

in order to convert land into cash, leading to significant increase in the cases of mass protest incidents.

Third: the "workplace unit" system was completely repealed. The state-owned enterprises were required to cut the number of employees to improve efficiency. Forty million workers became unemployed.

In the financial sector, policy-oriented banks were set up as distinct from commercial banks. State-owned commercial banks were then given free rein to profit-seeking and become alienated from industrial capital.

1996 China's Fiscal Revenue/GDP Ratio Declined to Historic Low; Public Services such as Education and Health Became Commodified

Macro-regulation measures by the central government to suppress inflation were strengthened. Both the investments and domestic demands declined while the economy became increasingly dependent on export. At the same time, local government's budget deficits and public debts increased substantially. Officials and cadres at the community level turned to the peasants with more taxes and levies as the way to cover the deficits. Mass protest incidents increased rapidly in number in both rural and urban regions.

1997 First Deflation Crisis in China: "Imported Deflation" due to the Asian Financial Crisis

No sooner had the government announced a "soft landing" of the economy than the Asian Financial Crisis broke out. What followed was a deflation lasting for four years.

Thanks to good harvest, food prices declined. The grain production in China reached a historic high. In addition, with the majority of the rural enterprises privatized, the rule of "the expulsion of labor by capital" resulted in a decline in the peasants' income over four years in a row.

In the report of the 15th Congress, the notion of "capital" was openly used in an affirmative manner, for the first time in the history of the

CPC. Then, under the pressure of mounting bad loans, the marketization reform was proposed so that state-owned banks would articulate with the financial capital system.

1998 China Initiated Infrastucture Ivestment through Public Debts in Response to Crisis, Striving to Keep the GDP Growth at a Level between 7 to 8%

The Yangtze basin suffered severe flooding. The central government deployed armies from around the country to deal with the emergency. It was a demonstration that the political authority was passed from one generation to the next. After most of the senior political leaders of the revolutionary generation had passed away, the centralized collective system was successfully inherited by the new generation and put into practice effectively.

China for the first time effectively deal with an exogenous crisis by adopting an expansionary fiscal policy by the central government. Facing a contraction in export, a proactive fiscal policy was urgently adopted involving the expansion of public debts to boost domestic demand. The goal was to maintain the GDP growth at least at 7% so as to keep a sufficient creation of new employment. Higher education institutes were requested to expand enrollment, so as to function as labor reservoirs. The result was the commercialization of education and over-borrowing by education institutes.

Other measures included: the monetization of housing; the dynamic integration of the unified purchase of grain with Agricultural Bank's funds into a closed circulation; the extension of the rural household contracts system; accelerating the WTO negotiations.

1999 The Euro Came into Existence along with the Balkan Crisis; Bombing of the Chinese Embassy

The Euro was officially put into circulation in 11 Euro zone countries on 1 January. Soon after that, the NATO intervened in the Kosovo War and the Balkan conflicts with air strikes against Serbia. The military expenditures were added to the fiscal budgets of the NATO members, including those in the Euro zone. The result was a 'lose-lose' situation for Europe: the collapse of the Milosevic government in Serbia and the damage done to the Euro. The exchange rate of Euro against the Dollar declined by more than 30%, from 1 Euro for 1.07 USD down to 1 Euro for 0.82 USD. Regardless of whether it was a conspiracy, the Balkan conflict in effect resulted in the failure of the Euro zone countries to meet the Maastricht criteria as dictated by the Maastrich Treaty—under 3% of GDP for the government deficit.

Yeltsin resigned and Putin came on the scene. Russia rose again as a power. The bombing of the Chinese embassy in Belgrade, Yugoslavia shocked the Chinese people. The post-cold war situation was steering towards a new trend.

2000   China Bidding Farewell to a Hundred Years of Shortage, Entering "Over-Capacity"

In the previous year, Ma Hong and Justin, Lin Yifu had raised the issue that China was entering the phase of industrial overcapacity. At the same time, China was faced with deflation amid depression and a general over-supply of consumer goods. In view of this, the government decided to increase the infrastructure investments financed by public debts by over 2 trillion yuan. That was on top of many existing large scale projects, for example the Great Western Development, forestry protection, and so on. The target was to drive GDP growth on one hand and re-balance regional disparity on the other.

2001   China Joined WTO; U.S. IT Bubble Collapse and the Outflow of Capital; Regional Wars in the Name of Anti-Terrorism Waged after 9/11

China's accession to the WTO coincided with the burst of the IT bubble in the U.S. which drove a large amount of foreign capital into China. The state managed to secure its currency sovereignty by absorbing these capital inflow with an expansion of domestic money supply as well as to keep the domestic capital market in the driving seat over foreign capital.

In the same year, the top leadership accepted the assessment that the *sannong* was in a dire situation.

The Asian financial crisis spread to other regions. Some countries such as Argentina encountered financial crisis.

The 9/11 Attacks happened. On 7 October the U.S.A. waged the war in Afghanistan in reprisal. China joined the international anti-terrorist movement yet was immediately faced with "double-standards". China's anti-terrorism moves were regarded as a form of ethnic suppression.

2002   China Proposed the Target of a 'Moderately Well-off' Society; Independent State-owned Commercial Banks were Born

The 16th CPC Congress put forth the development target of building an overall moderately well-off society as a new mission for the first two decades of the twenty-first century.

The government initiated the project to revive former industrial cities in the Northeast regions by investing over 1 trillion yuan through public debts, attempting to improve their infrastructure and economic conditions.

The commercialization reform of four major state-owned banks was completed. Ten years after having a money independent from the coupons mechanism, China finally had commercial banks that were relatively independent of the fiscal sector. Furthermore, there was not separation between commercial and investment banks right from the beginning.

2003   China Gave Top Priority to the *Sannong* Issue; The U.S.A. Invaded Iraq

In the Rural Region Working Meeting, the central leaders proposed for the first time to prioritize the "*sannong*" issues in party work.

The government launched the project to give impetus to growth in the central regions. The economy became over-heated by the infrastructure construction investments.

A large amount of foreign direct investments flowed into China under a worldwide overcapacity. As a result, foreign ownership accounted for a major share in China's heavy and chemical industries.

Following the completion of commercialization reform, the banking sector gradually became alienated from the real economy which was relatively having less liquidity. What came after that was the regional governments' pre-occupation with selling land to cash in and competing for credit support from commercial banks. The third round of land enclosure surged to a peak. The number of mass protest incidents relating to land appropriation in the rural regions notably increased.

The U.S.A invaded Iraq based on the fabricated "evidences" about weapons of mass destruction, which turned out to be non-existent. It successfully demonstrated to the world its unilateral military might capable of "winning two simultaneous wars".

2004   China Put Forth the Idea of Building a "Harmonious Society"; The Agricultural Tax Repealed

Towards the end of the year, the Fourth Plenary Session was convened in which the Central Bureau put forth the notion of 'harmonious society'.

Macro regulation were strengthened yet the economic over-heating still prevailed. The central government launched a strict investigation on the Jiangsu Province Tie Ben Company project, which had been initiated without the assessment and approval by the central. The project had appropriated 6000 *mu* of rural land illegally, forcing the relocation of more than 4000 peasants. It signified an alarm against regional government's third round of land enclosure.

2005   China Put Forward the National Strategy of Constructing the New Countryside

The central government affirmed the Construction of the New Countryside urban-rural rebalance strategy. However, the previous pro-people's livelihood strategies such as the Scientific Development Outlook and the Harmonious Society, as well as various macro-regulation measures proposed by the State Council, had difficulties in their execution.

The local pursuit for high GDP growth with the resulting high number of mass protest incidents was still prevalent. It was only after the Central increased the exertion of political pressure by purging major corruption cases in regions such as Heilongjiang and Shanghai that its macro-regulation could be effectively implemented.

China began to build its strategic oil reserve system. The exchange rate mechanism for RMB was reformed with the adoption of a managed floating rate system.

2006 China Launched Strategic Investments to Re-balance the Urban-Rural

The eight major strategies established in the eleventh five-year plan were officially launched. Among these, the investments into 'sannong' based on the use of public debts were expanded by a large extent, mostly put into infrastructure construction. Simultaneous to the abolition of the agricultural tax, the issue of public debts accumulated in rural grassroots-level was exposed, giving rise to a deterioration of governance. The serious drought in Chongqing exposed the shortcomings in privatizing the irrigation system.

2007 China Put Forth the Idea of Ecological Civilization Development; Sub-prime Crisis Broke Out in the U.S.A.

The market crash wiped out a total of 700 billion of net worth. Some foreign capital got trapped in China due to the stock market trough. The decline in the U.S. property market had led to the sub-prime crisis, which in turned burst the virtual capital bubble.

In the 17th Congress of the CPC the idea of Ecological Civilization was put forward. The goal was to develop an industrial structure with a growth and consumption model that was energy-efficient and eco-friendly.

The "Law of Specialized Farmers Cooperatives" and the "Labor Law of the People's Republic of China" were introduced after much anticipation.

2008 The Wall Street Financial Crisis; China Encountered "Imported Inflation"

The U.S. adopted an expansionary policy in response to the financial crisis. The cost of the bailout became rapidly transferred to the real economy—the prices of food commodities, energy, raw materials and precious metal all surged sharply, giving rise to hunger and famine in 37 countries. In China, two major state-owned oil companies incurred huge losses due to violent fluctuations in oil prices.

During the same period, the "China Threat" discourse was spread. The "3.14" incident in Tibet broke out. The Olympic torch relay encountered disruptions in the West but the Olympic Games were nevertheless conducted successfully in Beijing.

A major earthquake erupted in Sichuan, and the Central deployed the army from all regions around the country to engage in rescue effort. Court hearing on the case of Chen Liangyu, member of the Shanghai Political Bureau, ended.

The third plenary of the CPC 17th Congress affirmed the target of developing an ecologically conserving and environment-friendly agriculture by 2020. Yet the incident of melamine-tainted milk powder occurred at that time, arousing an unprecedented attention on the issue of food safety.

2009 Global Economic Crisis; Chinese Government Bailout with 4 Trillion

Tens of thousands of enterprises along the coast closed down under the global crisis, with 25 million workers laid off. China was faced with an exogenous crisis. Taking the experience from in response to the Asian financial crisis ten years ago, China turned this crisis into an opportunity through the adjustments made to the economic growth structure. The infrastructure investments in central and western regions as well as in rural areas continued to expand, giving unemployed migrant workers the opportunity to return to their home villages to set up businesses or find employment. Furthermore, the 13% tax rebate for promoting export was converted to subsidize peasants to purchase electrical appliances and cars as a way to stimulate domestic consumption.

A department director in the Ministry of Commerce was arrested on charges of bribery and abusing authority. The media's opinion was that it had to do with giving exceptionally favorable terms to foreign enterprises as compared to domestic ones. In the following year, China adjusted and tightened the conditions for bringing in foreign investments.

The "July Fifth" Incident broke out in Urumqi, Xinjiang. Three different forces, domestic and foreign, instigated Xinjiang separatism. The European sovereignty debt crisis began to unfold starting with Greece.

2010   The Global Crisis Deepened into an Across the Board Crisis of Western Modernization; China Maintained High Growth Rate; Then It Began to Decline

The World Expo was held in Shanghai. China's foreign currency reserve exceeded US$ 3 trillion and became the top holder of U.S. government bonds. The domestic money supply expanded in accordance with the proportion of foreign exchange reserve, which became the mother of inflation in China. Relying on China's stable, long-term investments in U.S. bonds, the U.S. adopted a "quantitative easing" policy, effectively transferring the costs of its crisis outward. Essentially it gave rise to persistent surge in global energy and grain commodity prices. Countries over-relying on food import were faced with imported inflation crises, which then transformed into street politics, and with a variety of background such as social, ethnic or tribal.

The European sovereignty debt crisis worsened among the EU countries due to their lack of a unified fiscal system. The contradictions between the global North and South were exacerbated.

2011 China Effectively Realized the Macro-regulation Target of Controlling Inflation yet the Real Economy Slumped into Depression due to Tight Monetary Policy; The Costs of U.S. Financial Crisis Transferred outward Creating Chaos around the World

Street politics that first started in New York took place in a large number of cities around the world. Pan-Mediterranean countries experienced street confrontations one after another. What it demonstrated was that there were two types of countries in the world that could not resolve the costs transferred outward by the US financial capital—the late-developing countries with a mono-product economy that were previously controlled by their colonizers, for example, Tunisia, Egypt and Libya, wherein either the governments were overthrown or the countries crumbled into chaos; then the veteran colonial suzerains such as Spain, Portugal and Italy where street confrontations broke out successively. These two types of countries generally formed a "Mediterranean Crisis Ring".

2012 Although its Debt Crisis Far from being Resolved, the U.S.A. Undertook its High Profile Asia-Pacific Rebalance Strategy, Relying on its Military Might

Japan announced the "nationalization" of Diaoyu Island and Sino-Japanese relations became mired in tension. The "10 + 3" alliance of the ASEAN and Northeast Asia at its embryonic form was aborted. That alliance should have had the potential to integrate the economies in the region into a unified trade and clearing system based on Asian currencies, similar to the EU. With the abortion of this potential alliance, the U.S. was able to secure the subordination of the West Pacific as a "Dollar Lake" in support of its financial hegemony.

2013 U.S. Federal Reserve Made a Plan to End QE; Imported Deflation Emerged in China; Chinese Government Proposed the Notion of "New Normal" for Economic Development; GDP Totaled 59.5 Trillion Yuan, 44.6 Trillion of which Came from Fixed Asset Investments in the Society

In June a temporary squeeze in money supply appeared in China's banking system. With immediate intervention by the financial authorities, China did not experience financial crisis in capital markets and sharp currency devaluation, as was the case in other "BRIC" countries. Towards the end of the year, the guiding principles of deepening the market reform were put forward, which did not learn the lessons from global financial crisis and caused heated discussions from all sides.

In August the State Council decided to set up the Shanghai Free Trade Zone, the first of its kind in China.

The wars in Ukraine and Syria broke out one after the other. Russia annexed Crimea resulting in sanctions by the West.

On 31 October, six major central banks, the U.S.A., Japan, U.K., EU, Canada, Switzerland, formed a long-term currency swap agreement, with the U.S. Federal Reserve at its core. It constituted a dynamic swapping network among the core countries, a vital institutional adjustment for financial capitalism.

2014 The Correlation between China's Real Estate Bubble and Local Governments' Effort in Appropriating Land to Support Debt is Gradually Exposed

The ratio of non-performing loans in the banking sector increased as a result of high leveraging, and economic growth slowed. The global demand declined and the crisis of overcapacity again surfaced. The fiscal and financial sectors made use of various policies such as the Shanghai Free Trade Zone, the Shanghai-Hong Kong Stock Connect, Shenzhen-Hong Kong Stock Connect, to push ahead with the deepening of financialization. International financial capital joined force to sell-short Chinese stock market.

China put forward the Belt and Road Initiative. The U.S. intervened in a high profile manner into the controversy over China's island and reef constructions in the South China Sea. At the same time the TPP negotiations accelerated.

From 2002 to 2014, with an accumulation of international balance of payment surplus, the Renminbi appreciated step by step, at one point reaching the peak of 1 USD to 6.05 Yuan.

On 31 October, one year after the six-party currency alliance came into operation, the U.S. formally announced the phasing out of the QE.

2015 New Form of Financial Capital Oversupply Crisis was in Incubation; Major Powers Made Adjustment in their Relationship

The capital funds released gradually out of the physical economy and real estate market were flowing into the stock market. The authorities liberated the futures markets on stocks and indices and permitted over the counter financing. The stock market was driven into a frenzy. In June, the stock market crashed and wiped out a net worth of tens of trillions Renminbi.

The Renminbi exchange rate reform on 11 August was regarded as the start of a devaluation cycle. Since then China had to engage repeatedly in the foreign exchange and financial markets to deal with the attempts to sell short the Renminbi by international investment funds.

In November the Leading Group for Financial and Economic Affairs' meeting report put forward the "supply side reform", along the line of pro-cyclical measures.

In December the U.S. Federal Reserve raised the interest rate for the first time in 10 years, which was generally regarded as the beginning of a new interest rate hike cycle.

Along with its military intervention into the South China Sea the U.S. completed the TPP negotiations with other countries. China accelerated the constructions of islands and reefs in the South China Sea. The Asia Investment Bank Agreement led by China came into effect in December. China's overseas investments as a proportion of the total volume in the world expanded rapidly. The number of incidents it therefore induced increased as well.

Russia intervened in the Syrian conflict with military actions. Europe faced the refugee crisis.

By the end of December, China's M2 supply reached 139 trillion yuan, with an annual growth of 13.3% while M1 grew by 15.2%. The total aggregate non-government financing plus the increment in local governments debt replacement reached 18.5 trillion. The total value of creditor's rights was 23 trillion yuan, with a year over year growth of almost 90%.

The Ministry of Finance began to implement 'local debt replacement', commonly called the 'revolving door'. The first batch being replaced in the year amounted to 1 trillion yuan.

2016   China Continued to Maintain Stable Economic Growth Using Policy-oriented Investments; Internal and External Pressure was Mounting up

The fixed asset investments reached 59.7 trillion yuan. The stock market circuit breaker mechanism was introduced in this year. The market continued to go down. The real estate prices in major cities kept skyrocketing. In August seven new free trade zones were set up, now a total of 11. In October the Renminbi was included in the IMF's Special Drawing Right (SDR). The pressure on the Renminbi to devalue persisted. The foreign exchange reserve continued to decrease while China's overseas investments kept expanding. The money supply continued to expand and so did the debts. The total debt to GDP ratio exceeded 340%. In December, the Central Economic Work Conference put forth the stance that 'houses are for people's accommodation, not for speculation'.

It had been 15 years since China's accession to the WTO. The U.S.A., the EU and Japan all refused to recognize China as a market economy, and maintained the anti-dumping "analogue country method" on China.

Food grain production decreased by 5.2 billion kilograms, the first decline in twelve years.

In November the central government initiated the reform to 'separate the three entitlements' on rural land—ownership, contractual right and management right.

2017   The New President Donald Trump Announced the United States' Withdrawal from the TPP; China Switched from Procyclical to Counter-cyclical Measures with Direct Government Intervention; US Government Redefined China as Strategic Competitor.

The US President Trump, taking an anti-free trade stance, withdrew from the TPP as promised in his election. A U.S. naval carrier entered the South China Sea island reef China claimed to have sovereignty.

In January to February the Renminbi continued to devalue. The central bank changed the mechanism for the intermediate price of Renminbi, reducing the computing time span for the basket of currencies. Strict measures were taken to control capital flights. The regulation over the offshore Renminbi market position was also strengthened. At the same time the notion of a "stable and neutral monetary policy" was introduced. In January the foreign exchange reserve balance was US$ 2.998 trillion, dropping below the 3 trillion level. Economic growth continued to rely on government investments. Among 23 provinces/cities/regions that disclosed fixed asset investments, the total volume already exceeded 40 trillion yuan.

2018   The Trump Administration Launched Trade War Against China.

In March the RMB Crude Oil Futures was listed on Shanghai International Energy Exchange.

2019   The US Attempted to Rip the Global Supply Chain.

US government launched a campaign to block Huawei, the leading Chinese IT enterprise, from access into the US and allies markets. The USA withdrew from several treaties and international organizations, seeking to reshape international order at a greater service to US interests.

2020   COVID-19 Plagued the World. The US Fed Initiated Unlimited QE. The US Government Forced through Reverse Globalization. Global Economy was at its Worst since the Great Depression. China Adopted the New strategy of Dual Circulation: Developing Domestic Economic Circulation Complemented by International Circulation.

In January, China and the US signed the phase one trade deal. COVID-19 epidemic broke out in China and the world with over 10.3 million infested and 506 thousand cases of death as of June. While the epidemic was successfully contained in China, the USA became the most seriously infected country in the world with a death toll of nearly 600 thousand as of May 2021. In May, China started its Digital Currency Electronic Payment pilot test. In June, the Beidou Global Satellite System was completed.

References

Most of the references are in Chinese and have not been translated into English. Their titles are translated for the readers' reference.

Bao, Youti (1988) 鲍有悌, "三省市乡镇企业发展外向型经济调查" (Survey on the Development of Export-Oriented Economy among Rural Enterprises in Three Provinces and Municipality), 宏观经济管理 (Macro-Economic Management), 1988(9).

Bo, Yibo (1991) 薄一波, 若干重大决策与事件的回顾(上) (Recollections on Various Major Decisions and Events, volume one). Beijing: Central Party History Literature Press.

Business Weekly (2011) "Special Report: Ten Years after Joining WTO," 商务周刊 http://finance.ifeng.com/news/20110321/3711209.shtml.

Cai, Wenxiang (1989) 蔡文祥, "也谈国际大循环" (On the Big International Circulation), 对外经济贸易大学学报 (Journal of University of International Business and Economics), 1989(3), pp. 23–27.

Chen, Tingxuan (1995) 陈廷煊 "国民经济恢复时期 (1949—1952年) 的商品市场与物价管理" (A Study of Commodity Market and Price Regulation during the Restoration of National Economy 1949–1952), 中国经济史研究 (Researches on Chinese Economic History), 1995(2).

© The Editor(s) (if applicable) and The Author(s) 2021
Wen Tiejun, *Ten Crises*, Global University for Sustainability Book Series,
https://doi.org/10.1007/978-981-16-0455-3

Chen, Xiwen (2004) 陈锡文, "资源配置与中国农村发展" (Resource Allocation and Chinese Rural Development), 中国农村经济 (Chinese Rural Economy), 2004(1), pp. 4–9.

Chen, Xiwen, Han Jun & Zhao Yang (2005) 陈锡文, 韩俊, 赵阳 "中国农村公共财政制度研究" (Study on Rural Public Finance System in China), 宏观经济研究 (Macro-economic Research), 2005(5).

Chen, Xubin (2015) 谌旭彬, "民国最凶险的一次死里逃生" (The Most Dangerous Narrow Escape of the Republic of China), 腾讯历史 (Tencent History), 短史记 (Short History), 302. http://view.qq.com/a/20150130/012199.htm.

Chen, Yun (1995a) 陈云文选第2卷 (Selected Writings of Chen Yun volume 2). Beijing: Remin Press.

Cheng, Shulan (1998) 程漱兰, 中国农村发展: 理论和实践 (Development of Chinese Villages: Theory and Practice). Beijing: China Remin University Press.

Chi, Aiping (2003) 迟爱萍, "新中国第一笔国债研究——兼谈陈云关于人民胜利折实公债发行思想" (Study on the First Public Debt in New China and Chen Yun's Thoughts on the Issuance of People Victory Bond), 中国经济史研究 (Researches on Chinese Economic History), 2003(3).

China Economic Yearbook 1981 (中国经济年鉴1981). Beijing: China Statistics Press, 1981.

China Financial Yearbook 1992.

China Real Estate Market Yearbook 1996.

China Statistical Abstracts 1993.

China Statistical Yearbook (various years).

China Textile Union (1996) "救救纺织行业困难职工" (Rescue the Textile Industry Workers in Difficulties), 改革内参 (Internal Reference on Reform), 1996(21).

Chinese Rural Enterprise Yearbook (1978–1987), China Agriculture Press, 1989.

Chronicles of Jiangsu Province—Chronicles of Rural Industries 江苏省志·乡镇工业志.

Coble, Parks M. Jr. (1987) *The Shanghai Capitalists and the Nationalist Government, 1927–1937* (Chinese Translation). Nanjing: Nankai University Press.

Contemporary China's Infrastructure Construction Book 1(当代中国的基本建设(上)). Beijing: China Social Science Press, 1989.

Cui, Xiaoli (1988) 崔晓黎, "统购统销与工业积累" (Unified Purchasing and Selling and Industrial Primitive Accumulation). 中国经济史研究 (Researches on Chinese Economic History), 1988(4).

Cui, Xinjing (2008) 崔新健 中国利用外资三十年 (China Making Use of Foreign Capital in 30 Years). China Financial and Economic Press.

Dong, Xiaodan & Wen Tiejun, (2008) "宏观经济波动与农村治理危机" (Rural Governance Crisis and Macro-economic Volatility), 管理世界 (Management World), 2008(9).

Dong, Xiaodan, Yang Shuai, Sit Tsui & Wen, Tiejun (2011) 董筱丹、杨帅、薛翠、温铁军, "中国特色之工业化与中国经验" (Industrialization with Chinese Characteristics and China's Experiences). *Remin University Journal*, 2011(1).

Dong, Xiaodan (2015) 董筱丹, 再读苏南——苏州工业园区二十年发展述要 (Reinterpreting Sunan Model). Suzhou University Press.

Dong, Zhikai (2009) 董志凯, 共和国经济风云回眸 (A Retrospect into the Republic's Economy). Beijing: China Social Sciences Press.

Du, Runsang (2005) 杜润生, 杜润生自述: 中国农村体制变革重大决策纪实 (Du Runsang's Narrative: Documentary on Major Decisions Regarding Rural Reform in China), People's Publishing House.

Duara, Prasenjit (1996) 杜赞奇, *Culture, Power and the State* (文化、权力与国家), Jiangsu People's Publishing House.

Fan, Gan (1994), "Soft Constraint Competition and Inflation of China in Recent Years," 金融研究 (Financial Research), 1994(3).

Faribank, John King (1992) *China: A New History*. Cambridge, MA: Belknap Press of Harvard University Press.

Financial Stability Analysis Group of the People's Bank of China (2005), 中国金融稳定报告 (China Financial Stability Report), China Financial Publishing House.

Friedman, Thomas (2006) *The World Is Flat: A Brief History of the Twenty-First Century*. London: Penguin Books.

Geng, Lei (2015) 耿磊, "朱理治与1941~1942年陕甘宁边区银行" (Zhu Lizhi and the Shaanxi, Gansu, Ningxia Border Bank 1941–1942), 史学月刊 (Historiography Monthly), 2015(6).

Gerschenkron, Alexander (2009) *Economic Backwardness in Historical Perspective* (Chinese version). Commercial Press.

Gu, Longsheng (1992) 顾龙生, 毛泽东经济思想引论 (Mao Zedong's Economic Thoughts). Shanxi Economic Press.

Han, Ping, Li Bin & Cui Yong (2005) 韩平, 李斌, 崔永, "我国M2/GDP的动态增长路径、货币供应量与政策选择" (M2/GDP Dynamic Growth

Path, Money Supply and Policy Options in China), 经济研究 (Economic Research), 2005(10).

Han, Yuhai (2009) 韩毓海, 五百年来谁著史: *1500 年以来的中国与世界* (China and the World since 1500). Jiuzhou Publishing House.

Han, Zhaozhou (1993) 韩兆洲, "工农业产品价格剪刀差的计量方法研究" (Studies on the Quantitative Method in the Price Scissors of Industrial and Agricultural Products). 统计研究 (Statistics Research), 1993(1).

He, Huili et al. (2014) 何慧丽等, "政府理性与村社理性: 中国的两大比较优势" (Government Rationality and Rural Communal Rationality). 国家行政学院学报 (National Administrative Academy Journal), 2014(6).

He, Shuijin (2008) 贺水金 "试论建国初期的通货膨胀及其成功治理" (Inflation During the Early Years of the Republic and Its Successful Management). 史林 (Historical Review), 2008(4).

He, Yunghong (2006) 何永红, 五反运动研究 (Research on the Wufan Movement). 中共党史出版社 (Chinese Communist Party History Publishing House).

History of Industrial Economy in PRC: October 1949 to 1998 (中華人民共和國工業經濟史).

Hu, Angang (2008) 胡鞍钢 *中国政治经济史论* (On China's Political Economic History). Tsinghua University Press, 2008.

Hu, Angang (1997) 胡鞍钢 "就业: 中国发展的第二号任务" (Employment: The Number 2 Mission of China's Development), 改革内参 (Internal Reference on Reform), 1997(12).

Hu, Sheng (1991) 胡绳 *中国共产党的七十年* (Seventy Years of CPC). CPC History Press.

Huang, Wei (2005) 黄蕙 "社会主义新农村——农村是拉动内需被忽视的动力" (Building the New Socialist Countryside—The Countryside was the Neglected Impetus in Domestic Demand Stimulation), 瞭望 (Outlook), 2005-11-23. http://www.agri.gov.cn/jjps/t20051123_500588.htm.

Huang, Philip C. C. (2011) 黄宗智 "重庆: 第三只手推动的公平发展?" (Chongqing: Equitable Development Pushed by the Third Hand?), 开放时代 (Ages of Opening), 2011(9).

Huang, Ray (1997) *1587, A Year of No Significance: The Ming Dynasty in Decline* (Chinese version). Beijing: Joint Publishing.

Hui, Po-Keung (1999) 许宝强, 发展主义的迷思 (The Myth of Developmentalism), 读书 (Dushu), 1999(7), pp. 18–25.

Ji, Yongming (1988) 季永明 "关于江阴市乡镇企业发展外向型经济调查之系列报告(续)" (Survey on the Rural Enterprise in Export-oriented

Economy Development in Jiangyang Township (cont'd)), 现代金融 (Modern Finance), 1988(10).

Jiang, Xingsan, Liu Shouying & Li Qing (2007) 蒋省三, 刘守英, 李青 "土地制度改革与国民经济成长" (Land System Reform and the Growth of National Economy), 管理世界 (Management World), 2007(9).

Jiangsu Province Rural Research Team (2003) 江苏省农调队课题组, 中国农村经济调研报告 (Research Report on Chinese Rural Economy). Beijing: China Statistics Press.

Jiang, Xingsan, Liu Shouying et el (2007) 蒋省三, 刘守英等 "土地制度改革与国民经济成长" (Land System Reform and Growth of the National Economy), 管理世界 (Journal of Management World) 2007(9), pp. 1–9.

Jin, Chong Ji & Chen Qun eds. (2005) 金冲及, 陈群主编, 陈云传 (Biography of Chen Yun Volume 1). Beijing, Central Literature Press.

Joint Survey Team of Henan Academy of Social Science and Henan Petition Bureau (1999) "关于当前农村社会稳定问题的调查" (Survey Regarding the Present Rural Social Stability), 调研世界 (The World of Survey and Research), 1999(1).

Ju, Hailong (2005) 鞠海龙 "破日本雁阵 中国—东盟布新局" (Breaking Japan's Flying Goose Formation: The New China-ASEAN Layout), 时代周报 (Time Weekly), 23-4-2009: Quoted by Jonathan Laing, "The Bubble's New Home," *Wall Street Journal*, 20-6-2005.

Lang, Xianping (2010) 郎咸平 "美国正把中国复制成第二个日本" (The USA Is Turning China into a Replica of Japan), 中国物流与采购 (China Logistics and Purchasing), 2010 (12).

Lewis, W. Arthur (1954) "Economic Development with Unlimited Supplies of Labour". The Manchester School 22, Issue 2: 139–191.

Li, Biao & Lu Zhihong (2004) 李彪, 卢志红 "我国国债发行规模中的协整和ECM实证分析" (A Co-integration Analysis and ECM Empirical Analysis on China's Debt Issuance Scale), *Journal of Anhui Agricultural University* (*Social Science*), 2004(4).

Li, Caihua & Jiang Dayun (2005) 李彩华, 姜大云 "我国大 '三线建设' 的历史经验和教训" (China's Three Defence Lines Construction: Experiences and Lessons), *Northeast Normal University Journals* (*Philosophy and Social Science*), 2005(4).

Li, Chenjie & Wen Tiejun (2009) 李晨婕, 温铁军 "宏观经济波动与我国集体林权制度改革" (Macro-Economic Fluctuations and China's Collective Forestry Rights System Reform), 中国软科学 (China Soft Science), 2009(6).

Li, Jingzhi & Pu Guoliang (2003) 李景治, 蒲国良 社会主义建设理论与实践 (Theory and Practice of Socialism Construction). Beijing: China Renmin University Press.

Li, Wenjing 李文晶 "中国FDI与经济增长的产业分析" (Industrial Analysis of China's FDI and Economic Growth), http://ems.nwu.edu.cn/economic/26/lianjie/papers/3.htm.

Li, Xingong (2009) 李新功 "美元霸权、金融发展差异与货币体系错配下中美经济失衡及调整" (Dollar Hegemony, Financial Development Differences and Monetary Systems Mismatch: Economic Imbalance and Adjustments in China and the U.S.A.), 现代经济探讨 (Modern Economy Inquiry), 2009(9).

Li, Ai (2005) 李爱 白银危机与中国币值改革-解析国民政府时期的政治、经济与外交 (Silver Crisis and Monetary Reform: An Analysis of Politics, Economy and Diplomacy in the Republic of China), PhD Thesis, Huadong Normal University.

Li, Chengrui (1962) 李成瑞 中华人民共和国农业税史稿 (PRC Agricultural Tax: A Preliminary History). China Fiscal and Economic Press.

Li, Guoding (1993) 李国鼎 台湾经济发展背后的政策演变 (The Policy Transformation of Taiwan's Economic Development). Nanjing: Southeast University Press.

Li, Tianni (1934) 李天倪 "提高粮米价格救济农村破产案" (Save Rural Bankruptcy by Raising Rice Price), 农村复兴委员会会报 (Rural Revival Committee Proceedings), April 1934, no. 11.

Li, Xia & Zou, Yingquan (eds) (1993) 李夏, 邹应泉编著, 突飞猛进一百年: 工业化进程 (Hundred Years of Industrialization). Hainan Publishing House.

Li, Yanling & Li Lutang (2008) 李艳玲 "李录堂, 农民工工资剪刀差的产生原因及对策" (The Cause of Price Scissors in Peasant Wages and Policy Response). *Anhui Agricultural Science*, 2008(5).

Liang, Guiquan (1988) 梁桂全 "不合国情的'国际大循环'构想——兼论开放的多元优势次阶跃推进战略" (The Big International Circulation Concept That Does Not Suit National Conditions), 学术研究 (*Academic Research*) 1988(4), pp. 19–24.

Liaoning Party History Research Laboratory (2009) "毛泽东在1964年的一个重大决策: 建设大三线" (Mao Zedong's Major Decision in 1964: Three Defence Lines Construction), 决策探索 (Policy Decision Exploration), 2009(2).

Lin, Yifu Justin (2002) "企业自生能力与改革的深层次问题" (Enterprises' Ability of Self-reliance and the Profound Issues of the Reform), 国研网 (National Research Network), 2002-03-28.

Liu, Guoguang & Liu Shucheng (1997) 刘国光, 刘树成 "论软着陆" (On Soft-landing), *People's Daily*, 7 January 1997, page 9.

Liu, Haiying (2002) 刘海英 "我们到底能做什么" (What In Fact Can We Do?), 中国改革 (China Reform), 2002(4).

Liu, Haiying (2003) 刘海英 "话说金融'故'事" (Old Stories of Finance), 中国改革 (综合版) (China Reform (General)), 2003(3).

Liu, Mou & Yi Yang (2012) "Commercialization Reform of State-Owned Banks and Future Trends," Master Thesis, University of International Business and Economics, May 2012 http://www.doc88.com/p-4827071198102.html.

Liu, Xiahui & Mo Rong 刘霞辉, 莫荣 "国有企业改革与职工再就业问题研究" (On SOE Reform and Workers Re-employment), Working Paper.

Liu, Yunzhong (2005) 刘云中 "1934年美国'白银收购法案'对中国经济的影响及启示" (Impact and Implications to the Chinese Economy of the U.S. Silver Purchase Act in 1934), 国务院发展研究中心调查研究报告 (State Council Development Research Center Research Report), November 28, 2005, Issue 200.

Ma, Hong & Lu Baipu (1999) 马洪, 陆百甫 中国宏观经济政策报告 (China Macro-Economic Policy Report). Beijing: China Fiscal and Economic Press.

Macfarlane, Alan (1978) *The Origins of English Individualism*. Oxford: Blackwell.

Mai, Jingnong (1997) 麦金农 经济市场化的次序——向市场经济过渡中的金融控制 (Order of Economic Marketization: Financial Control During Transition to Market Economy). Shanghai Joint Publishing House and Shanghai People Press.

Min, Jianshu (1988) 闵建蜀 "国际大循环理论之我见——香港中文大学工商管理学院院长闵建蜀教授谈国际大循环" (My Opinions on the Big International Circulation), 经济管理 (*Economic Management Journal*) 1988(7), pp. 62–64.

Ministry of Finance of the People's Republic of China (1959) "Report on 1958 Fiscal Revenue and Expenditure Settlement Account and 1959 Fiscal Budget Draft" (关于1958年财政收支决算和1959年财政收支预算草案的报告).

Ministry of Finance of the People's Republic of China (1994) 中国农民负担史 (A History of Burdens on Peasants). Beijing: China Fiscal and Economic Press.

National Bureau of Statistics (1984) *China Statistics Yearbook 1984*, Beijing: China Statistics Press.

National Bureau of Statistics (1987) 国家统计局国民经济平衡统计司编: 国民收入统计资料汇编 (1949—1985) (Collected Data of National Income 1949–1985). Beijing: China Statistics Press.

National Bureau of Statistics (1989) 中国农村统计年鉴(1989) (Chinese Rural Statistic Yearbook 1989). Beijing: China Statistics Press.

National Bureau of Statistics of the People's Republic of China (1980) 建国三十年全国农业统计资料 (1949—1979) (National Agricultural Statistics 1949–1979). Beijing: China Statistics Press.

New China 60 Years (新中国60年). China Statistics Press, 2000.

Nie, Minghua & Yang Feihu (2010) 聂名华, 杨飞虎 "劳动和资本双重过剩下的中国金融创新与经济增长" (Financial Innovation and Economic Growth in China Under the Over-Supply of Both Labor and Capital), 理论探讨 (Theoretical Exploration), 2010(3), pp. 65–69.

Nurkse, Ragnar (1953) *Problems of Capital Formation in Underdeveloped Countries*. Oxford University Press.

Pan, Zequan (2008) 潘泽泉 "全球化、世界工厂与中国农民工发展的经验教训" (Lessons from Globalization, World Factory and China's Migrant Worker Development), *Guangzhou Social Science*, 2008(1).

Peng, Chenggang (2006) 彭成刚 "斯大林模式在中国的历史考察" (Stalin Model in China: A Historical Survey), Wuhan Polytechnic University Master Thesis.

Peng, Tong & Liang, Shuang (2010) 彭曈, 梁爽 "外商直接投资在三次产业中的分布及评价" (Distribution and Evaluation of Foreign Direct Investments Among Tertiary Industries), *China Venture Capital*, 2010(4), pp. 47–50.

Polanyi, Karl (2001) *The Great Transformation: The Political and Economic Origins of Our Time*. Boston: Beacon Press.

Pu, Changmo (2010) 朴昌模 "韩中外资政策的演变及其效应的比较研究" (Comparative Studies of Changes and Effects of Foreign Capital Policies between Korea and China), Master Thesis, University of International Business and Economics, 2010.

Ramo, Joshua Cooper (2004) *The Beijing Consensus*, London: The Foreign Policy Centre.

Ren, Lixin (2011) 任立新, 毛泽东新民主主义经济思想研究 (Mao Zedong's Economic Thoughts of the New Democracy). China Social Sciences Press.

Selection from People's Republic of China Economic Archives 1949–1952: Infrastructure and Construction 1949–1952 中华人民共和国经济档案资料选编·基本建设投资与建筑业卷. Beijing: China Urban Economic & Social Press, 1989.

Selection from People's Republic of China Economic Archives 1949–52: General 1949–1952 中华人民共和国经济档案资料选编·综合卷. Beijing: China Urban Economy & Society Press 1990.

Selection from People's Republic of China Economic Archives 1949–1952: Industrial and Commercial Institutions 1949–1952 中华人民共和国经济档案资料选编·工商体制卷. Beijing: China Social Sciences Press, 1993.

Selection from People's Republic of China Economic Archives 1949–52: Transportation and Communication 1949–1952 中华人民共和国经济档案选编·交通通讯卷, Beijing: China Supplies Press, 1996.

Selection from People's Republic of China Economic Archives 1949–1952: Finance 1949–1952 中华人民共和国经济档案资料选编·金融卷. Beijing: China Supplies Publishing House, 1996.

Shanghai CPC History Research Office (1993) 中共上海市委党史研究室, 上海私营金融业的社会主义改造 (The Socialist Transformation of Private Financial Sector in Shanghai), in 中国资本主义工商业的社会主义改造, 上海卷(下) (Socialist Transformation of Industry and Commerce in China: Shanghai). Beijing: China CPC Party History Press.

Shen, Jiru (2004) 沈骥如 "中国外贸依存度解读" (Interpretation of China's Reliance on Foreign Trade), 招商周刊 (Business Weekly), 2004(41).

Shen, Zhihua (2001) 沈志华 "新中国建立初期苏联对华经济援助的基本情况——来自中国和俄国的档案材料" (Basic Situations of USSR Aid to China—From the Archives of China and Russia), *Russia Studies*, 2001(1–2).

Sheng, Laiyun, Wang Ran & Yan, Fang (2009) 盛来运, 王冉, 阎芳 "国际金融危机对农民工流动就业的影响" (Impact of International Financial Crisis on Flow and Employment of Migrant Workers), *Chinese Rural Economy*, 2009(9).

Shi, Lin (1989) 石林 "当代中国的对外经济合作" (Contemporary China's Economic Cooperation), China Academy of Social Science Press.

"State-owned Economy Steady, Non-public economy Rising" (数字看变化: 国有经济地位稳固非公经济比重上升). Beijing: People's Press, 1959. http://www.jiaodong.net/news/system/2002/10/08/00532129.shtml.

State Council of the People's Republic of China (1981, 1982, 1983) *Reports on the Work of the Government* 1981, 1982, 1983.

State Council of the People's Republic of China Research Team (2006) 国务院研究室课题组, 中国农民工调研报告 (A Research Report on Migrant Worker). Beijing: China Yanshi Publishing House.

Su, Guangping (2004) "Reflections on the IT Bubble", 2004-7-21, http://www.eepw.com.cn/article/27.htm.

Su, Hainan (2006) 苏海南 "保障农民工的劳动报酬权" (Safeguard Migrant Workers' Right of Remuneration). *Chinese Labour*, 2006(9).

Survey Report on Chinese Migrant Workers (2006) 中国农民工调研报告. China Yan Shi Press.

Sun, Jian (2000) 孙健 中国经济通史·中卷 (General Economic History of China Second Volume). China Renmin University Press.

Tang, Jianyu (1988) 唐建宇 "关于沿海地区发展外向型经济的几个问题" (Several Questions Regarding Export Economy in Coastal Regions), 亚太经济 (Asia-Pacific Economics), 1988(3).

Tao, Shigui (2013) 陶士贵 "地方政府控股下的地方银行制度变迁逻辑与风险防范" (Institutional Change of Local Banking System with Local Governments as Stock-Holders: Logic and Risk Prevention), *Nanjing Normal University Journal* (Social Sciences), 2013(5).

The Great Ten Years (伟大的十年), National Bureau of Statistics.

The World Bank's World Development Report 2005.

United Nations Conference on Trade and Development, *World Investment Reports* 2009 & 2012.

Wallerstein, Immanuel (2004) *World-Systems Analysis: An Introduction.* Durham, NC: Duke University Press.

Wang, Haibo (1998) 汪海波 中華人民共和國工業經濟史 (History of Industrial Economy in PRC). Shanxi Economic Publishing House.

Wang, Huihua (2015) 汪卫华 "群众动员与动员式治理——理解中国国家治理风格的新视角" (Mass Mobilization and Governance by Mobilization: new perspective understanding the style of China's state governance), 上海交通大学学报 (Jiaotong University Journal), 2015(05).

Wang, Jian (1988) "Choosing the Right Long-Term Development Strategy—Regarding the Conception of International Great Circle Economic Development Strategy," *Economic Daily*, 5 January, 1988.

Wang, Jian (2006) 王建 "产能过剩的后果与应对措施" (The Consequences of Over-Production Capacity and Response Measures), 中国金融 (China Finance), 2006(2), pp. 11–12.

Wang, Jian (2007) "防过热更需防过剩" (Caution on Overheat and More Importantly Overcapacity), 中国经贸导刊 (China Economic & Trade Herald), 2007(17).

Wang, Jian (2008) "关于设立珠三角金融特区的构想" (The Conception of Setting Up the Pearl River Delta Special Financial Zone), 中国宏观经济信息网 (China Macro-Economic Information), 4-8-2008. http://www.macrochina.com.cn/zhtg/20080804091350.shtml.

Wang, Jian (2008a) "关注增长与通胀格局的转变点" (Pay Attention to the Turning Point of Growth and the Inflation), 宏观经济管理 (Macro Economic Management), 2008 (8).

Wang, Liya (2011) "Reflections On State-owned Commercial Bank Reform Model," *Finance and Insurance*, 2001(11).

Wang, Peihua (2009) 黄佩华 "中国能用渐进方式改革公共部门吗?" (Can China Reform the Public Sector with a Gradual Approach?), 社会学研究 (Sociological Research), 2009(2).

Wang, Shaoguang (2009) 王绍光 "坚守方向、探索道路: 中国社会主义实践六十年" (Sixty Years of Socialist Practices in China), 中国社会科学 (China Social Science), 2009(5).

Wang, Shaoguang, Hu Angang & Ding Yuanzhu (2002) 王绍光, 胡鞍钢, 丁元竹 "最严重的警告: 经济繁荣背后的社会不稳定" (The Most Serious Warning: The Social Disability Behind Economic Prosperity), 战略与管理 (Strategy and Management), 2002(4).

Wang, Xiaohui (1999) 王晓辉 "教育财政体制改革应有新思路" (There Should Be New Ways of Thinking in Reforming Education Expenditures), 改革内参 (Internal Reference on Reform), 1999(22).

Wang, Shunseng & Li Jun (2006) 王顺生, 李军, 三反运动研究 (Research on the Sanfan Movement). Chinese Communist Party History Publishing House.

Wei, Dakang & Gao Liang (1988) 卫大匡、高梁 "投资海外带动出口——对国际大循环经济战略构想的补充" (Invest Overseas to Stimulate Export—Supplements to the Economic and Strategic Concept of Big International Circulation), 经济日报 (*Economic Journal*), 1988(1), p.10.

Wen, Tiejun (1993) "国家资本再分配与民间资本再积累" (State Capital Redistribution and Civil Capital Re-accumulation), 新华文摘 (Xinhua Digest), 1993(12).

Wen, Tiejun (2000) 中国农村经济经济制度研究—三农问题的世纪反思 (Studies on Chinese Rural Economic Institutions). China Economics Press.

Wen, Tiejun (2001) "周期性经济危险及对应政策分析" (Analysis on Cyclic Economic Crises and the Measures in Response), http://www.macrochina. com.cn/zhtg/20010608007807.shtml.

Wen Tiejun (2001a) "百年中国、一波四折" (Hundred Year in China—Four Twists and Turns), 读书 Dushu, 2001(3).

Wen, Tiejun (2003) "中国粮食供给周期与价格比较分析" (Comparative Analysis of China's Food Grain Supply Cycle and Price), 中国农村观察 (Rural China Survey), 2003(3).

Wen, Tiejun (2004) 解构现代化—温铁军演讲录 (Deconstructing Modernization). Guangdong People's Press.

Wen, Tiejun (2004a) "新中国三次对外开放的成本与收益" (New China's Three Rounds of Opening Up: Costs and Benefits), in 我们到底要什么 (What In Fact Do We Want). Huaxia Publishing House.

Wen, Tiejun (2008) "中国经验与比较优势" (Chinese Experience and Comparative Advantage), 开放时代 (Open Era), 2008(2).

Wen, Tiejun (2009) 三农问题与制度变迁 (Sannong Problem and Institutional Transition) 2nd edition. China Economics Press.

Wen, Tiejun (2011) 解读苏南 (Interpreting South Suzhou). Suzhou University Press.

Wen, Tiejun (2011a) "理解中国的小农, 四千年农夫中文版序" (Understanding Chinese Peasants—A Preface to Farmers of Forty Centuries), in 四千年农夫 (Farmers of Forty Centuries). Dongfang Publishing House.

Wen, Tiejun (2012) "全球资本化与制度性致贫" (Global Capitalization and Institutional Impoverishment), 中国农业大学学报 (China University of Agriculture Journal), 2012(1).

Wen, Tiejun et el (2008), "广东省产业结构和发展战略调整研究课题报告" (Report on Guangdong Province's Industrial Structure and Development Strategy Adjustments).

Wen, Tiejun et el. (2011) "Special Topic Report 2: From Central Government Corporatism to Local Government Corporatism," in *Interpreting Southern Suzhou*, Suzhou University Press.

Wen, Tiejun & Feng Kaiwen (1998) 温铁军, 冯开文 "农村土地问题的世纪反思" (Reflections on Rural Land Problem), 战略与管理 (Strategy and Management), 1998(4).

Wen, Tiejun & Feng Kaiwen (1999) 温铁军, 冯开文 "谨防重蹈旧中国农村破产的覆辙—从工商、金融资本对农村的过量剥夺谈起" (Be Mindful of the Danger of Rural Bankruptcy: The Overexploitation of Villages by Industrial, Commercial and Financial Capitals). 战略与管理 (Strategy and Management), 1999(1).

Wen, Tiejun & Zhu Shouyin (1996) 温铁军, 朱守银 "政府资本原始积累与土地'农转非'"(Government Primitive Accumulation of Capital and Converting Land from Cultivation to Non-agricultural Purposes), 管理世界 (Management World), 1996(5).

Wu, Cuifang et el (2007) 武翠芳等 "我国农村资金供求缺口分析" (Analysis of the Chinese Rural Fund Supply and Demand Gap), 金融理论与实践 (Financial Theory and Practice) 2007(5) pp. 65–66.

Wu, Chengming & Dong Zhikai eds. (2001) 吴承明, 董志凯主编, 中华人民共和国经济史 (1949—1952) (Economic History of the People's Republic of China 1949–1952). Beijing: China Fiscal and Economic Publishing House.

Wu, Chenming & Dong Zhikai eds. (2010) 吴承明, 董志凯主编, 中华人民共和国经济史(1949—1952) (Economic History of the People's Republic of China 1949–1952). Beijing: Social Sciences Literature Press.

Wu, Li (1995) 武力 "中华人民共和国成立前后的货币统一" (The Unification of Currencies around the Establishment of People's Republic of China), 当代中国史研究 (Contemporary China History Studies), 1995(4), pp. 1–12.

Wu, Yu (2014) Ye Jianjun ed. 吴珏著, 叶健君主编 三反五反运动纪实 (An Account of Sanfan Wufan Movements). Beijing: Dongfang Publishing House.

Xiang, Huaicheng & Ma Guochuan (2009) 项怀诚, 马国川 "改革是共和国财政六十年的主线(上)" (Reform was the Main Line for Fiscal Finance Over Sixty Years of the People's Republic (Part 1)), 读书 (Doushu), 2009(9).

Xiao, Guoliang & Sui Fumin (2011) 萧国亮, 隋福民 中华人民共和国经济史 1949—2010 (Economic History of the People's Republic of China 1949–2010). Beijing: Peking University Press.

Xie, Maoshi, Cai Zexiang & Wang Haiyan (2009) 谢茂拾, 蔡则祥, 黄海艳 "金融危机影响下农业就业的困境与新出路" (Predicaments and Solutions of Agricultural Employment Under the Impact of Financial Crisis), 中国发展观察 (China Development Observation), 2009(11).

Xie, Ping (1992) 谢平 "中国金融资产结构分析" (Analysis on China's Financial Asset Structure), 经济研究 (Economic Studies), 1992(11).

Xie, Yue (2005) 谢岳 "中国乡村保护主义政治及其后果" (The Politics of Chinese Rural Protectionism and Its Consequences), 江苏社会科学 (Jiangsu Social Sciences), 2005(2) pp.98–103.

Xietong Town Chronicle Editing Committee (2001) 斜塘镇志 (Xietong Town Chronicle). Beijing Local History Publishing House.

Xin, Jie (2005) 辛洁 "全球FDI向服务部门转移的趋势分析和对中国的政策建议" (Trend Analysis of Global FDI Shifts Towards Service Sector and Policy Suggestions for China), Nankai University Master thesis.

Xiong, Jingmin (2010) 熊景明 "先知者的悲哀" (The Sorrow of the Foreseer), 二十一世纪 (Twenty-first Century), June, 2010.

Xu, Hongyuan (2001) 徐宏源 "2000 年中国宏观经济形式分析与2001年展望" (Analysis of China's Macro Economic Form in 2000 and 2001 Outlook), Economic Forecast Department, National Information Center. http://www.cei.gov.cn/template/economist/yth_source/zgjj2001010203.htm.

Xu, Tao "Studies on China's State-Owned Banks Commercialization Reform," Master Thesis, Liaoning Normal University.

Xu, Yi, & Li Zheng Hua (2003) 许毅, 李正华 "陈云领导的上海米粮之战" (The Shanghai Grain War Led by Chen Yun). 文史博览 (Culture and History Vision), 2003(8). pp. 9–11.

Xu, Jianwen (2007) 许建文 中国当代农业政策史稿10 (A History of Contemporary Agricultural Policy, 10). Beijing: China Agriculture Press.

Xu, Lan (2010) 徐蓝 英国与中日战争1931—1941 (UK and Sino-Japanese War 1931–1941). Capital Normal University Press.

Xu, Zhongyue (2008) 徐中约 中国近代史: 1600—2000, 中国的奋斗 (第6版) (Modern History of China 1600–2000, sixth edition). Beijing World Books Publishing House.

Xue, Muqiao (1992) 薛暮桥 薛暮桥学术论著自选集 (Selected Academic Writings of Xue Muqiao). Beijing Normal University Publishing Group.

Xue, Muqiao (2006) 薛暮桥回忆录 (Memoirs of Xue Muqiao). Tianjin People Publishing House.

Yan, Jinmin (阎金明): "关于国际经济大循环理论的几点商榷" (Deliberations regarding the Big International Circulation Theory), 广州对外贸易学院学报 (Journal of the Guangdong University of Foreign Studies), 1988(4), pp. 15–17.

Yan, Ruizhen, Gong Daoguang, Zhou Zhixiang & Bi Baode (1990) 严瑞珍, 龚道广, 周志祥, 毕宝德 "中国工农业产品价格剪刀差的现状、发展趋势及对策" (Industrial and Agricultural Price Scissors in China: Status, Trend and Policy). 经济研究 (Economic Research), 1990(2).

Yang, Peixin (1988) 杨培新 "关于关于国际大循环问题的争论" (Debate over the Big International Circulation), 烟台大学学报(哲学社会科学版) (Journal of Yantai University, Philosophy and Social Science Edition), 1988(2) pp. 1–3.

Yang, Shuai & Wen Tiejun (2010) 温铁军, 杨帅 "宏观经济波动、财税体制变迁与三次圈地运动" (Macro-economics, Taxation Institutional Transition and Three Rounds of Land Enclosure), 管理世界 (Management World), 2010(4).

Ye, Yangbing (2003) 叶扬兵 "1956—1957年合作化高潮后的农民退社风潮" (The Tide of Peasants Withdrawing from the Cooperatives After the 1956–57), *Nanjing University Journal* (Philosophy, Human Sciences and Social Sciences), 2003(6).

Ye, Jingzhong & Sun Ruixin (2012) 叶敬忠, 孙睿昕 "发展主义研究评述" (Developmentalism Studies: A Critical Analysis). *China Agricultural University Journal* (Social Sciences), 2012(2).

Zhang, Daohui (2001) 张道卫 "为什么中国的许多林地不长树?" (Why Does So Much Forest Land in China Have No Trees?), 管理世界 (Management World), 2001(3), pp. 141–146.

Zhang, Jie (1998) *Analysis of China's State-owned Financial System Transformation.* Economic Science Press.

Zhang, Youyi (1997) 章有义 明清及现代农业史论集 (Essays on Ming, Qing and Modern Agricultural History). Beijing: China Agricultural Press.

Zhou, Yanling (2002) 周雁翎 "差异悬殊: 中国卫生保健事业面临严峻挑战" (Wide Differential: China's Medical Care Profession Facing Severe Challenge), 中国改革 (China Reform), 2002(4).

Zhou, Taihe (2005) 周太和 "陈云与新中国基本建设" (Chen Yun and China's Infrastructure Building), 党的文献 (The Party's Literature), 2005(3).

Zhu, Jiamu et al. (1999) 朱佳木等 陈云 (Chen Yun). Central Literature Press.

Zou, Quansheng & Wang Ying (2006) 邹全胜, 王莹 "服务外包: 理论与经验分析" (Service Outsourcing: Theoretical and Empirical Analysis). 国际贸易问题 (Journal of International Trade), 2006(05), pp. 54–61.

Name Index

© The Editor(s) (if applicable) and The Author(s) 2021
Wen Tiejun, *Ten Crises*, Global University for Sustainability Book Series,
https://doi.org/10.1007/978-981-16-0455-3

Subject Index

CPSIA information can be obtained
at www.ICGtesting.com
Printed in the USA
LVHW031136070622
720669LV00009B/401